A POISONOUS AFFAIR

In March 1988, during the Iran–Iraq war, thousands of people were killed in a chemical attack on Halabja, a remote town in Iraqi Kurdistan. In the aftermath of the horror, confusion reigned over who had carried out the attack, each side accusing the other in the ongoing bloodbath of the war. As the fog lifted, the responsibility of Saddam Hussein's regime was revealed, and with it the tacit support of Iraq's Western allies. This book, by a veteran observer of the Middle East, tells the story of the gassing of Halabja. It shows how Iraq was able to develop ever more sophisticated chemical weapons and to target Iranian soldiers and Kurdish villagers as America looked the other way. Today, as Iraq disintegrates and the Middle East sinks further into turmoil, those policies are coming back to haunt America and the West.

Joost R. Hiltermann is a seasoned Middle East analyst. While researching this book, he was working as Executive Director of the Arms Division of Human Rights Watch. He is currently the Deputy Program Director for the Middle East and North Africa for the International Crisis Group. His publications include *Behind the Intifada: Labor and Women's Movements in the Occupied Territories* (1991).

Frontpiece. March 1988 – Halabja: Chemical attack victims Nasreen Ahmad Abdullah and two children. (Reprinted with permission of the photographer, Ahmad Nateghi, and Ms. Abdullah's surviving relatives.)

A Poisonous Affair

AMERICA, IRAQ, AND THE GASSING OF HALABJA

Joost R. Hiltermann

CAMBRIDGE UNIVERSITY PRESS

Cambridge, New York, Melbourne, Madrid, Cape Town, Singapore, São Paulo

Cambridge University Press
32 Avenue of the Americas, New York, NY 10013-2473, USA

www.cambridge.org
Information on this title: www.cambridge.org/9780521876865

First published 2007

Printed in the United States of America

A catalog record for this publication is available from the British Library.

Library of Congress Cataloging in Publication Data

Hiltermann, Joost R.
A poisonous affair : America, Iraq, and the gassing of Halabja / Joost R. Hiltermann.
p. cm.
Includes bibliographical references and index.
ISBN 978-0-521-87686-5 (hardback)
1. Halabjah (Iraq) – History – Bombardment, 1988. 2. Kurds – Crimes against – Iraq.
3. Iraq – Ethnic relations. 4. United States – Foreign relations – Iraq. 5. Iraq – Foreign
relations – United States. I. Title.
DS79.9.H27H55 2007
956.7044′1 – dc22   2007001313

ISBN 978-0-521-87686-5 hardback

This book is respectfully dedicated to
F., O., R., T., W., and Y.,
who survived the Anfal killing grounds
and to all those who didn't.
And to all victims of Iraq's chemical warfare
in Halabja, on the warfront, and elsewhere.

CONTENTS

ABBREVIATIONS

BWC	Biological Weapons Convention of 1974
CIA	Central Intelligence Agency
CW	Chemical weapons
CWC	Chemical Weapons Convention of 1993
DIA	Defense Intelligence Agency
FBIS	Foreign Broadcast Information Service, a CIA translation service
FOIA	Freedom of Information Act
HRW	Human Rights Watch
IAEA	International Atomic Energy Agency
ICP	Iraqi Communist Party
ICRC	International Committee of the Red Cross
IRNA	Islamic Republic News Agency
IUMK	Islamic Unity Movement of Kurdistan
KCP	Kurdistan Communist Party
KDP	Kurdistan Democratic Party
KDP-I	Kurdistan Democratic Party of Iran
KPDP	Kurdistan Popular Democratic Party
KSP	Kurdistan Socialist Party
MID	Iraqi Military Intelligence Directorate
MSF	Médecins sans Frontières
NPT	Nuclear Non-Proliferation Treaty
NSA	National Security Agency
NSC	National Security Council
PKK	Kurdish Workers Party

PLO	Palestine Liberation Organization
POW	Prisoner of war
PUK	Patriotic Union of Kurdistan
RPG	Rocket-propelled grenade
SCIRI	Supreme Council for the Islamic Revolution in Iraq
UNSCOM	United Nations Special Commission on Iraq
WMD	Weapons of mass destruction

PREFACE

Journey to Halabja

Where were you on March 16, 1988? And where was I? Memory fails where conscience demands it.

March 16, a Wednesday, must have been an ordinary working day for most people, meriting no special attention. I happened to be in transit, somewhere between Palestine and California, about to finish my doctoral dissertation on labor and women's movements struggling under Israel's harsh military occupation. Was I in Washington, DC, that day? Given what transpired, that would not have been a bad place to be.

I must have read the papers in the next few days, but if anything registered, it did not remain. It took at least a week before the news emerged, but then the headlines were difficult to ignore: "Poison Gas Attack Kills Hundreds" (*Washington Post*); "Iran Charges Iraq With a Gas Attack And Its Grisly Toll" (*International Herald Tribune*); "Gas victims frozen in the agony of death" (*Times* of London); "Une ville kurde massacrée à l'arme chimique" (*Midi Libre*); "L'arme répugnante de Saddam Hussein" (*Le Nouvel Observateur*); "L'apocalypse de la guerre chimique" (*Quotidien de Paris*); "La guerra química llega al Kurdistán iraquí" (*El País*); "Es ist ein kurdisches Hiroshima" (*Wiener Zeitung*); and: "Il genocidio del popolo curdo" (*L'Unità*). A *New York Times* editorial proclaimed that Iraq stood "credibly accused of resorting to chemical weapons. . . . The deed is in every sense a war crime."[1]

A name appeared: "Halabja" – a place no one had ever heard of but said to be a village in Iraq's Kurdish region. In fact, it was a sizable town surrounded by resettlement camps housing the inhabitants of destroyed villages. Television began ladling out horrifying scenes from ground zero: the corpses of women and children piled in the back of a pickup truck, bodies strewn randomly along a mountain stream, a dead man prone on the ground cradling his infant son in a final embrace. Some of these images would become iconic – in Kurdistan. Elsewhere, they were soon forgotten. The world had its Babi Yar, its Srebrenica, its Timisoara, its Hiroshima and Nagasaki, its London, Dresden, and Berlin. The world also had its Halabja. But who now remembers?

In June 1992 I visited Iraqi Kurdistan as a consultant for Human Rights Watch in New York. My marching orders were to replace a colleague who had already spent three months there, and travel throughout the region to locate and interview survivors about the terrible events to which they had been privy in 1988. It was there and then that the name Halabja first entered fully into my consciousness, never again to depart. But another word took shape as well, a word that used to fill every Kurd with crushing fear: "Anfal." A counterinsurgency operation launched by the Saddam Hussein regime in the waning days of the Iran–Iraq war to decisively settle its Kurdish problem, the Anfal campaign led to the methodical murder of tens of thousands of Kurdish civilians – first flushed out of their villages by poison gas, then hauled to transit centers, sorted by age and sex, and carted off to execution sites in Iraq's western desert, far from Kurdistan.

Based on eyewitness testimonies and Iraqi secret police documents captured by the Kurds during their post–Gulf War uprising in March 1991, Human Rights Watch prepared a detailed study of the Anfal campaign, an account that was largely ignored when it was first published in 1993. The organization also attempted to mobilize governments to bring a case of genocide against Iraq at the International Court of Justice in The Hague, but found no serious takers. Only the regime's ouster in 2003 created the will to reopen the file of Halabja and Anfal, as well as the many other crimes that Saddam Hussein and his lieutenants committed during their thirty-year tyranny.

The Western world's pointed lack of interest in prosecuting the Iraqi leadership during the sanctions decade of the 1990s, when Saddam Hussein, following his invasion of Kuwait, had ceased to be America's friend, proved utterly frustrating. Having recorded these atrocities, sat with survivors who had lost their entire families, debriefed six men and a boy who had miraculously survived the killing fields (one of whom later died in internecine Kurdish fighting), and reported these events in great detail, I failed to grasp why no one would take an active

interest in what had transpired. Should the deaths of some 80,000 innocent people, including several thousand in a chemical attack against an
area saturated with civilians, remain a mere footnote in history? Why
did no one take notice?

And so, eight years after my first exposure to the Kurdish tragedy, I
set out to shed further light on these questions, to explore the context
in which Halabja and Anfal had taken place, and to address some of
the controversies that had started to whirl soon after the first images
appeared on television and before the world moved on to other matters.
Was Iraq truly to blame, or was there a hidden Iranian hand as well?
Were Western governments that tilted toward Iraq during its eight-year
war with Iran aware of Iraq's use of poison gas, not only in Halabja,
but throughout the eight-year conflict? Did the Reagan administration,
in particular, not only condone Iraq's behavior but actively encourage
it? How significant really was Iraq's use of gas on the battlefield and
against the Kurds? Apart from Halabja, were there any other allegations
that the Khomeini regime resorted to chemical weapons, and were these
credible? And my overarching question: Who knew what when, how
did they act on this knowledge, and was an alternative course of action
possible? This quest was, in some ways, a real whodunit.

In 2000, on a grant from the Open Society Institute, I visited Iran,
Kuwait, Jordan, and Israel in a first attempt to document this dark
period in the region's history, speaking to military and intelligence officers with specialized knowledge. With additional help from the John
D. and Catherine T. MacArthur Foundation, I visited Iran again two
years later, meeting with some of the surviving chemical victims still
laid up in Tehran hospitals or suffering at home from the delayed effects
of mustard gas, more than a decade after their exposure. From Iran I
crossed into Iraqi Kurdistan to find further witnesses, especially some of
the Kurdish commanders who had participated in the operation to drive
the Iraqis out of Halabja in the days before the chemical attack. This
journey became the first step in reconstructing what had happened –
an inspection, as it were, of the crime scene.

Tehran, May 2002

In my three weeks here, I have discovered the existence of a community
that until now has largely been known only to itself and a few outsiders.

They are Iranian doctors who have devoted their careers to the study of the long-term effects of poison gas on human physiology. Treating victims of mustard gas attacks to this day, these doctors could contribute enormously to medical knowledge. Regrettably, by publishing their findings exclusively in professional journals, they are spreading their expertise only to the specialized few. And although, for all practical purposes, the Iranian and Kurdish victims of Iraqi poison gas attacks provide the sole existing live laboratory for the study of chemical warfare today, only a handful of doctors, both in Iran and in Iraqi Kurdistan, have chosen this area as their vocation.

I find some of these people in Tehran's Sosan hospital thanks to Dr. Hamid Sohrabpour, a pulmonologist who trained at Mount Sinai hospital in New York City and Methodist hospital in Brooklyn in the 1970s. A kind and understated man, he has had an illustrious career. Returning to Iran coincidentally as the revolution broke out, he was chosen by the Iranian students who took over the US Embassy in 1979 to provide medical care to the hostages. Much later he became the official physician to the national soccer team: he fondly points to a photograph of himself with legendary striker Ali Daei in his clinic in an upscale Tehran neighborhood.

After war broke out with Iraq in September 1980, his expertise as a pulmonologist was soon in high demand. Early during the war he was called up to treat a set of patients with injuries he had never seen before. "I don't remember exactly when this was, but it was summer. These were Iraqi people from Haj Omran [a town just across the border from Piranshahr], Kurds who were fighting their own government. We didn't know what they were suffering from. It had to be chemicals, but what kind? We tried to get literature from abroad. Later on we saw our soldiers with the same symptoms. By then we knew what it was."

The Iraqi Kurds Dr. Sohrabpour saw were very likely the first documented mustard gas victims during the war. Iraq resorted to gas to counter an Iranian offensive in July–August 1983 in which allied rebels of the Kurdistan Democratic Party (KDP) guided Iranian forces through enemy territory. Mustard gas was a horrifying new weapon whose extensive use on World War I battlefields was unknown to the vast majority of Iran's young, and mostly uneducated, recruits. It sent Iran's medical establishment scrambling for information that would allow them to make the proper diagnosis and prescribe effective treatment.

The gas employed by Iraq in Haj Omran was, as they soon discovered, sulphur mustard (bis 2-chloroethyl sulphide), described in the literature as an "oily liquid with a garlic-like smell . . . [that] evaporates slowly enough for an area over which it has been scattered to remain dangerous for many hours, even days, yet fast enough for the imperceptible vapour that it gives off also to cause casualties. . . . Its burning effects are not normally apparent for some hours after exposure, whereupon they build up into the hideous picture of blindness, blistering and lung damage" observed among the Iranian victims.[2] It also kills, usually in slow motion and often only years after direct exposure, with unmitigated suffering along the way as victims succumb to respiratory disease or cancer. The only effective protection is a chemical suit covering the body. Treatment addresses symptoms only: washing the body, flushing the eyes, and treating the blisters as one would ordinary burns. Mustard gas caused an estimated 1,300,000 casualties, including 90,000 deaths, during World War I. The Haj Omran attack, more than sixty years later, was the first documented instance since the Great War in which chemical weapons were used in battle between two large conventional forces.

After Dr. Sohrabpour speaks for a while about the long-term effects of mustard gas and his work with chemical warfare victims, he offers to take me on a tour of some of his patients at Sosan hospital, which has a unit specializing in mustard gas injuries. To this day, more than fourteen years after war's end, mustard gas victims continue to seek help at medical centers throughout the country, and every year a number of them die as a result of complications from gas exposure. For example, several days later, as I discuss chemical warfare with Dr. Ja'fer Aslani at the Baghyatollah (military) hospital in Tehran, a man walks in with a constant, debilitating, wheezing cough. Dr. Aslani, a pulmonologist, examines him briefly, then says: "This is the patient's first visit. He says he was injured in Faw [a strip of land south of Basra taken by the Iranians in a lightning offensive in 1986], apparently from a relatively low dose of mustard gas. Today he is suffering from complications. What we do in such cases is treat patients for two to three weeks to a-symptomize them, then release them for out-patient follow-up. He may not even have realized in Faw that he was injured; he may have inhaled gas well after the attack; it tended to hang in the air and the trees because of the heat and humidity down there."

Some of the worst mustard gas cases come to Sosan hospital. The veterans' foundation that runs it, the Janbazan Bunyad (Foundation for the War Disabled), maintains a database that currently contains 30,000 hospital records of mustard gas patients. It has graded patients according to the severity of their symptoms, offering treatment to some 1,200 in the highest category, who typically suffer from a range of ailments from heart and respiratory problems to infections, infertility, and corneal ulcers, as well as malignancies such as lymphoma, aplastic anemia, and leukemia.

On the sixth floor of Sosan hospital I find three Kurdish women from the Iranian border town of Serdasht: Ghoncheh Hosseini (51), her daughter Sheveen (20), and her friend Pervin Karimi Vahed (36). Vahed in particular seems to have trouble breathing, turning herself on one side for comfort and to eye a visitor, but once we settle into the interview, her words begin cascading down. The story these women tell, substantiated in further interviews with doctors who were on the scene, in some way is frightening less by the nature of the horrors revealed than by the fact that it largely has not been told at all to an international audience.

It was, the women say, the seventh of the month of *Tir* in the year 1366 according to the Iranian calendar, or June 28, 1987. The war front was not far off, and Serdasht, a Kurdish town some 15 km (ten miles) from the border, had experienced frequent Iraqi air bombardments. The use of gas, primarily confined to the southern front, was largely unknown to the local population, or at least to these women. When Iranian troops encamped nearby suddenly donned gas masks as the chemical attack got under way, many townspeople did not even know what these outfits were for. "When soldiers started running through the streets yelling 'Chemical attack!' we had no idea what they meant," Hosseini recalls.

The attack, around four in the afternoon, caught her unawares, standing at the door of her home in the town's southern part, and when the bombs began to fall she realized that her son was somewhere outside. "I started running to look for him near the cinema, but suddenly my legs began to feel really hot. I thought, this must be from the running, but when I looked down they looked as if someone had poured boiling

water over them." She found her son, then returned home to fetch her
daughter Sheveen, five years old at the time, and together they made
their way to Laleh park, where men were burning car tires to create
fires, a minimal protection against gas exposure. According to Alastair
Hay, a chemical weapons expert at Leeds University (e-mail communication, 2002), "the heat from the fires would create an up draught that
would cause a vapour or gas to rise higher in the air. The heat might just
destroy some of the chemical."

"Soldiers were going around with loudspeakers saying that people
should move north to the elevated areas," Hosseini continues. "They
said everyone should leave, but we didn't have a car, so we stayed."
That night she went to the local sports hall, which had been turned
into a field clinic, for triage. Much later on she was taken to Tabriz, then
Tehran for treatment. She continues to suffer moderate health problems
and checks into the hospital occasionally to get boosters; both Sheveen
and her brother seem to have escaped the effects of the gas.

Vahed had arrived from Tehran, where her family had moved years
earlier, to visit relatives only two days before the attack. "I was taking a
shower when a bomb fell on my house," she recounts. "I stepped out of
the shower and noticed white powder everywhere. A piece of the bomb
had fallen on the TV table. We all laughed in relief at first because a
bomb had fallen on our house, and here we were, alive and well. But
then this white flour started spreading everywhere and when I walked
around I started developing burns and blisters, and I felt nauseated and
had to vomit."

"We somehow got into our cars," she continues, "and headed for
Mahabad" – the capital of a short-lived Kurdish bid for independence
after World War II. Here doctors gave them baths. She lost her eyesight
for a while and fainted. Today, fifteen years later, she continues to suffer
from severe respiratory problems. She is admitted frequently into the
hospital; her outlook, Dr. Sohrabpour tells me, is not good.

Halabja, May 2002

In the third week of May, I take an Iran Air flight from Tehran to the
Kurdish town of Kermanshah and from there drive two hours west
toward Qasr al-Shirin and the border. Signs along the way advise the

traveler of the diminishing distance in kilometers to Karbala and Najaf, Iraqi towns holy to Shi'ite Muslims who dominate Iranian political life (and constitute a majority in both Iran and Iraq). The green fields – fed by spring rains and buoyant with poppies – and undulating hills with imposing mountains behind them evoke memories of previous travels to Kurdistan, which I have visited frequently via Turkey.

The border crossing is a simple affair: my name is present on a piece of paper, having been telegraphed from Tehran. I sign a register that is promptly locked into a safe, aside from a table the only piece of furniture in the small shed that serves as customs post. The Iranian border guards engage in some patronizing backslapping of the few Kurds crossing that day; clearly there is no love lost between them. A Suleimaniyeh University professor is traveling in the opposite direction, returning to Germany with his family, but otherwise the border post is deserted.

The journey to Suleimaniyeh takes another two hours, and I arrive just in time for lunch. The menu in the restaurant at the top-range Ashty hotel offers, in the steak section, "Tornado with Mushrooms" and "Fillet Minion." I opt safely for Kurdish food – *kouzy* (lamb shank in tomato broth) – leaving my Kurdish companions to complain afterward how tough their tornados were.

I spend a week in Suleimaniyeh, a town of 700,000 set against a mountain range that forms the border with Iran, some twenty-five miles away as the crow flies. Not included in the US-imposed no-fly zone over Iraq, it lies exposed to Iraqi military action but has remained an oasis of tranquility since the end of the Gulf War, with only one exception – when KDP forces backed by Iraqi troops succeeded in briefly displacing Patriotic Union of Kurdistan (PUK) fighters in 1996. Here I meet, and interview, many of the original participants in the Halabja operation that preceded the chemical attack.

But my main target is Halabja. I am eager to see the town and to climb the hills behind it to appreciate how the capture/liberation of Halabja unfolded, who the participants were, where they had dug their positions, at what point during the military campaign the chemical attack occurred, what types of gases were used, and by which route the surviving inhabitants had sought to flee.

On a Saturday morning, four of us set out for Halabja – Ne'man the driver, my translator Muhammad, and Mam Hadi, a retired guerrilla who is affectionately known among his PUK friends as "the first partisan" in the Halabja area. He is a member of the Kaka'i, a small Shi'ite syncretist sect that is also known as the Ahl al-Haq. The Kaka'i inhabit three villages in the Halabja area, high in the mountains close to the Iranian border, but in recent months their inhabitants have faced expulsion from their homes by militants of Ansar al-Islam, a splinter group of the Islamic Unity Movement of Kurdistan (IUMK), which has its headquarters in Halabja. Aside from displacing villagers whose religious convictions they dislike and imposing Taliban-like rules, the militants have been accused of an unsuccessful attempt to assassinate the PUK prime minister in Suleimaniyeh, Barham Salih, my generous host during this visit.

We discuss these matters as we drive toward Halabja, a two-hour journey that carries us through a land of magpies, geese, and endless fields of sunflowers. We pass a number of small villages with low-slung houses. People in traditional dress tend their fields or herd flocks of sheep. At one point a gaggle of geese sits snugly in a circle on the road, facing inward as if in a mid-play rugby huddle. They all duck their heads in unison as we roar past but otherwise do not budge.

Halabja itself lies in a basin in front of towering mountains to its south and east (behind which is Iran). It is shielded from the rest of Kurdistan, to the north and west, by the man-made Sirwan lake that, fed by the Sirwan, Zalm, and Tanjro rivers, empties via the Darbandikhan dam into the Diyala river, then into the mighty Tigris as it flows toward the Persian Gulf. It is this area encompassed by lake and mountains that Iranian forces occupied in March 1988, driving Iraqi troops across the lake (where many drowned) or across the only all-weather bridge over the Zalm to positions at the small town of Sayed Sadeq, a third of the way back toward Suleimaniyeh.

Razed by the Iraqis after the Iran–Iraq war, Halabja has been largely rebuilt over the past decade. A new and glittering mosque is several months from completion. At the entrance of town I find a statue of a prone man embracing his child in death, asphyxiated in the chemical attack. Halabjans tell me that his name – and names and individual stories matter to the survivors – was Omar Hama Saleh, a baker who had suffered the great misfortune (by local cultural standards) of having had six daughters in a row but was then blessed, at long last, with a son. It was this son he was clutching when he died.

Hama Hama Sa'id, a local PUK commander, agrees to take me up the mountain to view Halabja from above (and Ansar al-Islam positions further up). Middle-aged and sporting a magnificent moustache, the commander once must have been a strapping guerrilla, but now his stride is slowed by a budding paunch, the flip side of ten years of peace. We bump along a dirt track up Shinirweh mountain. A machine gun mounted in the bed of the truck is manned by a handful of *peshmergas* (literally, "those who face death," the Kurdish designation for guerrilla fighters). "Here, in Abba Beileh village, was an Iraqi army post," my guide explains. "Over there, down below, was the large Iraqi artillery base at Delamar. And to the west, there, is Balambo mountain, where the Iranians overran another Iraqi position." At the top of the mountain we have a panoramic view of Halabja, Sirwan lake, and the valley stretching toward Suleimaniyeh. Ansar al-Islam positions are visible off to the east on heights closer to the Iranian border.

It is from Shinirweh, according to Hama Hama Sa'id and Mam Hadi, who both participated in the assault, that one column of Iranian forces descended on the Halabja area in the dead of night on March 12 or 13 (they are not very precise with dates), supported by artillery fire from positions inside Iran, and guided by PUK peshmergas. Other Kurdish parties, and even a unit of Iraqi Shi'ite Arabs of the Badr Corps, the military arm of the Tehran-based opposition Supreme Council for the Islamic Revolution in Iraq (SCIRI), accompanied Iranian forces in the descent from other points along the border. Capturing Iraqi army posts along the way, they converged on Halabja and Khurmal.

In Halabja itself, townspeople rose up in revolt against the hated Iraqi administration. They laid siege to the headquarters of the Ba'ath party, secret police (*Amn*), military intelligence (*Istikhbarat*), regular police, and the pro-regime Kurdish fighters known by the regime as *fursan* (knights) but in local parlance as *jahsh* (little donkeys), many of whom simply switched sides. (The people of Halabja had good reason to want to eliminate the regime's presence. Saddam's forces had carried out mass arrests and razed the town's Kani Ashqan neighborhood following protests over village destruction the previous year.) On March 15, the peshmergas joined them, victoriously touring the town accompanied by elements of Iranian intelligence. The main Iranian forces entrenched themselves in positions formerly occupied by their Iraqi foes at Delamar above Halabja, while others bypassed the town, heading for the lake and the Zalm bridge to eliminate the remnants of Iraqi troops.

Although the assault led to a rout of Iraqi forces, it was evident the Iraqis were not altogether unprepared. They had witnessed the buildup of Iranian forces on the border for days and had sent in tanks and armored vehicles as reinforcements in the days leading up to the attack. Some of the Kurdish commanders suspect, in hindsight, that they were being led into a trap. The area was self-contained, the lake forming a natural barrier to a further Iranian advance on either Suleimaniyeh or the strategic Darbandikhan dam – or toward the strategic road connecting Suleimaniyeh and Darbandikhan, which dips through a tunnel just as it reaches the dam. On March 16, one day after the Kurds liberated Halabja, the Iraqis retaliated, using the area's geography to their advantage.

Peshmergas holding the mountainous area northwest of Halabja and south of Suleimaniyeh, called Qaradagh, recall they witnessed Iraqi Sukhoy bombers flying overhead from the west, presumably from an airbase near Kirkuk, toward Halabja, whose contours shimmered in the distance. The planes nosedived during their bombing runs, leaving large plumes of dark smoke, then returned, flying back across Qaradagh. Faiq Golpy, a peshmerga doctor, watched the planes make their sorties that afternoon and subsequent days, but at first, he says, he did not realize what sort of payload they carried. Only when the guerrillas' radios started twittering with news from commanders at ground zero did he and his colleagues understand what had happened. Dr. Golpy is himself a Halabja native, and later, on furlough after Anfal (during which he was exposed repeatedly to Iraqi gas as he and his comrades fled through the countryside), he discovered that his mother, a brother, a nephew, and three other relatives had died in the chemical attack. Their bodies have not been found and presumably lie buried in one of the many mass graves.

As we come down Shinirweh, Hama Hama Sa'id steers along a dirt track leading from Abba Beileh through the foothills above Halabja to the villages of Jalileh and Anab, past carefully tended fields of wheat and other crops. As we get out, one of my companions picks some pods and we munch distractedly on the green chick peas inside. Jalileh is a hamlet of mudbrick homes tucked into the mountain's lap, a challenge to discern from afar against the weathered rock but, upon approach, a delight to behold, shaded by a clutch of trees and straddling a spring and a sparkling brook that nourishes these fertile lands. Villagers had to rebuild their homes after the Gulf War, as the regime razed most Kurdish villages during the 1980s counterinsurgency. Hamlets like Jalileh and Anab are micro-oases in an otherwise oft-unforgiving land, and it is to these springs that some of the surviving Halabjans came to seek refuge. It was their fate that the wind that day was blowing toward the north-east, right at Anab. The poison wafted down along the paved road leading out of Halabja and past the water sources where many had paused to wash themselves of the powdery substance sticking to their faces, limbs, and clothes, and to quench their thirst. Nothing lived: no humans, no animals.

A newly erected monument commemorates the victims of the attack. More jarring, though, are the mounds of dirt that line the road, marking the places where people fell and where, days after these indescribable events, survivors aided by Iranian troops and IUMK peshmergas buried them as they found them, in clumps. At first my companions have to point out these mounds, as they in no obvious way stand out from the surrounding countryside, but I soon get the hang of it. It is then I realize that from these mounds sprout the sweet young chick peas we have just consumed.

Today, life has returned to normal. The unmarked makeshift graves merge with agriculture and village life. As we drive slowly back to Halabja, nothing suggests the horrors that transpired here. Farmers seed the land, women take their washing to the spring, children play, and geese and chickens leisurely cross the road in front of us.

Amman, September 2006

One year later, the United States attacked Iraq and removed Saddam Hussein's regime. From that moment I was able to make regular visits to the country in my capacity as regional director of the International Crisis Group, a conflict prevention organization. During these trips I met several former officers and soldiers in the Iraqi army who were able to give me the kind of day-to-day operational detail about Iraq's chemical weapons use that was not available to the victims, and thus rounded out the picture for me.

This is where my story ends and that of others begins, the story told to me by Kurdish survivors, Iraqi perpetrators, Iranian medical personnel, American and Israeli intelligence analysts, and many others who shared their views and insights. It is also the story as recounted, if in a fragmentary way, in numerous intelligence documents, both American and Iraqi. And although their story has already been told elsewhere and shan't be repeated here (except in a brief synopsis in the Epilogue)[3], this book exists because of five remarkable men and one boy (now grown), and the inspiration they provided—Anfal survivors who through sheer pluck and a good dose of luck managed to escape from the killing grounds. I dedicate this book to them and their families with love, admiration, and gratitude. May this book, moreover, serve to keep alive the memory of all those who died in poison gas attacks, or perished facing the guns of Anfal.

Acknowledgments

The making of this book was a labor of love, eight years in gestation, another six years in production. If I finished it, it is only because of the support of a large cast of characters: family, friends, people who became friends along the way, and others who, clueless about who I was, nevertheless shared spontaneously and generously their time and insights, and otherwise offered energetic support.

The original impetus was provided by the organization of which I was a staff member in 2000, Human Rights Watch, and its director Ken Roth. Like all staff members, I was owed a paid three-month sabbatical after seven years of employment, and Ken encouraged me to start research for this book, which was based on a human rights investigation in Iraqi Kurdistan by a couple of colleagues and me in 1992–1994. It was Ken also who warned me early on, rightly, to avoid the trap of what is called in the United States "Monday-morning quarterbacking," a reference to American football: "The game's on Sunday. All the second-guessing comes on Monday." I hope I have succeeded.

HRW's flexibility and an Individual Project Fellowship grant from the Open Society Institute, awarded in 1999, allowed me to devote an additional three months to this project, including travel to Iran, Kuwait, Jordan, and Israel. My colleagues Steve Goose and Lisa Misol bore the burden of my absence, taking on responsibilities beyond their normal heavy workloads. I am grateful to them, as well as to my early collaborators on the Anfal project: George Black, Mawlan Brahim, Shorsh Haji, Paiman Muhammad, Jemera Rone, and Andrew Whitley. George showed me how a human rights report can be a beautifully written piece of work rather than a dull recantation of abuses; his *Iraq's Crime of Genocide* (cited previously) regrettably has been read by all too few people. Shorsh and Paiman deserve special mention as an ongoing source of inspiration, and vast knowledge, throughout this project.

Two years later, in 2002, the John D. and Catherine T. MacArthur Foundation provided me with a research and writing grant to complete the project. This included a month of research in Iran and Iraqi Kurdistan. For practitioners like me, who have full-time jobs and lack the backing of a university or a think tank, the support of foundations such as OSI and MacArthur is absolutely indispensable in freeing up time for research and writing.

In November 2003, a grant of the Rockefeller Foundation enabled me to spend a month as a resident at the foundation's Bellagio Study and Conference Center in Italy to write in quiet in the company of fellow researchers, as well as writers, musicians, and artists. I am particularly grateful to center director Gianna Celli for her support and good humor. Written recommendations from Shaul Bakhash, Ken Roth, Gary Sick, and Max van der Stoel were instrumental in persuading aforementioned foundations to support my work.

In the early stages of research, while I was teaching part time at Georgetown University's Center for Contemporary Arab Studies, I was aided by a series of graduate students who, for course credit, readily tracked down primary sources, many in Arabic, and summarized literature on the war: Krysti Adams, Julienne Gherardi, Ranya Ghuma, Rima Mulla, Mahasen Nasreddin, Rijin Sahakian, Sherene Seikaly, and Caitlin Williams. I thank them for the terrific job they did, and would like to single out Ranya as the research assistant par excellence who went far beyond what was expected, not only conducting serious research (long after her independent study with me had ended), but making the project her own and helping to shape the book's narrative logic. Others who assisted with sources were Niaz Khalid in Amsterdam (Kurdish) and Gheed Jarrar in Amman (Arabic). My niece, Roline Hiltermann, spent many hours typing up interviews, a numbing, thankless task.

William M. Arkin, Gordon Burck, and Michael Eisenstadt kindly gave me access to their files, while Joyce Battle of the National Security Archives at George Washington University and Kendal Nezan of the Institut Kurde in Paris readily opened the doors to their documents as well. Shafiq Ghabra, Giandoménico Picco, and Kazem Sajjadpour assisted in obtaining visas for Kuwait and Iran; I am grateful especially to Dr. Sajjadpour for overcoming Iranian bureaucratic hurdles when I inadvertently overstayed the period permitted by my visa.

Abd-al-Razzaq al-Saeidy (Baghdad), Muhammad Sleivani (Suleimaniyeh and Halabja), and Naghmeh Sohrabi (Tehran) served as my local interpreters and guides, doing a sterling job under sometimes difficult conditions. Several friends and acquaintances generously put me up and thus had to put up with me: Shorsh Haji and Paiman Muhammad in London, Ghanim Najjar in Kuwait City, Siamak Namazi in Tehran, Lilian Peters in Amman, Ruud Peters and Marlies Weyergang in Amsterdam, Susan Rockwell in Ramallah, and Barham Salih in Suleimaniyeh.

Jamal Aziz Amin (Suleimaniyeh), Hamit Bozarslan (Paris), Susan Meiselas (New York), Delphine Minoui (peripatetic), Jim Muir (Tehran), Susan Osnos (New York), John Packer (The Hague), and Fati Ziai (New York) helped out along the way. Jamal, in particular, has been a wonderful host on each of my visits to Suleimaniyeh; we spent many an evening over an abundant meal and a good glass of arak, if he wasn't taking me on a tour of Iraq's former security police headquarters downtown, where he had been severely tortured as a suspected member of the Kurdish underground.

After I moved from Human Rights Watch to the International Crisis Group in 2002, Rob Malley and Gareth Evans showed great flexibility and support in allowing me to take several short (not short to them) leaves of absence to complete the book.

Lisa Hajjar read an early draft of the manuscript and diplomatically suggested I radically revise it. I did so, and thanks to her, this became a somewhat more coherent and readable book. My wife and toughest critic, Patricia Gossman, then read a couple of new drafts from beginning to end, steering me away from foolish digressions and unnecessary rhetoric, and excising all the Dutchisms and most of the clichés – away with "genies uncorked" – that somehow had sneaked into the text. I am grateful, as well, to Marigold Acland, my editor at Cambridge University Press, for taking on this project and seeing it through; to my two anonymous readers, whose laudatory comments gave me a boost at a time when I was close to despair about the book's prospects; and to other staff at Cambridge, as well as at Aptara, Inc., who turned the manuscript into a fine-looking book. And I thank Isam al-Khafaji for conjuring up the book's title.

And then, my family: my wife and my children, Arent, Phoebe, and Aidan. My bill with them is way past due, and I owe them so much more than a few lines here. My absences were the worst of it; frequent absentmindedness was a close second. I'd like to think we are beyond that now and hereby commit to a full reengagement.

MAPS

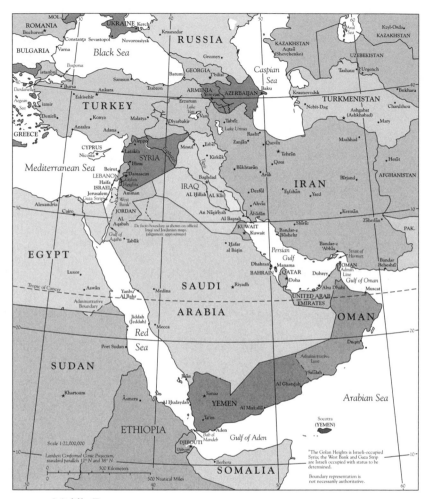

MAP I. Middle East

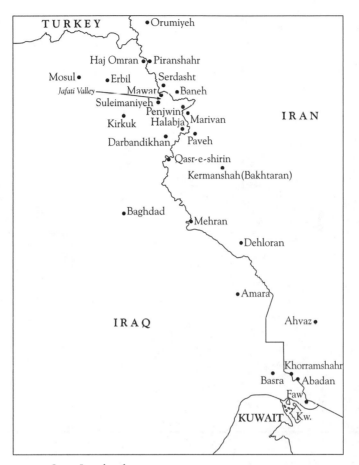

MAP 2. Iran–Iraq border

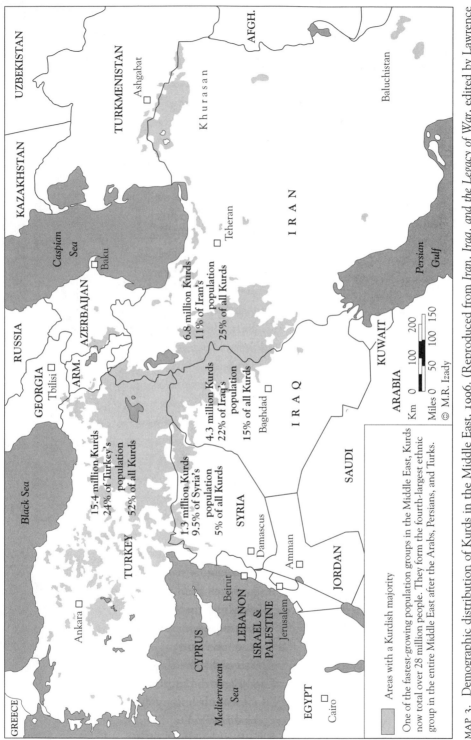

MAP 3. Demographic distribution of Kurds in the Middle East, 1996. (Reproduced from *Iran, Iraq, and the Legacy of War*, edited by Lawrence G. Potter and Gary G. Sick, Palgrave Macmillan, 2004, p. 72.)

MAP 4. Halabja district

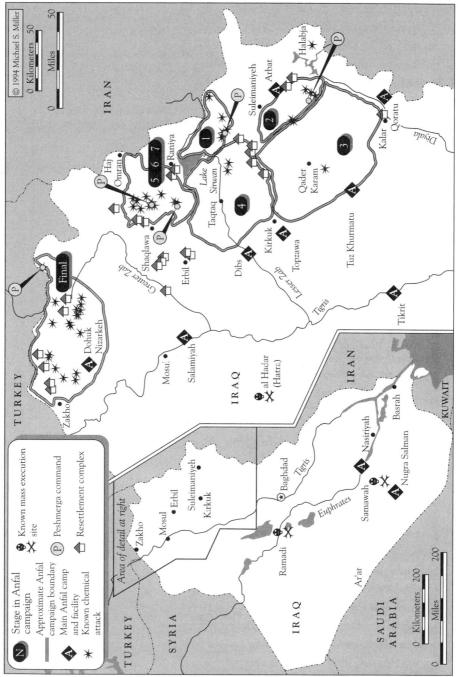

MAP 5. Area of Anfal operations (© 1994 Michael S. Miller)

xxxii

THE HALABJA CONTROVERSY

"I'm not afraid of anything but God – and poison gas."
– An Iraqi officer (Baghdad, 2003)

Witness to a Gas Attack

In March 1988 Ahmad Nateghi was chief of photography at IRNA, the Iranian news agency. The brutal eight-year war between Iran and Iraq was lurching toward an end, a fact evident to both parties. Iranian forces assisted by Kurdish guerrillas had just seized, or liberated, a large swath of territory in Iraqi Kurdistan, outgunning and overrunning Iraqi defenses at Halabja. Nateghi arrived at the border on March 15, just as some colleagues returned from the town with stories of how warmly its inhabitants had welcomed them and how pleasant its Turkish baths were. Eager to get a taste for himself, he set off early the next day, hitching rides with military vehicles and motorbikes. Truckloads of Iraqi captives were heading in the opposite direction to POW camps inside Iran.

At about 11 am, standing with three colleagues on a promontory, he took in the kaleidoscopic view of the sun-dappled valley below, then drove down on a truck that was taking food to Iranian troops who had established a front line on the shores of Sirwan lake and the Zalm river. They dismounted on the outskirts of Halabja, chewing on bread and snapping photographs as they walked along. Iraqi planes, suddenly appearing overhead, dropped a series of bombs. Nateghi, a four-year veteran of the war who had witnessed combat on numerous occasions, said it left him unfazed. "This was normal at the front," he remarked laconically.

I

It was early afternoon and Halabja's streets were as good as empty. "We took some pictures at a deserted day–care center and then decided to walk further into town. Soon I spotted another plane on a bombing run. I photographed the cloud its bomb left behind. Everything was ordinary. I opened the door to a house and saw a woman in the courtyard frying a chicken. She gave me a dirty look. We arrived at a T-junction and my friend suddenly said, 'Look over there, that girl is still alive!'"

In his Tehran office, Nateghi pulled out the pictures he had taken, first of a Kurdish girl prone on her face, then another of the same girl, this time visibly though barely alive, propped up against the wall of a house where Nateghi and his friends had carried her. Next to her is a boy, possibly her brother. Nateghi said he found the boy inside the house where he had gone looking for a mattress on which to lay the girl, and had carried him into the street. He noticed that a white powder covered the ground outside, as well as the children's faces. "I thought a bomb had struck a chalk factory," Nateghi recalled. He tried to wipe their faces clean, even as bombs continued to fall. "This was so normal that I didn't pay it particular attention. We moved on and then I saw this man." (Here he shows the picture, now famous, of a man stretched headlong on the ground cradling his infant son.) "I took their photograph and at that moment one of my friends, who had gone to find a car to evacuate the children, returned in a military vehicle. He was wearing his gas mask, and it was only then that I realized what was happening."

Nateghi never put on his own gas mask, even as he came upon ever more grisly scenes of sudden, instant, silent death – "a pickup truck with ten, twelve corpses inside, the driver barely breathing" – because, he said, it would have interfered with his work. Later that night, after a military helicopter flew him, his comrades, and a number of Kurdish survivors to Iranian positions across the border, he had to be treated for temporary blindness at a mobile clinic. When he revisited Halabja a second and third time during the next few days, he was overcome by persistent vapors as he toured the area in the back of a pickup truck, compelling him to return to Tehran.

The precise death toll from the Halabja gas attack is unknown but thought to be several thousand. Out of an area population of 70–80,000 and with the reported intensity of the bombardment this was perhaps a remarkably small number. Many survivors saved their lives by rushing inside as the bombs fell, shutting their doors and windows. Those to the south and west benefited from a wind that carried the poisonous gases east toward the border, an area that became saturated with casualties. Again others lived because Iranian troops evacuated hundreds of the injured to makeshift clinics on the border, where nurses washed their bodies and administered atropine, an antidote to nerve agents. For days, the border area overflowed with stunned and traumatized refugees who had climbed the mountain to find safety in Iran, a lukewarm ally of Iraqi Kurds in the best of times.

Ahmad Nateghi's story has been corroborated by numerous eye-witnesses: Kurdish survivors; Iranian medical personnel; Iranian scouts who visited Halabja before, during, and after the attack; Kurdish guerrilla commanders; and even an Iraqi general who says he was in the air operations room in the Republican Palace in Baghdad when the order came to chemically bomb Halabja. More generally, evidence of Iraq's use of poison gas during the war is contained in eight UN expert reports; admissions by Iraqi officials, military officers, and pilots; tons of Iraqi secret police documents captured by Kurdish rebels in 1991 and brought to the United States for safekeeping;[1] eyewitness accounts from Kurdish and Iranian survivors; soil samples;[2] hundreds of US intelligence and other government documents obtained under the Freedom of Information Act (FOIA);[3] and interviews with retired US and Israeli intelligence officers.

Yet the question of culpability for the Halabja attack is controversial. This is in part because Iranian forces controlled access to the area, which allowed Iranian journalists like Ahmad Nateghi to dominate early reporting. The Iranian military soon brought in by helicopter Tehran-based foreign correspondents whose reports and images flashed around the world. But no independent investigator could ever visit the area freely, at least not until late 1991, by which time the Iran–Iraq war was over and Halabja forgotten.

Iran's thirst for a quick propaganda coup damaged the Halabja story's credibility, especially after Iraq's friends in Washington went to work. While the international community was quick to condemn the Iraqi regime in the days that followed, within a week the US State Department began floating the suggestion that Iran had also played a role in the gas attack and even might be responsible for the majority of the chemical fatalities. This contention, which originated in the Pentagon, soon took on a life of its own and helped dilute a UN Security Council resolution that should have condemned Iraq. Waiting almost two months, the council eventually decried the continued use of chemical weapons "in the conflict between the Islamic Republic of Iran and Iraq" (failing to identify a culprit), and called on both sides to "refrain from the future use of chemical weapons," suggesting that Iran had shared responsibility.

The failure to strongly condemn the Iraqi regime for what should be considered a war crime and a crime against humanity had terrible consequences for the rural population of Iraqi Kurdistan, in whose midst a tenacious insurgency had burgeoned during the war years. Undeterred, the regime's forces were able to use poison gas repeatedly in the countryside during the next few days and weeks in an attempt to flush Kurds out of their villages. Precisely what happened in Washington and New York in the two-month period following the Halabja attack therefore merits a closer look.

The Fog of War

In the immediate aftermath of the Halabja attack, inchoate rumors and confused reports reached Tehran-based correspondents and editorial offices in Paris and London, Washington and Rio de Janeiro – reports of Iranian advances in northern Iraq, an Iraqi chemical attack on a Kurdish town with hundreds of casualties, a possible Kurdish role in the fighting near a strategic dam, and allegations that Iran, too, might have used chemicals. Initially the world was dependent on Iranian government sources for news. PUK leader Jalal Talabani, traveling in Europe, soon became a second source, taking a different line on what had happened based on reports he received from his comrades in the Kurdish mountains.

On March 16, hours after the chemical strike, the head of Iran's war propaganda machine, Kamal Kharrazi (later minister of foreign affairs), accused Iraq of carrying out a chemical attack on the town of Halabja "close to the zone of operations of the Iranian Val-Fajr 10 offensive." Kharrazi claimed that Iran had launched the offensive on Tuesday,

March 15, and that the Iraqi reprisal could be explained by the defeat of its forces.[4]

Val-Fajr X was the latest installment in the Val-Fajr series, which began early in the war. Whatever its target, Val-Fajr X was not, concluded the *New York Times* military analyst, Iran's "feared winter offensive."[5] Was it, as another analyst suggested, part of a shift in the way the war was being fought – away from major battlefronts and toward smaller encounters, as well as stepped-up attacks on shipping in the Gulf and the enemy's cities, in order to produce diplomatic and political advantage instead of territorial gain?[6]

Whatever Val-Fajr X's objectives or actual accomplishments, what stuck was that Iran had defeated Iraqi forces in an offensive inside Iraqi territory and this, above all, began to color interpretations of events in Halabja, Kurdish protestations notwithstanding. Interviewed in France, Talabani claimed that more than 2,000 Kurds had been killed during a chemical attack by Iraqi aircraft on Halabja, in an area he said had been taken "by Kurdish guerrillas with the assistance of Iran."[7]

Iraq countered by contending that, contrary to Iranian notions, there could not have been any fighting in Halabja and Khurmal, because "these areas have been cleared of our units. Our units do not exist there." Instead, the regime announced, Iran's claims derived from "an attempt to justify its despicable crime of destroying the town of Halabja and nearby villages, which its units occupied and destroyed."[8] Iraq's admission that its forces were not present in the area on March 16–17 turned out to be critically important, as we shall see.

On March 17, Iran's representative in New York informed the United Nations that "several civilians were murdered and injured" in an Iraqi chemical attack during Iran's Val-Fajr X operation and, a little later, that "Iraq used chemical weapons on a massive scale" in the Val-Fajr X operational theater "and also against Iraqi Kurdish areas." The next day, he reported the deaths of approximately 4,000 residents of Halabja, Khurmal, Dojeileh, and nearby villages.[9]

On March 21, IRNA claimed that a total of 5,000 Kurds had been killed in Halabja and the surrounding area – another bit of information that has stuck – from Iraq's use of cyanide, mustard gas, and nerve agents.[10] The reference to cyanide was particularly important, which also was to become clear later.

At this point the first victims reached Tehran hospitals. Here they were visited by Western correspondents who quoted Dr. Hamid Sohrabpour as asserting that hundreds of patients had arrived from Halabja, "the largest contingent of [chemically injured] civilians we have ever had." The Kurds told reporters that Halabja had been taken by Kurdish rebels twenty-four hours before the attack. According to the *Globe and Mail*, "Units of Iran's Revolutionary Guards apparently were battling the Iraqi army outside the city when the Kurdish rebels, perhaps in a jointly planned operation, took Halabja. Iran says that none of its troops were in Halabja during the subsequent bombing, which, if true, would imply that Iraq launched a chemical attack against a town full of its own citizens, albeit including rebel elements."[11] To put force behind the horrifying allegations, Iran released the first video images of the attack and its civilian victims, soon watched by millions of viewers across the globe. The Iranian representative at the UN urgently called for an investigation.[12]

In the meantime, Iran's Information Ministry had been working overtime to accommodate journalists' requests to visit Halabja. On March 20, helicopters airlifted the first group to the blighted town, nearly striking treetops in their effort to escape the notice of Iraqi warplanes circling overhead. Their stories soon appeared. The *Guardian's* David Hirst painted a particularly graphic picture: "No wounds, no blood, no traces of explosions can be found on the bodies," he reported. "The skin of the bodies is strangely discoloured, with their eyes open and staring where they have not disappeared into their sockets, a grayish slime oozing from their mouths and their fingers still grotesquely twisted. Death seemingly caught them almost unawares." Hirst quotes an Iranian doctor, Abbas Foroutan, as claiming the Kurds were the victims of cyanide gas: "One bomb holds a hundred litres and on a cold day the vapour can quickly spread 500 metres. These people had no chance."[13]

The uproar in the media, encouraged by Iran's propaganda machine, threatened to embarrass the Reagan administration, whose strong support of the Iraqi war effort – especially after the 1986 Iran–Contra scandal – was on public display as it pushed for an international arms embargo against Iran in the UN Security Council. Moreover, intelligence analysts estimated that Iranian troops advancing inside Iraqi territory might pose a direct threat to the Baghdad regime, Washington's ally. Fresh accounts, disturbing to those who feared an Iraqi military collapse, suggested that the Iranians were closing in on the strategic hydroelectric power station at the dam in the Darbandikhan reservoir, or Sirwan lake, that provided electricity to a vast region stretching as far as Baghdad, while the dam itself controlled the water level in the Diyala further down, a tributary of the Tigris. An Iranian capture of the dam, it was thought, would constitute a severe blow to the Iraqi regime and might even present it with an existential threat should the conquerors blow up the power station, open the dam, and flood Baghdad.[14]

Soon new reports insinuated themselves into the debate over the Halabja events, even as these events were still unfolding: reports of Iranian troop movements, heavy Iraqi resistance, and further chemical strikes. What to make of these reports? Journalists ferried into Halabja, whisked in and out by jittery escorts while under continuous Iraqi strafing and shelling, had little time for a thorough investigation. Who was where, doing what to whom? In the fog of war, these questions were nearly impossible to sort out.

In this confusion, on March 23 State Department spokesman Charles Redman condemned Iraq (of "a particularly grave violation of the 1925 Geneva Protocol") and in the same breath appeared to deflect Iraq's responsibility for the gas attack, saying there were "indications that Iran may also have used chemical artillery shells in this fighting."[15] Moreover (unnamed American officials soon suggested), the Iranians had used chemical shells on "very limited occasions" in the previous two years.[16]

The Iraqi regime, usually quick to the draw in countering Iranian accusations but oddly silent in the immediate aftermath following Halabja, now chimed in. Facing stiff criticism on ABC's "Nightline," Iraq's representative to the UN, Abd-al-Amir al-Anbari, grasped the lifeline thrown by the Reagan administration earlier that day: "Well," he said, "let me remind you that Mr. Redman . . . mentioned that there were some indication and some possibilities – actually, more than possibilities – that Iran used chemical shelling against Iraqi territories." He went on to assert that the Halabja accusation had been made only by Iran and by Jalal Talabani, "who's collaborating with Iran."

At this point Nightline's host, Ted Koppel, conceded, "There is some ambiguity in this particular instance." But if, he said, the ambassador was correct in suggesting that Iran, not Iraq, was to blame for Halabja, then surely the Iraqi government stood to benefit from a UN investigation. On this point al-Anbari ceded little ground. Instead he suggested, echoing earlier US assertions in the Security Council, that Iran's refusal to end the war superseded any atrocities Iraq might commit. "We have made ourselves clear," the Iraqi diplomat exclaimed, "and we will be ready to welcome any team, any solution, provided that it...not ... distract the Security Council and...world attention from the real cause – namely, the Iranian aggression and the war. We would like to cooperate with everyone regarding the chemicals or the prisoner of wars [sic] or the tankers, etcetera, etcetera, as long as the solution is to put a peaceful end to the war and to punish the guilty party."[17]

The Reagan administration's carefully worded accusation planted a seed of doubt in the minds of those who were willing to see an Iranian hand in evil acts. The media helped in spreading Washington's spin, with one paper quoting unidentified officials as saying they had "good intelligence indicating that Iran used artillery-delivered cyanide gas against Iraqi troops about the same time [as the Iraqi gas attack] as part of its offensive" in the Halabja area.[18] With the weight of the US government behind it, this version soon proliferated, becoming a respectable interpretation of events in the Western literature on the war and, in the absence of an independent investigation yielding contrary conclusions, framing the policy debate.

Sparring at the United Nations

The UN remained skeptical. Secretary-General Javier Pérez de Cuéllar, who had ordered several earlier investigations of Iranian claims that its forces had come under Iraqi chemical attack, felt he had sufficient indication of an Iraqi role in Halabja to condemn the Saddam Hussein regime. Citing "considerable and most serious evidence in the public domain" that Iraqi forces "again" had used poison gas, "causing a high number of casualties, including civilians," on March 25, while the debate over sanctions against Iran continued in the Security Council, his spokesman reiterated the secretary-general's long-standing position: He "consistently and unequivocally condemned the use of chemical weapons whenever and wherever this may occur."[19]

Pérez de Cuéllar's statement triggered a vituperative Iraqi response. Foreign Minister Tariq Aziz wrote to express his government's "bitterness and disappointment at the [statement's] biased and unbalanced nature," and assailed the UN's neglect of Iranian atrocities, most notably Iran's treatment of Iraqi POWs and its shelling of Iraqi towns. Rather than denying the Halabja accusation, he lashed out at the Iranians: "Out of our desire to emphasize the facts and in reply to the campaign regarding Iraq's use of chemical weapons, we would like to reiterate that Iran has used chemical weapons on the battlefronts several times. It has also used this weapon inside cities." Then he attacked the secretary-general: "We did not receive a quick and swift response from you exposing these barbaric and aggressive actions, and criticizing them with the same response and enthusiasm you have shown in your response to the desires of a barbaric regime that has shown a basic indifference to the organization of which you are the Secretary-General." Aziz ended with an allusive reference to Iraq's right to use chemical weapons: "Our people are determined to use all available capabilities and means against the criminal invaders."[20]

As grating to Iraq was Pérez de Cuéllar's decision to dispatch yet another investigative team to Iran. Unlike previous occasions, though, this team consisted of only a medical doctor with expertise in chemical injuries, not, to Iran's chagrin, a chemical weapons expert able to study expended munitions and identify the gases used.[21] Moreover, the doctor and accompanying UN political officer were unable to visit Halabja itself. The problem was that Halabja was an Iraqi town. UN deference to the principle of state sovereignty dictated that UN personnel could enter Iraq only with the Iraqi government's explicit consent. It was clear that as long as Halabja remained under Iranian control – as it would until the July ceasefire – the Iraqis would not grant such permission.

Meanwhile, Iraq stepped up its counterattack in the realm of rhetoric, firing off ominous warnings and new accusations. Quoting an "authorized Iraqi spokesman," at the end of March Jordan's official news agency reported that, "In response to Iran's chemical weapons attack on the border city of Halabjah and its destruction ... Iraq may select a number of major Iranian cities as targets for chemical weapons."[22] Thus, in an astonishing sleight of hand, the Iraqis first pinned responsibility for

Halabja on Iran and then used this as a pretext for an even more horrifying scenario: an all-out Iraqi chemical assault on Iranian cities to avenge the supposed Iranian atrocity in Halabja. Was this, perhaps, Saddam Hussein's latest bid to force the Iranians to accept a ceasefire?

Supposed evidence of Iran's culpability followed. It came in the form of Iraqi chemical casualties, soldiers alleged to have been wounded in Iran's latest chemical foray in Iraqi Kurdistan. On April 4, Foreign Minister Tariq Aziz notified the United Nations of Iranian chemical attacks by air and by artillery against Iraqi troops "in the Halabja sector on March 30–31," and called for UN experts to examine eighty-eight injured Iraqi soldiers.[23] The new allegation built on the State Department's March 23 claim to reinforce the notion of an Iranian role in the Halabja gassing, and possibly sought to telescope the March 16 and March 30–31 events in the minds of Western policy makers preoccupied with conflicts elsewhere.

Even if this was not the intent, it had that effect. Soon one could hear Iraq referring to "Iran's use of chemical weapons against Iraqi civilians in [the] Halabjah *sector* and other northern areas," and the "Iranian chemical bombardment of the Halabjah *area*," without specifying the dates of these supposed attacks.[24] Two years later, in a review of the Halabja gassing controversy, Patrick Tyler of the *Wahington Post* wrote, "Iraq asserted at the time that Iran also had used chemical weapons in the battle [over Halabja]."[25] Iraq, however, had never made such a claim, not in the spring of 1988, nor at any time since. If this was an attempt to obfuscate, it worked.

The UN immediately granted the Iraqi request for an investigation – to Iran's ire: The Iranians had begged for investigations repeatedly since 1983 but had been unable to extract more than one a year, and these usually came too long after the alleged attacks to be able to establish culpability. In the case of Halabja, it took ten days before the UN responded. Furthermore, Iran complained, the UN was conceding to an Iraqi request to examine Iraqi chemical warfare victims in hospitals in Baghdad, not in areas close to the supposed attacks, even though "it has been authoritatively and independently established that, owing to certain atmospheric conditions, Iraqi soldiers were in previous cases affected by chemical weapons that the Iraqi regime itself deployed." Therefore, Iran asserted, a simple visit to Iraqi soldiers in Baghdad hospitals would do little to clarify authorship of "this inhuman act."[26]

Keen on appearing evenhanded in a politically sensitive situation, the UN jumped at the opportunity presented by Iraq's request: A new investigation would offer the opportunity to spread the blame. To Iraq, moreover, it would also delay Security Council action. And so, Iran's remonstrations notwithstanding, the team returning from Tehran was promptly dispatched to the Iraqi capital, where it examined Iraqi casualties on April 8–11. It would take two weeks for its findings to be made public.

On April 25, the report was presented to the Security Council. In it the secretary-general expressed his "deep sense of dismay and foreboding" at the conclusion that "chemical weapons continue to be used" in the Iran–Iraq war, with an "apparent increase in the number of civilian casualties." The medical expert concluded that Iranian troops and civilians had been injured by mustard gas and a nerve agent in Iran, as well as in Halabja on March 16–18, and that Iraqi military personnel had also been injured by chemical weapons, primarily mustard gas. The latter claimed they had sustained their injuries in the Halabja area on March 30 and 31.[27]

It would take another two weeks before the Security Council finally took action, nearly two months after the Halabja attack. On May 9, the Security Council unanimously passed a resolution in which it noted an intensification of chemical weapons use in the war, condemned "vigorously the continued use of chemical weapons in the conflict between the Islamic Republic of Iran and Iraq," and called on "both sides to refrain from the future use of chemical weapons."

The statement was so weak and came so late – three weeks after Iraq began using chemical weapons in a key offensive against Iranian forces in Faw, and even as it was gassing villages in Kurdistan as part of the Anfal campaign – that it had zero impact. (By contrast, after the 9/11 attacks, events no more traumatic to Americans than Halabja was to the Kurds, the US invaded Afghanistan.) And so, as Iran and Iraq fought their final battles in this senseless conflict – soon agreeing to a ceasefire in their prewar positions – what had happened at Halabja became irrelevant. This obscured the chemical attack's critical role in allowing Iraq to gas the war to an end.

Why It Matters

Why focus on chemical weapons use in a war in which both sides perpetrated a host of atrocities? A number of answers present themselves. First of all, poison gas use was banned following the horrifying experience with gas warfare in World War I. To this day, mustard gas is often referred to as "yperite," after the Belgian village of Ypres that saw perhaps the worst of it.

In 1925, the world adopted the "Protocol for the Prohibition of the Use in War of Asphyxiating, Poisonous or Other Gases, and of Bacteriological Methods of Warfare," commonly known as the Geneva Protocol. In signing the convention, states declared that: "Whereas the use in war of [such weapons] has been justly condemned by the general opinion of the civilized world . . . this prohibition shall be universally accepted as a part of International Law, binding alike the conscience and the practice of nations."

Iraq is the first state since the treaty to have reintroduced chemical weapons on a major battlefield. (Italy allegedly used gas when it invaded Ethiopia in 1935–36.) Originating in Iraq's desire to have a counterweight to Israel's weapons of mass destruction, chemical weapons production accelerated after its forces breached the Iranian border in September 1980. The Iraqi leadership saw gas as the only effective answer to Iran's human-wave attacks – undulating hordes of ill-trained infantry troops prepared to sacrifice themselves for their leader, Ayatollah Ruhollah Khomeini, who had come to power in the 1979 Islamic revolution. After a few clumsy experiments in the early 1980s, Iraq first used mustard gas in July–August 1983. It then exhibited a swift learning curve in the face of Iran's perennial offensives, developing more potent agents (graduating from mustard to nerve gases; its use of tabun in February 1984 was the first recorded battlefield use of nerve gas in history) and using more sophisticated means of delivering these against enemy forces. Iraq would drop a quick-acting and nonpersistent nerve agent such as tabun or sarin along the front lines. This would set Iranian troops running but permit Iraqi ground forces to advance safely.

Iraq would simultaneously saturate Iranian staging areas with a persistent agent, such as mustard gas, thereby trapping the Iranians retreating from the front. Rear-area gas attacks, said a CIA analysis, were a "force multiplier" for Iraq, because Iranian support troops were less prepared than frontline forces.[28]

Seeing the powerful psychological effect of this weapon, Iraq later applied it in two novel ways: by smoking out Kurdish guerrillas barricaded in their formidable mountain strongholds, and – in a particularly cruel touch – by targeting civilian populations in both Iran (staging areas) and Iraq (villages nourishing the insurgency) in order to cause panic and to undermine popular support for continued fighting.

Chemical weapons are not considered effective killers, in part because they cannot be delivered efficiently. The early agents used by Iraq, such as mustard gas (a blister agent), were not even immediately lethal, although mustard is known to have long-term health consequences, fatal in many cases, and to possibly trigger genetic mutations that cause deformities and debilitating diseases. According to an Iranian medical census, some 34,000 people (soldiers and civilians) were exposed to mustard gas during the war – an astounding figure. Many who survived the attacks continue to die painful deaths from the delayed effects of mustard gas.[29]

Most of all, chemical weapons are enormously powerful instruments of terror. Iraq consistently used chemical weapons to sow terror in its enemies' ranks – with sensational results. Poison gas was the only weapon that proved capable of defeating a tenacious Kurdish insurgency. Fear of poison gas attacks flushed Kurdish villagers hardened to artillery and air bombardments out of the countryside in a matter of hours. A simmering Kurdish insurgency had started posing a serious threat to the Iraqi regime in the 1980s. Kurdish rebel parties took advantage of the war, specifically Iraq's preoccupation with Iranian offensives in the south, to seize control over large swaths of the Kurdish countryside. Recognizing the psychological impact of poison gas on Iranian soldiers, Iraq turned this weapon on its own Kurdish citizens in 1987 after Saddam Hussein appointed his cousin Ali Hassan al-Majid as overlord of the north. Within days, Al-Majid gave orders to use chemical weapons against the headquarters of the main Kurdish parties, the PUK and KDP, and against the PUK's regional command centers. In mid-April, several hundred Kurdish civilians were killed or injured in a chemical attack on villages located near a PUK stronghold. Other attacks followed but the main offensive came at the first melting of snow in 1988, first against the PUK's headquarters in Jafati valley, then Halabja, and finally on the first day of every stage of the six–month Anfal campaign.

Iraq's chemical weapons use likely was the qualitative factor that led to the Kurdish insurgency's collapse, as well as the Iranian leadership's decision to sue for peace. In particular, Iraq's April 1988 threat to strike Tehran with its new ballistic missiles armed with chemical warheads caused mass panic and fatally undermined support for the war.

When publicly confronted with accusations its forces had used chemical weapons, the Iraqi leadership issued stock denials. At the height of the initial accusations, however, in March 1984 the regime blithely referred to Iraq's right to use "insecticide" to "exterminate" this "swarm of mosquitoes," meaning the Iranian volunteers throwing themselves at Iraqi defenses.[30] And in July 1988, almost five years after Iraq's first use – when awareness of Iraq's chemical warfare had become commonplace – Iraq's foreign minister Tariq Aziz publicly acknowledged gas use against Iranian troops but justified it as a legitimate response to Iran's alleged resort to the same weapon, claiming that chemical agents were used "now and then" during the war and that Iran had used them "first, at the start of the conflict."[31] Two months earlier Tariq Aziz had already made an implicit admission by declaring, "Iraq has to repel . . . aggression, calling on all means including the use of chemical weapons against those who seek to occupy its territory."[32] The Iraqis never admitted to gassing their own citizens. The Kurds, though, knew very well who and what was hitting them.

Documents show that most of this information was also known to Western intelligence at the time. Later assessments (prepared in advance of the 1991 Kuwait war) show a full realization of the Iraqis' accomplishments: the use of chemical weapons as a force multiplier to compensate for their disadvantage in numbers. Iraq's chemical attacks were hardly "low-level" or "sporadic," as referred to in the literature.[33] The CIA, for example, credited Iraq with using chemical weapons "on a scale not seen since World War I," earning it "the dubious distinction of being the first nation to use nerve agents in battle." In an analysis from

1990, the CIA understood Iraq's deployment of poison gas against Iran to have evolved in three phases: defensively against Iranian offensives in 1983–86, preemptively against Iranian staging areas from late 1986 to early 1988, and offensively in 1988 when Iraq used "massed nerve agent strikes as an integral part of its well-orchestrated offensives."[34] Iraq's success in fully integrating chemical fire into its military operations is generally regarded as a feat unmatched in the annals of modern warfare.

Arguably, gas use is the worst of the war crimes either party committed during the war. This is why Pérez de Cuéllar dispatched chemical weapons experts to the Gulf eight times. Distraught by what the inspectors found in 1987, he stressed that violation of the Geneva Protocol constituted "one of the gravest infringements of international norms." The experts' own views bear quoting in full:

> While we are fully aware that all weapons are lethal and destructive, we wish to emphasize that chemical weapons are inhumane, indiscriminate in their action and cause long-term disabilities and suffering. It is vital to realize that the continued use of chemical weapons in the present conflict increases the risk of their use in future conflicts. . . . In our view, only concerted efforts at the political level can be effective in ensuring that all the signatories of the Geneva Protocol of 1925 abide by their obligations. Otherwise, if the Protocol is irreparably weakened after 60 years of general international respect, this may lead, in the future, to the world facing the spectre of the threat of biological weapons.[35]

The scientists were right: Iraq did develop biological weapons. Had the war not ended before Iraq achieved the capability to produce them, the world might well have seen their use in battle.

Several other factors should be remembered. First, the Iran–Iraq war witnessed the introduction of gases never seen in battle before, including possibly VX, a highly lethal nerve agent. Second, poison gas had never before been used against populated areas; in breaching this moral barrier, the Halabja attack set a dangerous precedent. And third, mustard gas victims are still dying horrible deaths today, nineteen or more years after their exposure. Which single weapon, other than the atomic bombs dropped on Hiroshima and Nagasaki, can take credit for such suffering? Moreover, the use or threatened use of poison gas so terrorizes its victims, especially unprotected civilians, that it prompts them to flee (even into the hands of their enemy, as during the Anfal campaign) or to abandon their support for the war (as did Iraq's threat to chemically bomb Tehran). "I'm not afraid of anything," an Iraqi officer declared (interview, 2003), "except for God and poison gas. It's like a ghost. You have no defense against it." This officer was not even a poison gas victim, but fighting on the perpetrators' side he had seen its effects.

Furthermore, chemical warfare was the war's only feature in which the international community had a moral and possibly a legal obligation to intervene and in which, at the same time, it had an active security interest because of the threat of proliferation and the development of more deadly weapons. Yet the world did nothing. Only after the war's end did the international community agree to impose multilateral constraints on chemical weapons development, stockpiling, trade, and use, enshrined in the 1993 Chemical Weapons Convention. This effort was only partly inspired by the Iran–Iraq war. According to Julian Perry Robinson (interview, 2001), a CW proliferation expert, the Iraqi experience added to the debate because of the obvious dangers arising from massive chemical weapons use on the battlefield and against civilians (Halabja being the symbolic turning point), but mostly because the world realized that Iraq, rather than remaining dependent on the Soviet Union, had acquired precursor chemicals, tools, and equipment from private Western companies to create an indigenous production capability. A strong condemnation at a time when Iraq was still experimenting with gas and probing international reactions could have restigmatized this weapon at no great diplomatic cost. The Security Council would have acted with the full moral weight of international law behind it.

As this book attempts to show, the absence of an early, strong, and unequivocal international condemnation of Iraq for its chemical weapons use, within the context of the Western tilt toward Iraq, had several dramatic consequences:

• It sent repeated signals to Iraq that the regime could continue, and even escalate, chemical weapons use – which it did, with the Halabja attack as climax. That event was later cynically deployed by George W. Bush as a justification for the 2003 war against Iraq, when he accused Saddam Hussein of being a man who had gassed his own people, eliding the critical role the US had played in encouraging the tyrant.[36]

- It enabled the genocide of rural Kurds during the 1988 Anfal campaign, as the tactical use of gas, aided by the Halabja demonstration effect, flushed terrified villagers out of the countryside. These villagers were gathered up and hauled to the western desert, where they were systematically murdered and buried in mass graves. In January 1991, coalition forces in Saudi Arabia and Israeli citizens prepared for Iraqi attacks with chemically tipped Scud missiles. Three months later, fear of renewed chemical weapons use drove tens of thousands of panicked Kurds into Turkey and Iran, as Iraqi forces advanced to crush the post-Gulf War uprising. In March 2003, just days before the US invasion, thousands of Kurds reportedly fled their homes again, citing a single fear: an Iraqi chemical attack.

- It also enabled Iraq to press for advantage against Iran, undermining support for the war by terrifying Iranian civilians into believing they would face gas attacks.

- It gave the impetus for Iraq's biological weapons program.

- More importantly, it stands at the root of Iranian programs to develop chemical, biological, and nuclear weapons, a legacy we face today.

- It may have misled Saddam Hussein, who got away with mass murder, to believe that he could also get away with invading Kuwait, precipitating an international crisis.

- It eroded international constraints on the use of weapons of mass destruction, as well as the credibility of international institutions such as the United Nations.

In sum, the Reagan administration's wartime collusion with Iraq and its virtual silence over Halabja amounted to a green light that culminated in genocide in Iraqi Kurdistan, WMD proliferation in the Gulf, and Iraq's invasion of Kuwait, the latter posing a direct threat to the West's access to oil. Iraq's chemical weapons use, a 1988 State Department letter to Congress forewarned correctly, "paints a grim picture of the direction war and terrorism may take in the future."[37] The US played no small role in encouraging this trend.

Rather than serving US strategic interests, these developments caused them irreparable harm. Today the world faces the prospect of a nuclear-armed Iran, which never again will allow itself to be caught so dangerously exposed to superior arms, illegal methods of warfare, and the world's tolerance of such. It also faces a chaotic Iraq that is sliding into civil war, having been destroyed by three wars and a decade of punishing sanctions for which, in addition to the Iraqi regime, the US and its allies also carry a significant measure of culpability.

This book's principal objective is to present the facts as they were available at the time and lay bare the debates that took place or should have occurred had these facts been publicly known. It also intends to make an argument that however unpleasant the alternatives, the decision to support Iraq and turn a blind eye to its worst atrocities had very specific, highly deleterious consequences, the blowback of which continues to haunt us today, creating unpalatable choices in a world that is giving every sign of becoming more destabilized and dangerous.

A Note on Sources and Methodology

A number of histories exist on the Iran–Iraq war, mostly written in the 1980s. Based primarily on media accounts, they are riddled with errors and elide both the important subnarrative of the Kurds as well as the pivotal role played by Iraq's chemical weapons use. Owing to the fog of war, to propaganda machines working overtime, and to the machinations of secret police, few of us have access to reliable information when two repressive societies face off. This does not, unfortunately, appear to be an obstacle in reporting events as established facts. For example, some accounts conflate Iranians and Kurds as Baghdad's common enemy, thus erasing the Kurdish independence struggle as an integral part of history. Kurdish names are frequently mangled and places are misidentified or mapped incorrectly.

Unlike other Iraqi military operations, the Anfal (which was announced – by that name – in banner headlines in Baghdad's daily papers at the time) did not merit a single mention in the literature until four years later. Chemical weapons attacks are attributed to Iran, invariably without evidence or specification of time and place (unlike Iraqi gas attacks). Because both Kurds and chemical weapons were deemed irrelevant to the war, and Kurds moreover were seen as allies of Khomeini's

Iran, few commentators rose to the occasion when Kurds were gassed. A number of works by US policy analysts are blatant apologia for the Iraqi regime, playing down its atrocities and heralding its rhetorical overtures as evidence of moderation.

Once Iraq invaded Kuwait, academic interest in the Iran–Iraq war faded. Histories of Iran and Iraq published since 1991, while devoting some space to the Kurds and mentioning chemical weapons, fail to give these issues due consideration and often get things wrong. Few good histories of the Kurds exist, and they tend to be weak on events in the 1980s.

This book does not aim to present a new history of the Iran–Iraq war or of US policy in the Gulf, but to fill a gap in our knowledge by restoring the role played by chemical weapons and the Kurds to their rightful place in that history. While much was known at the time, information was dispersed, difficult to obtain, and often secret. After 1991 much of this information became publicly available. Captured Iraqi secret police documents, US government documents obtained under the Freedom of Information Act, retired intelligence officers, Iraqi defectors, Kurdish witnesses (once their region fell free of Baghdad's control), Iranian witnesses, and (after 2003) Iraqi witnesses – these sources help to rebalance and clarify the historical picture and highlight the implications today of decisions made then.

Based on primary sources – government documents and eyewitness testimonies – this book seeks to determine what governments knew, and when, and what actions they took with that knowledge. This presents difficulties, as informants' memories may be colored by personal biases, subsequent developments, or by others' reports of the occurrences they themselves witnessed.

Official documents, while in many ways reliable attestations of historical events, carry a different set of problems. First, intelligence access to the two belligerents was poor. Intelligence assets were virtually nonexistent on the Iranian side and locked out for the most part in Iraq. "Access to Iraq was appalling," recalled a US intelligence analyst (interview, 2000). "The Iraqis didn't trust us and were afraid to talk to us; they had to get Foreign Ministry permission to see us. Getting information was like pulling teeth." David Newton, US ambassador to Iraq in the mid-1980s, recounted (interview, 2001): "We could leave Baghdad only with a permit, which would take seven days to obtain. A few times we didn't get permission. When we went out, we could see a lot but talk only to government people. In the north, for example, we only could speak with pro-government Kurdish militia leaders; these said very little and nothing critical of the regime. Information we obtained could not be verified. Access to non-regime sources was very limited."

Moreover, US friendship with Iraq de-emphasized collection of intelligence on Iraqi capabilities and performance. William O. Studeman, former head of the National Security Agency, has stated that, "During the Iran–Iraq war we viewed Iraq as an ally. So, Iraq was an area where we didn't have a lot of basic collection, or a lot of idea of the depth and breadth of the Iraqi capabilities. We had that on a monitoring basis, but few would call it in-depth knowledge of the target, the kind you would want to have if you go to war. We simply didn't have that."[38] This may explain the dearth of information on Iraq's chemical weapons use.

Secondly, although the Freedom of Information Act is tremendously useful in obtaining US government documents – the hallmark, potentially, of an open and democratic society – documents are often released selectively (perhaps reflecting the specific research agendas of the requesters) and, in many cases, heavily redacted. In addition, US Middle East policy is not made by the State Department but in interagency deliberations chaired by National Security Council officials. NSC documents are exempt from release under FOIA. Many available documents on the Iran–Iraq war are State Department documents that, taken at face value, do not represent an accurate record of US policy. Yet they are helpful in that they summarize past policy and describe ongoing diplomacy. Moreover, as a former US government contractor explained (interview, 2001), documents initiated by contractors (following a verbal request by a government agency) under a so-called omnibus contract – with no line items – cannot be obtained under FOIA as long as the government does not adopt them formally as position papers, but informally they are used as such all the time.

What emerges from US documents is not only how much the government knew at the time, but also – shockingly – how poorly it sometimes assimilated events, interpretations being colored by an author's knowledge, prejudices, and perhaps, in some cases, willingness to bend the facts. One State Department memo, for example, offering a thumbnail sketch of the Kurdish insurgency in Iraq, suggests that the reason for the 1975 collapse of Mustafa Barzani's rebellion was that "Saddam Hussein's regime so dominated the conflict that even Iranian military assistance was unable to prevent [the Kurds' defeat]."[39] The memo fails to highlight the US role in supporting the Kurds via the Shah and standing idly by as the Shah, having concluded a separate deal with Saddam Hussein, abruptly withdrew his backing from the Kurds who, left without support, were then easily subdued.

Lastly – and this is linked to the previous observation – US intelligence documents often are contradictory on key factual points and assessments (for example, on whether Iran shared responsibility for the Halabja attack), mirroring debates within the intelligence community. They are invariably labeled, "Not Finally Evaluated Intelligence," a standard disclaimer suggesting, according to a former intelligence analyst (interview, 2000), that the information is accurate but possibly incomplete, based as it is on "humint" (human intelligence). "There is no such thing as 'Finally Evaluated Intelligence,'" the analyst asserted.

In sum, the historian must take care not to generalize from the information available, conscious that it may represent only a partial reality, one side in a debate, or that which the government either wants you to know or does not mind you knowing. Hopefully, this book has withstood that test.

ONE

CROSSING THE CHEMICAL THRESHOLD

"Something sinister seemed to be going on in Iraq."
– US Secretary of State George Shultz, *Turmoil and Triumph*,
p. 238 (1993)

The Iran–Iraq War and Iraq's Need for a New Weapon

The Shah's fall and Ayatollah Ruhollah Khomeini's victory during the 1979 Iranian revolution brought dramatic change to the status quo in the Persian Gulf (called Arab Gulf by Arabs). One of the key pillars of US power projection in the region had fallen, a regime and a leader who had protected Western access to vast reserves of oil, thus guaranteeing a sustainable price. The Islamic Republic, by contrast, made no secret of its hostility toward Western interests, a fact graphically illustrated by the US embassy seizure and the ensuing hostage crisis. The first revolutionary years saw great violence and a succession of governments, as Khomeini's followers sought to impose their rule over other claimants. During this period, Iran was vulnerable to outside intervention.

When Iraqi forces thrust across the border in September 1980, the Iraqi leader, Saddam Hussein, claimed he was acting in self–defense against repeated Iranian provocations. In reality, he was motivated by a combination of fear and opportunity. The Iranian military, trained and equipped by the United States, remained a formidable power, while the new regime's revolutionary outlook constituted a potential threat. Yet the turmoil in Tehran offered an unusual opportunity. The Iraqi leader used it to make what he called border "corrections" in the

Iranian province of Khuzestan along its riverine boundary, the Shatt al-Arab (called the Arvand river in Iran). Saddam also, in the words of Israeli intelligence analyst Ephraim Kam (interview, 2000), wanted to "give a hard blow to the Iranian armed forces that would take them many years to recover."

Much to Iran's chagrin, the UN Security Council stayed virtually silent in the face of Iraq's aggression, authorizing only a statement of the council's president appealing to *both* parties to "desist from all armed activity" and "settle their dispute by peaceful means."[1] This, a US diplomat noted afterward, was "an exceptionally limp response to the outbreak of a war certain to have major consequences."[2] A subsequent Security Council resolution called for an end to the use of force, *not* for a withdrawal of Iraqi forces from Iranian territory.[3] No wonder, then, that throughout the war, Tehran's principal condition for a ceasefire was Iraq's formal designation as the aggressor. This, in Iran's view, was an "imposed" war, a term the Iranians canonized in official discourse.

In the early years Iran had the theoretical advantage of its strong and well-equipped military, but with the abrupt end to US assistance, warplanes and other equipment lost in battle could no longer be replaced, and spare parts gradually ran out. Meanwhile, the new Islamic leadership set off to purge the military, which they suspected of pro-Shah sympathies, and established the Islamic Revolutionary Guards (*Pasdaran-e Enghelab-e Islami*), a rival force with a separate command answerable directly to Khomeini. Iran's weakened military and its inability to obtain new war materials were the primary reasons why in the end it was incapable of winning the war.

Iraq, by contrast, had many friends, even if its earlier friendship with the Soviet Union had cooled after Saddam Hussein condemned the Soviets' 1978 invasion of Afghanistan and cracked down on the Iraqi Communist Party. Under the 1972 Treaty of Friendship and Cooperation, Iraq had been a recipient of vast quantities of Soviet weaponry, but now Soviet leader Leonid Brezhnev pledged neutrality in the war and refused to supply Iraq with arms. Still, Iraq had access to weapons from its Arab allies Saudi Arabia, Kuwait, and Jordan who, less out of love for the dictator than out of fear of Iranian expansionism, began bankrolling the war and serving as suppliers of and transit countries for arms, including from the US. Iraqi forces also had the psychological advantage of punching deep into Iran's Khuzestan region – oil-rich and ethnically Arab to boot – while Tehran was engulfed in violence and political uncertainty.

Within two years, however, the Iraqi advance had run aground, its forces receiving a severe thrashing from the Iranians who had managed to regroup. Rather than destabilizing the new order, the invasion served to rally popular support for Khomeini, who was able to defeat internal challenges – decimating opponents via mass executions, torture, and the like – and to mobilize young Iranians to fight at the front. Starting in May 1981, Iranian forces launched a series of powerful and increasingly successful counteroffensives. By the summer of 1982, they managed to push their adversary back across the border in a humiliating retreat, a disastrous reversal of Iraq's fortunes.

Had Iran savored this remarkable victory, Iraq might well have sued for peace – as it proposed on several occasions during the spring of 1982 – perhaps even on terms largely favorable to Iran. In fact, in an unprecedented challenge to Saddam Hussein's leadership, Iraq's highest decision-making organs offered to withdraw their forces to the international border and renege on all territorial claims. Had Iran accepted, Saddam Hussein would almost certainly have been forced to step down. As it was, the small group of clerics around Khomeini rejected the offer. Flush with victory, guided by a sense of revenge, and perhaps seeing an opportunity to spread the revolution to Iraq's majority Shi'ite population and thus bring about the collapse of the Iraqi regime, the clerics decided to press for advantage.

Scholars of Iranian history still see this decision as a tragic mistake. According to one Iranian analyst (interview, 2002), "some Iranian commanders wanted to enter Iraq to prevent Iraqi artillery attacks on Iranian cities, but soon they started talking about taking territory as a bargaining chip, then about going to punish the aggressor. If Iran had not invaded Iraq, Saddam Hussein might have fallen. Kuwait and Saudi Arabia had offered to pay Iran damages, but now they turned to support Iraq, and so did the United States, the Soviet Union, France, and Britain." Likewise, the Iran scholar Gary Sick has argued (interview, 2000) that the decision derived from "a foolish judgment that they could overthrow Saddam Hussein. They thereby prolonged the war for six years. All major atrocities of the war – the use of chemical weapons, the wars of the cities, the tanker wars, etc. – happened after that." Ever since Khomeini's death in 1989, a debate has raged inside Iran – not necessarily public but persistent in elite circles – over the wisdom of pursuing for six senseless years a war whose revolutionary fervor soon petered out in the absence of realistic objectives and as casualties mounted – a war, moreover, that rather than bringing Saddam Hussein's regime to an end, served to strengthen it.

On July 13, 1982, Iranian forces launched a large-scale offensive into Iraqi territory, aiming for the southern port of Basra, Iraq's second–largest city, whose capture (it was thought) would cut Baghdad's lifeline to the Gulf and precipitate the regime's collapse – a possibility viewed with alarm by Arab states and Washington. The next six years saw annual offensives, usually in late winter or early spring, in which untrained and essentially unarmed Iranian irregulars (the Pasdaran, but also *Basiji* volunteers recruited primarily from the villages, many mere teenagers) sought to wash over Iraqi defenses in "human-wave" assaults (*amwaj bashiriya* in Arabic) that incurred staggering Iranian casualties. The strategy was based on the calculation that Iraqi defenders would run out of ammunition before Iran, with its superior demographics, would run out of men willing to take the bullets. Iran seemingly had an endless supply of young zealots whose indoctrination and commitment were such as to ensure their willingness, even eagerness, to sacrifice themselves for nation and revolution.

Although Saddam Hussein had started digging in his forces on the Iraqi side of the border since 1981, these human-wave assaults caught the Iraqis by surprise, if only by their psychological effect. "I spent a lot of time at the front," Staff Col. Abd-al-Wahhab al-Saeidy, an Iraqi officer, recalled (interview, 2003):

> They'd come toward us and reach the minefield. The first one would try to move a mine with his foot and be blown up, but in doing so create a small gap, and then the next one would come, killing himself, and this is how they created corridors. We'd be firing at them with machine guns and other assault weapons and mortars and artillery. There'd be heaps of bodies and our weapons would heat up so much, they jammed. And still they kept coming, so we'd have to pull back and then start firing again, and this went on.

In response, Iraq brought all its conventional weaponry to bear. It initiated attacks on Iranian population centers and neutral shipping in an
effort to undermine the Iranian war effort by sapping civilian morale –
actions that were promptly copied by the Iranians and led, in 1984, to
the first "war of the cities." The war record shows an escalating pattern
of mutual atrocities. Iraq, said Awn al-Khasawneh (interview, 2000), a
senior advisor to Jordan's late King Hussein, "thought its invasion would
be a blitzkrieg. When this didn't happen, they became increasingly brutal. Targeting civilians was their specialty. They were desperate and
ruthless."

Yet Iraq had no effective response to the human-wave attacks. To save
his troops' lives, Saddam Hussein could mass artillery, of course, and he
did, but this became prohibitively expensive. His forces needed thousands of rounds to obtain an adequate "kill ratio" against the hordes
of Iranians rushing at their positions, unafraid to die. To overcome
Iran's psychological edge, Iraq required a weapon that would not simply kill greater numbers of enemy forces, but that by its ability to ter-
rify and cause severe and protracted suffering would diminish the Iranians' readiness to sacrifice themselves – a weapon, moreover, that would
allow the Iraqis to kill the maximum number of enemy at the lowest
unit cost. That weapon was gas. "We were using astonishing amounts
of ammunition, and still they would reach our positions," recalled an
Iraqi brigadier general (interview, 2004). "We faced serious shortages
and had to import from many places. Iraq then decided to experiment
with artillery-delivered mustard gas."

Iraq had launched a chemical warfare program well before 1980,
largely in response to well–founded suspicions that Israel was developing weapons of mass destruction: "Iraq initially sought to acquire a
CW capability to counter a perceived Israeli CW threat," said a 1988
State Department analysis.[4] In 1965 Iraq established the Armed Forces
Chemical Corps Directorate, modeled on the Soviet program. The next
year, Baghdad sponsored a training course for officers from friendly
Arab countries to enhance the Arab states' chemical defense capability, "due to Israel's suspected offensive capability."[5] Iraqi and Iranian
officers both participated in chemical defense training programs in
the US.

Closely aligned with the Soviet Union after the June 1967 war and
the 1968 Ba'athi coup, Iraq launched an all-out chemical weapons

development scheme, buying essential materials and precursors, even mustard gas stockpiles, from its primary ally and acquiring expertise in production and doctrine. Experts suspect that at the time of the Iranian revolution, Iraq had become self-sufficient in producing mustard gas. When it invaded Iran, it was ready to experiment, having succeeded in "weaponizing" gas – that is, in developing a weapon system capable of effectively delivering poison gas onto the regime's enemies. Given the limitations of mustard gas (a persistent agent that blocked Iraqi forces' access to areas they had saturated), Iraq began to diversify in 1982, seeking nerve agent ingredients and precursor chemicals from private Western suppliers who operated under the watchful but remarkably tolerant eyes of their governments.

Iraqi scientists' progress in chemical weapons production coincided with the military retreat from Iran and the onset of human-wave assaults. Iraq first deployed nonlethal tearing agents in its effort to stem the human tide sometime in July 1982 (data on the early attacks are few and far between) and put the Iranians on notice of its intentions. While tear gas can temporarily halt and disperse enemy forces, it does little to discourage zealots. Countermeasures are easily available, as onion–carrying Palestinian demonstrators discovered early on, and the absence of injuries allows a quick return to battle. Yet the early Iraqi experiments were successful beyond expectation, in part because the Iranians apparently believed they faced lethal agents. An entire division reportedly fled in panic. "This initial success," Andrew Terrill noted, "achieved with the use of a simple riot–control agent, undoubtedly encouraged an appreciation in Iraq of the potential of lethal synthetics on the battlefield."[6]

Once Iraq moved on to mustard gas the results were perhaps not sensational, but promising all the same. "Although the initial kill ratio was not very high – of 50,000 CW casualties only 10 percent died – the use of chemical weapons greatly disrupted the tempo of operations," explained Ahmed Hashim, a military expert (interview, 2000). "It reduced the mobility of the Iranians, forced to wear chemical suits in hot Gulf weather, by 40 percent. What took a while was for the Iraqis to get it right: to integrate chemical fire fully into their military operations." Over time, however, as Iraq gained more experience and better technology, chemical weapons became the cost-effective force multiplier it sought.

First Documented Mustard Gas Attacks: Summer 1983

One of Dr. Sohrabpour's students was to make a name for himself as the most widely recognized Iranian medical authority on chemical warfare. Abbas Foroutan, a physiologist by training, recalled being drawn into the new field of chemical casualty treatment after he, along with his mentor and other curious doctors, went in 1983 to see the Haj Omran victims, who were distributed over a number of Tehran medical centers. From there he went to the front. Gradually, in chemical strike after chemical strike, treating victims as Iraq continuously modified its tactics and deployed new gases, Foroutan became Iran's foremost expert and medical director of the Medical Association for Victims of Chemical Warfare.

Dr. Foroutan claims (interview, 2002) that Iraq may have used tear gas as early as 1980, as well as an agent that caused nausea and vomiting, most likely on an experimental basis:

> Iranian forces captured Iraqi troops equipped with very old Soviet gas masks, very old decontamination kits, and very old detector kits. These were found in Iraqi shelters. And although I never saw any medical cases before 1983 – I was working in regular emergency in Tehran and there was no central database for chemical attacks in those early war years – about twenty-five attacks have been recorded before August 1983 that produced casualties (twenty killed and forty injured) with wounds that were different from what you would expect from regular bullets and shrapnel.[7]

Before 1985, official Iranian sources listed twenty-nine uncorroborated gas attacks prior to July 1983, but later lists omit these early claims.[8] Credible reports of Iraqi mustard gas attacks emerged from late 1982 on. Although these attacks are poorly documented, we know that Iraq began storing chemical munitions near the front lines around this time. Col. Munqedh Fathi, a first lieutenant in the Iraqi army in the early war years, recalled (interview, 2003) that in a battle east of Basra in October (the first fighting in that area), his force deployed near the front line had rocket–propelled grenades (RPGs) containing mustard gas: "I received orders to check containers with RPG-7 grenades and mortar bombs. I smelled gas escaping from the valve of an RPG-7 and then my eyes began tearing and I couldn't stay there. It wasn't tear gas; I asked the guys in charge and they told me it was mustard gas. I don't think they used it during that battle, though." In December 1982, according to Terrill, battlefront reports suggested that, "Iraq was using limited amounts of crude sulphur mustard to repel night attacks and help break up Iranian human-wave formations."[9]

The first well-documented gas attacks occurred in July and August 1983, when Iranian and Iraqi forces fought a ferocious battle in the mountains above Haj Omran, a border town in Iraqi Kurdistan. The battle, part of Iran's Val-Fajr II offensive, was aimed primarily at dislodging Iranian Kurdish rebels of Abd-al-Rahman Qasemlou's Kurdistan Democratic Party of Iran (KDP-I), and extended across the border as the insurgents retreated to fallback positions inside Iraq. Iranian forces were joined in their assault by Iraqi opposition groups, most notably Masoud Barzani's KDP, but also elements of the fledgling Badr Corps (*Faylaq al-Badr*), the armed militia of the Supreme Council for the Islamic Revolution in Iraq (SCIRI), an Iraqi Shi'ite opposition group created under Iranian tutelage in 1982 and headquartered in Tehran. On the other side, Iraqi forces had the support of not only the KDP-I but also local Iraqi Kurds hostile to the KDP, specifically a force of the Bradosti tribe whose leader, Karim Khan Bradosti, was a *mustashar* (literally "advisor," but effectively commander) of a militia aligned with the Iraqi regime. Saddam later awarded him several medals for bravery.

The collusion between Iran and the KDP was particularly galling to the Iraqis. After the collapse of the Barzani revolt in 1975, the KDP leadership (having passed from Mustafa to his sons Idris and Masoud) had lived in Iranian exile. The Iraqi invasion lifted the KDP's hopes, and by 1983 it was providing active combat support to Iranian forces as scouts and guides. The Barzanis' thorough knowledge of the Bradosti tribal area in particular, which borders on their own, was a huge help to the Iranians, who succeeded in capturing Haj Omran and environs at the end of July. Cordesman and Wagner report that the Iranians advanced about ten miles into Iraqi territory, capturing "the Iraqi 1st Corps garrison of Haj Omran, the main heights and artillery positions in the area, some 43 Kurdish villages, a major headquarters of the KDPI, and much of the KDPI's equipment."[10]

Muhammad Ali Husein, a former Badr fighter, recalled (interview, 2002) how one day – he could not remember the date – Iraqi MiG-21s swooped over his small band of twenty-six Iraqis fighting alongside Iranian troops near Haj Omran at around 4:30 in the afternoon, dropping a load of bombs. One landed in their direct proximity, killing one fighter and injuring thirteen, including Husein:

> We didn't know about chemical weapons. We smelled garlic. After about six hours, the eyes of the fighters who had been lower down the mountain became inflamed; they were taken to hospital in Orumiyeh and then Torfa hospital in Tehran. We, who were near the top of the mountain, experienced some breathing problems. Some Iranians were also affected; I saw them later in hospital. I don't know what happened to our KDP friends, who were on the other side of the mountain. We withdrew after seven hours. Had we known Iraq was using chemical weapons, we would have pulled back much faster.

The symptoms that Husein and others described suggest that Iraq had used sulphur mustard, the same gas that had caused so many casualties in World War I trenches.

Dr. Foroutan remembered seeing forty-one chemical casualties in Torfa hospital. On the basis of their accounts, he placed the attacks in the afternoon of August 8 and early the next morning. The patients had skin lesions that initially baffled the medical experts. "I didn't know anything about mustard gas," he recalled. "The patients said they had seen smoke and smelled garlic. After three hours their eyes became irritated, they began to vomit, and their skin became itchy; the next day blisters appeared. When you pressed their skin, new blisters would appear. Some had severe pulmonary problems, but none of the ones I saw died. We knew the agent was quite stable because in some cases symptoms showed up only a month later. We didn't know how to treat these patients." Foroutan later wrote that Iraq had carried out a total of seven chemical attacks in the Haj Omran area during Val-Fajr II, and that civilians had also been injured.[11] He also said that he and his colleagues made an important observation: a garlicky–smelling clump of soil from the affected area that had been brought to the hospital in a plastic bag burned through the plastic. From this the military understood the need to use nonplastic materials for their troops' chemical warfare suits.

Not all participants in the Haj Omran battles agree that chemical weapons were used. An officer in the Bradosti militia that fought alongside Iraqi troops in Haj Omran swore (interview, 2000) that Iraq did not use chemical weapons on that occasion: "They didn't," he claimed, "because Iraqi troops were too close to the Iranians. I was there." Despite this denial, the claim that Iraq used gas at Haj Omran appears, on balance, to be correct. This was the first instance in which Iranian doctors unequivocally described poison gas symptoms. In the context of what preceded (and especially what was to follow), Iraq's use of gas at this stage in the war – and mustard gas in particular – was wholly consistent with its two-fold strategy of countering Iranian human-wave attacks and punishing Kurdish guerrillas for their treasonous alliance with the enemy. The contradictory accounts may be attributed to mountainous terrain in which one party might not be aware of the fate of another, or to the time lapse that occurred between the original Iranian assault, when the Iraqis aided by the Bradosti militia were putting up a stiff defense, and the Iraqi retaliation against the newly entrenched Iranian forces somewhat later. Alternatively, the Bradosti officer may have been less than candid in order to protect his tribe's standing with its ally, the PUK (itself the victim of numerous Iraqi chemical attacks), especially after the Iraqi regime's ostracism following the Gulf war.

The events at Haj Omran had three important consequences. To punish the KDP for facilitating the Iranian victory at Haj Omran, the Ba'ath regime arrested all male members of the Barzani tribe it could find, many of whom had been forced into resettlement camps around Erbil after the 1975 collapse of the Barzani revolt. Starting on July 30, between five and eight thousand Barzani men – precise figures are not available – were rounded up and taken away, never to be seen again. In a speech two months later, Saddam Hussein minced no words: "They betrayed the country and the covenant," he said, "so we punished them severely and they went to hell."[12] This reprisal bears an alarming similarity in method and result to the 1988 Anfal campaign: the Barzani massacre served as a warm-up for the regime and, for the Kurds, a small taste of what was to come.[13]

The Haj Omran events also deepened the split between Barzani's KDP and Talabani's PUK. The PUK, which had close ties with Qasemlou's KDP-I, initially was lukewarm toward Iranian entreaties and positively alarmed when Iranian forces launched operations in Iraqi territory the PUK considered its own. While the Haj Omran events were merely disturbing – the PUK had good relations with the Bradostis, both having a strong dislike of the Barzanis – a subsequent Iranian operation near Penjwin, a traditional PUK area east of Suleimaniyeh, was too close for comfort, and Talabani threw in his lot with the Iraqis, agreeing to fight Iran and engage in autonomy negotiations with the Iraqi regime. (These talks, in 1983 and 1984, collapsed over the thorny issue of Kirkuk and, as we shall see in Chapter IV, the PUK soon teamed up with Iran and the KDP after all.)

Finally, Haj Omran was a turning point, as Iraq decisively crossed the chemical threshold. Yet because Iraq's actions were barely reported they failed to make waves. The absence of international protest helped the regime realize it could use gas with impunity, especially if its targets were Kurds who, in their isolation, had little access to the media. Although most subsequent gas attacks targeted Iranian troops along the southern front, the Iraqis knew they could exploit the Kurds' vulnerability to poison gas later, when circumstances required it. More broadly, from August 1983 on, Iraq knew it could continue to experiment with chemical weapons. The following months thus witnessed a steady escalation as Iraq used mustard gas more liberally and then graduated to nerve agents.

The World's First Battlefield Use of Nerve Gas: Winter 1984

After Haj Omran, Iraq initially stuck to mustard gas, attacking Iranian forces in the third week of October. In its Val-Fajr IV offensive, Iran was again in pursuit of KDP-I guerrillas hiding in Iraq, now in the area of Penjwin. Cordesman and Wagner estimate that "this time [Iraq's] use of gas was effective" and that "Iran later claimed up to several thousand casualties."[14] Julian Perry Robinson, more carefully, lists only a handful of reported casualties.[15] Dr. Foroutan, who had started to follow chemical cases at this point, agreed that the Penjwin attacks were minor. In one case, he said, nine Kurdish villagers died from "severe respiratory insufficiency" within seventy-two hours of being hurt, while some of those who had buried the dead suffered other gas-related injuries.

Worse was to come. On February 22, 1984, Iranian forces launched a major offensive in two areas of the southern front east of the Iraqi towns of al-'Amara and al-Qurna, both of which sit on the strategic Baghdad–Basra highway. This vital north–south spine borders the vast Hawayza marshes that stretch east across the frontier toward the Iranian town of Ahvaz and sit atop one of Iraq's largest, only partially exploited, oil fields, containing perhaps up to 20 percent of the country's proven oil reserves. The first attack of what Iran called its Khaybar operation involved tens of thousands of troops surging forward in waves toward the highway. After a week of brutal fighting Iran had reportedly lost between 12,000 and 20,000 men to Iraqi gunners' withering fire and had accomplished nothing. A simultaneous Iranian marine thrust against oil–rig–bearing sand mounds in the marshes, called the Majnoun ("Crazy") islands, was more successful, and though suffering heavy casualties, the Iranians were able to hold on to their newly conquered "territory."

By now, Foroutan was right on top of it. "At the start of Khaybar," he said, "we were expecting a strong Iraqi counterattack with chemical weapons. We had an underground hospital in Jafeir outside of Ahvaz, where we prepared for CW casualties while treating the usual injured." At first, he recalled, Iraq used mustard gas in a limited fashion inside Iran, near the towns of Shatt-e Ali and Hoveyza; some unexploded munitions were later handed over to a visiting UN team. "On 7 Isfand 1362," he continued, or February 26 on the Western calendar,

> some wounded were brought in with unusual symptoms: projectile vomiting, redness, and smelling just like that clump of soil from Haj Omran. We realized that these were gassing victims and immediately spread our specially trained nurses over the area, using the Ahvaz soccer stadium for triage. In the first two days, aircraft dropped more than a hundred bombs with mustard gas. We treated 1100 cases, 150 with severe symptoms.

The doctor recorded another mustard gas attack, this time on the Majnoun islands, on 19 Isfand (March 9), involving three planes and yielding, he said, 533 casualties. Then a chemical artillery shell fired in the early morning hours on March 14 caused heavy casualties when it struck a prefabricated structure used by engineers to build frontline shelters.

Munqedh Fathi, an Iraqi officer who participated in the fighting, confirmed his side's use of gas at Majnoun. "The Iranians occupied South Majnoun and one-third of North Majnoun. I was on North Majnoun when our forces fired chemical shells at South Majnoun. We knew when a gas attack would be launched from the warnings [*shuhoub indhar*] we received: a white smoke grenade and a phone call. Our commanders were concerned about shifting winds and so we immediately put on our masks for a couple of hours."

Then the situation changed. "There were some other, minor attacks," continued Foroutan,

> but we quite knew how to handle it, and so on 27 Isfand [March 17] the nurses asked if they could go home for New Year's Eve [30 Isfand, or March 20]. Expecting further attacks, I told them no. And just then, around 11 am, we suddenly saw huge numbers of casualties coming in from the Jafeir area near us with completely unfamiliar symptoms: tearing, severe dyspnea [difficult or painful breathing], and a rapid initiation of symptoms. At first we thought this was perhaps a biological agent. But the casualties also had myosis – their pupils contracted – and we discovered that their enzyme levels were inhibited.
>
> Both these factors suggested something else, a nerve agent, and so we rapidly developed a treatment protocol. We administered atropine, an antidote to nerve gas. But we only had 1 mg ampules, hardly enough for these cases! We didn't know what kind of nerve gas we were facing, only that it was a G-agent [nerve gas], from our detection kits. Later we learned from the UN team that it was tabun. But the cases I saw were not so severe, and so I thought, if this is nerve gas, it's not a big problem!

What Dr. Foroutan saw were the victims of the first recorded battlefield use of a nerve gas in history. Tabun, also known as GA (ethyl NN-dimethylphosphoramidocyanidate), is a tasteless liquid poison with a somewhat fruity odor that interrupts the transmission of nerve impulses in the body and is so powerful that even short exposure to small concentrations "can result in almost immediate symptoms, felt first in the eyes (as a persistent contraction of the pupil) and chest (as a tightness or asthma–like constriction)," according to experts. Inhaled or absorbed through the skin, the poison triggers a sequence of manifestations, "some of great violence, including running nose, sweating, involuntary urination and defecation, vomiting, twitching, convulsions, paralysis and unconsciousness."[16] A gas mask offers effective protection. Developed by German scientists in 1936 and produced in large quantities during World War II – but never used – tabun is an organic compound whose chemical composition, containing phosphorus, resembles that of certain insecticides. Because of the rapid onset of symptoms, many victims die before they can obtain medical care. It is therefore likely that Abbas Foroutan remained unaware of the true toll, as most casualties probably never reached his underground clinic to receive atropine.

Iraq's rationale for using tabun was that unlike mustard gas it quickly dissipates, allowing soldiers to move swiftly into a contaminated area, even a heavily saturated one. It could therefore be used at the front. By contrast, the Iraqis had targeted mustard gas mostly at advancing Iranian troops as they themselves retreated, or at Iranian staging areas behind the front. But tabun use created a new problem: given the proximity of the front lines, it increased the risk that heavy winds would blow gas back at Iraq's own forces. Soon, according to eyewitnesses, this became a pattern (see Chapter VII).

There was a second nerve gas attack at 5 that afternoon, according to Dr. Foroutan, but none the following two days: "I would have known if there had been; we were the central infirmary." Now it was New Year's Eve (by the Persian calendar), and again the nurses asked to be allowed to go home, because the tabun casualties had all recovered. Again, the doctor refused. And again, the Iraqis attacked, this time targeting the Majnoun islands. Soon 370 tabun casualties were carried into the Ahfaz stadium. "It was a big emergency, because unlike with mustard gas the symptoms are instantaneous. We had some severe cases but not as many as expected. On Now Roz [New Year's Day] we were happy because there were only a couple of cases left in the ICU. Of these one died; the other survived with brain damage." Waleed Saleh, an Iraqi teaching at a Spanish university, later recalled a story (interview, 2005) that his brother once told him. Before he died of cancer, his brother had been a soldier in the war. Iraq used gas so intensively in the marshes, he had said, that Iraqi soldiers like him had to walk across Iranian corpses, as there was no space between them.

Iraq's prodigious and escalating use of gas could not continue unnoticed. For one thing, it had roused the Iranian propaganda machine. The country's diplomats received new marching orders: to bring this terrifying turn of events to the world's attention. And so they did, lodging vigorous complaints with the United Nations as well as a request for an independent investigation in the war zone. And although the international community, which was still deeply upset about the US embassy seizure and prolonged hostage crisis, initially paid little attention to the allegations, a small community of chemical warfare specialists, proliferation experts, and intelligence analysts began to believe Iran's allegations. Their assessments began to seep into the internal discourse of governments, the UN, and international agencies such as the International Committee of the Red Cross, fed by new accusations as Iraq expanded its chemical weapons use. It was only a matter of time before the world would become aware.

TWO

US RESPONSE: SETTING
THE VOLUME CONTROL

"We will never welcome the enemy with flowers."
 – Iraqi Gen. Hisham al-Fakhri, *La Stampa*, March 5, 1984

"The invaders should know that for every harmful insect there is an insecticide capable of annihilating it whatever their number and that Iraq possesses this annihilation insecticide."
 – Iraqi Maj.-Gen. Maher Abd-al-Rashid, News agencies,
February 21, 1984

Flushing Out the Reagan Administration

In February 1984, as Iran's Khaybar offensive got underway and renewed allegations of Iraqi gas use emerged, journalists started digging into the story, reckoning there had to be fire if there was that much smoke – which the Iranians were vigorously fanning. Reporters' questions were met with coy admission from Iraq.

In early March, having successfully defeated the Iranian advance on the Baghdad–Basra highway, the Iraqis allowed reporters access to the front and to battle commanders. On March 5, Turin's *La Stampa* published an interview with Gen. Hisham al-Fakhri, who admitted that at least some Iranian troops had reached the highway – their corpses were visible alongside it, lying in the sun. He estimated that the Iranians had deployed four divisions, each comprising 12,000–15,000 troops. "We completely annihilated them," he remarked calmly, claiming that Iran was sending only young boys and old men into battle. He dismissed the importance of the parallel attack against the Majnoun islands, saying the area was "of no consequence." At this point, a journalist asked:

Q: "Is it true that chemical weapons have been used?"

A: "We are now waging a war solely to defend our homeland, and we will never welcome the enemy with flowers, as he demands. I can assure you that if necessary we will use all the means in our possession."

Q: "You are talking about the future, but have you already used them?"

A: "I do not like these weapons. I can only confirm to you that I have ordered the same weapons used in past wars to be used here." (Note: The journalist does not appear to recognize this reference to World War I.)

Q: "Let us say, then, that you have not yet ordered their use. But does the same apply to the commanders on the rest of the front?"

A: "I must give you a political reply, as it is up to the government to decide whether or not it possesses chemical weapons. But I urge you to think about it for a moment: If ever there was a tactical opportunity favorable for such weapons, do you not believe that this battle of the marshes is the ideal opportunity?"[1]

This was the general's way of being candid. And he was simply echoing an earlier statement of Iraq's high command, which on February 21 had forewarned Iran that, "the invaders should know that for every harmful insect there is an insecticide capable of annihilating it whatever their number and that Iraq possesses this annihilation insecticide." As reports of chemical warfare multiplied over the following days, the media began a dogged pursuit of the story.

On March 3, Don Oberdorfer, a staff writer at the *Washington Post*, described in a front-page story the latest developments on the front, "the biggest offensive of the 41-month war." The Iranian "ground onslaught" and Iraq's threat to escalate air attacks, he wrote, "have created a new level of danger to the Middle East and the West's oil lifeline." Noting Iranian demands for a UN investigation ("seven times since Oct. 28"), he quoted an unnamed State Department official as giving "a certain amount of credibility" to Iranian allegations that Iraq was using chemical weapons. But, asserted Oberdorfer, "the Reagan administration, which is under heavy pressure from Iraq for political support on the battle against Iran, has said little about the poison gas charges. Asked about the allegations last Tuesday [February 28], State Department spokesman Alan Romberg said that, if the charges were true, 'we would find that a problem.' Asked to elaborate, he said, 'We would regret and oppose the use of such weapons.'"[2]

The State Department's tepid response raises the question: What did US officials know about Iraq's use of gas, and when did they know it? In an interview some sixteen years after the fact, the State Department's country officer for Iraq at that time, Francis Ricciardone, recalled (interview, 2000[3]) that he had received a call from Oberdorfer the day before his story appeared in print. At that point, he said, he and his colleagues had seen intelligence on Iraqi chemical attacks and shipments of precursor chemicals from West German companies since before Christmas 1983, but to protect sources and methods they could not make this information public:

> We were just starting the tilt toward Iraq. We didn't want Iran to win but also didn't want WMD [weapons of mass destruction] proliferation. We wanted the Iraqis to get rid of terrorists and improve human rights. We wanted to include chemical weapons in this but needed a peg. We knew the Iraqis would not be happy. I had told Nizar Hamdoon, the head of the Iraqi Interests Section [in Washington], that if there was anything to these accusations, there would be trouble and we would have to go public.
>
> We finally got a peg in February, when Saddam Hussein said in a chilling speech that for every insect there was an insecticide. We immediately hauled in Hamdoon and made clear to him that this was unacceptable – that the United States would have to condemn Iraq's use of poison gas. Two weeks later Hamdoon came back to us saying there was nothing to the story. Then came Oberdorfer's call. He had flushed out the intelligence report story. But because of Saddam's speech we were able to go public, and so we promptly condemned Iraq publicly. We also reiterated our condemnation of Iran for not accepting a ceasefire. It was a completely contrived statement that gave the appearance of balance.

And so, on March 5, in its first public acknowledgment of Iraq's resort to gas, the State Department declared that, "the United States has concluded that the available evidence indicates that Iraq has used lethal chemical weapons."[4]

The cat was out of the bag, with possibly embarrassing consequences for a Reagan administration that unmistakably had started tilting toward Iraq. In mid-March, *Time*, undercutting its own headline that there was "no conclusive evidence" of Iraqi chemical weapons use, quoted a senior US official as saying, "We have very conclusive evidence." "By January," the article continued, "the Reagan administration was sure that Iraq was using mustard gas, but did not know what to do about it." US officials had been reluctant to go public, the magazine claimed, "because they feared that to do so would diminish whatever limited influence the U.S. had in Iraq."[5]

The flurry of Iraq reporting exposed a fractious internal policy debate that came just as discussions about restoring diplomatic relations with Iraq were reaching maturity. This was, moreover, an election year, and even though Reagan was looking strong, it would be unwise to allow revelations of possible US complicity in Iraq's gassing of Iranian troops to get out of hand, however hated the mullahs might be.

A Growing Tilt

US support of Iraq in the 1980s was never wholehearted. Government officials intimated they were holding their noses even as Washington forged an alliance it considered tactically desirable. Officially, Washington stayed neutral, reflecting its preference that neither state win, but that each would wear the other down, neither one capable of mounting a threat to US strategic interests – Israel, and access to reasonably priced oil. What the Reagan administration clearly could not countenance, though, was an Iranian victory. Any tilt toward Iraq therefore served strictly to counter Iran's battlefield fortunes.

Washington's strong anti-Iranian animus derived from the ouster of its trusted guardian in the Gulf, the Shah, and the humiliating seizure of the American embassy. The drawn-out hostage crisis (November 1979 – January 1981) rendered rapprochement unthinkable, even if some administration officials toyed with the idea of boosting the perceived pragmatists around parliamentary speaker Ali Akbar Hashemi Rafsanjani against Khomeini's radicalism.

Iraq had broken off relations with the US and Britain in 1967 because of each country's support of Israel in the June war, and had signed a Treaty of Friendship and Cooperation with the Soviet Union in 1972 while also developing a relationship with France. It had maintained an Interests Section in Washington, though, and in 1972 the US decided to open its own Interests Section in Baghdad. The Shah's fall and the Iran–Iraq war propelled negotiations toward restoring relations. Who initiated these negotiations remains a matter of controversy. Iraq claims that the US pushed for a rapprochement, while the US says the initiative was Iraq's. Declassified documents and statements by key actors suggest that the emerging feelings were mutual, with each side reciprocating when the other offered an opening.

Iraq's invasion created tantalizing possibilities for political change in a volatile region. Soviet designs on the Gulf remained alive and its 1978 invasion of Afghanistan served as a reminder of the threat the Soviet Union continued to pose to Western interests. Yet neither revolutionary Iran nor nationalist Iraq was prepared to act as a superpower proxy. Iran had withdrawn into fervent isolationism, refusing even to attend discussions on the war at the UN Security Council, which it deemed a hostile institution. Its support of Lebanese guerrillas, who bombed the US and French embassies in Beirut in 1983 and took Western hostages, did little to improve Iran's standing. And Iraq under Saddam Hussein (who had formally assumed power in 1979) tried to ride a wave of Arab nationalism – rejecting the Camp David accords and Egypt's peace treaty with Israel and offering itself as a barrier to Iran's radical Shi'ism – to become the foremost Arab power. It needed the two superpowers to advance its own interests but was loath to act as a pawn in their geo–strategic power plays. A delicate game of chess followed.

The first indication of a thaw was the visit to Baghdad by Deputy Assistant Secretary of State Morris Draper in April 1981 to brief the Iraqi leadership on evolving US views. Ronald Reagan had just replaced Jimmy Carter in the White House, and the new administration was beginning to chart its own foreign policy, mostly in reaction to what it saw as Carter's dismal policy failures in Iran, Nicaragua, and elsewhere. The Reagan administration initially took a neutral stance toward the Iran–Iraq war, still reeling from the Islamic revolution's fallout while distrustful of Iraq, given its alliance with the Soviet Union and its opposition to the Camp David Accords. In a cable to Washington several days prior to Draper's scheduled arrival, the head of the US Interests Section in Baghdad, William Eagleton, remarked that "the important thing about Draper's visit is that it is taking place.... The atmosphere here is excellent following our decision not to sell arms to Iran, the increased Iraqi commerce and contacts with the US, mutual upgrading of diplomatic staffs and, most recently, the go ahead on five Boeing aircraft for Iraq. Although there remain a number of areas of serious disagreement on regional matters, we now have a greater convergence of interests with Iraq than at any time since the revolution of 1958."[6]

In dispatching Draper to Baghdad, US Secretary of State Alexander Haig informed his counterpart, Iraqi Foreign Minister Sa'doun Hammadi, that Washington wished to exchange views with Iraq in light of Iraq's "ambitious economic development program" and "capacity to influence major trends in the region."[7] The Iraqis reciprocated. In his meeting with Draper, Hammadi was at pains to put distance between Iraq and the Soviet Union and invited US companies to compete for contracts. Differences over Camp David were openly expressed but Iraq was urged – and it agreed – to keep an open mind. Concerning the Iran–Iraq war, Draper reiterated Washington's policy not to sell lethal equipment to either side, while seeking an early end to the conflict. On the evolving relationship Eagleton wrote that Iraq "is not yet prepared to resume full diplomatic relations but will resume and encourage a more systematic and more intimate dialogue at senior levels." Overall, he described the "atmospherics" as "good," the welcome as "genuine."[8]

The thaw continued, despite Israel's strike at Iraq's nuclear Osirak reactor in June 1981. In February 1982, the Reagan administration removed Iraq from the list of countries it regarded as supporting "international terrorism," canceling bans on US government–financed export credits and restrictive controls on arms sales and technology exports. Within a month, Washington reportedly offered direct support to Iraq's war effort, which was faring poorly. Staff Maj.-Gen. Wafiq al-Samarra'i, chief of the Iran section at Iraq's Military Intelligence Directorate in 1982, has claimed that at the end of March, as Iraq was witnessing "the most difficult times," the US began passing intelligence via Arab countries. Moreover, he wrote, that month "I was called to one of the luxurious houses on the bank of the Tigris in Baghdad to meet with three American CIA agents.... They said they had come to provide us with intelligence about Iran. . . . They brought with them precise maps and plans of Iranian sectors and regions, as well as satellite photographs. At that time we were in desperate need of this type of information."[9]

US support was too little and came too late from Iraq's perspective. By the spring of 1982, Iran was poised to retake its conquered towns and drive out the invaders. This led the White House to start referring to the situation in the Gulf as "the Iran threat."

The reversal of Iraq's war fortunes brought it additional support – from both the West and the Soviet Union. Arms started pouring in, and Iraq knew it could count on the backing of four of the Security Council's five permanent members, including (unusual for the Cold War) both the US and the USSR, with China staying largely on the sidelines. Washington was motivated by a desire to contain Iran and to alchemize, through a process of "constructive engagement," a pliable Iraqi leadership that would no longer block US efforts at settling the Israeli–Palestinian conflict and perhaps even become a partner in the peace process. There was also the expectation of increased business opportunities.

James Placke, a senior State Department official in 1982–85, recalled (interview, 2000) how the Iraqis approached the Reagan administration after Saddam Hussein had suggested in a speech that Iraq would change its position on Middle East peace and institute democratic reforms once the war with Iran ended: "He was making the right noises and he realized he was making the sorts of noises we wanted to hear."

George Shultz, who replaced Haig as secretary of state in 1982, described in his autobiography his initial approach to the Iran–Iraq war:

By the time I took office, the Iranians had driven Iraqi forces into their own territory, and the war had grown into a titanic struggle in which the Islamic but non-Arab Shiite fundamentalist regime of Ayatollah Khomeini was pounding hard on Iraq and thereby threatening the wealth, the religious legitimacy, and perhaps even the existence of Gulf Arab states. . . . The temptation was to stand by and watch this dictatorial and threatening pair of countries pound each other to pulp. But such a posture by the United States would have been inhumane and unwise. . . . U.S. policy, therefore, should be and was to try to stop the war. . . . Our only tactic, I felt, was to work to dry up the sources of weaponry that enabled both Iran and Iraq to render death and destruction in this seemingly endless war.[10]

Officially, the US approach toward the Iran–Iraq war in early 1983 remained unchanged from the day when Iraqi forces entered Iran, according to a State Department press guidance in February:

- The US supports the independence and territorial integrity of both Iran and Iraq, as well as that of the other states in the region.
- In keeping with our policy worldwide, we oppose the seizure of territory by force.
- We see the continuation of the war, as we have repeatedly said, as a danger to the peace and security of all states in the Gulf region, and we have therefore consistently supported an immediate cease-fire and a negotiated settlement.
- We have welcomed constructive international efforts to bring an end to the war on the basis of each state's respect for the territorial integrity of its neighbors and each state's freedom from external coercion.
- We have maintained a firm policy of not approving the sale or transfer of U.S.–controlled military equipment and supplies to either belligerent.[11]

Shultz's policy disguised the fact that the Iranian military, built up by the US during the Shah's reign, continued to rely heavily on US-made spare parts. Iraq, by contrast, had no US weapons and was therefore not dependent on the US. Moreover, it had ready access to weapons from other sources.

If this was false neutrality, now the outlines of an actual tilt emerged. As Shultz reasoned: "While the United States basically adhered to the policy of not supplying arms to either side, our support for Iraq increased in rough proportion to Iran's military successes: plain and simple, the United States was engaged in a limited form of balance–of–power policy. The United States simply could not stand idle and watch the Khomeini revolution sweep forward. . . . In this situation, a tilt toward Iraq was warranted to prevent Iranian dominance of the Persian Gulf and the countries around it."[12]

This approach gave rise to Operation Staunch, a US initiative to persuade its allies and other friendly nations not to ship arms to Iran. James Placke, who claims he gave the operation its name, recalled: "We had decided that the US had parallel – not identical – interests in preventing Iran from defeating Iraq. Iraq was seen as the first line of defense against the Islamic revolution. So we did not let the Iraqis buy guns in the United States – and they tried – but we told the Gulf Cooperation Council countries that we supported their support of Iraq. And we imposed an arms ban on Iran." Placke's State Department colleague Francis Ricciardone later recalled (interview, 2000): "Our position was not to sell arms to either side, but particularly not to Iran, because it had rejected the call for a ceasefire. We did complain to France about selling Exocet missiles to Iraq, because Iraq wanted to use these against shipping in the Gulf. We were not very crazy about that."

In addition to intelligence data, the US began providing Iraq with major economic aid. This initially included $210 million in credits to purchase US wheat, rice, and feed grains, access to Export Import Bank credits, and financing of agricultural sales by the Department of Agriculture's Commodity Credit Corporation. In the event, Iraq became the second–largest importer of US rice.

High-level meetings now became de rigueur: Sa'doun Hammadi visited George Shultz in Washington in mid-February 1983, and shortly afterward Iraq's under-secretary for multilateral relations, Ismat Kittani, introduced the newly appointed head of Iraq's Interests Section, Nizar Hamdoon, to Washington, meeting with an array of US officials and power brokers. Kittani recounted later (interview, 2000) that Hamdoon's assignment as Iraq's de facto ambassador was successful beyond expectation. By 1984 he had "taken the capital by storm, so when I went for a second visit [in November, to restore relations], I was able to meet with everybody," including Reagan himself.

In 1983, small events continued to delay the inevitable. In June, evidence emerged of an Iraqi bid to militarize its Hughes helicopters, which it had purchased from the US "for civilian purposes" in keeping with the US weapons–sales ban. Iraq denied the charge,[13] then countered with a concern of its own: It had received intelligence, buttressed by reporting in the US media, that the US was selling arms to Iran via Israel, and it could not believe that Washington was making good on its pledge to prevent such transfers.[14] Iraq would repeat this charge, and the US deny it, citing any number of countries that were supplying Iran, until the truth became known in 1986 that the US itself, via Israel, had also been arming the Iranians.

At the end of October, the UN Security Council expressed its dismay at the escalating conflict that now involved direct targeting of civilians. Condemning "all violations of international humanitarian law" in resolution 540, it urged "the immediate cessation of all military operations against civilian targets, including city and residential areas." No word, yet, about Iraq's use of poison gas, which had begun three months earlier.

Donald Rumsfeld Visits Baghdad

In October 1983, facing Iraqi gas at Penjwin, Iran ratcheted up its propaganda. Documents show that while US officials knew that Iraq had introduced chemical weapons into the war they were preoccupied with possible escalation in the Gulf. Iran was using a combination of military attrition (thrusts in the direction of Basra) and economic strangulation (preventing oil exports) to bring Iraq to its knees. In response, Iraq threatened to strike Iranian oil facilities and tankers with newly acquired Exocet missiles, hoping thus to disrupt world oil supplies and force the US to enter the war on its side.

These developments triggered a high-level policy review. A Reagan administration memorandum laid out the pros and cons of a progressive modification of the "qualified tilt." Ever since Iranian forces crossed into Iraq in 1982, the document noted, "the steps we have taken toward the conflict...have progressively favored Iraq." To prevent the US from being drawn into the war, Washington should now tilt further toward Iraq. Yet, the author recognized, such a shift itself also might pull the US into the war, for example, if it were forced to provide military protection to Gulf transport (a fear that was to become reality in 1987).[15]

The chemical weapons issue was subordinate to such concerns. Worse, it was seen as potentially obstructing the warming of relations. Documents suggest that as reports from the war theater multiplied, the administration sought to contain any fallout. Writing in hindsight, Shultz noted that, "Something sinister seemed to be going on in Iraq. In late 1983, reports drifted in that Iraq, desperate to stop the oncoming Iranian forces, had employed chemical weapons on the front lines."[16] These "sinister" developments evidently set off alarm bells in some quarters, most notably with officials seeking to stem the spread of weapons of mass destruction. In early November, Rear Admiral Jonathan Howe, director of the State Department's Bureau of Politico-Military Affairs, sent a memo to Shultz that deserves to be quoted in full: "We have," it begins, "recently received additional information confirming Iraqi use of chemical weapons. . . ."

> We also know that Iraq has acquired a CW production capability, primarily from Western firms, including possibly a U.S. foreign subsidiary. In keeping with our policy of seeking to halt CW use wherever it occurs, we are considering the most effective means to halt Iraqi CW use including, as a first step, a direct approach to Iraq. This would be consistent with the way we handled the initial CW use information from Southeast Asia and Afghanistan, i.e., private demarches to the Lao, Vietnamese and Soviets.
>
> As you are aware, presently Iraq is at a disadvantage in its war of attrition with Iran. After a recent SIG [Senior Inter–Agency Group] meeting on the war, a discussion paper was sent to the White House for an NSC [National Security Council] meeting . . . a section of which outlines a number of measures we might take to assist Iraq. At our suggestion, the issue of Iraqi CW use will be added to the agenda for this meeting.
>
> If the NSC decides measures are to be undertaken to assist Iraq, our best present chance of influencing cessation of CW use may be in the context of informing Iraq of these measures. It is important, however, that we approach Iraq very soon in order to maintain the credibility of U.S. policy on CW, as well as to reduce or halt what now appears to be *Iraq's almost daily use of CW*.[17]

On November 21, Howe and his colleague Richard Murphy, assistant secretary of state for Near Eastern and South Asian affairs, sent a modified version of Howe's memo to Under-Secretary of State Lawrence Eagleburger in which they refer to Iran's demand for a UN investigation and request approval to send a demarche to the Iraqi government, not only to deter future chemical weapons use by Iraq, but also to "avoid unpleasantly surprising Iraq through public positions we may have to take on this issue."[18]

It fell to the State Department's Iraq desk officer, Francis Ricciardone, to outline the new approach: "Our purpose is to deter further use," he wrote. Iran's appeal to the UN provides "both an opening and the necessity to raise this issue in Baghdad." However, the US should proceed carefully and not "play into Iran's hands by fueling its propaganda against Iraq." Iraq's foreign minister, Tariq Aziz, should be told that "continued Iraqi use of CW will play into the hands of those who would wish to escalate tensions in the region, as well as constrain the ability of the USG to play a helpful role." The US therefore believed, Ricciardone concluded, that "Iraq's scrupulous adherence to [the 1925 Geneva] Protocol is important to avoid dangerous escalation of the war, to maintain the hope of bringing Iran to the negotiating table, and to avoid providing Iran with a potent propaganda weapon against Iraq."[19]

In a background note to his memo, Ricciardone reasoned:

> Heretofore we have limited our efforts against the Iraqi CW program to close monitoring because of our strict neutrality in the Gulf war, the sensitivity of sources, and the low probability of achieving desired results. Now, however, with the essential assistance of foreign firms, Iraq has become able to deploy and use CW and probably has built up large reserves of CW for further use. Given its desperation to end the war, Iraq may again use lethal or incapacitating CW, particularly if Iran threatens to break through Iraqi lines in a large-scale attack. [Section redacted.] Nonetheless, on the basis of open source reporting now available there may be steps we and others could take to deter further Iraqi use of prohibited CW.[20]

In an e-mail communication in 2002, Ricciardone insisted that "our debates about what to say to Baghdad about CW and when to say it hinged almost entirely on the question of source protection." There may have been other factors at play, however.

On November 21, US diplomats in Baghdad handed a demarche to the Foreign Ministry outlining their chemical warfare concerns. There is no evidence, however, that rising US concerns over Iraq's "almost daily use of CW" prompted an active US approach, beyond the demarche, to put Baghdad on notice that continued resort to gas would be seen as a dangerous escalation. To the contrary, the issue did not appear in National Security Decision Directive 114 of November 26, which expressed concern over potential interruptions in the flow of Gulf oil and stated boldly that US policy was to "undertake whatever measures may be necessary" to keep oil flowing.[21] In that light, the demarche should be seen as the path of least resistance in a bureaucratic battle between those who had proliferation concerns and others, the dominant group, who saw an Iranian victory in the Gulf as the greater danger. A State Department assessment later concluded that the demarche had worked, as Iraq refrained from using chemical weapons – until Iran's offensive in February 1984.[22] But this ignores the fact that Iraq had no need to use gas in this period, as it did not come under sustained Iranian attack.

For the same geo-strategic reason, chemical warfare did not figure on the agenda for the most important meeting to date between US and Iraqi leaders Donald Rumsfeld and Saddam Hussein, in December 1983. Reagan had appointed Rumsfeld, secretary of defense under Gerald Ford, as his special envoy for the Middle East, and administration officials decided to work a Baghdad visit into his schedule. A key objective was to inform the Iraqi leadership of the results of the policy review. Talking points focused on regional issues (Israel and the Palestinians, Syria and Lebanon, Egypt's role in Middle East peace, and the US strategic relationship with Israel), as well as Iraq's support for terrorism, its ambitions to export oil via Jordan's Red Sea port of Aqaba, and the war. They made no mention of chemical weapons use.[23]

Rumsfeld, carrying a message from Ronald Reagan as well as a gift – a pair of golden spurs[24] – met with Saddam Hussein on December 20. According to notes memorializing the discussion, Rumsfeld and Hussein readily agreed on the need to re-establish diplomatic relations, with Rumsfeld indicating that Hussein should choose the time. Hussein accused the US of indifference during the war's early stages by letting "this group of lunatics bash each other." Rumsfeld responded that the conflict should be "settled in a peaceful manner which did not expand Iran's interest and preserved [the] sovereignty of Iraq." Hussein complained that US arms were reaching Iran; Rumsfeld pledged to put a halt to this. The notes suggest that chemical weapons did not come up.[25]

However, on the eve of seeing Saddam Hussein, Rumsfeld also met twice with Tariq Aziz, first in private and then with aides present. In his notes from his private session, Rumsfeld suggested that he did raise

Iraq's chemical weapons use but – judging from these notes – only as an afterthought. Rumsfeld said he signaled

> ...our desire to have the war mediated and end peacefully without further escalating tension in the Middle East. I offered our willingness to do more. [Section redacted.] I made clear that our efforts to assist were inhibited by certain things that made it difficult for us citing the use of chemical weapons, possible escalation in the Gulf [a reference to Iraqi attacks on civilian shipping], and human rights.[26]

That was all, and the discussion moved on. These notes suggest that when Rumsfeld had an opportunity to raise the issue of chemical weapons with the Iraqi leadership, he failed to do so in any meaningful way. Worse, he may well have signaled to the Iraqis that the US would close its eyes to Iraq's chemical weapons use. Rumsfeld, who later asserted that he was not the architect of US policy, certainly was the Reagan administration's most influential messenger to visit Baghdad. In an interview on CNN in 2002 as Washington prepared to oust Saddam Hussein, he moreover claimed that he had "cautioned" the Iraqi leader about chemical weapons use.[27] The available record shows differently.

Pleased with the results, William Eagleton concluded that, "Ambassador Rumsfeld's visit has elevated US–Iraqi relations to a new level." Yet, he noted, "We have received no commitment from the Iraqis that they will refrain from military moves toward escalation in the Gulf. Nevertheless the relationship being established with the US may have a restraining influence on the Iraqi leadership.... The Iraqis, however, do not consider attacking ships in the exclusion zone near Bandar Khomeini to be an escalation."[28] Nor, evidently, did the US deem Iraq's resort to chemical weapons an escalation. A status report prepared for Rumsfeld by Richard Murphy in January 1984 lists several ways in which the US had started implementing the further tilt toward Iraq: enforcing the arms embargo on Iran, imposing "anti-terrorism" export controls on goods to Iran, loosening export controls on Iraq (including, provisionally, military hardware), encouraging the Aqaba pipeline project, substituting new tanks for Iraq's old Egyptian ones, and increasing EXIM Bank financing to Iraq. It made no mention of a chemical weapons concern.[29]

Flush with delight over growing US support (soon-to-be-appointed US ambassador David Newton reported that anti-US floats suddenly disappeared from Iraqi parades in early 1984), Iraqi leaders may have felt they were not more but *less* restrained on the battlefield. Because Rumsfeld had mentioned chemical weapons merely in passing, and because his plea not to escalate the war clearly referred to attacks on oil tankers, the Iraqis must have realized that their battlefield experiments with gas had succeeded not only militarily but also politically. Moreover, following Rumsfeld's Baghdad visit, the US extended $2 billion in commodity credits for the sale of US farm products to Iraq. Newly confident, Iraq faced the Iranians as they launched the Khaybar offensive in February 1984. They did not even shrink from threatening Iran with "insecticides," a warning that Eagleton referred to in a cable as "chilling."[30]

Consummating the Affair: US Policy in 1984

"Flushed out" by the media in early March 1984, the State Department issued its first public statement on March 5. Concluding that Iraq had used lethal chemical weapons, it condemned "the prohibited use of chemical weapons wherever it occurs," and urged both states to respect their obligations under international conventions, "particularly those banning the use of chemical weapons."[31]

The Iraqis responded angrily at what they perceived to be a double cross, calling the US "hypocritical . . . , the last country with the right to speak about the ethics of war," given Hiroshima and Nagasaki. And Iraq insinuated that the US was trying to repair its relations with Iran.[32] Ismat Kittani, a senior Foreign Ministry official and later Iraq's envoy to the UN, put it more diplomatically, as reported by US diplomats in Baghdad. Kittani, their cable stated, "noted that the alleged chemical use had been on Iraqi soil" – and therefore somehow acceptable as self-defense – and "he compared it to use of nuclear weapons to shorten the war with Japan."[33]

In response, the Reagan administration engaged in damage control, formulating a two-pronged policy that one US official later characterized as "setting the volume control." First, it sought to appease the Iraqis, sending Rumsfeld back to Baghdad on March 26.

According to briefing notes, Rumsfeld was instructed to tell Tariq Aziz what Shultz had already told Kittani in Washington, namely that:

> Our CW condemnation was made strictly out of our strong opposition to the use of lethal and incapacitating CW, wherever it occurs. . . . Our interests in (1) preventing an Iranian victory and (2) continuing to improve bilateral relations with Iraq, at a pace of Iraq's choosing, remain undiminished. . . . This message bears reinforcing during your discussions.[34]

Rumsfeld's message deflected pressure on the Iraqis by referring to a general principle – "wherever it occurs" – rather than its specific application – Iraq's "almost daily" use against the Iranians. And it suggested to Iraq that the Reagan administration was prepared to overlook any transgressions for the sake of containing Iran. Rumsfeld later denied that he had in any way aided Iraq's WMD programs, and contended that he had spent the 1980s as "a private citizen," who assisted the Reagan administration only for a period of months.[35]

The administration, moreover, limited public criticism of Iraq by actively discouraging discussion of the CW question at international forums. In mid-March, for example, it opposed action against Iraq at the UN Human Rights Commission in Geneva, arguing that the commission was "an inappropriate forum for matters dealing with chemical weapons."[36] This was quite a rationale, given Iraq's violation of an international instrument, the 1925 Geneva Protocol, that by its explicit prohibition of chemical weapons *use* is a human rights convention, not a disarmament treaty.

To further appease Iraq – following a Security Council resolution, discussed below – the administration, in a new National Security Decision Directive (139, on April 5), carefully balanced its "unambiguous" condemnation of Iraq with the pledge to prevent Iraq's collapse and an instruction to "place equal stress on the urgent need to dissuade Iran from continuing the ruthless and inhumane tactics which have characterized recent offensives."[37] This, in other words, was a rebuke of Iran for its human-wave assaults and its use of teenagers as minesweepers – harsh words that aimed to soften the blow directed at Iraq.

The second prong of US policy was a ban on the export of key chemicals to both Iran and Iraq. This seems to have sent the strongest message to the Iraqis. In early March, before the ban, US Customs authorities had intercepted a large shipment of potassium fluoride at KLM's cargo facility at Kennedy airport. Potassium fluoride is a chemical needed in the manufacture of pesticides but is also a key ingredient in the production of the nerve agents tabun and sarin. This find in particular helped the administration understand the need for broader sanctions. So, at the end of March, the Department of Commerce instituted restrictions on the export of five (later expanded to eight) specified chemicals to Iran and Iraq. The State Department wrote to US companies urging them not to sell precursor agents to Iraq and met with diplomats of friendly countries to request that they, too, impose export controls. Britain soon complied, as did several European nations, Japan, Australia, and New Zealand, as well as the European Community.

Meanwhile, the US condemnation of Iraq, a UN Security Council resolution, and the new export ban raised many questions, which journalists increasingly began to pose: What did the administration know about Iraq's use of poison gas? Where had the Iraqis obtained these chemicals? From US companies? What was Washington doing to prevent further such shipments? Had it discussed preventive measures with its allies? Was it considering military strikes against Iraqi chemical warfare facilities? Was it asking Israel to carry out such attacks instead? At the question-and-answer session following the announcement of export restrictions, a journalist asked the State Department spokesperson why the US was punishing both Iraq and Iran. Is there, he asked, any suggestion that Iran has also used chemical weapons?

Answer (from John Hughes): "I'm not sure whether there is any suggestion that they have used them, but the intent would be to make sure that neither side uses them."

Q: "You're, in effect, punishing one side for doing something that it hasn't done?"

A: "There is a war going on that we would like to see ended. We're neutral in that war. We are opposed to the use of chemical weapons. . . . So we think that in this particular case it is intelligent and wise and prudent to ban exports to both."

Another journalist asked whether Iraq's use of nerve gas would affect the expanding relationship with Iraq, including its willingness to open diplomatic relations.

A: "No. I'm not aware of any change in our position. We're interested in being involved in a closer dialogue with Iraq."[38]

Initially, though, the Iraqis reacted with anger. "Hamdoon acted very surprised," recalled Placke, "and tried to persuade us that the chemicals they were importing were not intended for CW production. And so we told him that their *only* possible use was in manufacturing chemical weapons." Public condemnation hurt the Iraqis, Placke said, but the export restrictions "gave them a real shock." This was, he suggested, because Iraq's chemical industry remained heavily dependent on imported precursor agents.

In the end, the chemical weapons imbroglio in March 1984 turned out to be – through deft diplomacy – a mere hiccup in the process to restore diplomatic relations. "We were satisfied," Jim Placke concluded, that

Iraq was a growing trading partner. It was a barrier to Iranian expansionism. Formal relations would make us more effective in our representations in Baghdad – which I think we were. Plus keep in mind that in the Cold War ledger Iraq did come over to our side (even if they didn't break relations with the Soviet Union), and this made a difference.

As for the chemical weapons issue:

We agreed to disagree. We could not control all imports to Iraq. We took a rhetorical position against battlefield use. I'm not sure what more we could have done. Perhaps we could have made more of a public statement, but this would not have influenced their policy. They saw it as vital. If we had tried to make it a condition of restoring relations, relations would never have been restored.

Remarks by Tariq Aziz bear this out. In an interview in August 1984 he threatened that if the US made chemical weapons use the center of its policy, "I can assure you that the immediate conviction in Iraq will be that this is in preparation for an Israeli attack [against industrial complexes]. If so, it would poison the present constructive atmosphere between the United States and us."[39] Such an attack was being planned, Seymour Hersh reported, and Iraq had reason to pay attention, given the destruction of its Osirak nuclear reactor by Israel three years earlier.[40]

Ismat Kittani agreed (interview, 2000) that US–Iraqi rapprochement was "just a process that needed to happen, and in the end it was simply a formalization of a de facto situation that had developed." More surprisingly, however, Kittani also said that to the best of his recollection, "chemical weapons were not mentioned" in talks regarding diplomatic ties, and if they were mentioned, he said he doubted they had caused any delay.

US officials have taken a different view. David Newton, chargé d'affaires and then ambassador in Baghdad from June 1984 until July 1988, expressed world-weary frustration with his Iraqi counterparts: "We discussed the use of chemical weapons with them several times a year, but it was obviously a futile exercise. Yes, we had an interest in preventing the use and spread of such weapons, but gassing Iranians didn't send the kind of message that it would today. The general understanding [in Washington] was that the Iraqis would not stop anyway. We had to raise it but had no expectation they would stop." Francis Ricciardone, the State Department's country officer for Iraq, concurred (interview, 2000): "We held our noses a bit, but we ended up criticizing the Iraqis; we did demarches all the time. It became a big issue in our relations for a while. But thanks to excellent diplomatic work, we were able to upgrade relations in November 1984."

And so it transpired. George Shultz later wrote that in September 1984, "when Iraqi officials at the United Nations passed word to me that they would like to resume full diplomatic relations, I responded that we were willing to consider the idea." He raised it with Israeli Prime Minister Shimon Peres and Foreign Minister Yitzhak Shamir in October. They both agreed it "could be a positive development insofar as Israel was concerned." With the Israelis fully in the picture, there were no further obstacles, and on November 26, three weeks after Reagan's resounding reelection victory, Tariq Aziz, Ismat Kittani and Nizar Hamdoon attended a White House ceremony sealing the arrangement. "There were no stars in my eyes or in Ronald Reagan's," Shultz wrote later (*after* Iraq invaded Kuwait, crossing a US red line). "I simply thought we were better off with diplomatic relations with Iraq."[41]

Shultz claims he told Aziz that Washington "was unalterably opposed to the use of chemical weapons and that we would be watching Iraq carefully."[42] The public record is less explicit. It shows Shultz conveying to Aziz that, "Iraq can expect the U.S. to maintain its opposition to both the use and production of chemical weapons. This position is not directed specifically at Iraq, but is taken out of concern over this form of warfare all over."[43] Saddam Hussein, later called the "man who gassed his own people" by George W. Bush, was pleased to refer to his newly consummated relationship with the US as the "beautiful atmosphere between us."[44]

The UN Investigates

The use of nerve gas marked a distinct escalation in the war and it, along with the now almost routine use of mustard gas, prompted an avalanche of Iranian complaints. These, along with media reporting and the official US acknowledgment that Iraq was using poison gas, forced the hand of the International Committee of the Red Cross (ICRC), an organization that, in addition to providing humanitarian aid, monitors state compliance with the laws of war. It rarely goes public, preferring quiet diplomacy, but Iran's allegations provided an important opportunity. The ICRC's relations with the Iranian regime had declined over the issue of Iraqi prisoners of war, whom ICRC delegates were blocked from visiting. By publicly raising concerns over Iraqi chemical warfare the ICRC could improve its standing with the Iranians. On March 7, the organization issued a carefully phrased statement that its delegates had seen 500 wounded combatants in Tehran hospitals who presented a "clinical picture of such character as to support a presumption of the recent use of products prohibited by current international law."[45]

The ICRC's statement lent new credibility to Iranian claims and validated Tehran's assertion that chemical weapons use constituted a breach of the 1925 Geneva Protocol. The next day, Iran formally renewed its request for a UN investigation. And this time, having demurred repeatedly, the UN responded positively.

Getting the UN to act had proven to be a real struggle for the Iranians, who felt they had right on their side and interpreted UN reluctance as hostility. Sa'id Rajaie Khorassani, Iran's UN envoy, recalled (interview, 2002) that when he tried to raise the issue, he had to convince a hostile and skeptical world of the accuracy of Iranian claims at a time when the major powers had, for all practical purposes, lined up behind Iraq, angered by Iranian support of Hezbollah and apprehensive of the Islamic revolution's desire to extend its influence, via a conquered Iraq, to the fragile Gulf states.

A wiry man in his sixties, Khorassani served as Iran's permanent representative to the UN from 1981 till 1987 – the better part of the war. In his quest for a UN investigation, he said, he first had to overcome another major hurdle: his own government. The regime had learned to be distrustful of the UN, especially the Security Council, whose five permanent members were either hostile to Iran or, in the case of China, neutral to the point of being disinterested. Iran had instructed its diplomats to boycott Security Council sessions on the war, thereby leaving the field to the Iraqis. The latter, by contrast, were hyperactive and were led by a career civil servant, Ismat Kittani, who had been a UN assistant secretary-general before his country appointed him its representative. As General Assembly president in 1981, Kittani had even sworn in Javier Pérez de Cuéllar.

Khorassani claims that he tried to get around Iran's self-imposed restrictions by going straight to Pérez de Cuéllar, who, he thought, might be open to discussing verifiable violations of the laws of war, specifically the targeting of civilians – with any kind of weapon. Still he would need Tehran's green light. This came in the form not of a cable from his Foreign Ministry, but in a speech by the supreme leader:

> Khomeini made a speech in which he asked rhetorically: "Where are the international authorities to see what the Iranian people have suffered?" Until that moment I had no mandate, but after this speech I did: I was simply going to put into practice what the Imam had said. And so I made straight for the secretary-general to voice my request. He was absolutely delighted because he had been looking for a way for

the international community to get more involved. This was a good opportunity for him: He could establish the UN's impartiality, develop cooperation with us, and influence the Security Council to find a solution to the war. Within forty-eight hours he sent a delegation.

Khorassani's request was received by Giandoménico Picco, the assistant secretary-general for political affairs who was involved – at great personal danger – in efforts to negotiate the release of Western hostages in Lebanon. According to Picco (interview, 2000), the UN had to wring itself into all kinds of contortions to respond favorably:

> In 1983 we started to receive letters and verbal appeals from the Iranians. The idea of investigating chemical warfare accusations was very new, even though to the Western mind it's logical to investigate when you have an allegation. There had been no such investigations since the signing of the Geneva Protocol on gas warfare in 1925, and so when the secretary-general raised this with the Security Council in 1983, he encountered an antarctically cold atmosphere; the Security Council wanted nothing of it. The CW issue came up during the darkest hours of the Cold War – six months of Andropov's rule in the Soviet Union. Nobody in either Washington or Moscow gave a damn about the United Nations. It was equally despised by both.

Fortunately, said Picco, his colleague Iqbal Riza, then a Secretariat staff member (and Secretary-General Kofi Annan's chief of staff until 2004), decided to make an all-out push. "We said, 'What the hell? What have we got to lose?' In the end, it was Pérez de Cuéllar's decision – with great fatigue and political risk."

Iqbal Riza became the UN's most ardent advocate of investigations into atrocities committed in the Iran–Iraq war. "In 1983 it was our initiative to persuade the secretary-general, and in doing so we had to overcome quite a bit of resistance, even from many of his other advisors," Riza contended (interview, 2000). The mission that year, the first of nine, looked at civilian targeting, leaving aside the chemical weapons issue, which was still very new. Through this and subsequent missions, four of which he accompanied as political officer, Riza earned Iran's undying respect and gratitude. He had opened the door to the secretary-general's office, which over time became a significant counterweight to the Security Council's consistently pro-Iraqi stance.

To Riza, the repeated failure of peace efforts undertaken by UN envoy Olof Palme and others suggested that the UN should aim instead for "lesser measures" that had a better chance of succeeding, and to build on these to forge an overall peace. These measures should aim at bringing Iran and Iraq into compliance with their commitments under the laws of war, especially with respect to targeting civilians (the "wars of the cities"), attacks on merchant shipping, the treatment of POWs, and chemical weapons use. To Iran this approach was acceptable: It addressed some of its most pressing concerns – Iraqi advantages on the battlefield made possible through the routine commission of war crimes – while at the same time diverting attention from its steadfast refusal to negotiate an end to the war. The Iraqis, on the other hand, put up stiff resistance to Riza's approach. While Iraq had repeatedly raised the issue of Iran's treatment of POWs, it had no interest in international curbs on its methods of warfare. Instead, it wanted the Iranians to end their offensives and agree to a ceasefire. In sum, this was a diplomatic hornets' nest, but Riza pressed ahead.

"Under the 1925 Geneva Protocol on gas warfare there is no mechanism to investigate allegations of use," Riza explained. "So there was quite a sharp argument over instituting this. We advised the secretary-general not to seek Security Council authorization but to simply inform the council of his intentions. To his credit, he agreed."[46] In responding to the Iranian demand for an investigation, the UN made a point of asking Iraq's permission to visit Iraq as well but it was rebuked. And so, by dint of Iraq's refusal, the investigation had to be limited to Iran and the Iranian version of events.

Iqbal Riza may not have been altogether prepared for what he saw on his visit to Iran in March 1984. At a Tehran hospital, he says, the delegation saw a very badly injured chemical warfare victim. Noticing the foreign delegation, the soldier managed to raise his hand with great difficulty and make a victory sign. The man, Riza recalled, died two hours after their visit: "The image of this man raising his hand I will never be able to forget."

On March 26, Security Council members received a copy of the secretary-general's report, which concluded, on the basis of hospitalized casualties and debris picked up on the battlefield, that Iranian troops had been injured by air-delivered tabun and mustard gas. The bombs appeared to have been designed, the report said, "so that, when exploded, the liquid content would be dispersed over a relatively large area in the form of spray and vapour." The report, however, drew no conclusion about the perpetrator, or perpetrators, of these attacks, merely stating that "chemical weapons have been used," and then stressed:

> The Secretary-General attaches paramount importance to the strict observance of all the principles and rules of international conduct accepted by the world community for the overriding purpose of preventing or alleviating human suffering, whether they relate to the use of specific weapons, the treatment of prisoners of war or any other aspect of military operations.

It then added, "The Secretary-General remains deeply convinced that these humanitarian concerns can only be fully satisfied by putting an end to the tragic conflict."[47] In other words, the UN did not recognize an absolute prohibition on chemical weapons use, despite the explicit language of the 1925 Geneva Protocol.

The report might have been more forthcoming about the perpetrator, and the secretary-general might have been less eager to calibrate his statement in an effort to appear neutral, if the UN's experts had written in their report what they told diplomats in UN corridors in New York. Iqbal Riza, for example, told the US permanent representative, Jeanne Kirkpatrick, that the Iranians had shown the UN team "gas masks and associated gear, which they said had been captured from the Iraqis. The equipment was manufactured in Eastern Europe and bore Arabic script."[48] The finding was left out of the report because it did not constitute persuasive proof and, in the absence of additional evidence, might have been interpreted as an effort to smear Iraq.

Yet there was no doubt in anyone's mind about the perpetrator's identity. Ismat Kittani, who had already admitted Iraq's chemical weapons use in a meeting with US diplomats in Baghdad, later readily agreed (interview, 2000) that the UN report was objective and fair: "We took the reports seriously; they were scientifically based. Sure, we denied them, but our denial was thin. We virtually admitted chemical weapons use."

Now that the report had been handed to the Security Council and had been made public, negotiations started over an appropriate response. Kirkpatrick cabled Washington to convey the Iraqi government's "desire for 'restraint' in the handling of the issue and for action that takes into account the total context as well as beastial [sic] Iranian behavior."[49] In Washington, Nizar Hamdoon asked Jim Placke for a presidential statement rather than a Security Council resolution, or, failing that, a watered-down resolution that by its call on Iran to accept a ceasefire would de-emphasize Iraq's conduct. Moreover, Hamdoon pleaded, the resolution ought not to identify Iraq as the perpetrator, because neither had the UN team. According to US documents, Placke agreed but informed Hamdoon that the US would impose export licensing requirements on certain categories of chemicals and requested that Iraq halt its purchase of such materials. He concluded by saying: "We do not want this issue to dominate our bilateral relationship nor to detract from our common interest to see the war brought to an early end."[50]

On March 30, the Security Council president issued a weak consensus statement that strongly condemned chemical weapons use but refrained from naming Iraq as the culprit and directly linked cessation of "these humanitarian concerns" to efforts to end the war – doing, in other words, exactly what Iraq had requested.[51] To Ambassador Khorassani the resolution was disappointing, but, he said, for Iran "this was as much as we could get at the time."

A Missed Opportunity

That year, from April 1984 until the next Iranian offensive in March 1985, Washington had little cause to complain of further Iraqi embarrassments. Iraqi forces used gas only sporadically without affecting the military equation. And so the question must be asked: Did the combination of diplomacy and export restrictions work?

Some say they did, because Iraq effectively did not resort to chemical weapons for a year. Picco claims that as a result of UN efforts, "the use of poison gas stopped, at least temporarily."[52] Likewise, Ricciardone asserted (interview, 2000): "We told them to cut it out, and I think they did for a while." A military analyst, Andrew Terrill, also concluded that Iraq, facing an unexpected chorus of criticism in Europe and the United States, decided to lie low for a while.[53]

Others say, quite rightly, that while this may be true, Iraq was accommodated by the Iranians, who did not launch another major offensive until early 1985. At that point, the Iraqis once again resorted to poison gas, more massively than before, evidently undisturbed by US admonitions a year earlier. Dr. Foroutan speculated (interview, 2002) that Iraq did not use gas for a year because it needed time to improve its capabilities – which it did, as events in 1985 showed. And Iqbal Riza emphatically said "No!" when asked whether the Iraqis had heeded Washington's warnings, pointing at escalating chemical weapons use during the war's final years.

Moreover, while some US officials proudly refer to the administration's record on this episode,[54] the public condemnation was not repeated and US export restrictions proved largely ineffective. Much–touted demarches to the West German government apparently had little effect; West German companies, Iraq's primary import channel, continued to do business with the regime without interruption. As the 2005 trial and conviction of Frans van Anraat, a Dutch businessman accused of supplying Iraq with precursor chemicals, showed, much of the illicit trade circumvented European export controls by avoiding European ports.[55] Moreover, a State Department assessment contended, the dual–purpose nature of many chemical materials militated against an effective embargo.[56] Furthermore, Iraq's chemical weapons program was becoming increasingly self-reliant. The same assessment concluded that Iraq's chemical weapons capability had developed "in part through the unwitting and, in some cases, we believe witting assistance of a number of Western firms." Sanctions, in other words, were too little and came too late.

Furthermore, Iraq remained unaffected by the Reagan administration's decision to take its chemical weapons proliferation concerns to the UN Committee on Disarmament, where it proposed a worldwide ban on the production, stockpiling, trade, and use of chemical weapons. These concerns stemmed more from Soviet capabilities than Iraq's battlefield use, and negotiations were to last nine years, well beyond the Iran–Iraq war, the Kuwait invasion, and the Soviet Union's collapse.

Still, Terrill had a point. Although Iraq would not again face criticism for its chemical weapons use with the same severity, the immediate effect was that it did not press its counterattack against Iranian forces newly entrenched on the Majnoun islands, despite the significant loss of face and troop morale the Iranian success entailed. "The Majnoon Islands incidents," reasoned Terrill, "suggested a perceived threshold of 'military necessity' for Iraq to engage in the large-scale use of chemical weapons – i.e., in a situation where a significant Iranian territorial victory could not be overturned with conventional attacks. That threshold was then raised in response to unexpectedly harsh criticism from the West and the threat it foreshadowed for Iraq's essential supply channels and its general ability to continue the conduct of the war."[57] Iraq, in other words, traded tactical battlefield gain for a strategic relationship with the West. In so doing, it calculated correctly and benefited accordingly.

From Iran's perspective, things looked decidedly worse after the middle of 1984. The rapprochement between Iraq and the US gave little cause for optimism. Tehran dismissed US criticism of Iraq and export restrictions as "hypocritical," a mere "propaganda manoeuvre" aimed at concealing Washington's role in supplying chemicals to Iraq that were then used against Iranian troops.[58] Moreover, Iran had hoped for a strong UN rebuke of Iraq but instead won little more than a watered-down presidential statement. Sa'id Khorassani said he concluded from the episode that the UN was so preoccupied with bringing about a cease-fire that it was willing to overlook a serious breach of international law, and that perhaps it even believed that gas use, however disturbing, might help bring the war to an end.

If this was the thinking, there were certain to be consequences. Warnings about Iraq's resort to poison gas at a time when its capabilities were still limited and it was unsure of the West's reaction represented an early attempt to prevent worse. Instead, by being toothless, the Reagan administration's weak condemnation deflected attention and allowed Iraq to escalate chemical weapons use. The Defense Intelligence Agency concluded in September 1984 that Iraq was likely to continue to develop its conventional and "formidable" chemical capabilities, and would "probably pursue nuclear weapons." It also, with commendable foresight, painted a postwar scenario that, we know now, hit the mark: "Once the war ends," the assessment predicted, "Iraq's intransigence in settling territorial claims to two islands (Bubiyan and Warbah) with Kuwait, despite Kuwaiti support during the war, suggests that Baghdad's relationship with the Arab Gulf states will continue to experience strains."[59]

In an independent analysis, Julian Perry Robinson and Jozef Goldblat predicted that Iraq's unprecedented battlefield use of tabun suggested that "there may well be powerful incentives operating upon the Gulf War belligerents to introduce even deadlier nerve gases that offer still more potential for rapid mass destruction: agents such as the sarin, VX and, reportedly, soman stockpiled by the USA, France and the USSR." Their forecast, too, was eerily precise, as Iraq soon began using those very nerve gases.

The two researchers made an even more ominous prediction, one that in hindsight is as brilliant in its prescience as it is disturbing in its unacknowledged implications. "Against unprotected people," they warned, "an aircraft armed with sarin could be as destructive as the nuclear bomb dropped on Hiroshima."[60]

In 1984, the world was well on its way to Halabja, and all the warning signs were there, visible to those who cared to see.

THREE

CHEMICAL INTERLUDE

"If the world does not deal with the emerging nexus between terrorist networks, terrorist states and weapons of mass murder, terrorists could one day kill not more than 240 people, as in Beirut, or more than 3,000 people, as on Sept. 11, but tens of thousands – or more."
– US Secretary of Defense Donald Rumsfeld, *Washington Post*, October 26, 2003

The Badr Offensive (March 1985)

Slapped on the hand but facing no serious penalty, and confronted with a fresh Iranian offensive, Iraq relapsed as soon as its defenses came under renewed assault. Iraq increasingly resorted to gas, especially nerve agents.

The March 1985 offensive, named Badr by the Iranians, was almost a replica of the previous year's, with Iranian forces – Pasdaran and Basijis, but also Iraqi fighters of SCIRI's Badr Corps – stealing through the reed-covered Hawayza marshes in small boats to seize the Baghdad–Basra highway. To heighten the element of surprise, Iran carried out a diversionary artillery attack on Basra and an air raid on Baghdad. The offensive soon ran aground. Some units reached the highway, but their supply lines were weak; once they reached open terrain they became easy targets for Iraqi gunners.

The Iranians also tried again to overcome Iraqi positions at Majnoun but found their adversary fully prepared. When the attack ended, it proved to have been as fruitless as the previous one, and apart from the shocking loss of life, the situation remained unchanged. A Basiji platoon commander, Hadi Farajvand, readily described his frontline routine (interview, 2002):

> At Majnoun early in the spring, I was charged with preparing infrastructure. Early in the morning, I'd take my platoon (about twenty-two men) in a small boat some 3–4 kilometers to the front line and return late afternoon. Some days I had to go 10–20 kilometers to the rear to get what I needed. At the front we were safe, because our positions were so close to the Iraqis' that they were afraid to use gas, as the wind might blow it back at them. The only danger came from conventional weapons. But at the rear the Iraqis used to hit us with chemical shells all the time. Whenever this happened, we'd climb on top of our shelters to minimize the risk: we'd have suffocated inside and we had no IPE [Individual Protective Equipment]. The only thing we had was our scarves (shafiyeh). I inhaled gas several times and am lucky to be alive. Some fourteen of my men were injured, four severely. We received protective gear only about a month after the offensive began.

An Iraqi officer, Staff Col. Abd-al-Wahhab al-Saeidy, confirmed Farajvand's story (interview, 2003). "The weak point in Iranian strategy," he said, "was that they could not keep on advancing because our air force attacked their supply lines and reserve troops with gas. We had to saturate their staging areas with gas in order to disrupt their operations. And in the marshes, the Iranians usually created only a single track, so if we saturated that with gas, too, we could stop them."

Abbas Foroutan again was at the front. When the Iranians launched their offensive on 19 Isfand 1363 (March 10, 1985), he stood ready with a team of 120 medical students, all outfitted with gas masks and other protective equipment. One of them, Mahmoud Abassi, remembered (interview, 2002) that he used to wear his gear at all times, even when sleeping: "Dr. Foroutan would scream at us if we didn't!"

Typically, Foroutan said, the Iraqis waited two or three days before using gas against Iranian onslaughts. The first chemical attack during Badr came at 4 pm on 22 Isfand (March 13). The Iraqis used tabun, causing many casualties. Out of 2,231, thirty-two died, Foroutan reported.[1]

Foroutan noted two significant improvements in Iraqi capabilities. First, the Iraqis had overcome problems with the munitions' timing fuses. A bomb with a timing fuse is designed to detonate not on impact but at a preset time, usually just before it reaches the ground, so as to maximize casualties. If the fuse is defective or it malfunctions, the munition will land harmlessly as a dud, though it remains armed and dangerous. During Khaybar, Foroutan had observed many such duds but now the bombs "exploded very well." This means that the Iraqis had either managed to repair the timing fuses or had switched to impact fuses, some of which were found by a UN team a year later.

A second improvement involved the use of tabun. During Khaybar, the Iraqis had not yet managed to disperse the liquid gas effectively across the battlefield, but now it appeared to be of finer quality and saturated a much wider area. Despite tabun's greater lethality, however, mustard gas remained the Iraqis' weapon of choice because of its persistence, which forced Iranian troops to vacate affected areas for long periods, especially in rear staging areas where most support forces other than medical personnel lacked proper protection.

In addition to tabun and mustard gas, Foroutan also reported the use of a new chemical agent that he tentatively identified as cyanide gas, a blood agent: "I remember an attack in which the victims died very rapidly," he recalled (interview, 2002). "Our monitoring device [Chemical Agent Monitor, or CAM] failed to identify the gas. Cyanide is highly volatile, dissipating very fast, so you have to be at the impact site right away. Alternatively, a high nerve gas concentration might have the same effect."

Iraq's use of cyanide gas during Badr, or at any stage during the war, remains unproven. Because the Iranian military lacked an adequate chemical defense system, identification was a serious problem faced by medical doctors who had little prior expertise and encountered new generations of Iraqi gases every year. Moreover, nerve agents are swift killers; those who survive by injecting themselves with atropine rarely exhibit lasting symptoms.

Cyanide gas kills faster than tabun, often in one or two minutes. Because cyanide attacks hemoglobin – the oxygen carrier in the blood – a victim suffocates inside his body rather than from lack of air. Immediate care can save a patient. The typical medical response is to administer a serum, amyl nitrite, by inhalation. If the patient recovers, doctors can be fairly confident that their diagnosis was accurate. During the war, Iranian doctors sporadically reported the effective use of amyl nitrite in some cases and therefore suspected cyanide gas. Moreover, Iran flew several victims to European hospitals – for treatment but also for propaganda advantage. Most of these cases concerned mustard gas, but both a Viennese doctor and a Belgian toxicologist, Aubin Heyndrickx, reported that their patients suffered from "some agent containing cyanides."[2] However, it is highly unlikely – for reasons discussed in Chapter VIII – that Iraq ever used cyanide gas. These medical observations must therefore be treated with a good deal of skepticism.

In a vigorous protest to the UN in March 1985 in which for the first time it threatened "retaliation in kind," Iran claimed a total of thirty-two separate chemical attacks during Badr, including at Majnoun, involving both mustard and cyanide gas.[3] Because the fighting had not ended by the time Pérez de Cuéllar visited the region in early April, Iran could communicate its outrage directly, reminding the secretary-general pointedly of the UN's obligation to monitor compliance with international conventions and then demanding a new investigation.[4]

Acknowledging developments on the battlefield, the Reagan administration weighed in, reiterating its earlier position against chemical weapons use but failing to impose real sanctions against the perpetrator, Iraq. Noting that "it is our conclusion that the Iraqis have used chemical weapons against the recent Iranian invasion attempt," Assistant Secretary of State Richard Murphy asserted: "We condemn the use of chemical weapons in violation of international law and conventions whenever and wherever it occurs, including in this latest instance. We initially raised our concern about the possible use of chemical weapons with the Iraqi Government in late 1983 and were the first to condemn their use publicly when our information became conclusive in March 1984."[5] To the Iraqis, this was steady state, and so they saw no need to change their policy.

Pérez de Cuéllar proved willing to take the matter a step further, however. His visit convinced him that the Iranians had a point when they argued that international treaties should be observed even without agreement to move toward a ceasefire. Until the end of the conflict is achieved, he explained, he was "legally obliged . . . to try to mitigate its effects, in areas such as attacks on civilian population centers, use of chemical weapons, treatment of prisoners of war, and safety of navigation and civil aviation."[6] In that spirit, he ordered another investigation of chemical warfare claims. This time, however, rather than sending experts to the region, he dispatched a medical doctor to European capitals to question Iranian victims, who had been sent there by a regime intent on scoring a propaganda coup, as well as the doctors treating them.

The doctor reported back at the end of April. The hospitalized Iranians clearly were victims of chemical warfare, he concluded – of mustard gas, to be precise – but without hard evidence he could not support Iran's contention that the culprit was Iraq or that types of gas other than mustard had been used. In sum, he asserted blandly, chemical weapons "were used during March 1985 in the war between Iran and Iraq."[7]

UN action was correspondingly feeble. In a "note," the Security Council president declared that Council members were "appalled that chemical weapons have been used against Iranian soldiers during the month of March 1985" and condemned "all violations of international humanitarian law," which they urged "both parties" to observe.[8] Iraq thus understood that while the council abhorred chemical weapons, it nonetheless seemed to turn a blind eye to their use in countering what the Iraqis deemed an existential threat.

And so it continued. In the absence of another major Iranian offensive, reports of further chemical weapons use trickled in sporadically. Iran accused the Iraqis of firing chemical shells at its forces in May and November 1985, and again in January 1986. None of these attacks triggered an international response. Then came Faw.

The Occupation of Faw (February 1986)

To the Basijis, the battle over Faw (Fav, in Persian) was at once exhilarating and terrifying. For the first time in five years, Iran acquired major Iraqi territory, but victory came at a tremendous cost. This was Iran's Val-Fajr VIII operation, which sought to deal a devastating blow to Iraq's pride, if not to its security. The Faw peninsula, south of Basra, is Iraq's only outlet to the Gulf; the country is otherwise landlocked. Faw's loss would choke Iraq's oil exports, rendering them wholly dependent on pipelines leading through Saudi Arabia, Jordan, and Turkey. It would also bring Iranian forces to the gates of Basra and, by threatening that city, would mount a most dangerous challenge to the regime. Finally, it would put Iranian troops in close proximity of Kuwait and Saudi Arabia, states that were financing the Iraqi war effort precisely to prevent an Iranian advance in the direction of their oil fields.

The assault began in the early hours of February 11, 1986, when Iranian troops crossed the Arvand river (the confluence of the Tigris and Euphrates, known otherwise as the Shatt al-Arab) by boat and over makeshift bridges. After some early setbacks, they gained a significant foothold.

Taghi Aghaei was a Basiji volunteer who spent the better part of the war as a military reporter near the front. "I loved it, even after I lost my hand to shrapnel," he declared (interview, 2002). "I insisted on going back. It was a harsh life but we got used to it, and" – clearly a matter of intense pride – "I never killed anyone."

Describing how he forded the Arvand, Aghaei recalled:

> It was very windy and we lost many men. Some of our divers were carried off by the strong current. But many of us made it across. We surprised the Iraqis and captured the area up to the salt factory, which was full of landmines. Two days later – the moon was full – they fired chemical shells at us, and we fled back toward the river. I couldn't put on my mask because of my hand. As we pulled back, many of our men had blisters on their faces and were choking. The doctors at the mobile hospital were completely overwhelmed. It was a total disaster. Over half of our men died. There simply wasn't enough care available. I also saw real courage: Some of these guys would give their masks to their friends and then die. It was unbelievable!

Ahmad Nateghi, the Iranian news agency's chief of photography, had similar memories. He used to make quick frontline visits from Tehran. Early during the Faw operation he crossed the river in the company of French journalists. Iranian forces had built two bridges. One, for tanks and armored vehicles, consisted of metal pipes soldered together with sand poured on top; the second was a string of cork rafts covered with steel, kept along the Iranian side and pulled across the river by small boats when it was safe. The French journalists were stunned by the Iranian operation's success. The Iraqis had "Raziq" radars, they said, that could detect even minute troop movements. How could they not have noticed the Iranian assault? Nateghi remembered witnessing two chemical attacks, one on the Iranian bank, the second on its field clinic on Faw in which Nateghi's cousin sustained mustard gas injuries. Nateghi deduced from the numbers of casualties that the volume of chemical munitions was uncommonly high.

Dr. Foroutan, also present at Faw, remembered the chemical attack of 23 Bahman, or February 12, three days into the offensive, as one of the longest and most intense of the entire war. The weather was pleasant, he said, about 20 degrees centigrade with a gentle breeze. At around 5 pm some thirty-two aircraft organized in small formations carried out a constant gas bombardment that saturated the area. "At first we had 2,500 cases but because the mustard gas hung in the palm trees, it went up to about 8,500 in a couple of days. We couldn't decontaminate the area and smelled mustard gas for a month afterwards. We kept praying for a rain, which finally came and washed the chemicals away. But in that period, we saw many new mustard cases."

He diagnosed cases of nerve agents as well. The clinical picture was so severe in some patients that he suspected, with hindsight, that they had inhaled sarin, a gas even deadlier than tabun. First developed in Nazi Germany, sarin is a highly volatile toxic compound that appears in liquid or vaporized form and, when inhaled, can cause severe damage to the respiratory system, then death. Released in the Tokyo subway by a Japanese cult group in March 1995, it killed twelve and injured 5,500. Six-tenths of a milligram is sufficient to kill an adult. A gas mask is the most effective protection. Following exposure, immediate injection of atropine and the administration of oxygen may save the victim.

Another doctor observed the massive chemical attack of February 12. To Dr. Ja'fer Aslani, a fresh medical graduate familiar with victims of gassing from his internships with Abbas Foroutan in Tehran, Faw was his first direct encounter with war. He was assigned to a chemical warfare emergency unit attached to the Fatma e-Zahra hospital, a major mobile facility built partially underground. "I saw so many gassing victims," he recalled (interview 2002), "all soldiers. One day, some twenty Iraqi planes bombed the area right near the river. It was full of troops. We received 4,000 chemical casualties on a single day! They had different symptoms, mostly from mustard gas, but also nerve gas and some from cyanide poisoning."

Six days into the offensive, February 15, the Iraqis attacked the Fatma e-Zahra hospital directly. "They came four times over a period of twelve days," said Foroutan. "They may not have realized it was a hospital." The first time, aircraft dropped small phosphorus munitions, followed soon by a plane that dropped a chemical bomb. Owing to the wind, the gas dissipated fast and there were no victims. A second gas attack two days later also proved harmless. On February 19, there was a third attack, involving not gas but high-explosive (HE) munitions that killed several Iranians. The last attack, on February 27, was the worst. Ten aircraft first dropped conventional munitions and then chemical bombs. "One exploded 15 m near the door leading to the emergency room. Mustard gas wafted underground, injuring many surgeons, anesthesiologists and nurses." Iran later claimed to have suffered 12,000 casualties at Faw from chemical weapons alone.

Not only Iranian soldiers fell victim to Iraq's gas attacks, but also Iraq's own troops. "We treated quite a few Iraqi POWs with mustard gas injuries," said Foroutan. "They told us that their pilots had been aiming at the front line; the Iraqi and Iranian positions were very close to each other, and anyway it is not a straight line."

The appearance of Iraqi chemical warfare casualties stirred a good deal of controversy. Iran claimed they were "friendly fire" victims, while Iraq offered them as proof that Iran was also using gas. A UN experts' team investigating the claims agreed with the Iranian viewpoint. Seventeen years later, an officer in post-Ba'ath Baghdad concurred (interview, 2003), saying he had many friends who were injured by Iraqi gas at Faw: "They told me the wind changed and they smelled gas."

After ten days of fighting, and despite intense chemical bombardments, the Iraqis realized they had lost part of the peninsula. The battle cost them thousands of men, with many more injured. An Iraqi surgeon treating the wounded in Basra reported (interview, 2006) that he saw "thousands of injured, perhaps ten thousand," and that he alone carried out an astounding 250 amputations in two weeks. The defeat set off unprecedented criticism of Saddam Hussein among his military commanders, who felt he micro-managed them despite his lack of military credentials. It also triggered fear in neighboring Saudi Arabia and especially Kuwait, where the thudding impact of artillery fire 40 km east clearly could be heard. They promptly appealed to the West by raising the specter of an Iranian thrust toward the oil fields. The result was a new Security Council resolution calling for a ceasefire, a position supported by Iraq but rejected by Iran, which insisted that Iraq should first be named as both the original aggressor and a repeat violator of the laws of war. By its failure to do so, Iran charged, the council was responsible for the war's continuation. But it welcomed the secretary-general's efforts to prevent further escalation.[9]

The reference was to Pérez de Cuéllar's decision to conduct a new investigation of escalating Iranian claims that Iraq was using chemical weapons. And this time Iran accomplished what had eluded it so far: direct identification of Iraq as the perpetrator. The expert team traveled to the front in March, where it visited the Fatma e-Zahra field hospital and interviewed poison gas victims, including Iraqi POWs. Most importantly, the team met with a captured Iraqi pilot who, "responding freely and voluntarily and without duress," confirmed he had participated in two "special missions" using chemical bombs.[10] His testimony proved most harmful to the Iraqi regime.

By failing to identify Iraq as the perpetrator in 1984 and 1985, the Security Council had sent the Iraqis a signal that it supported its efforts to contain Iran. But now an investigative team sent by the secretary-general had forced the council's hand, and it had no choice but to acknowledge the facts. In a presidential statement on March 21, the council expressed concern that "chemical weapons on many occasions have been used *by Iraqi forces against Iranian forces*" and "strongly" condemned the continued use of gas.[11] Such a "note," though, was of lesser standing than a council resolution, which would have been legally binding. Moreover, the council diluted its condemnation by adding, in reference to Iran's occupation of Faw, that it called "upon the two sides to respect the territorial integrity of all States." The council also pointedly stated that Iraq, unlike Iran, had accepted its earlier call for an immediate ceasefire. By these actions the council showed that the Iranian success at Faw had raised the threshold of its tolerance of Iraqi methods of warfare. While it could no longer skirt the truth, the council's feeble rebuke underscored its growing fear of an Iranian victory.

To Iran, however, the team's assessment constituted progress, and it thanked the secretary-general for his "well-balanced and fair" report.[12] To Iraq, the council's nod to Iran set a dangerous precedent. Accusing the council of lacking the "required degree of balance," Tariq Aziz lashed out at the fact that "certain international parties which shed crocodile tears for international agreements are the same parties which provide the barbarous Iranian regime with the means to evil and aggression, including arms, ammunition, spare parts and military equipment."[13] To

Aziz, the use of chemical weapons was a secondary issue, a distraction from the council's overriding task to pursue an end to hostilities. And what if Western states were arming Iran?

Betrayal: The Iran–Contra Affair

The renewal of US–Iraqi diplomatic relations in November 1984 was followed by an upswing in Iraq's fortunes. The Reagan administration promptly increased credit guarantees and other financial assistance. Embassy staff in Baghdad swelled from sixteen in 1984 to thirty-five in 1988, including a CIA bureau chief, the defense attaché who was a senior Defense Intelligence Agency (DIA) officer, and an Air Force officer. On the other side, Iraqi officials led by their dynamic, smooth, urbane ambassador Nizar Hamdoon found open doors in Washington. An architect by training, Hamdoon was a Ba'ath party man from a family of cavalry under the Hashemite monarchy, loyal to his country and leader. From the moment he arrived in 1983, he embarked on a charm offensive that was remarkably successful in keeping public criticism of Iraq to a minimum.

Despite Hamdoon's best efforts, however, the US never had any illusions about the Iraqi regime's nature and what it was capable of doing. Few saw in Iraq an ally, even less a friend. Yet as a bulwark against Iran's Islamic revolution, Iraq was seen as deserving US help. Many in the nation's capital therefore held their noses at this unsavory regime while closing their eyes to its worst brutalities, all in the cause of protecting the Gulf. A September 1984 DIA assessment of Iraq's economic and military prospects simply *assumed* Iraq's continued chemical weapons use.[14] Another intelligence analysis, of late 1986, noted coolly that Iraq was developing sarin.[15] Chemical weapons use stayed on the agenda but enjoyed no great priority as relations blossomed.

Ambassador David Newton, who promoted and facilitated much of the business that came with the tilt, later claimed (interview, 2001) that he raised chemical weapons "several times a year" with his Iraqi counterparts, and that "it wasn't pro forma: We had an interest in preventing the use and spread of these weapons. But it obviously was a futile exercise. Their perspective was: 'You want us to win the war, so. . . .'" Nor did the Iraqis usually admit to chemical weapons use, alluding instead to their need to use "all necessary means" in holding off the enemy. Only once, Newton recalled, did Tariq Aziz drop his guard. During a visit to Baghdad by Les Aspin, chairman of the House Armed Services Committee, Aziz, a man who "usually keeps his cool," became exasperated, exclaiming: "Yes of course we use chemical weapons! These are savages and we need to defend ourselves. We would use *nuclear* weapons if we had them!"

As the Iraqis realized, Washington's diplomacy was all carrots and no sticks. The Reagan administration cared only about Iraq's position on the peace process and its support for international terrorism. What it chose to do on the battlefield had no impact on US policy. Chemical escalation was a concern, but those in the administration who followed WMD proliferation had no influence on Iraq policy, which was tightly controlled by the geo-strategists. A June 1985 speech by one such official gave expression to their frustration:

> I want to emphasize why, ultimately, we feel the problem is so dangerous. Last year Iraq employed chemical weapons against Iran. This year, in spite of international protest, they have used it again. . . . Yet Iraq has suffered no real penalties, and in fact, continues to deny any wrongdoing. Plainly, condemnation is not working. . . . Proliferation will lead to use, which in turn, will lead to more proliferation. . . . The dynamic becomes a self–perpetuating one. . . . Proliferators and users like Iraq basically pay few penalties for their irresponsible behavior; certainly not enough to dissuade others from seeking to obtain such a capability. I think we can all agree this has got to change and quickly.[16]

A CIA assessment of late 1986 questioned the effectiveness of Iraq's chemical weapons use, citing "poor tactical employment, lessened element of surprise, increased Iranian preparedness, [and] possible problems with munitions, agents, and delivery techniques." But, the assessment continued, "because the political costs of continued CW use have been so small, we doubt that Iraq will abandon its use of chemical weapons in the foreseeable future."[17]

Iran's victory at Faw far overshadowed any proliferation concerns the US might have had. A second Iraqi setback in July sent further shivers down the spines of Washington's war watchers. Two months earlier, Saddam Hussein, in a pique of wounded pride and to show his generals he understood their *métier*, sent his forces to seize the Iranian border town of Mehran. They succeeded in a swift offensive, and the

Iraqi leader cried victory. The Iranians, though, were almost as quick in recapturing the town, driving Iraqi forces back across the border. This second debacle reignited tensions between Hussein and his senior military commanders, who feared defeat as long as he remained in charge of military strategy. For a moment it looked like the regime was tottering. In Washington, Assistant Secretary of State Richard Murphy, one of the geo–strategic view's main proponents, immediately called for a renewed US effort to "bolster the Iraqi will to resist, both psychologically and militarily . . . [and] pressure Iran to wind down – or end – the war."[18]

Another view existed in the Reagan administration, however, one that had been outvoted in policy debates. Frustrated, some of its advocates embarked on their own secret foreign policy. In November 1986, a Lebanese newspaper reported that the US was pursuing two contradictory approaches toward the Iran–Iraq war: A secret arms channel to Iran directly undercut the pro-Iraq tilt. This was the Iran–Contra affair.

What emerged from Congressional hearings was that a cabal inside the National Security Council (including National Security Advisor Robert McFarlane), with Reagan's ostensible approval, had funneled US weapons to Iran via Israel for over a year in an apparent bid to gain the release of US hostages held by Iranian proxies in Lebanon; proceeds from the sales were intended for US proxies, the Contras, fighting Nicaragua's Sandinista government. Israel had been supplying Iran since the start of the war, including spare parts for US–made Phantom bombers. In Israel's assessment, shared by elements in the CIA and NSC, helping Iran might tip the balance toward the regime's perceived moderates (Speaker of Parliament Ali Akbar Hashemi Rafsanjani vs. Supreme Leader Khomeini and President Ali Khamene'i) while creating a counterweight to Soviet influence. Moreover, the preferred Israeli scenario in the Gulf was a war without end in which two exhausted adversaries would pose no strategic threat. In this view, the Iraq tilt was unwise. There were, moreover, those in the Reagan administration who wanted to contain Soviet influence; they regarded simultaneous US and Soviet support of Iraq unnatural.

Iran–Contra contradicted the Reagan administration's stated policy of isolating Iran (via Operation Staunch and otherwise), violated US law against arms transfers to Iran, and subverted democracy. Moreover, as one administration official warned when the deal was put in motion, the supply of TOW missiles and maps depicting the order of battle on the Iran–Iraq border signified a tilt "in a direction which could cause the Iranians to have a successful offensive against the Iraqis with cataclysmic results. . . . Providing defensive missiles was one thing but when we provide intelligence on the order of battle, we are giving the Iranians the wherewithal for offensive action."[19] Yet the culprits, who had seemingly enjoyed the president's blessing, escaped punishment.

To the Iraqis the disclosure was an enormous shock. Not only had their purported ally been duplicitous, but it had provided Iran with key intelligence as well as with two pivotal weapon systems that allowed Iran to fight the Iraqis in areas in which they had been unchallenged. US Hawk anti-aircraft missiles diminished Iraq's overwhelming air superiority, and TOW missiles countered its huge advantage in armor. Iran received 2,008 TOWs and 235 Hawks and it deployed them as soon as shipments started arriving in 1985 – with immediate results. In hindsight, therefore, the defeat at Faw was painful not only because of the slap to Iraq's pride but also because the loss was made possible by collusion between Iraq's enemy and the superpower that had pretended to be its friend.

David Newton, the ambassador in Baghdad, remembered (interview, 2001) the sudden pall that fell over relations:

> The Iraqis never quite trusted us but had some confidence in their ability to predict us. But they could not have predicted Iran–Contra, which was an irrational policy. So it really shook them. It caused real damage and casualties in the war, and those who had favored closer relations with the US on the argument that it was less threatening than the USSR – Tariq Aziz, Nizar Hamdoon, and others – suffered at the expense of Latif Jasem, a real snake, and [Deputy Prime Minister] Taha Yasin Ramadan, whose old prejudices about the US being an imperialist pro-Israeli power now were reconfirmed. Iraq's intelligence services had seen the US as helpful: While they did not want foreigners in Iraq, they grudgingly accepted US diplomats. Now all of this was gone. I never thought Iraq would be in a position to take the high road with us, but they did.

Setting a New Course

The Iran–Contra affair completely destroyed the network of relations that underlay the tilt and sundered the brittle trust between the two nations. It likely accounts for the Iraqi leader's erratic behavior toward the US in the interwar years (1988–90), if not his decision to invade Kuwait.

Now Washington had to bend over backward to prove that its Iraq policy was genuine – and this had consequences. In a December 1986 memo ominously titled "U.S.–Iraqi Relations: Picking Up the Pieces," Richard Murphy warned, in the first sentence: "U.S.–Iraqi relations are in crisis, with potentially serious consequences for U.S. standing in the Gulf region and U.S. policy on counterterrorism." To restore trust, Murphy suggested giving Iraq "a powerful political signal of U.S. confidence in Iraq's future" in the form of new Exim Bank credit guarantees.[20] Subsequent memos about Iraq's commercial relations with the US highlighted the new concerns. Delays in the issuance of Department of Commerce licenses for export of US products to Iraq suddenly were said to have "disruptive consequences both for American exporters and for our relations with Iraq," requiring "an immediate NSC review. . . . A significant gesture is especially important and urgent right now."[21]

David Newton said it took six months to rebuild the relationship. Institutionally, the DIA replaced the CIA as the primary US liaison with the Iraqis. The DIA's Iraqi counterpart was the Military Intelligence Directorate (MID), or *Istikhbarat*. According to retired US officials, the two established a working relationship that lasted till the end of the war. On the Iraqi side, the principal interlocutor was the MID's deputy director, Staff Maj.-Gen. Wafiq al-Samarra'i; for the Americans it was a succession of defense attachés.

Politically, Washington had to grant Iraq's dual request for an immediate reinstatement of Operation Staunch and a UN Security Council resolution calling for an end to the war. The Reagan administration did put its support behind a new Security Council resolution, which passed in July 1987 and was eagerly embraced by Iraq. Although Iran rejected it, Resolution 598 became the blueprint for the August 1988 ceasefire that ended the war. The administration also restored Operation Staunch and went even further: It mobilized Security Council support for an arms embargo against Iran and, perhaps most importantly, it stepped up its sharing of intelligence with the Iraqis. This latter practice had started as early as 1982, but few within the administration were aware of it. It was discovered and exposed by journalists investigating Iran–Contra, prompting an outcry from the Iranians.

George Shultz outlined the administration's rationale a month after Iran–Contra broke:

- The provision of limited, but useful, amounts of intelligence to Iraq is something which I approved – and continue to approve.
- Our policy of neutrality on the war remains. We favor an end to the war with neither a victor nor a vanquished and with the independence and territorial integrity of both Iraq and Iran intact.
- Our policy on the war is clear – we want it ended at the earliest possible time. Iraq has been willing to negotiate an end to the war for the past several years. Iran has been the recalcitrant party – and continues to be. We look for ways to pressure Iran to reconsider its stubborn commitment to the war – through Operation Staunch and through diplomatic pressures. Iraq is the only country which can exert direct military pressure on Iran. We decided that the stakes involved in the outcome of the Iran–Iraq war were great enough to justify supplying some intelligence to Iraq.[22]

Sporadic though intelligence sharing may have been from 1986 onward, the data provided to Iraq was directed toward convincing Iran to accept a ceasefire. According to a US intelligence officer (interview, 2001), it comprised "intelligence reports and line drawings of [Iranian] facilities . . . critical to . . . the impending Iranian offensive." Paul Wolfowitz, the undersecretary of defense for policy, and Richard Armitage, assistant secretary of defense for international security affairs, the officer added, "supported the Department of Defense's assistance program . . . and arranged for Secretary of Defense Frank Carlucci, under his own authority . . . to direct – not 'authorize' but 'direct' – the DIA to release information to Iraq that would prevent an Iranian victory." Another former intelligence analyst said (interview, 2001): "What we gave the Iraqis was unattributable. We just gave them the information without the source. But obviously, satellite photos come from satellites."

Increasingly confident that it could deal the Iranian enemy and their Kurdish proxies a decisive blow, Iraq escalated the war in 1987. It had vastly improved its capabilities after Saddam Hussein belatedly delegated war strategy to his military commanders following the twin defeats at Faw and Mehran, including the authority to launch chemical attacks. Moreover, Iraq had a fresh crop of recruits ages fourteen and up. And US intelligence on Iranian rearguard facilities proved critical in accurately directing Iraqi chemical strikes. The Iranians, by contrast, were exhausted. They had lost tens of thousands of "volunteers" (many also mere teenagers, often used as mine-clearers) to Iraq's withering fire without any significant territorial gain apart from Faw, let alone the regime's collapse. Iranian offensives targeting Basra in late 1986 and early 1987, which leaders referred to as "final," ground down just as quickly as had their predecessors, despite early advances that overcame, in Cordesman and Wagner's words, "massive amounts of [Iraqi] firepower, air power, and poison gas."[23]

Iran's drive on Basra touched off a new round in the "war of the cities," as Iraq launched air and missile strikes against Iranian towns, killing hundreds of civilians. Iraq also continued its attacks on Iranian shipping and oil facilities. Iran in return fired Scud missiles at Baghdad and Basra and started attacking ships in the Gulf belonging to Iraq's allies, especially Kuwait, scoring a number of painful hits. This brought the US into the war. In July 1987 the US placed its flags on Kuwaiti tankers and provided them with naval escorts. At the same time, the Reagan administration started pressing for a diplomatic solution at the UN, an effort that culminated in Resolution 598.

The Iran–Contra affair, in sum, derived from an intra-bureaucratic battle between two factions, each of which looked at the Iran–Iraq war through a Cold War lens and sought to strengthen its side by providing material aid to its preferred proxy. When the conspiratorial effort to arm Iran collapsed, the administration's pro-Iraq tilt was reinforced. Its advocates received a virtual carte blanche to assist Iraq, and although limits remained on what was permissible, the bar was raised. This gave the Iraqis leverage to draw the US into the war. Ironically, therefore, covert support of Iran spelled the beginning of the end of the Iranian war effort, even if the Iranians managed to slog on for another year and a half. At the same time, enhanced US support of Iraq, with no questions asked, led to Iraqi excesses and greater US tolerance thereof. This, too, had an opposite effect. When the Iraqis, realizing their newly won impunity, overreached by gassing Kurdish civilians, US administration officials who had found the alliance necessary but distasteful remained silent at first, but once the war ended they pushed strongly to cool relations, setting Iraq on a collision course with its wartime ally.

FOUR

WAR IN KURDISTAN

"The essential point [about Saddam Hussein] is that he's a thug who has been willing to murder some of the people closest to him, who has used chemical weapons against his own people, who has invaded his neighbors. He is probably the most dangerous individual in the world today. . . . The question of Saddam Hussein is at the very core of the war against terrorism. . . . He is the symbol of defiance of all Western values.
— Richard Perle, chairman of the Defense Policy Board, PBS
Frontline, November 8, 2001

Gas Attacks against Kurds in Iran

Civilian immunity is a cardinal principle of international humanitarian law, also known as the laws of war, the primary sources of which are the four Geneva Conventions of 1949. It is also one of the prohibitions most commonly violated. The Iran–Iraq war proved no exception. Both sides committed atrocities that amounted to war crimes.

Soon after its forces were expelled from Iranian territory in 1982, Iraq began attacking Iranian civilians and civilian structures, usually in response to Iranian military thrusts. Iran retaliated with outrages of its own, prompting the UN to plead with both sides to protect civilians. Because of rising tit-for-tat attacks on civilian areas, the UN sent a team of experts to the Gulf in 1983 to investigate. Touring the war zone, the experts concluded that Iraq had repeatedly acted without regard for civilian lives, using cluster munitions in residential areas, attacking hospitals, and so forth, and had razed Iranian towns before withdrawing in 1982. As for Iran, the team suggested it had paid insufficient regard to civilian lives when targeting Iraqi industrial complexes and oil facilities.[1]

At various times during the war, the UN was able to broker bilateral agreements to halt attacks against residential areas. This put restraints on the two belligerents – but only until one side managed to advance militarily, which provoked a counterattack against civilians, which then prompted an in-kind retaliation that restored the balance of terror. Morally repugnant and cowardly as it was, targeting civilians had a military objective: to undermine support of the war by damaging people's morale. During the course of the war both sides escalated this tactic, causing greater destruction, larger numbers of casualties, and more terror affecting larger population groups, including residents of major cities like Tehran and Baghdad.

Understanding terror's potency, Iraq soon advanced its use of chemical weapons from the battlefield to threaten vulnerable civilians. By 1987, Iran had announced improvements in its chemical defenses, so as to raise troop morale and discourage Iraqi CW use as futile. Ironically, this may instead have persuaded the Iraqis to target civilians as a way of putting new pressure on Iran to end the conflict.

The majority of civilian gassing victims were Kurds, both in Iran and Iraq. The first such gas attack, however, seemed to target Iranian towns in the south, far from Kurdistan. In April 1987, Iran's foreign minister, Ali Akbar Velayati, claimed that Iraq had "repeatedly resorted to chemical warfare on a very large scale" against residential areas, killing and injuring civilians in Abadan, Khorramshahr, and Mared. UN failure to condemn earlier Iraqi gas attacks, he charged, had "eroded the authority of all rules and principles of international humanitarian law," and he called on the Security Council to recognize its "moral and constitutional responsibility in the face of this dangerous qualitative and quantitative escalation of the use of chemical weapons."[2] The three towns largely had been evacuated, however, and the majority of casualties were therefore likely Iranian troops.

Still, noting an alarming escalation on the southern front, Javier Pérez de Cuéllar dispatched yet another team of experts. Iranian rhetoric peaked in the days before the team's arrival in Tehran, with the accusation that Iraq's gassing of civilians constituted war crimes.[3] The investigation confirmed the team's worst fears. Observing that the number of chemical casualties among Iranian troops and the severity of their injuries were "considerably less" than the previous year (presumably because of improvements in protective gear), the experts nonetheless said they were "very disturbed" to find "numerous civilian casualties" from mustard gas attacks.[4]

On May 14 the Security Council issued yet another presidential note in lieu of a resolution, in which it restated the now standard language condemning both the "repeated use of chemical weapons" and the "prolongation of the conflict" – in other words, castigating Iran and Iraq in equal measure.[5] To both sides the text must have sounded like a broken record, though the Iraqis could take heart from the council's failure, once again, to attach any form of sanction to their grave violation of the laws of war. And so the stage was set for further atrocities.

In the meantime, Iraq had started to extend its chemical warfare northward, to the Kurdish regions of both Iran and Iraq. New Iranian accusations reached the UN on an almost daily basis, mostly concerning Iraqi chemical attacks in Iranian Kurdistan: an attack on villages in the Baneh area on April 16 (ten villagers reported injured); attacks on villages near Baneh, Penjwin, and Serdasht on May 7 and 8 (at least ninety-two reported civilian injuries); and an attack on the town of Serdasht on June 28, killing more than a hundred and injuring thousands, the majority civilians.

The latter attack was of considerable significance. Serdasht, a Kurdish town near the border and close to the front, had become both a refuge for displaced villagers and a regular encampment for Iranian troops, who used it as a staging area. Serdasht had experienced frequent air bombardments, and in the days prior to the chemical attack, Iranian and Iraqi forces had been battling on nearby Mamanda mountain, then the front line. At first, the Iranians, joined by PUK peshmergas, prevailed, blunting an Iraqi assault. But, recounted Hama Hama Sa'id, a PUK participant in the battles (interview, 2002), Iraq's forces regrouped and rebounded, taking full control of the area. It was then that Iraq launched a chemical attack on the town (see Preface). Witnesses in Serdasht claim that Iraqi planes discharged several chemical bombs, then circled for a full twenty minutes before disappearing over the horizon.[6]

For a direct attack on a town that, unlike many towns on the southern front, had not been evacuated, the casualty toll in Serdasht was fairly low, certainly if measured against the standard that would be set by Iraq in Halabja a year later. By conservative accounts, only thirty civilians died on the day of the attack, another sixty-six within the first month, eight more within a year, and another seven in the next thirteen years – a total of 111 (in 2002).[7] Although these deaths reportedly all involved mustard gas, there may have been victims of nerve agents as well, as eye-witness accounts suggest; these victims may have been Iranian troops, who were not included in the Serdasht body count. Yaghoub Ghotsian, an Iranian nurse, described (interview, 2002) how, when serving in one of the army's emergency clinics in Serdasht, he rushed to the chemical weapons unit when the attack started. There had been regular gas attacks on Iranian troops in surrounding areas in previous days, he said, and so the army was well prepared:

> The first thing I saw was a soldier who came running in, yelling there had been a chemical attack. Within two minutes he died. He was a young, healthy person, well built, and he had no symptoms, so this was a surprise to us. It must have been nerve gas. We treated some 2,000 patients in twelve hours. Many died on the spot; I saw perhaps a hundred. We assumed these were nerve gas victims. The others we divided into two groups. Those with skin problems we assumed to have mustard gas injuries, so we gave them a bath and administered thio-sulphate. The second group had no symptoms. We gave them a sugar and saline solution intravenously, assuming they were merely hysterical.

Many observers at the time saw the Serdasht attack as a dangerous escalation. The Iranians attributed it directly to the Security Council's failure to act against Iraq's earlier gas attacks: The council's "feeble statement" of May 14, Foreign Minister Velayati charged, was interpreted by Iraq as "a carte blanche for its continued resort to chemical weapons."[8] Yet the literature on the Iran–Iraq war contains only fleeting references to the Serdasht attack. Seen in the context of all Iraqi chemical attacks, perhaps the event appeared routine. Nevertheless, Velayati referred to it as a "tragedy [that] should be recorded in encyclopaedia and history books alongside of Hiroshima and Nagasaki as the first city in the world which fell victim to chemical bombardment." Apart from the hyperbole, he had one thing right: This was indeed the first gassing of a town in history. As such, it foreshadowed the Halabja attack the next year.

As it turns out, it was Serdasht's bad fortune not only to be at the receiving end of an Iraqi gas attack but also to find its story overshadowed in Kurdish lore by the Halabja atrocity. The Iranian government did not broadcast news of the attack, fearing it might trigger mass panic and erosion of popular morale, according to a Foreign Ministry official (interview, 2002). By contrast, Iranian newspapers covered chemical attacks on the southern war front routinely and in detail. Soon, what happened in Serdasht had been forgotten – except, of course, by its victims, who till this day hold an annual commemoration.[9] One reason Serdasht was forgotten was that it was a Kurdish town; inhabitants claim that the Iranian regime cared little for the Kurds and after the war neither drew public attention to the attack, nor provided aid to the surviving victims. The other reason was what happened in Halabja.

The Spreading Rebellion in Iraqi Kurdistan

Most Iranians had some inkling of the attacks in Iranian Kurdistan (even if these did not receive extensive coverage) by way of, for example, accounts of soldiers returning from the front. It is unlikely, however, that they knew how extensive Iraq used gas against Iraqi Kurds, at least before Halabja. The world knew a little more, in part because of Iranian complaints to the UN. These lacked detail and accuracy, however, based as they were on accounts by traumatized refugees conveyed to medical personnel who were unfamiliar with conditions across the border. Iraqi Kurdistan remained hermetically sealed to outsiders throughout the 1980s, except for a few reporters brought on regime-guided tours that revealed none of the cruelties visited on the population. It was only after Iraqi forces withdrew from Kurdistan in late 1991, well after the Gulf war, that independent investigators gained access to the region and could verify some of the earlier claims. In doing so, they had to brush up on their Kurdish history – a history suppressed and distorted by the states in which the transborder Kurdish populations lived.

The Kurdish national movement in Iraq arose, along with the Iraqi state, from the ruins of the Ottoman Empire. Post–World War I maneuvering by the victorious powers England and France yielded new states with new borders, as well as stateless people living across newly drawn international frontiers. The Kurds were the largest such nonstate nation, inhabiting a vast territory that comprised significant parts of Turkey, Iran, Syria, and Iraq. Feeling cheated out of independence by the postwar powers, the Kurds fought for greater freedoms in each of these countries during the twentieth century. In so doing, they repeatedly forged tactical deals with disparate parties: the regimes under whose repressive yoke they labored; regimes of neighboring states; and Kurdish movements in adjacent parts of Kurdistan with whom they shared language and culture, but each of which had its own battles to fight with its central authorities. From the Kurds' perspective, their modern history is a litany of promises made and then betrayed, agreements sealed only to be undone, and long periods of relative peace punctured by insurgencies, massacres, the destruction of villages, and, in most cases, utter defeat.

The first Kurdish rebellion occurred in the early 1920s under the leadership of Sheikh Mahmoud Barzinji, who titled himself "King of Kurdistan." His movement was suppressed only when the British mandatory authorities brought in RAF bombers. In the 1940s, a young Kurdish leader emerged who fought the monarchy from his base in Barzan and then Suleimaniyeh. His name was Mullah Mustafa Barzani, and he became the father of the modern Kurdish national movement in Iraq. Forced into exile in Iran in 1945, he helped establish the ill–fated Mahabad Republic the next year and founded the KDP, which promptly split into Iraqi and Iranian wings. Barzani was able to return home only after the monarchy's collapse in 1958; in 1961, he relaunched the national movement in Iraqi Kurdistan.

Barzani's movement was able to grow in the vacuum of post-monarchy Iraq when successive, short-lived, and weak republican regimes proved unable to impose their will, even though they tried – raiding, bombing, and ultimately razing entire villages. The Ba'ath regime that seized power in 1968 was so weak that it soon settled for an autonomy agreement that, on paper, devolved significant authority to a Kurdish regional government. The key sticking point then, as in later negotiations, was the status of Kirkuk, an oil-rich region claimed by both the Kurds and Iraq's Arab regimes. In 1974, the question of Kirkuk led to the collapse of the agreement and to a Kurdish revolt that could be crushed only when the Kurds' principal ally, the Shah of Iran, made a separate deal with the Ba'ath regime and withdrew his support. The KDP was defeated, its fighters dispersed, its people relocated to camps in southern Iraq, and its leadership forced to rebuild the movement from exile in Iran.

Immediately following this disaster, the KDP broke up, with younger cadres, led by Jalal Talabani, challenging Mullah Mustafa's leadership and establishing the PUK. This development represented not only a generational but also a cultural and linguistic split. From its founding, the PUK predominated in Suran, the western part of Kurdistan centered on Suleimaniyeh, where the Surani dialect is spoken. The KDP's base, however, remained in Kurmanji-speaking Badinan, especially around the village of Barzan, the home of the KDP's founder and the son who succeeded him, Masoud Barzani. Since its inception, the KDP has remained essentially a family affair, even if it has drawn in tribal leaders, professionals, and intellectuals from Dohuk and Erbil. The PUK, by contrast, has had a broader, more urban base, although Talabani's leadership has been largely undisputed.

Iraq's 1980 invasion of Iran revived these two parties' fortunes. For eight difficult years, the Iraqi regime was preoccupied with fighting the war. It sought to keep things under control in Kurdistan by buying off tribal leaders, whom it referred to as "Counselors" (Mustasharin) and whom it charged with policing the countryside with tribal recruits, called Fursan (Knights) by the regime but jahsh (little donkeys) by nationalist Kurds. The regime succeeded in maintaining control only in the lowlands; the more mountainous terrain became the domain of the peshmerga ("those who face death"), guerrillas deployed by the two main parties and a host of smaller ones – the Kurdistan Communist Party (KCP), the Kurdistan Socialist Party (KSP), the Kurdistan Popular Democratic Party (KPDP), the Islamic Unity Movement of Kurdistan (IUMK), and others.

These fighters moved around with great freedom, putting significant pressure on pared-down Iraqi forces. But even as the KDP and PUK relaunched their insurgency, they also confronted each other in a pattern that remains largely unchanged today: at times fighting, at other times negotiating, occasionally engaging in a tactical alliance when the broader political situation demanded it – but never overcoming a deep–seated rivalry and distrust.

Throughout the 1980s the KDP enjoyed a warm relationship with the Iranian regime. The party had its headquarters in the village of Slivana near Ziveh, a small Iranian town not far from the border with both Turkey and Iraq. When Iraq invaded Iran, the KDP saw an opportunity to avenge the humiliating defeat of 1975 and reassert its control in Badinan, if not all of Iraqi Kurdistan. When the Iranians, having repulsed the Iraqis in 1982, sought to push Iraq onto the defensive, the KDP was eager to assist. Thus, in the summer of 1983, KDP fighters and scouts accompanied Iranian forces in their offensive at Haj Omran. Following this partially successful battle, the Iranians made several further attempts, in alliance with the KDP, to thrust into Iraq more deeply. Each time these efforts ran aground, until Iranian forces were beaten back decisively in 1986.

The Haj Omran offensive gave the KDP a chance to settle scores with the Bradosti tribe, an old rival that, because of its position between the Barzani domain and the Iranian border, could limit the KDP's access to its headquarters in Iran. Allied with Baghdad, the Bradosti militia played a key role in defending its tribal homeland. The nature of Kurdish politics was such that the KDP's animosity toward the Bradosti tribe and the historical enmity between the KDP and the PUK spawned a tactical alliance between first the PUK and the Bradostis and then the PUK and the regime in Baghdad.

Such an alliance was encouraged by the PUK's difficult relationship with Khomeini's Iran. The Iranians had repeatedly asked Talabani to take up arms against Abd-al-Rahman Qasemlou's KDP-I, an Iranian Kurdish rebel party that had long been a thorn in the Khomeini regime's side. Talabani and Qasemlou were old friends, though, and the two parties shared an urban secular socialist ideology. Talabani balked at Iranian pressure and allowed the KDP-I and six other Iranian Kurdish opposition groups to establish their headquarters in the PUK's stronghold in Jafati valley, high in the mountains north of Suleimaniyeh, nicknamed "Valley of the Parties." Iran's continuing attempts to insert troops into northern Iraq – in pursuit of the KDP-I and other rebels but also hoping to take advantage of Iraq's Achilles' heel by taking chunks of Iraqi territory with the help of the KDP – soon pushed the PUK into Baghdad's arms.

In July 1983, just as the Haj Omran battle got under way, Talabani's chief negotiator, Faridoun Abd-al-Qader, began informal talks with the regime, meeting three senior Iraqi intelligence officers at a KDP-I base in the Alaan area, due west of Serdasht inside Iran. Soon he was invited to Baghdad. Staying at Qasemlou's house in Baghdad, Faridoun held a series of talks with Tariq Aziz and other senior leaders in October and November. They told him, he claimed later (interview, 2002), that everything was negotiable: parliamentary elections in Iraq, release of Kurdish prisoners, expansion of the Kurdish autonomous region, even the status of Kirkuk. In early 1984, Jalal Talabani and Saddam Hussein met in Baghdad to discuss Kirkuk, the potential deal breaker. According to Faridoun, Saddam said he was pleased with the progress made and appeared ready to make a significant concession on Kirkuk, saying: "I don't want to say Kirkuk is an Arab city, but it also isn't a Kurdish one. It cannot fall within the Kurdish autonomous zone, but it also does not have to stay under central control. We can work out a joint administration." But the regime issued a warning as well. According to Neywshirwan Mustafa Amin, Talabani's deputy (interview, 1993), Tariq Aziz told the Kurdish leaders: "If you help us, we will never forget it. But if you oppose us, we also will never forget it. And after the war is over, we will destroy you and all your villages completely."

These talks came at a time when Iraq was faring poorly in the war and Saddam Hussein needed all the allies he could find. Moreover, the negotiations allowed Iraqi forces to be shifted from Kurdistan to the southern front. But soon after Iraq, using mustard and nerve gas, successfully blocked Iran's Khaybar offensive in March 1984, PUK negotiators noticed that their counterparts began using delaying tactics. Negotiations stretched over the entire year and, depending on Iraq's battlefield fortunes, either progressed or stalled, recalled Faridoun. A final round of talks in November, just as Iraq and the US resumed diplomatic relations, collapsed after twenty days. Further low-level contacts failed to reverse the downward path, and when the pro-government Kurdish militia of Tahsin Shaweis killed a senior PUK commander, Mama Risha, in January 1985, daggers were drawn. In skirmishes in February, PUK guerrillas defeated Iraqi troops near Jafati valley, where they now returned to reestablish their headquarters.

Fearing a rapprochement between the PUK and Iran, Iraqi forces furiously attacked the mountain chain stretching from Suleimaniyeh to the border, destroying all the villages and relocating their inhabitants to large, bare-bones complexes (mujamma'at) in the lowlands. Outside this cordon sanitaire, the PUK managed to extend its writ over large swaths of rural territory, leaving the Iraqis in control only of major towns and the roads connecting them. Clashes were continuous in a low-level insurgency that Iraq could not end and the peshmergas could not win.

Unable to fight a two-front war, the PUK soon began to explore better relations with Iran. Their main interlocutors were intelligence officers in the Karargeh Ramazan ("Ramadan Command"), a Pasdaran security force with primary responsibility for Iraqi Kurdistan that controlled the Kurds' access to Iran, collected data on their movements, and generally kept them in check while fighting dissident Iranian Kurds. Sherdel Abdullah Howeizi, the PUK's liaison with the Karargeh Ramazan, explained the mutual benefits that would flow from better relations:

> According to Iranian propaganda, we still had relations with the Iraqi regime. At one point an Iranian group came to reconnoiter the area of Jafati valley and visited us, meeting with Mr. Talabani. That day, Iraqi jets bombed the area of our headquarters, and so the Iranians understood our new situation. They also could see that we had peshmergas based near the towns who could put pressure on the regime. After this, our relations began to improve. We needed Iran, especially to obtain medicines and treatment for wounds. There was also a lively smuggling market in the area, plus Kurds in both countries maintained close bonds. And it was important to us that we could travel abroad via Iran and that Westerners could reach us as well.

When the PUK asked for military support, the Iranians made a stipulation, said Faridoun. They wanted the PUK to assume a greater role in the war: "The Kurdish insurgency was not enough; they wanted to see a major attack on Iraqi forces." This suited the PUK, which ever since the failed negotiations, had wanted to strike the Iraqi regime where it hurt the most: Kirkuk. The Kirkuk oil fields had become strategically critical to the regime because of continuous Iranian attacks on oil installations at Basra. The Pasdaran liked the PUK's proposal but needed reassurance it was realistic, so a handful of senior Pasdaran officers, including Muhammad Ja'fari, the commander of Karargeh Ramazan, joined a PUK group on a reconnaissance mission to Kirkuk. "When they saw with their own eyes that our forces were close to Kirkuk," continued Faridoun, "they pledged their full support. They offered us more than fifty tons of weapons and explosives, as well as training in the use of Estrellas," shoulder-fired heat-seeking missiles. (An Iraqi pilot, interviewed in 2000, recounted that the Kurds had managed to bring down several helicopters and Pilatus planes with Estrella and SAM rockets.)

In October 1986, the peshmergas, driving over unpaved roads between the villages and helped by friends inside the pro-regime *jahsh* militias, in a single night hauled some forty tons of weapons to Kirkuk: GRAD and Katyusha rockets and 80 mm and 120 mm mortars. Sherdel Howeizi, who had obtained a degree in field artillery at Iraq's military college in the 1970s and participated in the attack, said he knew the enemy well. The Iraqi commander in charge of Iraq's Oil Protection Forces in Kirkuk was Gen. Bareq al-Haj Hunta, "a good artillery man who graduated with me." Untrained in the use of these weapons, however, the two thousand or so peshmergas who carried out the raid were accompanied by close to a hundred Pasdaran fighters and explosives experts, whom they referred to as a "technical force" (*quwa-t-al-fanniyin*).

The attack took place in the early hours of October 12 and was, according to Sherdel, a lightning strike intended to do some damage but, most importantly, to send a message to Baghdad that the Kurds had a claim on Kirkuk and had allies who could help them take the area. The Kurds, Sherdel claimed, lost only six or seven fighters, the Pasdaran lost none, and they were gone at dawn. Exulting in the strike's success, the Pasdaran allowed the Kurds to keep the weapons and started training them in their use. Iranian propaganda later glorified the attack as a major Iranian operation, called Fatah 1, whose objective was to "destroy the economic and military installations of Kirkuk."[10] In fact, the operation was a pinprick that caused only minor damage. Miqdad Bayes, a Kurd who witnessed the raid from his home in Kirkuk and whose brother, a PUK peshmerga, participated in it as a guide, remembered (interview, 2005) a multipronged attack originating in Kurdish areas east of Kirkuk that targeted military posts near his neighborhood. The Iranians, he said, instructed Kurdish fighters in the use of mortars.

Regardless of its scope and impact, the strike represented a stunning upset for the Iraqis, as it caught their forces defending the oil fields by complete surprise. It also sent an unambiguous warning that a potent new Kurdish–Iranian alliance could open a second front in a war in which Iraq, following the debacles at Faw and Mehran, was not doing well. For the regime the Kirkuk attack could not have come at a worse time. It was another blow to the nation's pride and this, added to a sense of deep betrayal, goes a long way in explaining the depth of anger that informed the regime's military response once it was capable of launching one.

Chemical Ali's Reign

The successful raid on Kirkuk earned the PUK new Iranian respect for its capabilities and sealed a far-reaching cooperative accord that would define the relationship between the two until the end of the war. According to Neywshirwan, it included a reciprocal commitment that if either party faced a serious military threat, the other would open a second front to relieve the pressure – a significant agreement that helps explain the events in Halabja in 1988. Invited to Tehran, Jalal Talabani, Faridoun Abd-al-Qader, and other senior PUK officials met with the Iranian leadership, including the powerful parliament speaker (and future president), Ali Akbar Hashemi Rafsanjani. "From then on our relationship was very strong," recalled Faridoun. "But when we returned to our bases in Jafati valley, we said to each other: 'The Kurds really have bad luck. The whole world supports Iraq against Iran, and now we have decided to support Iran against Iraq.' "

In their Tehran talks, the PUK negotiators managed to overcome one sore point that had blocked a closer alliance: the PUK's friendship with the Iranian Kurdish parties. Talabani later declared that it took him two years to persuade Iran that the PUK would not attack the KDP-I and Komala, a smaller party, on its behalf.[11] Another hurdle was the KDP. Iran's prodding helped push the two parties back into each other's arms. In an Iranian-brokered reconciliation in November 1986 that included reciprocal prisoner releases, the parties set up the Kurdistan Front, a coalition that incorporated several smaller parties as well.

From then on, the peshmerga forces started operating jointly, seizing effective control of the entire region demarcated by the defunct autonomy agreement of 1974, minus the larger towns and main roads.

They ran active underground operations that launched urban attacks and staged popular protests. The peshmergas also established, trained, and armed "backing forces" in the villages – civil defense units of able-bodied men, including many army deserters and draft dodgers who had found refuge there. Thus reinforced, the peshmergas attacked Iraqi military positions and camps, harassing army convoys and putting great pressure on the jahsh militias. A mustashar might be firmly in Baghdad's camp, having been bought with a hefty salary and expensive gifts, but his foot soldiers often suffered from divided loyalties. Many surreptitiously aided their rural relatives. Even some of the mustashars covertly negotiated deals with the rebels to secure their relatives' survival, quietly supporting the insurgency as it gained strength while running checkpoints on the main roads and at the entrances to towns to keep up appearances.

These developments further raised the threat level for the Iraqis, who not only saw their control of Kurdistan shrinking by the day, but also realized that the Kurds were approaching Kirkuk by infiltrating the surrounding countryside and bringing the population over to their cause. The regime took a good look and found wanting its "super-governor" in Kirkuk, Muhammad Hamza al-Zubeida, who oversaw counterinsurgency efforts. The man chosen to replace him was Saddam Hussein's cousin, Ali Hassan al-Majid, a coarse and brutal man who headed Iraq's secret police, the Amn. On March 18, 1987, Iraq's ruling Revolutionary Command Council appointed al-Majid chief of the Ba'ath party's Northern Bureau in Kirkuk, granting him broad latitude to suppress the rebellious Kurds.

Al-Majid understood from his predecessor's failed performance, which he decried in his speeches, that the guerrillas derived much of their strength not just from the mountainous terrain but also, critically, from the population's support. He therefore needed to break the nexus between guerrillas and villagers. His chosen weapon was gas. Its widespread use in the Kurdish countryside in 1987–1988 would earn him the nickname "Ali Kimiyawi," Chemical Ali.

Al-Majid's use of gas was an integral part of a two–pronged strategy to defeat the insurgency. One component was to depopulate the countryside. To this end, al-Majid undertook a three-stage village destruction campaign in the spring and summer of 1987. Army engineers equipped with bulldozers and dynamite and backed by military forces first moved into villages and subdistrict towns (*nahyas*) located on paved roads that were easy to reach. Then they moved against villages nestled against the mountainsides, where guerrillas used the tall vegetation to spring ambushes on poorly motivated Iraqi troops. The third stage, aimed at villages in the higher mountain valleys, could not be accomplished in 1987 and was postponed for a year. Human Rights Watch later concluded that al-Majid's destruction campaign was "an extraordinarily thorough enterprise," the evidence of which was "visible all over Iraqi Kurdistan, with many villages not so much demolished as pulverized."[12] Moreover, al-Majid declared the entire countryside, whether destroyed or yet untouched, "prohibited." Villagers stayed there at their own risk, targeted by helicopter gunships, army units on patrol, or roving bands of jahsh fighters.

The other component of al-Majid's strategy was to decapitate the Kurdish leadership – to cut off the "head of the snake." Air bombardments, artillery shelling, and infantry assaults had all proven incapable of dislodging the rebels from their many redoubts. Al-Majid now tried to use gas to smoke them out, funnel them into open terrain, and defeat them there with conventional forces. Topography, however, worked against this strategy. Gas hung like a cloud low in the valleys, rarely reaching into the caves or drifting upward. The peshmergas learned to find uncontaminated air simply by climbing up the mountainsides.

The regime soon realized that the peshmergas' main vulnerability was the rural population that sustained them, and that by gassing civilians it could break the rebels' fighting spirit – demoralize them to the point of paralysis. After all, the Kurdish parties justified their insurgency as necessary to protect the people. Chemical weapons' brutal effectiveness would expose the hollowness of this claim. The Iraqi discovery emerged gradually over the year, and then, merging with the frustrated objective to depopulate the entire countryside, mutated dangerously into another idea altogether: Use gas to flush villagers from their homes, gather them up, take them to faraway sites, and dispose of them – bury them under the desert sands and thereby end the Kurdish rebellion forever.

No one expressed his intentions better than al-Majid himself. In a speech to the party faithful in 1987, he warned that no one in rural

Kurdistan would be spared, not even the allied mustashars and their followers if they failed to leave their villages:

> I told the mustashars that they might say they like their villages and that they won't leave. I told them: "I cannot let your village stay. I will attack it with chemical weapons. Then you and your family will die. You must leave right now. I will not be able to warn you on the day I decide to attack with chemical weapons." I will kill them all with chemical weapons! Who is going to say anything? The international community? Fuck them! – the international community and those who listen to them. . . .
>
> This is my intention. . . . As soon as we complete the deportations, we will start attacking them everywhere according to a systematic military plan, even their strongholds. In our attacks we will take back one-third or one-half of what is under their control. If we succeed in taking two-thirds, then we will surround them in a small pocket and attack them with chemical weapons. I will not attack them with chemicals just one day, but I will continue to attack them with chemicals for fifteen days. . . . Then you will see that all the vehicles of God himself will not suffice to carry them all.[13]

The idea for the Anfal campaign was born.

"Special" Communications Channels

In the spring of 1987, however, both sides were still feeling each other out and experimenting with new methods of attack and defense. Gas had yet to be used. If al-Majid wanted to decapitate the Kurdish leadership, Kurdish leaders in turn wanted to remove as quickly as possible the virtual chokehold the Iraqi military held on their main headquarters. The army built positions on mountaintops ringing the Jafati valley, holding it under continuous siege and controlling the points of access (though not smugglers' paths).

On the night of April 13–14, a force of PUK peshmergas engaged Iraqi troops in the mountains surrounding Jafati valley – the "Battle of Dastani Rezgari" – pushing them out of military camps at Azmar, Chuarta, Mawat, Jabel Spi, and elsewhere. According to one of the Kurdish participants, Jamal Hama Karim (interview, 2000), the guerrillas almost reached, and seized, the road linking Suleimaniyeh with the town of Dukan on the edge of Dukan lake, where a dam on the Lesser Zab (a tributary of the Tigris) yields energy for the region.

The Iraqi counterattack came the same day and included al-Majid's first signal that times were changing. Though unsuccessful in retaking lost territory, the attack saw the first recorded use of gas in Kurdistan that was not, as at Haj Omran and Penjwin in 1983, primarily directed at Iranian forces. In it, Sherdel Howeizi became, as he later called it, al-Majid's "first chemical weapons casualty." As a long-time peshmerga he had grown accustomed to the scent of phosphorus, which he likened to the smell of onions. In the evening of April 15, as he hunkered down in Jafati valley expecting an Iraqi counterattack, shells started to rain down. This did not concern him greatly, as surviving artillery attacks had become as ordinary as going fishing or bringing in the harvest. However, "the explosions sounded strange to me," Sherdel recalled:

> These were not normal shells. They produced smoke. I smelled onions. Some of our men were slightly injured. In the morning I noticed that my hand had blistered and my head hurt. I went to see Mam Jalal [Talabani] and Kak Faridoun at once to tell them we had been attacked with phosphorus. But my cousin, Shalow, who is a doctor, was there. He took one look at my hand and said: "That's mustard gas." Mam Jalal instructed me to tell no one. We were the only four who knew. The next day there was more shelling, and then it dawned on everyone that these were chemical weapons. We had no experience!

The guerrillas may have lacked experience but not forewarning. Faridoun said he had received a message from al-Majid a month earlier – messages were being passed routinely through informal channels – in which he said: "You have made fine shelters for your pershmergas. We will use weapons that will kill you inside your shelters." "We realized then that the regime would use gas," Faridoun said. "But we decided not to tell the men, concerned about the effect on morale." Al-Majid had a similar recollection. In a Northern Bureau meeting later in 1987 he explained: "Jalal Talabani asked me to open a special communications channel with him. That evening I went to Suleimaniyeh and hit them with special ammunition" – chemical weapons.[14]

Shortly afterward, the Iranians sent a medical team to treat their Kurdish allies, give them gas masks, and train them in chemical defense. "They explained to us the different types of gas and how they each smelled," remembered Sherdel. "They told us to wash ourselves when attacked, to make fires, to wrap ourselves in wet blankets, and put wet scarves around our heads."

Sherdel soon observed a disturbing modification in Iraqi tactics. Iraqi gunners used to fire conventional shells to drive the guerrillas into their shelters, followed by a chemical volley to kill them inside. "So of course, as soon as we heard the softer sound of chemical shells, we'd rush outside and move up the mountainsides. But then they started using conventional and chemical shells simultaneously. This made things very dangerous." He also noticed that the Iraqis used self-propelled 152 mm shells with a curve range, "fired by an unusual artillery unit brought in specifically for these attacks and then immediately withdrawn." These shells would reach deep into their hiding places.

The PUK's headquarters and nearby peshmerga positions were not the only targets of al-Majid's first use of gas, nor were Kurdish guerrillas its sole victims. On April 16, shortly after Sherdel Howeizi incurred his unfamiliar injuries, Iraqi forces launched a major gas attack against a set of villages in Balisan valley, base of the PUK's regional command (malband) for Erbil. The valley is far from the border but constitutes a critical link in a chain of valleys between Suleimaniyeh and Badinan. The peshmergas lived interspersed with the local population, but they say they were absent on the day of the attack. Human Rights Watch offers a detailed description of what happened:

> In the drizzly late afternoon . . . the villagers had returned home from the fields and were preparing dinner when they heard the drone of approaching aircraft. Some stayed put in their houses; others made it as far as their air–raid shelters before the planes, a dozen of them, came in sight, wheeling in low over the two villages [Balisan, with 250 households, and Sheikh Wasanan, with 150] to unload their bombs. There were muffled explosions.[15]

A videotape made by a jahsh fighter recorded the attack. Witnesses later recounted a cool spring breeze and an attractive scent of smoky clouds drifting down, but also hideous injuries and great suffering. Scores of villagers died on the spot. Many of the injured were able to reach the nearest towns, helped by peshmergas.

What happened to the survivors is a dramatic story all by itself: many died during flight, and most of those who arrived in Erbil were seized by the Amn and disappeared. Significantly, however, a small number were able to reach the border, where Iranian doctors treated their wounds and evacuated them to the regional capital Bakhtaran.

The Iranians made no secret of what had happened in Balisan. The UN's Iqbal Riza remembered (interview, 2000) that in an April 1987 visit to the Iranian Kurdish town of Baneh, itself a frequent Iraqi target, the UN team was shown Iraqis – "civilians as far as we could make out" – who had slight gas injuries. "The Iranians told us these people had been found inside Iraq. But this was not really within our mission's terms of reference." The problem was that the UN had a mandate to investigate chemical weapons use in the context of the Iran–Iraq war, an international armed conflict to which the 1925 Geneva Protocol fully applied. But the Protocol contains no provisions for chemical weapons use in the context of *internal* armed conflicts, such as rebel warfare or counterinsurgency campaigns. And so the team, already caught in tensions between the Security Council and the General Secretariat, was at a loss how to report the new casualties. "We were not inside Iraq," Riza explained, "but we thought that these people's injuries might be incidental to the war. So we signed a separate letter to the secretary-general to inform him of what we had seen. This information did not make it into the final report. It was never made public, and it was not made available to the Security Council."

The evidence of this new atrocity was so weak – accounts by civilians injured in circumstances that could not be verified independently – that it was easily ignored, despite vigorous media campaigns by Kurdish political representatives in European capitals that triggered the occasional parliamentary question. Iraq's leadership thus understood once again that, literally, it had gotten away with murder. It must therefore have felt totally uninhibited in its ambition to finish off the Kurdish insurgency in the shortest time possible with whatever means it had. It had reason for optimism. Life, according to Barzan Qader Muhammad, a peshmerga at the time (interview, 2004), was very tough in the villages and morale was low. Chemical weapons were a new phenomenon, and Kurds did not yet know how to protect themselves. "Fear was therefore great. The regime sent its agents into the villages to warn of impending chemical attacks and urge people to move into the complexes to save themselves."

By June 1987, the Iraqi advance on the Kurdish strongholds had run aground in the face of stiff resistance. Although many rural inhabitants had been moved to mujamma'at, many others simply fled to higher elevations, finding shelter in villages that the army had been unable to reach. They were joined by growing numbers of army deserters and draft dodgers, men who harbored no loyalty toward the regime and refused to become its cannon fodder in a war that did not represent their interests as Kurds. In response, Ali Hassan al-Majid, lord of all he could survey from his hilltop villa in Kirkuk, issued two standing orders that should be considered "smoking gun" documents. The first order, of June 3, further defined the prohibited zones. Paragraph 5 reads: "Within their jurisdiction, the armed forces must kill any human being or animal present within these areas. They are totally prohibited."

The second order, of June 20, is even more sweeping. Its paragraph 4 instructs corps commanders to "carry out special strikes by artillery, helicopters and aircraft at all times of the day or night in order to kill the largest number of persons present in those prohibited zones, keeping us informed of the results." Its paragraph 5 should be seen as the blueprint for the Anfal killings the next year: "All persons captured in those villages shall be detained and interrogated by the security services and those between the ages of 15 and 70 shall be executed after any useful information has been obtained from them."[16]

The reader may be excused for failing to note the coded instruction in paragraph 4. "Special" strikes (*darabat khaseh*) and "special" munitions (*e'taad khaseh*) were euphemisms for gas attacks, as senior Iraqi commanders well knew. This emerges unambiguously from security police and military intelligence documents, and has been confirmed by both UN chemical weapons experts and various Iraqi defectors, including MID's Wafiq al-Samarra'i and pilots who flew wartime missions.

If no significant gas attacks occurred in the prohibited zones between June and year's end, it was because Iraq was preoccupied with other matters: shepherding a ceasefire resolution through the Security

Council (July), managing a volatile naval standoff and superpower rivalry in Gulf waters, conducting its decennial census (October), countering Iranian pinprick attacks along the front, preparing its forces for Iran's next "final" offensive, and waiting for the snow to melt in Kurdistan.

An Internal Matter

In the summer of 1987, the Reagan administration was in active pursuit of an end to the war, which was drawing US forces into the Persian Gulf, where the Soviets also maintained a significant presence. Reagan wanted a ceasefire on terms largely favorable to Iraq, thus to contain Iranian expansionism and restore stability to a region that is home to the West's principal sources of oil. In the words of the UN's Giandoménico Picco, it was "the disruption in the flow of oil out of the Persian Gulf that would finally concentrate the minds, if not the hearts, of the global community on the Iran–Iraq war."[17]

To what extent was Washington aware of events in Kurdistan? Western news reporting was vague and distorted, given the difficult access. But a Joint Chiefs of Staff intelligence report gives us an indication of how much the administration knew. The beginning part has been redacted, but the declassified part reads:

> The fighters of the Patriotic Union of Kurdistan, who have become the predominant factor within Kurd resistance movements, and the Kurd Democratic Party have succeeded in extending their area of control which mainly covers the mountainous border region east of the line Arbil–Kirkuk–Sulaimaniyah and north of Al Amadiyah–Dohuk. In order to counter the spreading insurgence, the Iraqi authorities embarked on a resettlement campaign, flattening some 300 villages and destroying residential areas in frequent air raids. [Section redacted.] Despite the ruthless repression, which also includes the use of *chemical* agents, and the reinforcement of the armed forces by several brigades of the Presidential Guard, Iraqi security operations, coordinated by Ali Hassan Al-Majid, have failed to stifle the Kurd insurgence so far.[18]

Likewise, a CIA report dating from late 1987 or early 1988 that provides a detailed assessment of Iraqi capabilities and actions shows considerable knowledge of events in Kurdistan. Iraq had gassed the Kurds, it suggested, to:

> ...minimize the diversion of troops from more critical fronts and the losses that might occur in inaccessible areas that favor guerrilla forces.... Since April 1987, a military campaign has been waged to eradicate village bases of support for Kurdish guerrilla groups. To minimize losses of men and materiel, Iraqi troops have used riot control agents and possibly chemical weapons repeatedly when conventional weapons have not sufficed to subdue villagers before razing their dwellings.[19]

Moreover, the CIA warned with accurate foresight, "there is evidence that Iraqi CW attacks may be evolving [from strictly defensive use] to include preemptive uses. If Iran were to threaten Iraqi perceived strategic positions, we believe that Iraq might authorize massive chemical employments, as implied by Iraqi politicians.... We should also expect to observe the introduction of more lethal agents such as VX." The report then cautioned: "As currently employed, chemical weapons will sometimes allow technical advantage, but are unlikely to affect the war strategically. Baghdad, thus far, has not shown the intention to commit the full CW resources necessary to gain a true strategic advantage."[20]

Documents show that other government branches were also well informed. In early September, Peter Galbraith, then an aide to Senate Foreign Relations Committee chairman Claiborne Pell, made a brief journey through Iraq accompanied by an embassy political officer, Haywood Rankin. Rankin's unpublished report, "Travels with Galbraith – Death in Basra, Destruction in Kurdistan," noted how Galbraith "was able to observe first hand that the security situation...has deteriorated markedly," since his previous trip three years earlier. Restricted to the main roads, the two men nonetheless were able to report:

> Destruction of the houses was thorough, as we observed in all of the Kurdish towns and villages we saw destroyed – 23 in all. After another mile, we passed through another large Kurdish town, this time completely destroyed. There was rubble as far the eye could see through the dust haze. No walls were left standing.... In this zone and everywhere else along the highways in Kurdistan, we observed

military forts about every kilometer interspersed with single–man posts which are often manned by [pro-regime] Kurds. . . . What was odd [on the way from Darbandikhan to Suleimaniyeh] was the complete absence of human habitation, not even a single herd or herdsman. . . . Stretching for miles south of the large Kurdish town of 'Arbat, we saw a great concentration of new construction, a series of towns [mujamma'at] being laid out on the undulating plain. . . . On the road [from Suleimaniyeh to Kirkuk, there was again a ten–mile zone of destroyed villages. . . . This wide plain which in normal times would be an excellent agricultural basin today sports not only destroyed Kurdish villages but a massive military presence, one army camp after another.[21]

For a whirlwind tour of the north, these observations were remarkably spot-on. Had the two men been free to travel into the countryside, they might have discovered even more. Iraq, however, permitted no such access.

The State Department's annual human rights report also signaled awareness of events in Kurdistan, referring to "widespread destruction and bulldozing of Kurdish villages, mass forced movement of Kurds, and exile of Kurdish families into non-Kurdish parts of Iraq."[22] Ambassador Newton later claimed (interview, 2001) that Washington had been very much aware of Iraq's counterinsurgency campaign:

It was clear that it targeted the countryside. It was clear that they were destroying orchards and fields. It was a campaign against anti-government Kurds. But it was also clear that this was an attempt to reduce the rural population and take away the guerrillas' support base. And it was clear that it was an inhumane program. I can't remember, however, that we raised it with the Iraqis. We had no grounds. Unlike their use of chemical weapons [against Iran], this was an internal matter.

In the 1980s, notions of sovereignty were not what they would be a decade later: Iraq's invasion and subsequent defeat in Kuwait triggered a UN inspections regime unprecedented in its intrusiveness. The fall of the Berlin Wall and the rise of the human rights movement made it difficult for Western governments to hide behind the excuse of "internal affairs" to justify their client states' brutalities. But in 1987 Iraq's internal affairs triggered only public silence. There is no indication that the

Reagan administration in any way sought to signal its displeasure at the regime's response to the "Kurd insurgence." Doing so might have upset difficult negotiations at the Security Council that, in July, finally led to Resolution 598, which laid out the terms of the ceasefire.

The administration did something else, though. In a speech in Israel in October 1987, Secretary of State George Shultz publicly criticized "both Iran and Iraq" for using poison gas.[23] The accusation at Iran's expense, in the absence of proof or even strong evidence that the Iranians had used gas, served to deflect questions about Iraq, to whose brutalities on the battlefield the world had become inured. Impossible to disprove, the charge was sufficiently plausible – following Iranian threats that it might respond to Iraqi gas attacks in kind – that administration officials could employ it in both bureaucratic and public battles over the US role in the war, as the parties entered the endgame in late 1987. Given Iraqi intentions, the gambit did not come a moment too soon.

FIVE

HALABJA

"[I'm concerned about] Saddam Hussein using weapons of mass destruction against his own people and blaming it on us, which would fit a pattern."
     – US Secretary of Defense Donald Rumsfeld, *New York Times*,
                    February 18, 2003

"...The Iraqi regime...was supported by the Americans and the British during the war against Iran. No one talked about Iraq when it used chemical weapons against the Kurdish people...."
     – Osama bin Laden, *Newsweek*, January 11, 1999

The peshmergas roaming Kurdistan's mountains were accompanied by a man with a video camera who documented their every exploit – victories and defeats, advances and retreats, and the common people in between. His name was Abbas Abd-al-Razzaq Akbar, but his comrades called him "Abbas Video." He was in Sheikh Wasanan during the Iraqi chemical attack in April 1987, where he filmed the demise of a man named Shams-al-Din who, injured by mustard gas, died a hideous death after ten days of intense torment.

On March 16, 1988, Abbas Video crossed through Iranian territory from Jafati to Halabja, hoping to rejoin his friends, who along with Iranian troops had seized the area a day earlier. Delayed by bureaucracy, Abbas entered Iraq four days later. On his way to the border he encountered Kurdish refugees straggling into Iran; many bore signs of mustard gas injuries.

Informed of the Halabja events, Abbas nevertheless was unprepared when he entered town (interview, 2002):

> I saw whole families – mothers with their children – that nobody had touched. One of the first survivors I met was a young woman whose father I had known, a photographer named Omar Rassam. She took me to the cellar of her house. Inside, everyone was dead. She was the only survivor. All the people I met were in shock. In another cellar a dead woman was holding her son, her arm outstretched as if to beg for help. I felt as if this were my family, and so I touched her hand. It was soft. I then thought, "This is the end of all life," and I had a strong desire to lie down next to her and not get up again.

Yet he kept going, documenting the horrific scenes of sudden death, with some corpses frozen in the midst of daily routines: sitting in their courtyards; behind the wheel of their cars; holding infants to their breasts. Others, it seemed, had been caught in mid-flight as they ran to escape the poisonous clouds that arbitrarily killed some people while sparing others. Outside town, Abbas Video recalled:

> The gas had killed all natural life, animals and trees. I saw thousands of goats and sheep, all dead. Also wolves. I saw a dead cow whose calf was still alive, trying to suckle. I filmed hundreds of dead animals on the roads around Halabja. I couldn't hear anything. No birds. There was absolutely no sound. Everything had died. I had to leave town every so often to go to an area where I could hear birds, because the silence drove me crazy.

A Marriage of Convenience

In early 1988 the peshmergas effectively controlled most of rural Kurdistan, including the undulating hills of Germian (literally: "warm"), a region stretching from Suleimaniyeh westward to Kirkuk. This the Iraqi regime could not accept. Preoccupied with the war, Iraq had been unable to send forces to subdue the Kurds, but now its fortunes were turning. The Iranian military machine – Pasdaran, Basiji volunteers, and poor army foot soldiers – increasingly looked like a spent force, waiting to trudge home to family and loved ones. The Iranian spring offensive, an annual ritual, failed to materialize. And so, confident of US support, the Iraqis girded themselves for the showdown, setting their sights on not only the Iranian adversary but also the enemy within, the treasonous Kurds, a fifth column of "saboteurs" and their families who had tried Baghdad's patience far too long.

At the first melting of snow, the regime launched a full-scale air and artillery assault on PUK headquarters in Jafati valley. The date was February 23, and the rebel leader in charge was the PUK's number two, Neywshirwan Mustafa Amin. (Jalal Talabani was in Europe rendering an account of village destruction and chemical attacks.) The operation took almost four weeks, but what caused the guerrillas' defeat was not the military onslaught, which soon ground down in the face of determined resistance in difficult terrain, nor the Iraqis' intensive use of poison gas, but the utter collapse of the peshmergas' morale. And the single reason why these hardened fighters suddenly gave up was the news they received from Halabja on March 16.

What led to the Iraqi gas attack on Halabja is controversial, a fact that helps explain subsequent confusion, disinformation, and the absence of international condemnation. It is therefore important to describe at some length the developments that preceded it.

In interviews with scores of persons either present during the attack or involved at some level of Iraqi command responsibility, no one has credibly claimed that Iran shared responsibility for the gassing on March 16. The only accusation one hears is that Iraq's brutal reprisal was a predictable consequence of the audacious Iranian–Kurdish seizure of Halabja, and that therefore the operation should never have been carried out. In Iran the matter is not subject to public debate, nor has it the same relevance, but Iraqi Kurds have been engaged in a lively discussion about the wisdom of liberating Halabja, with one leader (Shawqat Haji Mushir, a Halabja native and the PUK commander in charge of the Halabja operation) publishing a detailed version of events that amounted to an extended apologia.[1]

By all accounts, the Halabja operation arose from a convergence of interests between Iran and the Kurdish parties, the PUK in particular. What is controversial first of all is the precise role each played in the attack. PUK cadres are divided between those who say the affair was an Iranian military initiative – that the Kurds, once again, were pawns in a game whose objectives they never fully grasped – while others insist that the Iranians, for their own reasons, embraced the Kurdish plan – that it was a desperate move reflecting the Kurds' realization that the war was coming to a close and their options were rapidly diminishing.

A second controversy – over who actually entered Halabja – is even more serious, as it goes to the heart of fundamental questions of collusion and treachery. After all, the PUK had earned the official Iraqi designation "Iranian Agents" (*'Umala Iran*), while the KDP was labeled the "Offspring of Treason" (*Salili al-Khayaneh*), a direct reference to Masoud Barzani, whose father, Mullah Mustafa, had been in cahoots with the Shah during the ill–fated Kurdish revolt in the mid-1970s. There was considerable pressure on Kurdish leaders, especially from within PUK and KDP ranks, to keep their distance from Iran, lest the Kurds be seen as proxies to a foreign power, not as a political movement with its own military capabilities that had legitimate claims to territory and political status – not, in other words, as a movement of national liberation.

What is not in doubt is that each side was seeking to solve a specific problem. Iran was under tremendous political and military pressure. Its economic facilities were under attack, the US was policing the Gulf, and the UN Security Council was preparing to impose an arms embargo. Rather than launching its spring offensive, Iran matched up with Iraq in another ugly round of the "war of the cities." On February 29, Iraq launched a massive strike on Tehran, for the first time using ballistic missiles. In the next ten days, Iran fired twenty-two missiles against Iraq's sixty-eight, until both agreed to a ceasefire. The exchange affected Iraqi morale less than it did Iran's. Iraqi strikes killed many and terrorized all, compelling a fair portion of Tehran's inhabitants to flee. By contrast (according to a CIA assessment), "almost all the 20 Iranian missile attacks on Baghdad hit lightly populated areas southeast of the city," causing no public panic. As a result, "no significant number of people have left Baghdad."[2]

Another CIA report insightfully explained Iran's options, suggesting that by carrying out attacks short of a major offensive, Tehran was hoping to limit both international and domestic criticism: "The attacks may be away from the southern front to soothe Gulf Arab nerves and possibly limit damage to relations with Moscow and Damascus," the report said. Moreover, "by avoiding an assault on a heavily defended strategic target, the regime would be more likely to avoid high casualties in the period leading to the parliamentary elections," scheduled for

April.[3] In this assessment, an incursion into Iraqi Kurdistan would fit the bill, threatening no major international interests while casualties would accrue primarily to the Kurds, who were expected to do most of the heavy lifting.

Such a maneuver would also help Iran in reducing heavy pressure on the southern front by forcing Baghdad to send troops north. Moreover, with the war drawing to a close, Tehran may have sought last–minute advantage in future negotiations by acquiring Iraqi territory. It must have dawned on Iran's leadership that the insurgents had been a good deal more successful in wresting territory from the Iraqi regime than had Iranian forces in the south, and that the Kurds, unlike Iraq's Shiʻite population, had proved far more willing allies. An added advantage, from a propaganda perspective, was that Iraqi citizens – the Kurds – would do the lion's share of fighting, thus underscoring the Iraqi regime's lack of legitimacy. (Likewise, the Iraqi media gave prime coverage to the role of Kurdish jahsh militias in the Anfal campaign to suggest that the peshmergas were outlaws enjoying little popular support.)

In the Iranian scenario, Halabja was an obvious candidate: Sheltered from the rest of Iraq, its capture would enable a natural defense against an Iraqi counterattack. Moreover, Iran's Kurdish allies were enthusiastic to take Halabja, for reasons explained below. Finally, Halabjans themselves would likely greet the Iranians as liberators – a propaganda coup. Only a year earlier, the Iraqi regime had destroyed the town's Kani Ashqan neighborhood in reprisal for street protests over Ali Hassan al-Majid's village destruction campaign. In messages passed to the guerrillas, Halabjans indicated they were itching for revenge.

In addition to these factors, the theoretical prospect of reaching the Darbandikhan dam may also have proved appetizing to the Iranian leadership. This was certainly the view in Washington and Baghdad. A CIA assessment at the end of March warned that the ongoing Iranian offensive along the southern bank of the Darbandikhan reservoir would put their forces "in excellent position to capture Salim Pirak, the dam, and possibly cross to the west bank of the reservoir north of the dam."[4] Iraq, according to US Ambassador David Newton (interview, 2001), saw an Iranian capture of both the Darbandikhan and Dukan dams as a real threat. Iraq therefore drained the two reservoirs in March to prevent the Iranians from attempting to flood Baghdad.[5]

Some Kurdish commanders clearly understood the dam to be one of Iran's prime objectives. Muhammad Haji Mahmoud, leader of the Kurdistan Socialist Party (KSP), asserted (correspondence, 2001) that Iran sought to reduce the risk of an Iraqi counteroffensive in the south by widening the battlefield, but also wanted to capture the dam. Control over the water flow in the Diyala river would give Iran significant political leverage. Moreover, capture of the Suleimaniyeh–Baghdad road adjacent to the lake would give Iranian forces free passage to rebel-held Qaradagh and from there to Germian and the ultimate prize, the Kirkuk oil fields – a possible substitute for elusive Basra. PUK commander Shawqat Haji Mushir (interview, 2002) likewise claimed that Iran had express designs on the dam: "We discussed it many times with them. They wanted to blow it up, but we did not agree."

This is not the Kurdish consensus view, however. At least one PUK commander, Hama Hama Sa'id, has argued (interview, 2002) that if the dam was an Iranian objective, Iranian forces came ill-equipped: Engineering teams specialized in demining and road clearing were deployed only around Halabja and between Halabja and the border, not in the direction of the dam. Moreover, he said, the Iranians never made a serious effort to take Shakh Shemiran, a mountain overlooking the lake, without which they would not have a prayer of getting even near the dam.

Hadi Farajvand, a Basiji platoon commander, recalled (interview, 2002) that the regime had considered blowing up the dam but decided against it: "Friends of mine in the Karargeh Ramazan studied the possibility of placing explosives, but they checked with Ayatollah Khomeini. He asked where the water would go, and then denied permission." Khomeini apparently feared that a swollen Diyala would cause damage to Shi'ite holy shrines downstream. (In any event, Iranian forces never reached either the dam or the highway. In a post-battle review aired on Iranian television, though, Pasdaran commander Mohsen Reza'ie boasted that they had come to within ten kilometers of the road, putting it within reach of Iran's medium–range artillery.[6])

After overrunning Halabja, Iranian forces stayed put lakeside until the end of the war, giving no hint of broader aspirations. Sheikh Mowla, a senior leader of the Supreme Council for the Islamic Revolution in Iraq (SCIRI) who was at the Iranian headquarters in Dizli (near Marivan) during the Halabja operation, insisted (interview, 2002) that the Iranians never intended to blow up the dam, but instead planned to destroy the tunnel connecting Suleimaniyeh with Darbandikhan (and Baghdad). Some have suggested that the massive chemical strike on Halabja sabotaged such plans. It could also be argued that the Iraqis themselves did not appear overly concerned about an Iranian attack on the dam. Instead of attacking Iranian forces around Halabja, the Iraqis gassed the Kurds, leaving the Iranians in control of the area for a full four months without even a hint of wanting to dislodge them.

Iran did have another important objective, one it did not report to its Kurdish allies but that became evident as soon as its troops entered Iraq: to decimate Iranian Kurdish rebels who used Iraqi Kurdistan as a launching pad for insurgency in Iran. Both the KDP-I and Komala had bases close to Iraqi troops in the Halabja area. As Iraqi defenses crumbled, Iranian troops surging into Halabja went after these rebels. More about this later.

On the Iraqi Kurdish side, the PUK's motivations were equally complex. Most critically, Iraqi pressure on its Jafati headquarters was so desperate that the PUK needed to draw Iraqi forces away. PUK commander Hama Hama Sa'id explained that during the Halabja operation the PUK deliberately refrained from coding wireless communications between its forces there and in Jafati, "so that the Iraqis knew we were attacking Halabja. This way, we hoped, they would withdraw from Jafati. But they didn't."

To the Kurds, too, Halabja was an obvious candidate. The scheme to liberate Halabja coincided with an older plan to which all the Kurdish parties subscribed and which they had designed to preempt an equally old Iraqi plan aimed at razing Halabja and border towns. Iraqi forces had already leveled Penjwin, Chuarta, and Mergasur. The Kurds suspected that Halabja and Qala Dizeh would be next. (In any event, Iraqi forces destroyed Halabja after retaking it from Iran at war's end in July 1988 and razed Qala Dizeh a year later.) "We had," recalled Shawqat Haji Mushir, "a written agreement with the Iranians to jointly liberate Suleimaniyeh governorate. First we would seize the area between Qala Dizeh and Haybat Sultan [a mountain separating Suleimaniyeh from

Erbil]. Then we would take the area of Halabja and Darbandikhan, and cut off the Suleimaniyeh–Kirkuk road at Darbandi Bazian."

Observing the emerging alliance between the Kurds and Iran, the Iraqis decided to preempt their plans by attacking the PUK in Jafati. Iraq brought in two army corps (*faylaq*). One came from Ranya, thereby thwarting any Kurdish plan to liberate the area between Qala Dizeh and Haybat Sultan, which was now crawling with Iraqi troops. "We canceled step one," Shawqat explained, "and because the pressure on our headquarters was so severe, we proceeded directly with step two: Halabja's liberation." Shawqat's deputy (and cousin), Hamid Haji Gali, had a slightly different version (interview, 2000). The original decision was to open three fronts, he said: at Qala Dizeh, Halabja, and Haj Omran. But "after discussing these three areas' relative merits, the leadership settled on Halabja, because its population had swollen in 1987 [as a result of village destruction]. These discussions were all conducted in code [*jifra*] by wireless."

The Kurds were motivated by something else as well, suggested Shawqat: Until then, only the PUK was based in Iraq. The other Kurdish parties were eager to establish their own headquarters inside Iraq as well. The capture of territory would allow this. "There was," he said, "a common interest to hang onto, or acquire, additional liberated area."

At its most realistically ambitious, the Kurdish plan was to liberate all of Suleimaniyeh governorate, seizing control of both the Darbandikhan and Dukan dams and cutting the Suleimaniyeh–Kirkuk road. This was only meant to be the prelude, though, to a plan reflecting the Kurds' wildest dreams: to seize Kirkuk.

Early in 1988, the Kurdistan Front began a series of meetings with the Iranian leadership. The front's coordinating council comprised the KDP's Babaker Zeibari, the KSP's Shirwan Shirawandi, the PUK's Faridoun Abd-al-Qader, and Mullah Ali Abd-al-Aziz, leader of the Islamic Unity Movement of Kurdistan (IUMK). SCIRI was represented by Ali Mowlani; the Iranians sent Pasdaran commander Mohsen Reza'ie and several others. The final decision to liberate Halabja was taken, according to KSP leader Muhammad Haji Mahmoud, on March 7, after a frantic appeal for help from the PUK. This set in motion the final preparations for Iran's Val-Fajr X offensive.

Conflicting Accounts

From this point the question of the nature of Iran's contribution is highly contested. The Kurds say they developed an elaborate division of labor among the parties and with the Iranians: 200 KDP peshmergas led by Hamid Effendi and Nader Ali Howramani would take the town of Khurmal; 100–150 KSP guerrillas commanded by Muhammad Haji Mahmoud would seize the strategic Zalm bridge, thereby cutting the Halabja–Suleimaniyeh road; 500 PUK guerrillas would head for Halabja; 100–150 IUMK peshmergas led by Mullah Ali Biyari and Mullah Ali Abd-al-Aziz would provide logistical support to the PUK; and a contingent of 1,000–1,500 of SCIRI's Badr fighters led by Abu Ali and Abu Zeinab (both *noms de guerre*) and accompanied by Kurdish scouts would seize Shakh Shemiran. In Halabja, the rebels had distributed weapons to their friends in the underground and had spoken with local jahsh commanders to see if they would switch sides.

The PUK assembled a force of 450 men, drawn from different parts of Kurdistan (not wanting to weaken its troop strength in Jafati), near Hawar village in the mountains above Halabja. Hamid Haji Gali, who led the group, said they reconnoitered the area and removed antipersonnel landmines. "I and about five other PUK commanders sneaked into Halabja and spent an entire week coordinating the attack with the underground. We gathered information on Iraqi troop strength and took photographs and video images of Iraqi army bases and camps." The Iraqis had an army artillery brigade (*liwa'*) in Delamar, above Halabja, and four battalions (*afwaj*) in Rostam Beg north of Khurmal, in Halabja proper, in Zammaki just north of Halabja, and in Chemi Palania near the destroyed town of Tawela on the Iranian border – a total of 3,500 troops. Moreover, there were four jahsh battalions in Halabja, each with 800 to 1,000 men. Hamid Haji Gali reckoned that three-quarters of the fighters, including junior commanders, would join the guerrillas; only the mustashars – Hassan Mahmoud Beg, Khaled Jalilei, Ibrahim Naser al-Din, and Hama Reza Namdar – and some of their lieutenants would stay loyal to the Iraqi regime. Finally, Iraq's Military Intelligence Directorate was thought to have about seventy, and the Amn about sixty, armed agents stationed in Halabja.

According to Shawqat, Iranian forces were largely absent from the Halabja area during the operation, at least until the Iraqi chemical attack. In his version, which is supported by Hamid Haji Gali, the Kurdish forces, backed by Iranian artillery fire from batteries inside Iran, routed the Iraqis and liberated Halabja in a lightning strike on March 14–15; the Iraqis counterattacked the next day, dropping poison gas from the air; the Kurds fled and were replaced by Iranian troops, who streamed into the area from the border, lest they lose the large territory captured by the Kurds. Initially, the Iranians played only a supporting role, Shawqat claimed, providing ammunition, food, and clothes, as well as battle coordination by wireless: "There were large Iranian forces on the border inside Iran: near Marivan, Nowsud, Paveh, and Jwan Roh. These did not enter the area until after the chemical attack, when the situation spun out of control." He counted on his hand the Iranians in his entourage as they descended toward Halabja on March 15: a radio operator, Mahmoud Reza'ie; an artillery spotter, Ali Reza; two video operators who filmed the chemical strike; and a man who carried the radio. Each Kurdish force was accompanied by a similar Iranian team, he said. Lt. Col. Muhammad Tehrani was the overall Iranian field commander in charge of the operation; Ali Shamkhani, an Arabic–speaking Iranian later to become minister of defense, commanded Iranian forces at Paveh.

Hamid Haji Gali described the attack as follows: At 1 am on March 14, his force

> . . . crossed the border and took Iraqi positions on the peaks surrounding Halabja. We finished by early morning. It was a total success. Then we decided to initiate phase two: to take Halabja. There were scattered battles with the Iraqis – they brought reinforcements by helicopter – but on March 15 we liberated Halabja. There was a big celebration: The townspeople were dancing, clapping and singing. In the late afternoon, Iraqi batteries fired shells from Darbandikhan and Sayed Sadeq, and this continued until the next morning. Because of this many Halabjans went into their shelters.

It was then that the chemical attack began.

All along, Hamid Haji Gali said, the Iranians only provided artillery support: Their gunners rocketed the Delamar base, the Halabja area, and the Zalm bridge. The gun emplacements were inside Iran, especially at Dizli, the highest mountain overlooking Halabja. There was nothing extraordinary about this, he asserted: The Iranians had been shelling the Iraqis for years from these positions, but now their fire was more concentrated and continuous. The Iraqis barely put up resistance. Many surrendered; others withdrew toward Sayed Sadeq, trying to cross the Zalm bridge, fording Sirwan lake, or hiding in destroyed villages near the lake waiting for reinforcements. The main Iranian force entered Iraq only after the Iraqi chemical attack on March 16, moving thousands of troops into the greater Halabja area and digging trenches along the Zalm down to the lake – the new front line. This was, according to Shawqat, three days after the chemical attack. The Iranians tried to overcome Iraqi defenses and reach Sayed Sadeq and Penjwin, but were beaten back at the Zalm. This view accords with news reports of "the fifth stage" of Iran's Val-Fajr X, launched early on March 24.[7]

To other Kurdish participants this version is highly self–serving: by glorifying Kurdish military feats it played down the Kurds' role as Iranian proxies who shepherded enemy troops into Iraqi territory during a war that threatened the Iraqi regime, thereby triggering a justifiably power-ful, if exceptionally brutal and patently illegal, response. But this version might have the virtue of carrying at least a kernel of truth. It is supported by at least one other senior leader, Kosrat Rasoul Ali, the PUK com-mander in Erbil and later (2006) vice president of the Kurdistan region under Masoud Barzani (interview, 2000). The account is also backed by two Iranians who took part in the operation. Muhammad Zahidi, a nurse in an emergency unit called Imam Riza near Nowsud, just inside Iran from Halabja, recalled (interview, 2002) that he was assigned to an emergency clinic established for Val-Fajr X two or three days before what he considered the start of the main Iranian assault on Halabja: "We were preparing for an offensive, but it didn't happen. Instead we learned that chemical warfare victims were coming to us. Then men, women, and children started arriving in all sorts of vehicles. Only after this, the offensive began." Likewise, an Iranian Pasdar who assisted in evacuat-ing injured Halabjans and burying the dead claimed (interview, 2002) that when the chemical attack began, there were no Iranian troops in the town of Halabja, only intelligence agents, and that Iranian troops poured into Iraq only afterward, making straight for the lake.

The record of Iranian war reporting suggests a version at the opposite extreme: an almost exclusive Iranian role in Halabja's capture. But it also reinforces the idea that the main Iranian force did not arrive in the town until after the chemical attack.

On March 13, Iran announced the launch of its Zafar 7 offensive in the direction of Khurmal, a town located on the Zalm in the same basin as Halabja. The operations were said to be led by Iraqi opposition groups – SCIRI's Badr Division 9, units of the IUMK, KDP, PUK, and unspecified Suleimaniyehbased peshmergas – "with the support" of units of the Pasdaran's 75th Zafar Brigade. Later IRNA reported an operation by Pasdaran troops "in league with" Iraqi fighters and Kurdish peshmergas, suggesting a different division of responsibility. The operation's objective, the Iranians said, was to avenge "Iraqi chemical bombing of over 15 Kurdish–populated villages in northern Iraq [the previous week] . . . as a result of which 8,000 Kurds became homeless" – a probable reference to the shelling of villages in Jafati valley, whose inhabitants had begun to flee toward Iran.[8] Stage one aimed to conquer Iraqi bases on the peaks overlooking the plain, a task accomplished by March 15; stage two was directed at Khurmal, which Iran reported taking the next day.

At this point, IRNA announced the launch of Val-Fajr X "in the Khurmal region," during the night of March 15–16. Iranian forces that had previously taken Khurmal now fanned out in all directions, overrunning Iraqi troops and seizing (destroyed) Kurdish villages. At this point, Iranian military communiqués stopped referring to their Iraqi allies' exploits, but only to "the courageous [Pasdaran] warriors," while calling on the Kurds merely to "use the favorable conditions provided by Iranian combatants and escalate their anti-Ba'thist regime guerrilla warfare."[9] The implication was that the peshmergas played at most an auxiliary role.

On March 16, Iran claimed it had seized the road between Khurmal and Sirwan and was advancing on the lake. This meant they were making headway. By this maneuver they cut off the only viable escape route for Iraqi forces in the Halabja area. As a result, Iraqi morale crumbled and most troops simply surrendered. The next day Iran announced that its forces were heading for Halabja from Sirwan and were also attacking Iraqi positions on Balambo, a hill directly west of Halabja. The capture of Balambo heights was announced early on March 17; the seizure of the "strategic garrison" of Zammaki, on Halabja's northern outskirts, came an hour later.

Later that afternoon, Iranian forces were said to be "advancing on the besieged northeastern Iraqi city of Halabja from several points." Moreover, reported IRNA, "Simultaneous with the advance of the liberating forces Halabjah residents are fighting the hard-pressed Ba'thist troops inside and have killed and wounded several of them. Local residents are jubilantly accompanying the Muslim forces to the city."[10] At 4:20 pm GMT (7:50 pm local time) on March 17, an exultant Tehran radio announced: "God is greatest! God is greatest! God is greatest! O heroic Iranian nation! O brave men of the land of martyrs! My sisters and brothers! The strategic city of Halabjah has been liberated!"[11]

The next day, Iran announced it had taken Tawela and Biyara, two Iraqi Kurdish towns above Halabja near the border, as well as Nowsud, a nearby Iranian Kurdish town held by the KDP-I (with Iraqi help). This suggested that Iran's forces had completed a pincer movement that Pasdaran commander Reza'ie later described as follows: "On one side, [the enemy] was hemmed in by the hills, and on the other side there was the lake. Since we had occupied the [Zalm] bridge, it was as if the enemy had been trapped in a pocket, and we had closed the flap of the pocket."[12]

One important aspect of Iran's account appears incongruent. Iran claimed to have taken Halabja on March 17, with local residents "jubilantly accompanying" its forces. Yet that same day, IRNA reported that Iraq had "chemically bombed Halabjah town . . . twice Wednesday evening" – March 16 – killing and wounding "hundreds of . . . defenseless women and children." Following the attack, "thousands of residents of Halabjah and surrounding areas left their homes in groups Thursday morning and walked towards the western Iranian border lines." Iran then reported a second round of Iraqi chemical strikes on Khurmal, Sirwan, and Halabja on Thursday morning.[13] The notion that civilians fleeing a chemical bombardment simultaneously would be jubilantly escorting Iranian forces into the targeted town strains belief. Either these forces entered Halabja before March 17, or the account of jubilant townsfolk must be dismissed as war propaganda.

Or perhaps the Iranians did not take Halabja at all. If we accept both Iran's chronology and Kurdish claims to have taken the town without significant Iranian assistance, the Iranian advance on March 17 would have been on a town already in Kurdish rebel hands, empty of its inhabitants after the gassing a day earlier.

Middle Ground

An alternative narrative that falls somewhere between the versions advanced by Iran and senior PUK commanders is offered by lower-level PUK commanders who participated in the assault, as well as by townspeople interviewed by Human Rights Watch in 1992 and by members of other parties that had forces in the area, all of whom agree that some Iranians did enter Halabja before March 16. While these observers saw large numbers of Iranian troops in the Halabja *area*, the troops did not enter the town, at least not prior to the chemical attack.

According to this version, too, local preparations started well before March. Mam Hadi, a PUK peshmerga who grew up in the area, roamed its countryside after signing up in 1976, and knew it like his back pocket, claimed (interview, 2002) that Iranian intelligence agents had begun scouting the area three months earlier: "There was a unit commander named Daoudi with five or six men who came perhaps ten times, staying a couple of days at most. They would go with local PUK peshmergas to Iraqi military posts, taking photographs and drawing maps. A similar group went with the KDP in the area they controlled" – above Khurmal.

Hama Hama Sa'id, the PUK subcommander in Halabja, described an unambiguous division of labor between Iranians and Kurds. Yes, he said, elements of the Karargeh Ramazan – radio operators, photographers, and motorcycle messengers – did accompany Kurdish forces that liberated the area, but separately, Iranian troops guided by Kurds attacked the large Iraqi bases outside Halabja well before the chemical attack: "I was responsible for the area behind Halabja [near the border]. Our first objective was to attack Balambo and Shinirweh mountains jointly with Iranian forces." To provide cover to their ground forces, the Iranians lobbed shells from Dizli, Kani Khiyaran, Hirweh, and Du Awa inside Iran, according to Hama Hama Sa'id: "We had an Iranian artillery spotter with us – his name was Ahmad – and he would con-stantly report back our positions by wireless."

On March 14 Sa'id's group of close to 200 peshmergas, accompany-ing 150 Pasdaran, started advancing from the border village of Hawara Kon ("Old Hawar") to Shinirweh mountain and attacked Iraqi mili-tary positions at Chadergah, Dara Rash, and Hawargey Boynian. By next morning, they fully controlled the area. Another Pasdaran group attacked Iraqi tanks in the Nowroli area between the villages of Hassan Awa and Prees on the lower slopes of Balambo, while in Delamar, "it was the Iranians, and only the Iranians, who attacked the Iraqi artillery base there," Sa'id contended. "A number of them were killed in battle." Delamar housed an Iraqi brigade headquarters and served as Iraq's main artillery base in the area, with eight tanks and six long-range artillery pieces. If there was any Iraqi resistance to the joint Pasdaran–peshmerga advance, it came from Delamar, but even here the battle was over in a matter of hours. The Iraqi commander, a brigadier general, was taken prisoner and transferred to Iran.

Mam Hadi similarly asserted that the peshmergas left the fighting to the Pasdaran, and "once Iraqi defenses at Delamar collapsed, the pesh-mergas went into Halabja." This version is also supported by Sherdel Howeizi, the PUK's liaison with the Karargeh Ramazan, who stated emphatically (interview, 2002) that there were "a lot of Iranian troops" in the Halabja area before the chemical attack.

On March 15, Sa'id continued, "I received orders from Kak [brother] Shawqat via the wireless to proceed to Halabja," because the Iranians and the Kurds had taken the Zalm bridge. "The Pasdaran stayed behind on Shinirweh." The only remaining obstacle was the jahsh battalion at the Anab resettlement complex guarding the dirt road between Halabja and Delamar. Once they realized, however, that their protectors were gone, the jahsh "threw down their weapons and became indistinguish-able from ordinary Kurds. Many fled, others surrendered to us, and again others had been working secretly for us all along, and they now joined us openly." As for the Iraqis, Sa'id claimed, "we took the weapons from those who surrendered and let them go. Some managed to get across the Zalm to rejoin their forces; others fled to the border once the chem-ical attack started." Again others hid in destroyed villages. In one such village, Kheli Hama (between Halabja and Khurmal), "some 200 Iraqi troops surrendered to us only after five days. We told them we didn't have food for them, so we let them go and they went to Iran." Many Iraqi soldiers preferred exile as POWs over being returned to the front.

And so, in the mid-afternoon of March 15, the victorious PUK pesh-mergas entered Halabja. "The people came out to welcome us," Shawqat recalled. They helped the peshmergas seize government buildings and capture Iraqi security personnel. "It was like an uprising," he said. Then, in the late afternoon, senior Kurdish commanders convened a meeting. They decided to distribute their forces over the town, protect the pop-ulation, eliminate remaining pockets of resistance, and remove heavy weaponry. Using loudspeakers, they urged people to stay calm, to turn in any weapons they might find, to hand over Iraqi security agents, and not to rob government offices or otherwise engage in looting. "We assured them we would not leave and warned them they should take precau-tions, as we thought the Iraqis might retaliate," declared Shawqat a decade later, after he had come under criticism for exposing the pop-ulation to danger. "We encouraged them to join their relatives in the [surviving] villages but to stay off the roads because of Iraqi shelling and air attacks that targeted the town and the roads."

From interviews with townspeople four years after the events, it appears the rebels were accompanied by Iranians. What remains unclear is precisely how many or what role they played. Eyewitnesses inter-viewed by Human Rights Watch in 1992 say they saw Pasdaran "openly parading through the streets" on the evening of March 15, "greeting the townspeople and chanting 'God is great! Khomeini is our leader!' They billeted themselves on local Kurdish families and ordered them to prepare dinner. Some rode around Halabja on motorcycles; others were very young, barely teenagers, and carried only sticks and knives. Many also carried gas masks. They asked bewildered people in the streets how far it was to the holy cities of Karbala and Najaf."[14]

Beyond such sightings, however, there is no indication that signif-icant Iranian forces entered Halabja before March 17, a day after the chemical attack. Tehran's reporting from the war theater seems to con-firm this – minus the jubilant crowds that gave good propaganda value and fed Iran's self–image at home. There may have been welcoming crowds on the evening of March 15, but it is safe to assume that the Halabjans reserved their joy for the rebels, many of whom rejoined their families for the first time in months or years, and not for the Iranians – Persian–Shi'ite radicals viewed with suspicion by Kurdish Halabjans, who themselves were practicing or secular Sunnis. The conclusion must be that the Iranians who entered the town of Halabja on March 15 most likely were no more than an advance party escorting Kurdish peshmergas.

"To Protect Our Own People"

Halabjans had much to cheer about when the town's hated administration collapsed. Yet at the same time, residents were gripped by a deep foreboding about Iraqi retribution. Some left that same evening or the next morning, despite the danger on the roads leading out of town: Iraqi gunners lobbed shells from positions at Sayed Sadeq and Darbandikhan. Many others stayed behind, either having no easy access to transportation or perhaps calculating that their best chance lay in the bomb shelters they had dug underneath their houses and courtyards long ago to protect against Iranian shelling.

"We did not," Shawqat insisted, "expect Iraq to use chemical weapons against civilians. On the battlefield, yes. That's why we all had gas masks and atropine injectors." Defending his cousin, Hamid Haji Gali claimed that many Halabjans heeded Shawqat's warning to evacuate, and that this saved the majority of the population. The KSP's Muhammad Haji Mahmoud, also a Halabja native, remembered it differently, contending that both Iran and the rebels "were expecting the chemical attack," because it was consistent with what they knew about the Iraqi regime: "That's why we prepared ourselves with atropine and gas masks and warned the people of Halabja. But they didn't leave. Otherwise, this great number of people would not have been killed." Hama Hama Sa'id presented a more damaging critique. Shawqat, he said, did not urge Halabjans to evacuate. To the contrary, "on his orders we advised the people of Halabja *not* to leave when the shelling started on the evening of the 15th because, we told them, we would protect them. I disagreed with Kak Shawqat, but he was in charge." Moreover, Sa'id asserted, the Iranians did not help: Of those refugees who fled toward the border, many were forced to return, having been refused entry by Iranian authorities.

Another PUK commander, Omar Fattah, who as acting head of the PUK's first *malband* (regional command center) in Qaradagh technically was Shawqat's superior, claimed that Shawqat asked the PUK's political bureau for instructions on the evening of March 15, reporting by wireless that Halabja was very crowded and that he expected Iraqi retaliation. "I was copied, so I responded," he recalled. "I advised Kak Shawqat to evacuate the city, but he replied that it was raining and people had no place to go. I responded that it was better to be exposed to rain than to bombs. But he was accountable directly to the political leadership [headed by Neywshirwan in Jafati], and I don't know what advice they gave, because I was not copied in on the reply."

Wednesday, March 16, was a cold but pleasant late-winter day, according to Shawqat. There were small clouds and a light wind. In the morning, the market was open; people were dancing. "We were being thronged by well wishers," he recalled. Sa'id's recollection of weather conditions differed slightly: "There was alternating sun and rain, with a mild wind from the southwest." He was on Ashkohol mountain (behind Anab) when the chemical attack began, on his way to disarm three Iraqi battalions that had surrendered. It was then, he said, that he saw six Soviet made Sukhoy bombers fly over, then another three separately, and another two. They dropped their bombs over Halabja. "Smoke rose: some was white, some black, some red, some mixed. I saw people putting their hands over their faces."

In Halabja itself, Shawqat, accompanied by his cousin Hamid Haji Gali, had just greeted the Pasdaran commander, Lt. Col. Muhammad Tehrani, when the chemical attack started: "I had radioed him to say we had taken Halabja and sent Kak Hamid to collect him by car so he could see for himself how much in control we were." At 5:20 pm, Shawqat said, on a day of intermittent Iraqi shelling and air attacks, a new group of bombers came in low: "The sound of the explosions was unlike that of conventional bombs, more like a 'tap.' The smoke went up, then down to the ground." Tehrani and Shawqat, realizing they were under gas attack, donned their chemical gear, shut their car windows, and drove north. The chemical strikes continued intermittently until the next morning, he said. "People tried to leave town. Most of those who died were on the roads outside Halabja; others died inside their shelters."

Shawqat claimed he stayed in the area to direct relief efforts and regroup his panicked fighters, while Tehrani returned to Iran to coordinate evacuation efforts. Hamid Haji Gali went to Ahmad Awa (a village and famous picnic area on the Zalm's banks just above Khurmal) to assemble peshmergas who were fleeing along the paved road to Dizli, the way Iranian forces and KDP and KSP fighters had descended a few days earlier. Shawqat sustained chemical injuries the next day when three Iraqi jets bombed Abba Beileh village, where he happened to be. Several villagers were killed, and his Iranian artillery spotter, Ali Reza, was badly injured. Reza was transferred to the rear of Iranian forces inside Iran, where Abbas Foroutan and his team ministered to the many wounded. Shawqat reported another chemical attack in Anab later that afternoon that killed 300 people. Hama Hama Sa'id similarly mentioned three or four chemical attacks on the 17th, including a chemically loaded shell fired at Hawara Kon, the Iranian staging area near the border. A Khurmal resident who lost twenty-six relatives in the Halabja attack (interview, 2005) reported that Ahmad Awa was one of the places hit.

After the 17th, the chemical strikes ceased. By then, most civilians had been evacuated to refugee camps in Iran. The Iranian troops that now streamed into the Halabja basin apparently did not merit an Iraqi chemical assault or a military counterattack of any sort. The Iraqis were preoccupied elsewhere, pressing for advantage against the demoralized Kurdish insurgents. And so the Halabja area remained quiet till Iranian troops withdrew shortly before the end of the war in July.

The Iranians used the opportunity to strip Halabja and Khurmal of everything that was movable – cars, electrical pylons, office equipment – and to loot a wide range of buildings including banks, police stations, secret police headquarters, the courts, hospitals and clinics, petrol stations, the tobacco company, and ordinary shops, before blowing them up with TNT. Moreover, they destroyed both the Zalm bridge and the bridge over the Sirwan at Tawela. Not surprisingly, they also hauled away the security agencies' files, which gave them detailed information about armed opposition groups allied with Iraq, such as the KDP-I, Komala, and Mujahedin Khalq. At the end of March, Iran's interior minister, Ali Akbar Mohtashemi, pointedly warned "members and advocates of counter-revolutionary grouplets" to surrender, as their identities were known from membership lists found in Halabja.[15]

And so, if the peshmergas were full of praise for Iran's evacuation of civilians from Halabja, they bitterly railed against being subsequently barred from the region, which gave Iranian troops the freedom to pillage. "It started as ordinary looting," Shawqat recalled, "but then they brought trucks. It was clearly organized. They even removed the carpets from the mosques. We quarreled with them but were vastly outnumbered." Halabjans, who pride themselves on being among the most literate of Kurds, have lamented in particular the theft of their books.

The wanton destruction of Halabja and Khurmal remains a festering wound in Iranian–Kurdish relations. It also became grounds for another accusation against Kurdish leaders, Shawqat in particular, who led the Iranians into Iraqi Kurdistan. But even Hama Hama Sa'id, otherwise so critical of his commander's decisions, saw it necessary to justify the Kurds' association with Iran: "The Iranians told us they were going to attack the Halabja area one way or another," he said. "We had to join them to protect our own people."

In any event, the Kurdish parties proved spectacularly unsuccessful in protecting Halabjans from either Iraqis or Iranians. After the Iranians withdrew, the Iraqis returned in force and, according to Sa'id, who had lingered in the region, leveled whatever remained. The Iraqis resettled returning refugees in new complexes constructed across the lake or even as far away as Erbil, and barred government employees from their jobs for a year.

The different versions of Iran's role in Halabja appear irreconcilable, although it is likely that in the difficult terrain and chaos of war not every commander was aware of what happened in areas not under his personal control. A careful reconstruction suggests that the most credible scenario is this: Swift-moving KSP and KDP units accompanying a large force of Iranian Pasdaran, Basijis, and army troops burst upon Iraqi positions guarding Khurmal and the Zalm bridge, cutting off the Iraqis' only escape route from Halabja. Iranian Pasdaran aided by PUK guerrillas simultaneously seized key peaks from Iraqi forces south and east of Halabja and then successfully stormed the heavily fortified artillery base at Delamar. Iraqi resistance crumbled throughout the area, and Halabja fell easily into the peshmergas' hands. The Iranians sent intelligence personnel to guard key interests but otherwise the town held little interest. By March 16, the fight was over. Targeting Iranian Kurdish rebels as well as fleeing Iraqi troops, the Iranians conducted mopping-up operations along the lakeshore and in the geographically isolated border area around Nowsud, Tawela, and Biyara, preparations for which were observed by Muhammad Zahidi, the Iranian nurse. The blow-by-blow Iranian media reports elided both the part played by the Kurds in Khurmal and the role of Pasdaran units fighting their way down the slopes of Shinirweh and Balambo, favoring reportage of the main force's advance along the lake.

It may not be possible to reconcile the competing narratives of Shawqat Haji Mushir and Hama Hama Sa'id. The latter had a limited view of the war theater; he was in communication solely with his immediate commanders while rushing headlong into Halabja, then retreating along with a hysterical populace. Shawqat, who communicated routinely with other senior commanders, must have had a fuller view. But as the operation's senior commander, he bore much of the blame for what some see as the Kurdish parties' strategic error of bringing the war into Kurdish urban areas, thereby provoking the Iraqis to retaliate. Till his death in 2003 he remained extremely defensive about his role.

In any case, the debate is in some ways academic: Regardless of Iran's role, Iraq consciously and deliberately retaliated with a poison gas attack against a civilian population, a crime against humanity that cannot be justified by the defeat of its ground forces. But whatever their differences on the details of battle, Kurdish commanders agree on two key points that are not solely of academic interest: Apart from reconnaissance and intelligence officers, the main Iranian invasion force did not enter the town (as opposed to the area) of Halabja before the chemical attack, and it was Iraq, and only Iraq, that used chemical weapons in Halabja and the surrounding region.

Today, a new generation is questioning the aging PUK leadership's wisdom in conceiving the Halabja feint and carrying it out in league with the Iranians, to whom the operation was nearly cost free while yielding enormous benefits. Some see it as a disastrous miscalculation for which no one has been held accountable. As Mam Hadi put it, "A tragedy happened in Halabja, and nobody has explained why, or come to our aid."

SIX

THE HALABJA DEMONSTRATION EFFECT

"There's a danger that Saddam Hussein would do things he's done previously – he has in the past used chemical weapons."
– US Secretary of Defense Donald Rumsfeld, Associated Press, November 15, 2002

Blowing Smoke

The stakes were high in the spring of 1988. Javier Pérez de Cuéllar, pursuing peace on the basis of Resolution 598 (passed in July 1987), intended to sit separately with the two belligerents to identify common ground. Security Council members were debating an arms embargo against Iran – a measure that the Soviet Union opposed. A week after the Halabja attack, Iran threatened that it would refuse to attend peace talks if the UN failed to order an investigation. The *New York Times* reported that the US and France had put pressure on the secretary-general not to send an investigative team to the Gulf, "arguing that the visit would divert attention from the peace process." When Pérez de Cuéllar, acting on his own initiative, gave the green light anyway, it set the stage, the *Times* suggested, "for possible disclosures about the Iraqi war effort that might embarrass western members of the Security Council as they try to impose an arms embargo on Iran."[1]

The single medical expert dispatched visited both Iran and Iraq. His report, released in mid-April, was difficult to disregard. What had happened in Halabja was so graphic and egregious it could not be ignored. Now, having ordered the investigation and found that chemical weapons use had caused unprecedented numbers of civilian victims, the UN had to act. Moreover, in inveighing against Pérez de Cuéllar over ordering the Halabja investigation (see Introduction), Iraq's foreign minister Tariq Aziz incurred Security Council members' severe displeasure. A heavily redacted State Department cable reported that Aziz's letter had drawn criticism from "virtually all delegations – including some of Iraq's closest Arab friends," and would "almost certainly lead to some new SC action on CW."[2]

So it looked as if Iraq, for the first time, would become the target of a resolution condemning its use of gas. But while Washington could not prevent the resolution and the UN's subsequent action, the accusation (promoted vigorously by the Reagan administration) that Iran shared at least some of the blame for the Halabja attack served to dilute both. Declassified US State Department documents show how the Iran accusation was molded into a diplomatic maneuver designed to let Iraq off the hook.

On April 5, the US embassy in London reported that Her Majesty's Government had summoned the Iraqi ambassador to "protest strongly Iraq's apparent use of chemical weapons in Halabja." Noting that the United Kingdom had specifically named Iraq, not Iran, as the culprit, the US ambassador requested "an early readout [phrase redacted] on chemical weapons use in the Gulf and more details on the evidence of Iranian use of chemical weapons."[3] The cable, in other words, hinted at the evident contradiction between the welter of international indictments against Iraq and Washington's assertion that Iran, too, was to blame. A clarification was in order.

In response, the State Department produced the following internal statement, listing what it referred to as the "elements of our policy" concerning Halabja, to be used as guidance by US diplomats:

- Both Iran and Iraq are parties to the 1925 Protocol banning chemical warfare.
- We have condemned Iraq for use of chemical weapons against the civilian population of Halabja.
- We believe that both Iran and Iraq used chemical weapons in the fighting around Halabja.
- Use of chemical weapons against civilian populations is a particularly grave violation of the Geneva Protocol.

- This incident makes implementation of [resolution] 598 all the more urgent.
- FYI: *Evidence of Iranian use is convincing, but we are not now in a position to discuss the evidence publicly.*[4]

In "talking points" circulated to its embassies around the world a week later, the State Department asserted: "The U.S. believes that both Iraq and Iran used chemical weapons in the fighting around Halabja. (*For use only if pressed for further information: While we have concluded there was Iranian use, we cannot discuss the information from which we have drawn our conclusion.*)"[5]

Although the US, like other governments, customarily declines to disclose intelligence information to protect sources and methods, its decision to issue a blanket accusation without any form of substantiation was striking. In any event, the strategy bore fruit. US diplomats soon were able to report back allied governments' new positions. Portugal, for example, supported a European Community demarche to the UN secretary-general strongly condemning chemical weapons use in the war. The Portuguese official relaying the action to the US embassy "underlined that the EC declaration did not single-out [sic] one specific country but rather was directed at both."[6]

US diplomacy also shaped the form of Security Council action on Halabja. Stating that the US preferred a presidential statement to register its protest of chemical weapons use, Secretary of State George Shultz explained:

> If widespread support exists among Council members for a resolution, we believe it would be in our interest to go along. We want to be clearly on record on this issue, though we need not get out in front of other UNSC members if there is widespread reluctance on a resolution. Others might perceive any U.S. attempt to block a resolution as evidence of lack of conviction on the CW issue or as an attempt to protect Iraq. Thus [US] Mission [to the UN] should try, by its actions, to assure no such interpretation is credible.

Then Shultz came to the crux of the matter:

> We have previously stated our conclusion that Iran, as well as Iraq, used chemical weapons in the Halabcha [sic] incident. It is our assessment that both sides have previously used chemical weapons during

the war, and both have the capacity to launch similar attacks in the future. Therefore we believe any resolution/statement should cite both Iran and Iraq for CW use.[7]

And so, thanks to hard work by US diplomats, Resolution 612 (May 9) condemned "the continued use of chemical weapons," and urged "both sides to refrain" from future use. In a separate public statement, the Reagan administration emphasized: "We condemn without reservation illegal use of chemical weapons by both sides in the Gulf conflict." This was a bone tossed to the Iraqis, aimed at softening the blow of Washington's censure that followed: "In particular," the statement read, "use of chemical weapons against non-combatants is an egregious offense against civilization and humanity." Because both the administration and the Iraqi regime knew who had committed the offense (Washington never denied that Iraq had used gas in Halabja), Iraq could understand this to be a pointed warning that gassing civilians constituted a red line. Yet the statement's overall effect was to reassert the tilt toward Iraq by its reminder that "the horror of this recent illegal use of chemical weapons underscores the urgency of achieving a negotiated settlement to the Gulf war as soon as possible through implementation in full of UNSCR 598" – the ceasefire resolution that Iraq had accepted and Iran had snubbed.[8]

As a US diplomat wrote later, this was the first time that the council had responded to Iraq's chemical weapons use with a resolution rather than a presidential statement, "but the text was neither vigorous nor indignant."[9] It was the minimum necessary morally, the maximum possible politically, and far from sufficient to deter future Iraqi use.

By causing diplomatic confusion, the Iran accusation, first aired by the State Department's spokesperson on March 23, won Iraq a two–month reprieve. Unencumbered by unanimous condemnation of its warfare methods, it could now trigger the war's endgame. And so, in this crucial breathing space, Iraq launched a powerful series of counteroffensives on the southern front under the code name "Tawakkulna 'ala Allah" ("We place our trust in God") – its way of saying the regime was going for broke. It also extended its Anfal counterinsurgency campaign from Jafati to the vast Kurdish countryside. Within six months it was all over. Few factors contributed more to Iraq's breathtaking twin victories than the demonstration effect of the Halabja chemical attack and the international community's near silence in its aftermath.

Gas: Integral Part of Anfal

If Anfal started three weeks before the Halabja attack, its first victory came three days afterward – a direct result of the gassing that triggered the peshmergas' total collapse of morale. "Halabja had an impact on our defensive posture," said PUK commander Kosrat Rasoul Ali (interview, 2000), who was in Jafati in March 1988. "We were not defeated militarily in Halabja: Very few of our peshmergas were killed; most were not even inside the town or nearby resettlement camps. But we didn't want to cause even more casualties, especially among civilians. So we decided to withdraw and evacuate the townspeople." Halabja had an even greater impact, he suggested: "It brought into sharp focus the reality of Saddam Hussein's regime – that it had a new policy of annihilating the Kurdish people."

Chased from their Jafati mountain stronghold by Iraqi ground troops, the demoralized peshmergas and the villagers under their care fled toward Iran; many died in harsh winter conditions at high elevations. On March 19, Iraqi radio jubilantly proclaimed the fall of the PUK's headquarters in the "Anfal operation" following "a brave and avenging battle with the traitors."[10] Baghdad dailies carried headlines such as: "The Anfal Operation Crowns Our Mountains with a Great Iraqi Victory."[11] A security police memo later reported that the PUK had lost some 600 fighters in Jafati and Halabja, and that rumors were circulating that the regime was planning to destroy Suleimaniyeh after attacking it with chemical weapons.[12]

Such was the fear – instinctive, overpowering – of further gas attacks that a decades-old guerrilla movement, one that had gained control over much of the countryside in the span of three years, suddenly suffered total disintegration. An Iraqi military intelligence assessment from that period concluded that "the use of special ammunition in strikes on saboteur headquarters and other places where they congregate has caused casualties among the saboteurs, has terrified and panicked them, and has weakened their morale, forcing many to return to the national ranks" (a regime euphemism for "surrendering").[13]

The ramifications soon became evident. Conscious of its new psychological advantage, the regime now pressed for total victory. On April 2, the military announced the end of "the second Anfal operation" in Qaradagh, south of Suleimaniyeh.[14] Six more Anfal operations followed, covering rural Kurdistan, each limited to a defined geographic area that had its own local peshmerga command.

This is the critical point: On the first day of each stage of Anfal, the Iraqi military fired gas shells or dropped bombs containing poison gas, usually against one or two clusters of villages where the peshmergas had their bases. Iraqi ground forces and their allied Kurdish jahsh irregulars had to do no more than surround the targeted area and wait for terrified villagers to run straight into their arms. And they did, in droves, panicked and desperate, taking only what they or their tractor–drawn carts could carry. This was the pattern in the second Anfal in Qaradagh (end of March); the third and fourth Anfal in the vast Germian plain east of Kirkuk (April/May); Anfals V, VI, and VII in, respectively, Smaquli valley (end of May), Balisan and Akoyan valleys (June/July), and the area of Qandil mountain (August); and the "Final Anfal Operation" (*Khatimat al-Anfal*) in Badinan, the KDP-controlled region that borders Turkey (late August, early September). In each case, the tactical use of gas, mostly targeted at peshmergas but mainly killing and injuring civilians, served – by causing mass panic – to flush out of the countryside in a matter of days, sometimes hours, villagers who had been hardened to years of air and artillery attacks.

Faiq Golpy, the peshmerga doctor in the Qaradagh mountains who had seen airplanes streaking overhead on their way to bomb Halabja on March 16, was attached to a peshmerga band that directly experienced four stages of Anfal, fortunate (unlike many hapless villagers) to elude the army's dragnet each time, but unfortunate to keep fleeing into the next area to be "Anfalized." On March 22, Golpy recalled (interview, 2002), he was in Balagjar (a Qaradagh–area village that had suffered a mustard gas attack a month earlier) when he heard the sound of explosions. Looking outside, he saw clouds over nearby Seyw Senan, a village that was home to the local PUK base:

The first victim, a farmer named Kamal, reached us after about an hour. His pupils were constricted; he was partially blinded and had trouble breathing. 'This must be nerve gas,' I remember saying, because mustard gas does not make the eyes contract. I gave him atropine and we washed him.

We had warned people that Iraq might attack with chemicals. We had distributed pamphlets about chemical protection to the bigger villages. Those who could not read clearly had not absorbed this information. I know cases where families died but the man survived because he had read how to protect himself.

That night and the next day, we received about 300 chemical victims in different clinical states. All of them recovered; by chance we had just received 2,000 ampules of atropine. Still about seventy people died in Seyw Senan, mostly women and children.

Iraq's military intelligence later stated in a quarterly report on "saboteur" activity that in March "our aircraft bombed the headquarters of the sabotage bands in the villages of Saywan [sic] and Balakjar in a chemical strike. This resulted in the deaths of fifty saboteurs and the wounding of twenty other saboteurs."[15]

Panicked by news of the gassing, and aware of what had happened in Halabja less than a week earlier, villagers streamed out of Qaradagh. Shortly afterward, Golpy said, Iraqi troops launched Anfal, advancing from all directions.[16] He and his comrades escaped westward to Germian, setting up a field clinic south of the destroyed town of Sengaw. But to their misfortune, Anfal arrived there as well (the third stage), about ten days later, forcing them to move on. Golpy was not aware of any chemical attacks in this part of Germian. There are several eyewitnesses, though, to a chemical attack on the first day of Anfal III. Iraqi planes bombed the village of Tazashar, a local PUK stronghold close to the road from Tuz Khurmatu to Qader Karam. The peshmerga defenders died, as did goats, cows, and birds.[17] The effect was the same: mass panic and flight.

Ahead of Iraqi troops, Golpy and his comrades crossed the Suleimaniyeh–Kirkuk highway north to the Aghjalar area, halting only after fording the Lesser Zab in Kuzlu, a village on the river's banks. "I was in Kuzlu on May 3 when, in the late afternoon, four airplanes came and started bombing," he recounted. "Because the sound was low, I suspected a chemical attack. About half an hour later we learned that [the villages of] Goktapa and Askar on the other side of the Zab had been hit. Many were killed there. One of the injured crossed the river by boat, but the Iraqis opened the sluice at the Dukan dam, raising the water level and thereby making it impossible for others to cross. The water was unusually high and moved very fast. Anyway, I had no atropine left. Anfal [IV] started the next morning; the army reached Goktapa after several hours." At least 158, and perhaps as many as 300 villagers were killed in Goktapa and Askar in what was probably the most directly lethal chemical attack during the entire Anfal campaign.[18]

Golpy and his peshmerga group fled again, this time in the direction of Smaquli valley (which connects Erbil and Shaqlawa to Dukan). Here, in the village of Khateh, they got caught up in Anfal V, which had started with a nerve gas attack on the villages of Wareh, Warta, Nazanin, and Golan in mid-May. Again they were forced to flee, now toward Qandil, a mountain on the border with Iran. Chemical attacks and Anfal (VI and VII) followed them through the mountain valleys, until August, when the PUK insurgency at last was defeated, its fighters dispersed, and exile in Iran its last remaining prospect.[19] The military's final target was KDP-dominated Badinan. The army pushed in that direction after the war had ended, in late August, bombarding villages with chemical weapons before mopping up panicked Kurds who failed to reach the Turkish border.

In a strange twist in the pattern, Iraqi aircraft erroneously gassed fighters of the allied Iranian Komala, a Kurdish rebel group based in the village of Boteh in Akoyan valley, in August. Najmaddin Fakeh, an Iraqi Kurd who stayed with these Iranian insurgents and witnessed the attack from nearby Golan, claimed (interview, 2006) that twenty-two Komala fighters died and many more were injured. Komala later complained to its friends in Baghdad, and the Iraqis admitted their mistake, Fakeh said, but the Komala leadership has never openly discussed the incident.

After the initial chemical attacks, the pattern was the same for each stage of Anfal: Fleeing villagers reaching the paved road were gathered up by Iraqi troops and pro-regime Kurdish militias. They were herded to temporary holding centers, then driven by truck to the Popular Army base at Topzawa just outside Kirkuk. Here males between the ages of fifteen and sixty were separated from their families and hauled off to execution sites in western Iraq, where they were killed and buried in mass graves. Older men and women were dispatched to Nugrat Salman, a notorious prison located in the desert west of Samawa in southern Iraq. Those who survived the prison's extreme hardships (little food, no medical care, harsh climate) were released in a September 6 amnesty marking the end of Anfal. Then they were sent to live in a resettlement camp.

The fate of women and children depended on their place of residence. If they were from areas of Anfal II, V, VI, or VII, they were sent to an army base in Dibs, north of Kirkuk, also to be released in the amnesty and relocated to camps. If they were from the area of Anfal VIII, they were detained in a prison camp at Salamiyeh, near Mosul; survivors were released in the amnesty. If, however, they were from Germian (Anfals III and IV), in most cases, they were treated like the men and carted off to execution sites for mass killing. Those from the area of Anfal II who fled to Germian and were scooped up during Anfal III also were sent to their deaths.

Perhaps as many as 80,000 Kurds, the vast majority civilians, were thus killed. Only six men and one boy returned – miraculously – to tell their story.[20]

Staff Maj.-Gen. Wafiq al-Samarra'i was deputy director of Iraq's Military Intelligence Directorate (Istikhbarat) in 1988, overseeing the war with Iran and the campaign against the Kurds. He denied (interview, 1997) any personal involvement in Anfal, an assertion that, given his job description, strains credulity. He had two lines of responsibility, he said: one to the MID director, Sabr al-Duri, and the other directly to Saddam Hussein, who trusted him and would see him at least once a day.

While denying any role in Anfal killings, al-Samarra'i said he was willing to explain the reasons for Anfal and its consequences, in part because he had been friendly with the Kurds and, according to PUK leaders, had sent them warnings throughout the 1980s. His words are significant – and are therefore quoted here extensively – given his proximity to both the Iraqi regime and the events that unfolded on his watch.

Saddam Hussein's rationale for Anfal was threefold, a-Samarra'i said:

First, he decided to reduce the Kurdish threat, because before March 1988 the Iraqi military position was very weak and the Kurds had forced the army to send many units north [when they were needed on the southern front]. Secondly, he wanted to re-impose his authority.

And third, he wanted to punish the Kurds severely for their treachery. He was motivated by revenge when he decided to kill all the Kurds in the prohibited zones. Anyway, the Kurds are lucky, because 3 million of them could have been killed. Human life means nothing to Saddam Hussein.

As for the fate of the *Anfalakan* (as Kurds call Anfal's victims), al-Samarra'i said:

We received memoranda saying they were buried in mass graves. The Kurdish leaders asked us about them during the 1991 negotiations [after the post–Gulf War uprising]. We told them that none were in Baghdad. Then Saddam Hussein issued an order: "Release all the Kurdish prisoners." None appeared. So then we knew they had all been killed. They were no longer in Iraq. They were under the ground. Saddam Hussein and Ali Hassan al-Majid said there were tens of thousands of them. Nobody knows the exact number. Everybody was killed in Anfal: men, women and children.

If that was not sufficiently chilling, al-Samarra'i explained the selective killing of women and children as an integral part of the regime's Arabization of Kirkuk: The ones who were killed came from areas close to Kirkuk, he said, and were targeted expressly to reduce Kirkuk's Kurdish population:

You can kill half a million Kurds in Erbil, but that won't do anything: It would still be Kurdish. But killing 50,000 Kurds in Kirkuk will finish the Kurdish cause forever.

Through Anfal, in other words, the regime took Kirkuk's Arabization to its logical conclusion.

It is not known how many Kurds died during Anfal, but it is possible to make an educated guess. Early on, the PUK claimed 182,000 dead, a figure that has assumed mythical status among Kurds but is based on an extrapolation of assumed average village size in 1988 and has no relation to actual disappearances or killings. Human Rights Watch, relying on a careful but incomplete survey conducted by a human rights organization in Suleimaniyeh, the Committee for the Defense of Anfal Victims' Rights, proposed a death toll of "at least fifty thousand and possibly as many as a hundred thousand persons."[21] The committee documented only 63,000 "disappeared" (*mafqoudin*), but did not include Badinan (Anfal VIII, estimated at seven or eight thousand).[22] Its estimate of no more than 70,000 dead, published in Kurdistan in 1995, proved highly controversial and forced its director (interview, 2006) to leave the country. Tellingly, Ali Hassan al-Majid himself, during negotiations following the 1991 uprising, reportedly exclaimed in reference to the number of Anfal victims alleged by the PUK: "It couldn't have been more than 100,000!"[23]

The Iraqi regime could not have systematically murdered this many Kurds if it had not been in a position first to flush them out of their villages – a feat it had signally failed to accomplish in the army's perennial attempts to subdue the countryside, due to the difficult terrain and strong peshmerga resistance. During Anfal the selective, tactical use of chemical weapons, building on the Halabja demonstration effect, was the qualitative factor that changed the rural equation. It enabled the systematic mass killing of tens of thousands of rural Kurds in what Human Rights Watch and the Legal Office of the US State Department during the Clinton administration determined to amount to genocide.[24] Said the PUK's Kosrat: "The chemical factor was decisive. We didn't think we would be defeated, but they wanted to teach us a lesson. Our plan was to defend ourselves as long as we could, and when we reached the limit, we had to withdraw."

Anfal and US Intelligence

Did the world, or at least US intelligence, know about Anfal and what it was, beyond a mere counterinsurgency campaign? The answer is both yes and no. Media reports mentioned chemical attacks in Kurdish areas, including Qaradagh. Jalal Talabani, touring Europe, referred to gas attacks in meetings and public events. Iranian diplomats reported on Iraqi chemical strikes in angry communications to the UN. The Iraqi military openly reported its progress in the Anfal operations – remaining silent, however, on its use of poison gas. The sad truth is that very few reports emerged about Anfal and chemical strikes in Kurdistan at the time, and certainly none from independent observers, given the difficulty of access. Worse, the name Anfal apparently never entered the lexicon of US officials watching Iraq and the war.

Thirteen years later, David Newton, the US ambassador to Baghdad in 1988, said (interview, 2001) that the word Anfal had meant nothing to him at the time, or that if it did, "it didn't leave an impression." It turns out that Newton did hear about Anfal and clearly it did not leave an impression. According to meeting notes, a KDP-I representative in Baghdad, visiting the US embassy in April 1988, mentioned to Newton "the recent Iraqi campaigns 'Anfal-1' and 'Anfal-2' against the PUK Kurds east and south of Sulaymaniyya."[25]

The name Anfal otherwise does not appear in many US intelligence documents or ring a bell with intelligence analysts, despite its wide coverage in the Iraqi media, translation of which was provided by the CIA's Foreign Broadcast Information Service (FBIS). From the end of March 1988, Iraqi papers reported routinely on Anfal. The headline in the daily *Al-Thawra* (April 3), for example, read: "The People of Suleimaniyeh, Dohuk and Erbil Greet the Heroic Anfal Operation." In a paean to Anfal and the Kurdish jahsh on April 16, the paper quoted allied Kurds as blessing the Anfal operations for promoting – of all things – Kurdish unity. Reflecting some recognition, a "top secret" analysis attached to a September 1988 State Department memo did refer to Anfal VIII at the end of August as "the fifth in [Iraq's] 'Anfal' series of counterinsurgency operations."[26]

A US government analyst with top–level security clearance recalled (interview, 2000) he had been aware of large-scale village destruction. (The US had satellite imagery of the destruction taking place in the countryside.[27]) But, the analyst said, his understanding was that the inhabitants were being resettled: "I never heard about mass disappearances and killings." A Joint Chiefs of Staff document on "Iraq's resettlement policy," written at the height of Anfal III, when large numbers of Germian Kurds were being ferried to their deaths, estimated that "an unknown but reportedly large number of Kurds have been placed in 'concentration' camps located near the Jordanian and Saudi Arabian borders."[28] In September 1988, after Anfal had ended, a State Department official quoted KDP leader Masoud Barzani as writing to Pérez de Cuéllar that men captured in the military campaign "were taken to an unknown destination," resulting in "grave concern about their fate."[29] To the US, however, these men (no mention of women and children) were relocated "to the flat, desert areas of western and southern Iraq, where they can be more easily controlled."[30]

Other US intelligence analysts monitoring the war also claimed ignorance about Anfal. For example, Stephen Pelletière, who had taken a post at the US Army War College in early 1988 after a long stint covering Iraq at the CIA, said (interview, 2001) that he had never heard of the name Anfal. In a 1990 after-action study, he and two colleagues claimed that: "Initially, reports circulated that the Kurds were being forcibly driven from their mountain homes and relocated in the desert lands of the south. Subsequently it developed that this was not the case. In fact, they were being directed to new towns which the Iraqi government had built throughout the Kurdish area."[31] In fact, they were neither, at least not before the September amnesty.

US Defense Intelligence Agency analyst Rick Francona, who spent considerable time in Iraq as the DIA's liaison with Iraqi Military Intelligence in 1988, also expressed surprise (interview, 2000): "Did the Iraqis call it Anfal? I thought it was the Kurds themselves who did so. When I was in Iraq, I didn't hear about Anfal. I found out about it from the Kurds later [after 1991]." A postwar DIA appraisal of developments in Kurdistan suggested that villagers were divided into two groups, loyal and disloyal. Those "thought to be neutral or loyal to Baghdad have been moved to a number of new towns built in the north" with good facilities. Disloyal Kurds, however, "are transferred to holding camps and later moved to facilities deep in the south."[32] In reality, "loyal" Kurds were resettled in camps in 1987; most "disloyal" Kurds – that is, those who defied the regime's orders to move – were taken to the desert to be executed, not resettled.

Walter (Pat) Lang, chief of the DIA's Middle East section, later claimed (interview, 2000) that his agency's ignorance of Anfal should be attributed to the Pentagon's preoccupation with the southern front: "The CIA and State Department were much more interested in the Kurds than the DIA." Yet he expressed no surprise at the mass executions of Anfal once he heard about them during an interview for this book, describing them as "very Hitler-like" and "implicating everyone" – consistent with what was known about the Iraqi regime.

From his vantage point in Baghdad, Ambassador Newton said he had concluded:

> We *did* know that villages were being razed and that people were being taken to the desert. We had the impression they were being executed. This was a logical deduction, not a conclusion based on empirical evidence. It didn't make much sense for them not to [kill them]. We also knew about the Barzanis who never came back [in 1983]. What nobody realized at the time was the scale of the campaign. Even people in intelligence and government who knew the Iraqis well all were surprised later when they discovered the scale and intensity of the brutality.

In sum, the reason for weak US knowledge of Anfal and zero intervention, even at the diplomatic level, may have been Washington's preoccupation with the southern front, as well as its strong support of the Iraqi war effort. The Kurds, after all, were Iran's allies, and whatever the Iraqi regime was doing to them Washington considered an internal matter. Aware that it had a free hand, Iraq disposed of its internal problem once and for all by using gas to scare villagers into its arms. At least it must have thought it had fixed this nagging question for good. If the 1991 Gulf War and its aftermath had not given the Kurdish national movement a new lease on life, Kurdistan would have remained a wasteland, Halabja forgotten, and Anfal concealed by layers of desert sand.

The Use of Gas to End the War

By the third week of April 1988, several factors reinforced Iran's view that Washington now wanted Iraq to win the war: international silence on Halabja, US attacks on Iranian ships and oil platforms in the Gulf, and, perhaps most importantly, the perception that Washington had aided Iraq in recapturing the Faw peninsula a few days earlier. "Although the United States maintains official neutrality in the Iran–Iraq war, the Reagan administration's gradual tilt toward Iraq is beginning to look like a full–fledged embrace," wrote Elaine Sciolino in the *New York Times*.[33] This was also the Iraqi perception. A high-ranking diplomat at Iraq's Washington embassy in 1987–1990 recalled (interview, 2004) that, "Washington always said it was neutral. In reality, they were closer to us. In 1987, Secretary of Defense Caspar Weinberger, a nice person who was always happy to see me and continually used to praise me, gave an order while on board an American ship in the Gulf to fire at an Iranian oil platform. This is a good example of how they sided with us."

Following on the heels of the Halabja gassing, knowledge of which was widespread in Iran, Iran's loss of Faw marked both a military and a powerful psychological reversal. Faw had been the only significant territory Iran's forces managed to seize (certainly compared to the strategically insignificant sliver around Halabja). The CIA reported that Ayatollah Khomeini had not appeared in public "since Iran's military defeat at Al Faw and Iran's losses to the US naval forces in the Gulf earlier this week; he often appears during periods of tension in an effort to shore up the regime's leadership. . . . His silence at this time is noticeable."[34]

Iraq's counteroffensive that started at Faw in April was the first stage of its "Tawakkulna 'ala Allah" campaign. Four stages followed, in which it managed to push back Iranian forces on all fronts. These crucial military victories are attributable to several factors: better training and discipline, more substantial hardware, the element of surprise, and growing popular disaffection in Iran. But two additional factors, not always accorded their due weight, should be mentioned: Iraq's access to hair-sharp satellite images of Iranian positions and troop movements – courtesy of the DIA – and Iraq's massive resort to chemical weapons in Faw and afterward.

Military analysts Pelletière, Johnson, and Rosenberger, who had no access to the Iranian side and, by their own admission, had a cropped view of Iraqi military thinking, claimed to "have seen no convincing evidence that gas was used to recapture Al Faw; if it was used it was in connection with one of the four subsequent battles."[35] Others also have cast doubt on the Faw claim. Their assessment, however, not only contradicts Iran's startling accusation that Iraq's chemical attacks "were so heavy. . . . that toxic gases contaminated parts of the southern Iranian port city of Abadan, across the Arvand river,"[36] but also the DIA's findings. The Iraqis, observed Pat Lang, "used a hell of a lot of gas" in Faw.

Lang's principal source was the DIA's man in Iraq, Rick Francona. As liaison officer to Iraqi military intelligence, Francona's biography states, he traveled extensively in combat areas as an observer of Iraqi military operations against Iranian forces, and flew sorties with the Iraqi air force. In fact, Francona was part of a team of more than sixty DIA officers who, according to the *New York Times*, provided the Iraqis with "detailed information on Iranian deployments, tactical planning for battles, plans for airstrikes and bomb-damage assessments for use of chemical weapons."[37] In a 1999 book about his experiences Francona writes, "Iraqi use of chemical warfare agents at Al-Faw was obvious."[38] Recalling his visit to Faw in the battle's immediate aftermath, Francona said (interview, 2000): "I personally picked up used atropine injectors off the battlefield and from captured Iranian vehicles. I personally observed Iraqi attempts to decontaminate captured Iranian equipment – no need to do so unless they knew they had used chemicals."

In a separate interview (2000), Francona explained that expended atropine injectors strongly suggested that nerve gas had been used, because the cure is almost as bad as the disease: Iranian soldiers would not inject themselves with atropine, which could make them very sick, unless they were fairly certain they were being attacked with a nerve agent. The DIA traced the injectors back to European manufacturers, who had indeed sold them to Iran. A US intelligence document provided the following evidence:

> . . . the absence of insect and bird population for several days after the battle, a very low number of Iranian prisoners of war, evidence that Iranian battle gear had been abandoned with little sign of use in battle, and an Iraqi request for bulldozers to be brought in . . . [a request] believed to be for the establishment of mass graves as there were no road barriers or other obstructions that required removal. Observers were not allowed into the Al Faw battle area until after Iraq had ample opportunity to clean up.[39]

Another US intelligence document stated that Iraq fired close to 2,000 122-mm rockets containing mustard, sarin, and CS tear gas during its Faw offensive.[40]

Sheikh Mowla, a Badr Corps commander in Faw, recalled (interview, 2002) two separate Iraqi chemical attacks, involving both mustard and nerve gas. In the first attack, he said, a strong wind blew gas back at Iraqi forces, killing many; the second attack caused mostly Iranian casualties. An Iraqi pilot claimed (interview, 2003) that Ilyushin cargo aircraft had also gassed the Iranians: "The planes ascended to a very high altitude. With the cockpit pressurized, they opened the back, flew at an angle, and let barrels filled with gas roll out. It was saturation bombing meant to cause mass panic. This was something that was discussed openly between us [pilots]. It was a big thing. The cargo pilots were proud that they, too, had been asked to carry out a bombing run. I visited Faw afterwards; it became a very famous place." The use of 55-gallon drums filled with chemicals and dropped from Iraqi helicopters is described in US intelligence documents.[41]

Reports surfaced that Iraq used a new nerve agent, VX, at Faw. Gen. Wafiq Samarra'i, for example, the former MID chief, told reporters after his 1994 defection that Iranian resistance at Faw collapsed because of Iraq's use of VX. Developed by the US and Britain in the 1950s, VX is a quick-acting, highly lethal nerve gas – a single drop can kill – that, like mustard gas, is also persistent and hangs around on the battlefield. "VX was used in the battle of Fao on 17 and 18 April," he said. "We put it in long-range artillery shells and [also] dropped it from aircraft. This is what caused the panic among the Iranian Revolutionary Guards. . . . We won because we used VX."[42]

Samarra'i's claim has not been corroborated, and US intelligence assessments of Iraqi capabilities before the Kuwait war suggest that Iraq's VX program was still in the developmental stage in 1990.[43] The DIA's Lang, however, also recalled that Iraq had used VX in Faw, and there were reports of VX use during several of the following Tawakkulna 'ala Allah stages as well: at Fish lake in May, Majnoun in June, and possibly in Mehran later that month.

Interviews with Iraqi officers suggest that, just like in Anfal, the Iraqis used chemical weapons primarily on the first day of each of the five stages, killing many Iranian soldiers and causing mass panic, which destroyed morale. Then they moved in ground troops in what became virtual mopping-up operations, capturing enormous amounts of abandoned military equipment. Kamel Anwar Boutros, an Iraqi soldier fighting in all five offensives, remembered (interview, 2004): "We used chemical weapons on the first day of the Faw attack, at five in the morning. All our *rajima* [artillery launchers] were firing chemical shells. After that we fired conventional rockets, because there no longer was a need for chemical weapons. All the Iranians died. In each operation we only used chemical weapons in a single massive salvo on the first day." "The Iranians fled like maniacs," a senior Iraqi officer recalled (interview, 2004). He said many Iranians were killed by Iraq's gas but many Iraqi soldiers also suffered gas-related injuries.

Ja'fer Aslani, an Iranian doctor (interview, 2002), noted cases in the second Tawakkulna 'ala Allah operation at Fish lake with atypical symptoms that "came on very rapidly and heavily: lachrymation, vomiting, seizures and mental changes. Patients' response to treatment with atropine was very poor or nonexistent, and a lot of soldiers died." These were possibly VX cases, he said. Based on his frontline experience, Abbas Foroutan also reported VX cases.[44] Iraqi reports seem to confirm this. Mohamad Hanon, an Iraqi infantry soldier, said (interview, 2003) that during the third stage in June, at Majnoun, there had been "heavy, heavy use of chemical weapons by our side. We wouldn't have taken the area if it hadn't been for chemical weapons. We were told by our commanders it was VX and that we had to wear our masks, because the terrain was flat and the wind was changing by the minute." He noted that during chemical defense training, soldiers like himself used to be given lectures on VX, along with other gases. The Iranians claimed that hundreds of their troops had died from gas at Majnoun;[45] a UN team of experts later examined some of the surviving casualties.[46]

From Mehran (stage four) also came hints of VX use, but no confirmation. Iraqi Staff Col. Abd-al-Wahhab al-Saeidy recounted (interview, 2003) that he and his men were issued rocket–propelled grenade (RPG) launchers with chemically filled grenades and were instructed to use these once they received a special order. The order never came, he said, but friends told him Iraq did use gas during the battle: "And why not? We were attacking Iranian cities and killing civilians. So why wouldn't we also use chemical weapons? What's the difference?" He did not recall what type of gas it was, he said, and "we were not permitted to open the boxes. But I learned later what kind of gas we had in our arsenal, because I had to teach chemical defense at the Staff College in the 1990s. We had mustard and nerve gases, including VX. I don't know if we ever used VX, though," an Iraqi brigadier general said (interview, 2004): "My understanding was that VX was *routinely* used.

At least, this is the term that everyone employed from 1984 or 1985 on."

By training their men in VX defense and propagating the idea they had this gas in their arsenal, Iraqi commanders may have wanted either to confuse their adversaries, forcing them to be prepared for any gassing eventuality, or to raise the terror level by making them believe they were facing VX. The unusual symptoms noted by Iranian doctors may be attributed less to VX than to the fact that the Iraqis increasingly resorted to a cocktail of gases for which the Iranians could not be appropriately equipped except by donning prohibitively cumbersome chemical body-suits.

Iranian troops in the south were not the only gassing targets during the war's waning days. So were troops fighting in the north, and there, Iranian Kurdish civilians were often caught in the downdraft, if not targeted outright. Iranian complaints to the UN revealed a disturbing pattern of repeated gas attacks on Kurdish villages around towns such as Marivan, Serdasht, and Baneh, and directly on the town of Oshnaviyeh. The final UN report on chemical weapons use was devoted entirely to the Oshnaviyeh attack in July.[47]

The Marivan attacks appeared particularly extensive. In the days before and after the Iranian offensive against Halabja, the roads around Marivan, a town just across the border inside Iran, were teeming with Iranian troops, whose local headquarters was in Dizli. These staging areas became targets for Iraqi chemical attacks. Iraqi pilots and gunners apparently did not look too carefully, however, when they dropped or fired their munitions or wanted to send a message. While acknowledging the presence of Iranian forces around Marivan, both Dr. Foroutan and local residents reported direct hits on villages that had no troop presence. Two days before the Halabja attack, for example, Iraqi forces struck the area between Qalaga and Qala'ji. No one died, but most villagers fled into the nearby forests, mountains, and caves. Those who stayed in their homes were caught in a second gas attack the next day, which killed twenty, including five members of one family. "On the radio we had heard army announcements that we should go to higher ground during a chemical attack," said Bahman Sultani, a villager who returned to help carry eight bodies to the local mosque (interview, 2002). "But people were not prepared." Several days after the Halabja attack, villagers in Nijmar suffered a chemical strike that killed twenty-two. In nearby Kani Dinar, five died from a gas attack around the same time.

While the Iraqi air force denied using chemical weapons in Marivan,[48] Abbas Foroutan, working in the army hospital there, described symptoms "that did not fit nerve gas and thus were treated for cyanide poisoning. After a while they responded to treatment." Yet he did not exclude the possibility of a new, fast-acting type of nerve agent, the likes of which he had not seen before, possibly VX.[49]

The Threat to Gas Tehran

Cumulatively, these final massive gas attacks helped bring the war to an end, but only after Iraq coupled them with a threat to chemically attack Tehran and other cities. This was not an empty threat. The Iraqis had developed a dangerous new capability. They modified their Soviet-made Scud missiles to extend their range, and now the Iranian capital became a push-button target. The first conventionally loaded ballistic missile struck Tehran on February 29. Now the Iraqis warned that they might place chemical warheads on these long-range missiles.[50]

The CIA was monitoring these developments closely. In early April, having absorbed the Halabja attack's significance, the CIA warned that "the risk is growing" that smaller population centers might be attacked with chemical weapons:

> A strategic breakthrough by Iran in the ground war would be the scenario most likely to drive Iraq to chemical attacks on Iran's major cities. Iraq probably would use chemical weapons in a battle for a major Iraqi city such as Al Basrah or As Sulaymaniyah if Baghdad believed Iranian forces were on the verge of seizing control.

If, the agency went on, the international community failed to respond with sanctions, "the chance of chemical strikes on larger cities would increase significantly."[51]

The images from Halabja matched with Baghdad's warnings triggered mass panic in Iran, whose urban population was already being hammered. The New York Times reported that Tehran radio had "demonstrated a new signal of three beeps to warn of a chemical attack and detailed steps civilians can take to protect themselves," and that perhaps as much as half the city's population, estimated at six million, had fled because of conventional missile attacks.[52] There is a famous story of a Tehran bakery being hit by a missile; the flour that swirled up triggered a panicked evacuation of the neighborhood. Dr. Hamid Sohrabpour helped prepare medical teams for a chemical strike: "We were expecting mass casualties," he recalled (interview, 2002). "There was a real fear this would happen. Meanwhile, of course, conventional missiles were raining down on us. . . . "

In any event, no chemical strike against Tehran occurred. One could plausibly argue that Iraq did not gas the Iranian capital because it had not yet developed chemical warheads for its missiles. Yet the mere threat overwhelmed the Iranians with fear, sapping whatever support remained for the war. When Iraq launched its final series of counteroffensives, Iran's response capability collapsed. The Faw attack had a domino effect that obviated the need for chemical escalation beyond the immediate battlefield. The CIA's prediction of a chemical war of the cities was premised on Iranian battlefield advances – which never came.

There are those in both Iran and Iraq who strongly believe that Iraq's mix of bluster and the tactical use of gas, more than any other factors, brought the war to an end. "We sent a signal to Khomeini that if he didn't put a halt to the war, we would fire chemical weapons at Iranian cities," said Staff Col. al-Saeidy. A CIA analysis concurred: "Iran's defenses soon collapsed everywhere. Chemical weapons ended the war. . . . The success of offensive operations in the southern sector in mid-1988 ultimately caused the Iranians to cease hostilities. The use of chemical weapons contributed to the success of these operations."[53] A postwar intelligence assessment was even more explicit:

> We believe chemical agents were critical to Iraq's willingness to launch military offensives that recaptured significant pieces of Iraqi territory this year. We further believe that chemical warfare played a decisive role in curbing the threat to the Iraqi Government from Iranian–backed Kurdish rebels in northern Iraq.[54]

An Iranian chemical weapons experts took a more nuanced view (interview, 2002): "What brought Iran to a ceasefire was a combination of Iraq's chemical weapons use and the war of the cities," he said. "The

gas attacks broke soldiers' morale and made new recruitment very difficult, while the missile attacks broke the backbone of popular support
for the war. The specter of mounting chemical warheads on these missiles was very much alive in people's minds." To that expert, however,
the clincher was the shooting down of an Iranian airliner by the US
in early July, which many Iranians interpreted as a message that Washington, acting on Iraq's behalf, was prepared to do anything to end the
war. Col. Ephraim Kam, then deputy head of Israel's Military Intelligence, cited Iran's inability to acquire new weapons as the primary reason for its decision to sue for peace. But, he said (interview, 2000), Iraq's
Scud attacks on Iranian cities and the fear that Iraq would use chemical
weapons was a close second.

It is unlikely that any single factor accounts for Khomeini's decision
to – in his words – finally "drink from the cup of poison" and consent to a (humiliating) ceasefire. Iran had never recovered, militarily
or psychologically, from the failure of its "final" offensives the two previous years and it was facing recruitment problems. Meanwhile, Iraq
had gained a significant edge with its ballistic missiles, its ability to fully
integrate chemical weapons fire, its air supremacy, its superior battlefield armor, and its ability to swiftly move armor across the country.
"The Iraqi military steadily increased its competence during the war
and quickly became the most effective and efficient force in the region,
scaring the hell out of the Israelis," the DIA's Pat Lang said (interview,
2000). Moreover, US intervention in the Gulf put an end to Iran's naval
advantage and threatened further escalation. Facing such odds, the
Iranian leadership must have wondered what greater purpose continuing the war would serve. The prospect of victory after a long battle of
attrition had vanished – the attrition now harming the Islamic Republic itself as well as the very revolution that had given it life. What ended
the war, therefore, was the clerical leadership's acute insight into what
the Republic had to do to survive.

But consider this: If by the summer Iraq had succeeded in repelling
its enemy from the small territories it had acquired, what more had it
gained than enormous amounts of abandoned Iranian armor? Both sides
had suffered huge losses in lives. Iraq, moreover, had incurred debts it
could not soon repay, even if its oil sector recuperated. And although
both regimes stayed firmly in place, when they signed the ceasefire

accord in August they were back to the same international border of old, a fact that underscored the war's futility. This, then, was not an Iraqi victory as much as a belated Iranian realization that it could not win. Rather than vanquished, Iran was merely deterred from pressing on indefinitely. To bring the Iranians to their knees would have required much more than the Iraqis could muster, a vastly larger allocation of resources, and a far more explicit US–Iraqi alliance. Seen in this light, Iraq's combined threat and use of chemical weapons was a precipitating factor, more than a cause, of ending the war, because it served as an indispensable – if overdue – reality check for a regime bent on achieving an impossible victory.

SEVEN

IRAN AND THE USE OF GAS

The Security Council "condemns vigorously the continued use of chemical weapons in the conflict between the Islamic Republic of Iran and Iraq," and "expects both sides to refrain from the future use of chemical weapons."

– UN Security Council Resolution 612 (May 9, 1988)

Black Sheep Bleating

In the 1980s the Cold War was waning. Leonid Brezhnev died in 1982. He was succeeded by two ailing leaders until the arrival of Mikhail Gorbachev in 1985. Soviet troops were mired down in Afghanistan, where US-backed Islamist resistance fighters (the *mujahedin*) made their lives miserable and their prospects of successful extrication bleak. The situation in the Israeli–occupied territories continued to be unstable. Israel's unceasing policy of building new Jewish settlements on Palestinian land inevitably triggered resistance, which the army crushed, in 1985, with a brutal "Iron Fist" policy of deportations, detentions without trial, and house demolitions. The Israelis also occupied part of Lebanon, having invaded to expel the Palestine Liberation Organization in 1982. This gave rise to Shi'ite resistance, including bombings and kidnappings attributed to Hezbollah, an indigenous movement drawing strong political and material support from Iran's clerical leadership. In Tehran the mullahs made noises of wanting to spread the Islamic revolution, defeating both the Zionist entity and the corrupt rulers of the oil sheikhdoms in the Gulf.

If, in this period, the Iranian leadership came to the United Nations to complain that Iraq violated the basic precepts of international humanitarian law, why should anyone listen? By taking Western hostages, supporting Hezbollah's violent tactics, and threatening the Middle East with an Islamic makeover on the Khomeini model, Iran found itself ostracized and locked out. Effectively it had lost its standing at the UN, certainly as a petitioner on human rights. Tehran reciprocated by cold–shouldering the international community, ignoring Security Council resolutions when they did not suit its interests, and parlaying its imposed isolation into an ideological virtue consistent with its puritanical worldview. Unsurprisingly, therefore, Iranian remonstrations about Iraq's chemical weapons use fell mostly on deaf ears, especially in the early stages – in 1983–1984 – when Iraq started probing both new technologies and international tolerance of its behavior, and when intervention could have made a significant difference.

Iran was right to complain, though, of such blatant violations of a recognized UN instrument, the 1925 Geneva Protocol. The UN's failure to halt Iraq's chemical weapons use had appalling consequences, something the Iranians articulated with growing sophistication as Iraq's use of poison gas escalated. The irony is that Iraqi actions were so barbarous that Iran could report them without apparent embellishment. Iraq, by contrast, banked on its international support to counter these charges with only the crudest denials and most transparent subterfuges – except when it went overboard, as it did in Halabja. Then deliberate obfuscation was the only way out of scandal. But by 1988 it was arguably too late to reverse the alarming chemical escalation.

The UN's mishandling of the chemical weapons issue damaged its standing as an arbiter of international peace and security and undercut any pretensions it might have had of being a human rights champion – at a time when human rights had yet to become a household phrase and UN leadership could have put the concept out in front. If anything saved the UN from an embarrassing tarnishing of its reputation, it was Secretary-General Javier Pérez de Cuéllar.

In protesting Iraq's gas use, Iran was its own best advocate, even as it also was its own worst enemy. Starting in the summer of 1983, Iran's pleas increased commensurately with Iraqi gas attacks. Finding no audience in the Security Council, Iran appealed to the secretary-general for his personal intercession. While sloppy in their details – dates wrong, place names mangled, gases misidentified – these supplications were invariably on target, or at least were never proven wrong in their central contention that Iraq had, once again, used chemical weapons. On each of its missions, dispatched on Pérez de Cuéllar's own authority, the team of experts concluded that Iranian troops had indeed been affected by poison gas and that, from 1986 on, unequivocally the culprit was Iraq.

Moreover, Iran became increasingly skilled at embedding its complaints in international law, specifically the Geneva Protocol. As Iraq started gassing civilians, Iranian diplomats resorted to an even more basic moral precept, the prohibition on attacking civilians – with any weapon – encapsulated in international humanitarian conventions. Over time, Iran's argumentation metamorphosed from its humble beginnings – that brutality left untreated breeds impunity, and then worse atrocities – to a canny disputation on the military and moral consequences of casting aside international law. Thus, Iran's response to the first confirmed Iraqi chemical attacks in the summer of 1983 was to say, on the basis of previous Iraqi conventional strikes on Iranian population centers, that "the acquiescence of the Security Council and the indifference of the international community has been an encouragement for the ruling régime of Iraq to continue its savage atrocities."[1]

The Iranians refined their impunity argument over the years; the unprecedented gas attack on the town of Serdasht in June 1987, in particular, helped sharpen the argument's focus. This attack, the Iranians contended, constituted a "turning point in the history of the use of chemical weapons," and gave a "green light" to the Iraqis to repeat their breach of international norms, "thereby ridiculing world consciousness."[2] Moreover, they said, the Security Council knew full well that its "feeble statement" in response to the UN experts' report in May 1987 "would be interpreted by Iraq as a carte blanche for its continued resort to chemical weapons – *and it was indeed interpreted as such.*"[3] By the time Iraq struck Halabja, the impunity argument had begun to lose force. After all, what worse could there be than the gassing of a town that large? All Iran could say was:

It is now abundantly clear that the failure of the United Nations machinery to take the Iraqi régime to task for its genocidal use of chemical weapons in Halabja and other large-scale resorts to chemical warfare against both Iranian and Iraqi targets is at least partially responsible for the continuation and escalation of the criminal behavior shown by Iraqi aggressors.[4]

Iran also developed a corollary argument: The Security Council's silence in the face of Iraqi atrocities implied its "complicity in these heinous crimes."[5] By their diplomatic stance and active military and financial support of Iraq, council members had become parties to the conflict and thus shared responsibility for Iraq's conduct – deeds that Iran referred to as war crimes, crimes against humanity, and genocide.[6]

In 1983, Iran argued, rather than punishing Iraq for using gas, the Security Council rewarded Iraq with resolution 540, which failed to mention chemical weapons. "Owing to such encouragement," Iran contended, "the rulers of Iraq felt free to open new avenues of crime and to resort to the use of chemical weapons."[7] Indeed, Iraq graduated from mustard gas to nerve agents soon after.

It could have turned out differently, the Iranians contended. They noted, for example, that the council strongly condemned chemical weapons use only in 1986, after UN experts found that Iraq was responsible. Despite the council's failure to condemn Iraq, Iran was mollified but, as its foreign minister observed ruefully, "Had this condemnation been effected three years ago when the régime of Iraq introduced these prohibited weapons into the conflict, the continuation and extension of the use of chemical warfare by the Iraqi régime would obviously have been prevented."[8] Even if such a result was not necessarily "obvious," it was at least plausible, and the action should therefore have been attempted.

One measure that Iran argued the council could have taken was to station chemical weapons experts in Tehran who could produce real–time assessments via on-site inspections whenever Iraq used gas. This would have allowed for more accurate diagnoses (given the quick dissipation of nerve agents and possibly cyanide gas), and provided stronger impetus for international action if the problem's true scale was understood.[9] The idea, echoed by UN inspectors only in 1988,[10] proved unattractive to a Security Council that tilted toward Iraq. More punitive Iranian proposals – a mandatory export embargo on chemical agents and technology to Iraq[11] or even a comprehensive arms embargo[12] – were similarly ignored. All the secretary-general was prepared to do was send experts to the region, and all the council would do was condemn chemical weapons use and urge *both sides* to refrain from chemical warfare, even if Iraq alone was guilty.

In the process of doing nothing, Iran alleged, the council lost its standing as an international arbiter: "When political considerations predominate an international organ," its diplomats argued, when the council fails to "discharge its constitutional duties" in the face of gross violations of international law, then "the very *raison d'être* of the organ becomes its immediate victim."[13] Just as seriously, Iran said, the continued international indulgence of Iraqi violations of the Geneva Protocol had "eroded the authority of all rules and principles of international humanitarian law."[14] This, in turn, was serving to lower "the abhorrence of these horrifying weapons."[15]

Rightly – all too rightly, with the advantage of hindsight – Iran was raising the specter of chemical weapons proliferation, the development of even more deadly weapons, and a more widespread use of these lethal technologies. "It is feared that quite soon we will witness a tremendous international race in the field of chemical weapons," Iran contended.[16] Evidence suggests that Iraq did develop more immediately lethal nerve agents, such as VX, and also started producing biological agents. Had it not made the foolish mistake of invading Kuwait, Iraq might also have succeeded in building a nuclear weapon. Iran, too, launched a chemical weapons development program and was suspected, after the war, of starting biological and nuclear weapons programs as well.

Iran never found an effective answer to Iraq's chemical weapons use. Iranian leaders repeatedly stated that Iran would not use poison gas out of respect for "humanity, Islamic principles and international law," even though, they claimed, they had the capability – probably a bluff.[17] Occasionally, though, they dropped hints that Iraqi gas attacks, and the international community's "passive reactions," left Iran with no option but to respond in kind.[18] Particularly after the Serdasht attack, which they declared was as significant as the Hiroshima and Nagasaki bombs, Iran registered a "temporary reservation" to its signature to the Geneva Protocol, thereby signaling its right of chemical retaliation, "as long as practical measures to prevent Iraq from further chemical attacks have not materialised."[19] The Geneva Protocol prohibits the use of gas in international conflict, but many countries attached a reservation when they signed, stating that the protocol would "cease to be binding" in case an enemy violated it. Iraq, which ratified the convention in 1931, had made such a reservation; Iran had not. But now, circumstance forced Iran to issue a reservation as well.

To put weight behind its threat to resort to gas warfare, Tehran boasted it had an active chemical weapons program. Indications are that indeed it did, at least toward the end of the war; its declarations under the 1993 Chemical Weapons Convention bear this out. Iran maintained this rhetorical position – "we have *not* used them and *will not* do so out of principle, but we *may* use them because we can, and we *may have to* use them because you leave us no choice" – throughout the war. Unlike the Iraqis, Iran not once even so much as hinted that they ever used chemical weapons, which suggests they did not.

If they truly never used gas, it was because Iran realized it could not effectively counter Iraqi gas attacks with a chemical response, given its belated arrival to the development of these weapons. According to Ambassador S. R. Tabatabaei, a Foreign Ministry official (interview, 2002), Iraq began its chemical weapons program in 1970. By the time Iran got wind of it, in the early 1980s, it was thirteen years behind. Iran then developed "two pilot plants that could produce limited amounts of mustard gas. Then we produced some other chemical agents, but we never weaponized them." Instead Iran decided to mine the propaganda value it thought would accrue from exposing Iraq's repeated gas use. This strategy had limited success, because Iran was the international community's black sheep. Even if its accusations had a basis in fact, who was Iran – a republic of Islamic zealots, hostage takers, and supporters of terrorism – to raise an outcry over Iraqi crimes? Apart from some UN officials working for the secretary-general, chemical weapons experts, and those working to halt WMD proliferation, no one seemed to care. This had damaging consequences for Iran: Its failure to convince the world that Iraq's use of chemical weapons had to be stopped set the stage for that country's massive gas use in the war's final battles and its threat to target Tehran.

Iraq mostly ignored Iran's UN demarches or dismissed them without bothering to argue specifics. One favorite response was to accuse Iran of hypocrisy, contending it had targeted civilians (with conventional weapons) from the war's outset.[20] Another was to remind the international audience that Iraq's very existence was at stake in the face of a merciless invader: "It is only natural that Iraq, which is the victim of aggression, should resort to *all necessary means* to defend its security, its vital interests, and its existence."[21]

The Iraqi response went further, and in this Iraq found the Security Council's support. Iraq's argument also drove the Iranians into the arms of the UN secretary-general as the only acceptable alternative. The debate that evolved concerned means versus ends or, put differently, the partial versus the full implementation of Iranian and Iraqi international obligations. Or, put another way, a sequential versus a comprehensive and simultaneous approach to ending the conflict.

The Iraqi argument went as follows: Iran invaded Iraqi territory (in 1982) and was the original aggressor in September 1980; Iran was obliged to comply with Security Council resolutions calling on both parties to end the conflict but failed to do so; and Iran should not be permitted to pick and choose among various international conventions, accepting the laws of war (prohibiting chemical warfare) as legitimate, while rejecting (by persisting in its breach of international peace and security) the UN Charter. For example, Iraq argued that:

> ... any appeal to legality presupposes respect for the norms of international law and the Charter, which prescribed a central role and authority for the Security Council in situations of armed conflicts. In its contemptuous defiance of the authority of the Council, and its rejection of the Council's unanimous resolutions on the settlement of the armed conflict it imposed upon Iraq, the Iranian régime is the party to be condemned on the very legal basis it has appealed to.[22]

Iran responded by claiming the cards were stacked against it in the Security Council, yielding resolutions that invariably favored its adversary. "It appears," Iran complained as early as 1983, "that the Security Council, in dealing with the Iran/Iraq conflict, functions on the basis of a different Charter of the United Nations from the one to which Iran had adhered." The apparent bias arose, Iran said, from the fact that Iraq, "the aggressor," was involved in the drafting process while Iran, "the victim," was excluded.[23]

Iran had a point, but it neglected to mention that Iran had excluded itself from the process, shunning the council as long as that body failed to declare Iraq the aggressor. It was this chosen exile from council deliberations, as well as growing alarm over attacks on civilians, that prompted Pérez de Cuéllar to investigate the early gassing charges. In so doing, he cited a mandate obligation to ensure compliance with all relevant international law, not only to "seek to end the conflict," but also to "try to mitigate its effects, in areas such as attacks on civilian population centers, use of chemical weapons, treatment of prisoners of war and safety of navigation and civil aviation."[24] The secretary-general apparently hoped that by engaging Iran's leaders on an issue they cared deeply about, he could draw them into the diplomatic process and thus negotiate an end to the conflict. His initiative took on a life of its own, however. As Iraq escalated its chemical weapons use the Iranians, rather than being drawn back in, were convinced they were the victims not only of aggression but also of illegal methods of warfare.

The laws of war (also known as international humanitarian law) are a set of international conventions negotiated by states on the basis of wartime experiences, in particular the realization that their vital interests are served by constraints on the means of warfare. Most of these constraints come in the form of treaty obligations, most famously the four Geneva Conventions of 1949, but some are deemed so fundamental as to have attained the status of universal application regardless of whether a state has signed the conventions. The prohibition on attacking civilians is one such universal constraint, and violation of it amounts to a war crime.

The laws of war are separate from the UN Charter, which prohibits acts of aggression. Given Iraq's repeated chemical weapons use, its preference for the charter was not surprising, because even if Iraq was the aggressor, antipathy toward Iran was such that the Security Council left the issue undecided. Only after Iraq's 1990 Kuwait invasion did Pérez de Cuéllar, in one of his final acts before leaving office, publicly identify Iraq as the aggressor in the previous conflict.[25]

Iran relied on the UN investigations to embarrass Baghdad. This infuriated the Iraqis. In 1986, after the UN accused Iraq of being the source of Iranian soldiers' chemical injuries, the Iraqi regime decried Pérez de Cuéllar's "step-by-step" method as undercutting support for the diplomatic process aimed at ending the war and thus giving Iran time to prepare new military offensives. Iraq reminded the Security Council that its resolutions, adopted unanimously, dealt with the Iran–Iraq war "within a comprehensive framework" and called for an end to the war "in accordance with the principles laid down in the Charter of the United Nations, international law and relations among States." Iran (Iraq said) should not be permitted to apply a "selective method of interpreting" these resolutions as a way of continuing the war.[26]

Over time, though, the Iraqis learned to play the game. From 1987 on they tried to manipulate UN investigations to their advantage, referring to the same rules Iraq had denounced until then. In April 1988, for example, Iraq, which all along had appealed for implementation of the third Geneva Convention regarding POW treatment,[27] declared: "We have made it clear on many occasions that the Iranian régime, *while committing criminal acts which are in violation of the principles of international humanitarian law*, makes spurious complaints about the non-implementation of those principles in order to cover up its crimes and divert attention from its policy of prolongation of the war, aggression and expansion."[28]

In the end the Iraqis won. The Security Council tolerated Iraq's chemical weapons use by condemning both parties equally and failing to punish the proven offender. Iraq was able to gas with impunity until the end of the conflict, arguably gassing the Iranians to the negotiating table. Iran was forced to swallow its pride and accept a ceasefire. This, claimed Iran's UN ambassador Sa'id Khorassani (interview, 2002), may have been precisely what the council intended – that the only way to bring Iran to its knees was by unleashing Iraq's chemical arsenal.

In pursuit of this objective, international humanitarian law – the only mechanism the world has to keep belligerents from committing the worst abuses – was severely weakened. The Iranians pointed out that the Security Council took the position that "the only way to prevent the repetition of the use of chemical weapons by Iraq is to terminate the war."[29] Such an approach made a mockery of the very *raison d'être* of the laws of war, they argued: Mitigating suffering in warfare by eliminating unconscionable methods can advance the cause of peace by dampening passions and breaking the cycle of mutual recriminations. Moreover, allowing practices such as chemical weapons use was likely to have serious consequences beyond the scope of this particular battlefield, as the Iranians also argued, because it lowered the threshold of acceptability.

Did Iran Use Gas?

In the spring of 1987, just when Iraq's chemical weapons use became of such magnitude – attacking Iranian troops, Kurdish guerrillas, and civilians – that the world had to take notice, the Iraqi leadership began accusing the Iranians of similar practices. Supported by Washington, Iraq found that few people required evidence: it was expected and readily accepted that Iran would use chemical weapons. Now the Iranians had to deny perpetrating precisely the kinds of atrocities from which they had avowedly refrained out of deference to moral principles rooted in humanity and religion – but in reality because they lacked the capability. Whatever voice they had on chemical warfare – the only rhetorical edge they had over Iraq – they now lost to claims directly challenging the moral high ground they had taken.

There is, however, no convincing evidence that Iran ever used chemical weapons. This view is supported, after the fact, by a range of Iraqis interviewed for this book – military officers and soldiers, a chief of military intelligence, a defense attaché in Washington, a senior diplomat at the UN, and a senior advisor to Saddam Hussein, all of whom either fought for or otherwise served their country during the war. None is known to harbor pro-Iranian sympathies; to the contrary, some were open about their intense dislike of the Iranians and said they were prepared to fight them again. Those among them who came to oppose the regime in Iraq and defected in the 1990s made clear they were Iraqi nationalists all the same, ready to defend their country. Some justified Iraq's chemical weapons use as an unpleasant but necessary element of a brutal war. Few expressed sympathy for the Kurds. Their emphatic judgment that Iran did not use gas, or was unlikely to have done so, should therefore be taken as "statements against interest" in light of their own indirect complicity in their country's gassing of Iranians and Iraqi Kurds.

These Iraqis include:

• Staff Maj.-Gen. Wafiq al-Samarra'i, Iraq's deputy head of Military Intelligence in the 1980s, and later its chief before his defection (interview, 1997): "Iran never used chemical weapons in the war and did not possess chemical weapons. They developed these only afterwards."

- A high-ranking Iraqi officer, an information commander at the front in 1980–1986 (interview, 2004): "During the entire period I was at the front, Iran did not use gas, according to my personal experience and information."

- Ambassador Ismat Kittani, a Kurd who, as Iraq's permanent representative to the UN in the 1980s, repeatedly accused Iran of chemical weapons use (interview, 2000): "I really don't know whether Iran used chemical weapons. The only thing I could go by was the American assessment. Ambassador Newton [discussing Halabja] said both sides had used chemical weapons. I don't have any evidence myself. I always referred to the Americans."

- Mukarram Talabani, advisor to Saddam Hussein and the regime's liaison with the Kurdish rebel parties (interview, 2003): "Iran never used chemical weapons."

- Staff Col. Yaser al-Gailani, an Iraqi fighter pilot flying a MiG-21 interceptor in the 1980s (interview, 2000): "I never saw evidence that Iran used gas during the war, and so I don't think they used it. I never heard this. If they had, Saddam Hussein would not have been silent; he would have made a lot of noise about it."

- Col. Munqedh Fathi, a mechanical engineer in the Iraqi 2nd Army Corps in the 1980s (interview, 2003): "I never heard that Iran used chemical weapons. We received a lot of chemical defense training, but we never had the expectation of an Iranian chemical attack. The Iraqi leadership was lying. The Iranians didn't use chemical weapons. I hate the Iranians very, very, very much. But this is the truth." He also said that he had participated in all five Tawakkulna 'ala Allah offensives in 1988 and that to the best of his knowledge, the Iraqis found no trace of a chemical arsenal among the vast amounts of Iranian equipment and weaponry they captured.

- An Iraqi battalion commander (interview, 2004): "Iran never used chemical weapons. I was in the war from 1980 till 1988, starting as a first lieutenant until I became colonel. Never. Nor did I ever hear anyone say that Iran used chemical weapons elsewhere along the front."

- Mohamad Hanon, a private first class deployed at the front lines during the war (interview, 2003): "From day one till the end – and while I don't like the Iranians – I never heard they used chemical weapons. I am not aware of any Iranian chemical weapons use, ever."
- Mu'ath Abd-al-Rahim, an anti-Saddam Iraqi nationalist with Iyad Allawi's Iraqi National Accord, who was a journalist in Iraq in the 1980s (interview, 2000): "We never heard [from friends or colleagues] that Iran used chemical weapons. The government used to say this but provided no evidence. As journalists, we often discussed chemical weapons use. Our children, who were in the army, told us about it. They used to say that the wind carried the chemicals back to the Iraqi side. This happened a lot."
- Kamel Anwar Boutros, an artillery man who participated in all five Tawakkulna 'ala Allah operations (interview, 2004): "I never saw Iranian chemical weapons use during the entire time I was at the front. It is possible they used chemical weapons, but I never saw or heard about it."

Other Iraqis were less certain. Speculating that Iran might have used gas, they knew of no specific examples. One officer, Col. Abd-al-Wahhab al-Saeidy, claimed (interview, 2003) to have observed an Iranian gas attack once, when an Iranian plane, he said, fired a rocket at a mountainside near Seif Sa'at during the fourth stage of the Tawakkulna 'ala Allah campaign in July 1988. He cited the black mushroom cloud caused by the rocket as evidence, though he had no detail beyond his visual impression and knew of no Iraqi casualties from the attack. He did acknowledge Iraq's own chemical weapons use during the same operation, and was able to cite previous incidents in which he knew Iraqi soldiers had been injured by Iraqi gas that had wafted back into their trenches. "I am one hundred percent certain that Iraq used chemical weapons," he concluded, "and I am not one hundred percent certain that Iran did."

An Iraqi fighter pilot remembered (interview, 2003) visiting the Al-Rashid hospital in Baghdad when there were a large number of Iraqi victims of mustard gas. "I understood they were victims of an Iranian chemical attack," he said. But in his two years of flying during the war (1987–1988), he could not cite a single incident involving Iranian gas use. By contrast, he was aware of several cases in which Iraqi gas had blown back on Iraqi troops.

Gen. Nizar al-Khazraji, army chief of staff in 1987–1990 who claims he was the Tawakkulna 'ala Allah campaign's principal architect, asserted following his defection that Iran had used chemical weapons, but only "rockets and artillery shells, and this was not as effective as when you attack from the air." He readily acknowledged Iraq's gas use in the five Tawakkulna 'ala Allah offensives, "but only on Iranian reserve forces in rear areas.... It was too dangerous for us to use chemicals on the front lines where both sides were close together."[30]

A statement from as senior an officer as Khazraji should be taken seriously. However, in 2002 Khazraji was being investigated for war crimes in Denmark, where he was seeking asylum, and had an obvious interest in playing up Iranian gas use as a way of justifying Iraq's. Moreover, given his ambition to rebuild and lead the Iraqi army following the impending US war, he also had reason to play down the gross negligence exhibited by Iraqi pilots who gassed Iranians massed along the front lines, killing or injuring many Iraqi infantry troops. This does not mean that Khazraji's statement should automatically be assumed to be mendacious, only that it should not be taken at face value, as it cannot be considered a statement against interest.

What about US policy makers and analysts? Among them the view predominates that Iran probably carried out some chemical attacks of its own, but only infrequently, on a small scale, using simple chemical agents (reflecting the infancy of its chemical weapons program) or firing captured Iraqi munitions back at Iraqi troops. These officials expressed a good deal less certainty in the early 2000s than US officials did at the time itself. A sampling:

• David Newton, US ambassador in Baghdad (interview, 2001): "There was a general feeling [in Washington] that both countries were developing a chemical weapons capability, but that Iran was very much behind. So there was a general feeling that Iran wasn't entirely clean in this regard. There is some evidence that Iran also used chemical weapons, but it is very limited."

• Jim Placke, deputy assistant secretary of state for Near Eastern affairs (interview, 2000): "Iran was endeavoring to use chemical weapons but hadn't gotten the hang of it. In reaction to Iraq's chemical weapons use, Iran hastily started its own program, but by the end of the war they had not developed either the weaponry or the doctrine to use chemical weapons. They have probably done so since."

- Frank Ricciardone, speaking years after his service as the State Department's Iraq desk officer, recalled (interview, 2000): "I never saw any evidence of Iranian chemical weapons use."
- DIA analyst Rick Francona (interview, 2000): "We know Iran used chemical weapons [in Halabja]." Upon further probing: "We were very confused. The area was contested. We saw some of the [Iraqi] victims [in Halabja]. They didn't look like victims of mustard or nerve gas. I don't think we were ever sure. I think what we'll find is theory, not fact. We didn't have access to the Iranian side . . . and in Iraq we were escorted everywhere by security guards."
- Robert Mikulak, an official in the State Department's Bureau of Arms Control who played a prominent role in negotiations over the 1993 Chemical Weapons Convention (interview, 2000): "I don't recall anything specific. There was some evidence of Iran capturing Iraqi munitions and sending these back to the Iraqis."
- Ahmed Hashim, a military analyst (interview, 2000): "Based on US sources, Iranian use was episodic. Possibly captured Iraqi stock. That would have been the only way. The Iranians only had tear gas. No cyanide."
- A CIA analyst (interview, 2000): "According to our intelligence, both Iran and Iraq used chemical weapons." When pressed, the analyst demurred, referring to Seth Carus at the National Defense University as *the* US authority on the subject.
- Seth Carus, a military analyst in the 1980s (interview, 2000): "We knew exactly what was going on at the time. The alleged use by Iran is a controversial matter. There are people in the US government who are sincerely convinced that Iran used chemical weapons. I am extremely skeptical because there is no evidence that they had the capability. If they did use it, it would have been on a very small scale. The evidence may exist in intelligence documents, but if that is the case, I haven't seen them."

Declassified postwar DIA and CIA reports accuse Iran of occasional chemical weapons use but invariably do not provide examples (locations and dates) and note that, if anything, Iran's was a rudimentary capability. Typically, the language in these documents is carefully calibrated to allow for the possibility of Iranian use even as it belittles its significance. In one example in August 1990, the CIA reflects that Iraq's wartime chemical weapons use "was enhanced by the limited Iranian CW protective capability and Iran's inability to retaliate in kind on any appreciable scale."[31] Likewise, a DIA document states, "there was no credible threat of Iranian retaliation with chemical weapons."[32] Another CIA document states that Iran was not enthusiastic about using chemical weapons but "felt they were forced to in retaliation for Iraqi attacks. Iran used chemicals only 'once or twice,' however, on troop concentrations, and with little effect."[33] This assessment must be questioned, given its apparent reliance on a local source and mysterious dating of the Halabja attack as having occurred in August 1987. All three documents are replete with detailed descriptions of the Iraqis' chemical weapons programs and instances of use, with the latter CIA memo explicitly declaring that Halabja was "heavily attacked" by Iraq with chemical arms.

A respected military expert, Anthony Cordesman, has claimed, "Iran made its first confirmed use of chemical weapons in 1985, using mortars and artillery to deliver gas rounds. Some of these rounds may initially have been captured from Iraq."[34] However, he did not say who confirmed this, or where or when this alleged incident took place. This highlights a problem with all the Iran allegations: unlike the accusations laid at Iraq's door, they invariably lack specificity. In the same vein, a 1986 US army analysis said, referring to mustard and tabun gas in unexploded Iraqi munitions: "*It is assumed* that the Iranians collected some of the agent fills for their own use. Iran is also *reportedly* making efforts to obtain CW agents and the chemicals and equipment to make their own agents. The status of this effort is not known." The same document is more assertive and detailed about Iraqi capabilities.[35]

Experimentation on Kurds?

There is another possibility that must be considered. Quite apart from the Iran–Iraq war theater, Iran had its own Kurdish insurgency to contend with, and although it never assumed the dimensions of its Iraqi Kurdish counterpart, the insurgency was irksome to the Iranian leadership all the same. In the early 1980s in particular, the Iranians carried out a series of assaults on hideouts of the main rebel party, the Kurdistan Democratic Party of Iran, KDP-I. Subsequently, KDP-I officials made repeated allegations that Iran used chemical weapons against their forces. KDP-I leader Abd-al-Rahman Qasemlou, for example, claimed from his headquarters in Baghdad in September 1988 that Iran used poison gas against his forces twice: in 1982 and again on August 13, 1987, the KDP-I's founding anniversary.[36]

Qasemlou was assassinated by Iranian agents in Vienna in April 1989 and therefore can shed no further light on his claim. Hashemi Karimi, a member of the KDP-I's political bureau in London, said (interview, 2003) he was unable to back up the late leader's contention but claimed to have been an eyewitness to another Iranian chemical attack. It took place, he said, in the winter of 1983 in the Gowra Deh area near Mawat (inside Iraq, not far from Jafati valley), where the KDP-I had a base: "The Iranians attacked our group from the air with a lot of conventional bombs but also some gas. Two or three of our peshmergas were injured, suffering skin discoloration and infections. There was a French doctor with us who told us these injuries were from a chemical agent. We made fires and a lot of smoke, and this helped." A second KDP-I official, Mowloud Swara, mentioned (interview, 2003) another Iranian gas attack, one involving artillery shells fired at Mirawa village between Serdasht and Piranshahr inside Iran in 1980 or 1981. This may have been one of the attacks to which Qasemlou referred.

Sadeq Zarza, a KDP-I official living in the Netherlands, described a third attack that occurred in the late fall of (he could not remember the year) 1982 or 1983 (interview, 2003), when he commanded a group of some eight hundred men in Saqqez district in Iranian Kurdistan:

> We were in the area of Shakala when I heard airplanes overhead on a bombing run; it sounded like regular bombs, nothing unusual. Then we learned that the nearby village of Bayanjan had been attacked with chemical weapons. There were at most two peshmergas there. We went to take a look in an area near the village where casualties were arriving at our mobile clinic. We heard that seven villagers had been killed and many others injured. Two or three had been blinded; maybe nineteen others suffered from a combination of shrapnel wounds, skin irritation, and blistering. One person lost a leg and a hand. These people told us it was a chemical attack; we didn't know what it was.

What they did know, he said, was that Iranian planes had carried out the attack. The Iranians, he surmised, might have wanted to terrorize Kurdish villagers and so turn them against the peshmergas.

The Bayanjan gassing, if that is what it was, hit the news at the time. The KDP-I, broadcasting from exile, claimed that Iranian aircraft "dropped some type of bomb which gave off a lot of smoke," killing eight persons in Bayanjan. The report insinuated that recent Iranian charges of Iraqi chemical weapons use were an attempt to "shift responsibility" for these attacks.[37] The Iranians, in turn, blamed the Iraqis for the Bayanjan attack, alleging, "Iraqi warplanes suddenly swooped down on Bayanjan village near Baneh" on October 25, 1983, "and dropped chemical bombs containing arsenic and mustard gases on the unsuspecting civilians. As a result a group of peaceful villagers were martyred or wounded."[38]

The KDP-I's accusation must be taken seriously, as the Iraqis would have had little reason to strike the Bayanjan area in October 1983. Its KDP-I officials insist that there were no Iraqi Kurdish peshmergas in those parts, nor was it an obvious staging area for Iranian troops. On the other hand, no one has ascribed a chemical weapons capability to Iran as early as 1983. The answer may be that whatever injured or killed the villagers was not Iranian gas but an incendiary agent, such as napalm or phosphorus, or a combination of phosphorus and conventional bombs (given the shrapnel injuries). Perhaps not coincidentally, Iranian forces were pursuing the KDP-I as part of the Val-Fajr IV offensive near Penjwin inside Iraq. If their airplanes carried out a simultaneous attack in the vicinity of a KDP-I group in the Baneh area, it may have been to prevent these men from rushing to their comrades' aid.

Did Iran use chemical weapons against its own Kurdish insurgents and population? The only responsible answer is that the jury is still out. Concerning the reported attacks in 1982 (one) and 1983 (two), eyewitness accounts make them plausible except that there is no evidence that Iran had started producing chemical agents at that time, let alone had the capability to weaponize them. It is possible that Iran, coming under Iraqi gas attacks, started developing chemical agents and experimentally used them against its Kurdish rebels. In the absence of more detailed and consistent eyewitness accounts and corroborating evidence from doctors present on the scene, the KDP-I's allegations are insufficient to prove its case. As for the 1987 gas attack on the KDP-I's headquarters alleged by Qasemlou, KDP-I officials have indicated they know nothing about it.

The Blowback Deception

During the war, Iraq also alleged that Iran was using gas. In the earlier years these accusations, by their crudeness, could only be described as transparent attempts to divert attention away from Iraq's own battlefield use of gas. In 1986, for example, as Iranian forces occupied Faw despite intensive Iraqi gassing, the Iraqis claimed an Iranian chemical attack, offering no detail: "The Iranian régime," they complained, "because of the heavy losses that it has suffered, actually made use of chemical weapons against us yesterday and this morning, under the delusion that such a vile maneuver would extricate it from its dilemma and its deadly predicament."[39] But soon the Iraqis realized that chemical casualties emanating from their own gas could be turned into evidence of Iranian use, and that the UN could be duped into seeing an Iranian hand.

More importantly, the knowledge that Iran was not retaliating in kind when Iraq was relying so heavily on gas not only hurt Iraq's propaganda effort, but had the potential of embarrassing Iraq's main patron, the United States. It was then, in the fall of 1987, that Washington began airing suggestions that Iran, too, had gone chemical. In a speech at the Weizman Institute of Science in Israel in October, Secretary of State George Shultz publicly criticized "both Iran and Iraq for their alleged use of chemical weapons in the Persian Gulf War."[40]

"Alleged" use? Who had made the allegation? Shultz's accusation was the first by a senior US official. Earlier in the year, Iraq had charged Iran with using mustard gas and phosgene, a choking agent also used in World War I that causes severe and painful tissue damage, in "chemical raids" on the southern battlefront.[41] This was the first specific Iraqi accusation during the war, vague only in that it failed to identify the incident's location. It may have been true. If so, the evidence has yet to be presented. However, Iraq may also have tried to prepare international visitors for the sight of Iraqi chemical casualties.

In April 1987, in response to increasing Iraqi chemical attacks – now reportedly also affecting civilians – and mounting Iranian pressure, the UN secretary-general once again sent a specialist team to the region. But this time Iraq also opened its doors to the experts. The team was taken on a tour of hospital wards in Baghdad and Basra and briefly visited the front east of Basra. In their report, released a month later, the experts concluded that some Iraqi casualties had been affected by mustard gas, others by "a highly aggressive irritant, probably phosgene."[42]

The report bears close reading. Referring to their visit to Iran, the experts highlighted chemical attacks on both military positions and civilians, and used weapon fragments to show that Iraq was the perpetrator. Concerning their Iraq visit, by contrast, the team wrote that around Basra, "Iraqi forces have been affected by mustard gas and a pulmonary irritant, possibly phosgene. In the absence of conclusive evidence of the weapons used, it could not be determined how the injuries were caused."[43]

Furious, Tariq Aziz protested the report's wording, which, he charged, "amounts to a serious shortcoming . . . and is in fundamental conflict with some reliable evidence of which the mission had knowledge and from which it could have deduced that Iran is indeed using chemical weapons." What is more (he asked), if the report failed to mention phosgene as an agent in the Iranian arsenal, how then "can one account for the fact that Iraqi military personnel have sustained injuries from it?"[44]

This is how it could have happened: Iraq had a ready supply of troops who had sustained chemical injuries – either from gas dispersed incompetently by Iraq's own forces or from gas leaking from poorly manufactured munitions. There is substantial evidence that Iraqi bombers repeatedly gassed their own forces during the war. Often this was due to shifting winds and thus especially likely to occur along the front where both sides' troops were entrenched in close proximity. The problem became more acute when Iran acquired Hawk anti-aircraft missiles from the United States (as part of the Iran–Contra affair). Iraqi bombers were then forced to fly at much higher altitudes, greatly enlarging the field of dispersal and making it more likely that gas would waft over both Iraqi and Iranian troops.[45]

A post-war CIA report confirms the blowback problem. In attacking Iranian troops with chemical weapons, Iraq paid

> ... relatively little regard for the safety of [its] own troops who were in or near the chemically contaminated area. ... Iraq's willingness to use chemical weapons on or near its own troops apparently varied depend[ing] to an extent upon how well prepared a given group of soldiers was to survive a chemical attack. This reticence did not preclude Iraq from using chemical weapons on combat zones where its own exposed soldiers were fighting on several occasions. ... Regardless of Iraq's rationale, *large numbers of Iraq's own troops were killed or injured during Iraqi chemical attacks*.[46]

Iraqi soldiers and pilots corroborate this assessment. One pilot, Staff Col. Yaser al-Gailani, asserted (interview, 2000) that Iraqi planes accidentally bombed their own forces on many occasions with both conventional and chemical weapons, and even once, in the southern marshes, with napalm. These mistakes, he said, caused many casualties. Moreover, he charged, "Saddam Hussein was able to use the Iraqi victims as evidence of *Iranian* chemical weapons use." Chapter III showed how Iraqi soldiers were injured by their own gas at Faw. Iraqis have reported similar incidents in other battles as well (interviews, 2003). Typically, soldiers were forewarned of impending Iraqi gas attacks through a series of signals: two blows on a whistle, thrice the yell "Gas!" (*Ghaz!*), and sometimes also a couple of strokes with a stick against a car wheel. This was a sign they had to put on their gas masks, but often they did not do this, as in most cases the chemicals did not come their way. They rarely bothered to don other chemical gear such as ponchos, boots, or gloves; the masks usually sufficed. This made sense: The Iraqis used quickly dissipating nerve agents along the front lines especially, as a way of killing Iranians while minimizing the risk to their own men. Mustard gas was dropped on Iranian rear bases; as it lingered, it sent Iran's supply lines into disarray. Mustard gas required full bodysuits, while for nerve agents gas masks sufficed.

Yet shifting winds were liable to screw up any precautions and warnings. An Iraqi battalion commander (*amer fawj*) recalled (interview,

2004) a battle near the (devastated) Iranian town of Muhammara and
the Karoun river in April 1987:

> I was on Um Rsas island in the Shatt al-Arab. One day, I saw two of
> our planes dropping chemicals on the Iranians in Muhammara and
> Jasem river. I could smell it. The Iranians fired a Hawk missile, bring-
> ing one of our planes down, a MiG-23. It exploded and crashed into
> the marshy ground. I went to take down its registration, along with my
> bodyguard, Khaled, a Kurd from Kalar. As we stared at the wreckage,
> his helmet fell into the water. He put it back on, water dripping along
> the sides of his face. As we got back to the battalion, he told me he
> couldn't see any more. I took him to the field hospital, where they put
> him in an ice pool. He relaxed, but once he came out, it restarted. He
> was evacuated by helicopter and spent six months in hospital. He had
> blisters all over – mustard gas. A day earlier, sixteen of my men had to
> be hospitalized with chemical injuries.

An Iraqi brigadier general recalled (interview, 2004) that at the beginning of the war, after its disastrous reversal of fortunes in 1982, Iraq
started experimenting with gas loaded into 122 mm, 130 mm, and 155
mm artillery shells, and 120 mm mortar shells. The reason Iraq chose
artillery over chemical air bombardments was this, he said:

> No-man's-land was very small. If we used chemical weapons at close
> range, nobody would know who was responsible, and we could blame
> Iran. But if we bombed deep behind the lines, it would be clear it
> was us, and it would cause a scandal. We saw that it worked; peo-
> ple at headquarters were encouraged to proceed. Some commanders
> were enthusiastic about gas use, while others were concerned about
> the danger of hitting their own men.

A second source of self-inflicted chemical injuries was leaking munitions, which posed a danger to those handling them or forced to be in
their vicinity. A former fighter pilot recalled this as a recurring problem
(interview, 2003):

> Whenever gas was used at the front, we used to joke: "They are using
> Bif Baf!" [Arabic pronunciation for Pif Paf, a cockroach killer on the
> Arab market]. We were not allowed to discuss "special strikes" with
> the pilots who flew them, but there was a lot of chatter anyway. We

used to call these bombs "Abu Khat al-Aswad" [Daddy Black Stripe] because of their black markings. At times we were blocked from certain areas of the airbase until a mission was over, or the telephones were cut temporarily. That's how we knew these were chemical missions.

But after a while they weren't special anymore, and pilots didn't like to go on them, because there were many accidents; they were afraid. It was dirty work. The bombs were prepared in a hurry, and they leaked as a result. I heard from a pilot friend that one of the bombs he was meant to carry had started to leak. The mission was delayed, so he had to get out of his plane and wait in its shade. He became unwell and started developing blisters on his behind and could no longer bend his fingers. That's just one story involving a person I know, but we heard many such stories.

This pilot's recollections are corroborated by a CIA document of the late 1980s. It states that designated units used to transport chemical bombs, referred to as "special bombs," that required careful handling because "many of them leaked." These leaks caused accidents: "Exposures resulted in burns, blisters and oozing sores. Chemical defense units were required to cleanse and treat the burned soldiers."[47]

An Iraqi soldier in the 1988 Tawakkulna 'ala Allah campaign, recalled (interview, 2004) that while Iraqi forces had fired ready-made Italian chemical rockets during the first stage, at Faw, in later stages they resorted to US-made rockets whose warheads he and his comrades had to remove and replace with shells filled with liquid gas. "We had been using these rockets for eight years, but with conventional shells," he said. "This was the first time that we fiddled with them." The problem, he said, was that they tended to leak. This led to accidents in all four battles in which he participated:

Men from National Security [Amn Qawmi] dressed in civvies would bring these rockets in trucks, supervise their handling, and tell us not to talk about them. We knew they contained chemicals, because they told us so, without specifying what kind. We used to cradle these rockets like we cradle small children. At one point I warned them that they would not reach the Iranian side, but fall on our own forces. The supervisor [mushrif] responded: "If out of those forty rockets ten reach their target, it would be enough." After every attack our field hospitals were filled with Iraqi chemical casualties. The wards were full to overflowing. They *had to be our own* casualties, because so many of these rockets misfired. The chemicals would land right in front of our positions.

In July 1988, during the campaign's fifth stage in the Hawayza marshes near Qal'a Saleh, he himself was injured "when we were filling chemical rockets into the artillery piece, and one leaked":

> There were nine of us, plus two officers. We were first taken to a cleaning tent, and then to a special chemical warfare hospital in al-'Amara. We had trouble breathing and were given cortisone shots. For two days we were unable to eat or drink. The others also received atropine injections, but when the medical officer heard my name, he said, "You are a Christian. You don't get one."

The soldier suffered no after-effects and was never told what kind of gas had caused his injuries, only that it was "kimiyawi" – chemical. He returned to the front, arriving only days before the August 8 ceasefire.

The 1987 UN report does not say that Iraq was cheating in presenting its chemical casualties. All the same, it goes to some length to discredit, in neutral terms, the supposedly incriminating evidence presented by the Iraqi military. This included two 130 mm shells (or fragments thereof) that, according to the Iraqis, had contained mustard gas but had since been decontaminated; these, the report noted, had "no internal chemical–resistant coating," carried no trace of mustard gas, and were shells "normally used for filling with high explosives." In other words, these shells were unlikely to have contained a chemical agent. About the second piece of evidence, a shell crater near Basra, the report concluded that, "craters of this depth and diameter are not normally associated with ordnance designed to disperse chemical agents over a surface area."[48] High-explosive munitions are particularly unsuitable to carry chemical agents, as the latter would be destroyed in the explosion and thus fail to spread. Gas is therefore commonly dispersed by spray tanks or in containers that break on impact or via a small explosion triggered by a time fuse. In other words, the report suggested, whatever the Iraqis were offering as evidence, it was unlikely to be related to chemical weapons use. Moreover, the Iraqis failed to present any remnants of Iranian mortar bombs containing phosgene.

Few observers of the Iran–Iraq war were likely to read a UN report in that sort of detail. What the world came away with is what was contained in the cover letter that the UN secretary-general sent to the Security Council when he transmitted the report. It said that, "the specialists' findings that chemical weapons were again used against Iranian forces by Iraqi forces, also causing injuries to civilians in the Islamic Republic of Iran *and that now also Iraqi forces have sustained injuries from chemical warfare* must add new urgency to the grave concern of the international community."[49] There was a subtle difference here, too subtle for the lay observer, and therefore useful to those who wanted to deceive.

More Iraqi attempts at subterfuge followed – simple accusations without detail and a stock request for a UN investigation.[50] In July 1988, the Iraqis succeeded, and the UN agreed to send a mission to Iraq for the sole purpose of investigating a specific allegation of an Iranian chemical attack. This time, too, the experts pointedly refrained from assigning responsibility for the casualties they examined,[51] but the fact that the UN devoted an entire investigation to a claim it then failed to debunk could only serve to reinforce the allegation. Instead of lending credence to the Iraqis' evidence – 81-mm mortar shells containing mustard gas allegedly fired by Iranian forces – the team raised significant doubts, such as that the shells were "in such a bad condition that their use as munition would, for safety reasons, be precluded," and that the shells appeared to have been filled with an incorrect mixture.[52]

Shultz's 1987 assertion of Iranian chemical weapons use may have been rendered plausible by a combination of factors. This was the first specific Iraqi allegation of its kind. The Iraqis used it to invite UN investigators to Baghdad for the first time. Here, they received evidence that might look credible to a layperson. That it could also suggest, to the contrary, that Iraq was trying to frame Iran, does not emerge unambiguously from the team's findings.

If the Iraqis were engaging in a deception, their timing was opportune: The Iranians had started making noises that if the UN failed to halt Iraqi gas use, Iran might have to respond in kind, based on the country's right of retaliation under the 1925 Geneva Protocol, "as long as practical measures to prevent Iraq from further chemical attacks have not materialized."[53] It was generally assumed that Iran was developing chemical agents, and the perception therefore existed that Iran would also start using gas soon. Repeated Iranian assertions that the Islamic Republic had decided not to retaliate in kind fell on deaf ears.

The 1987 UN report's careful phrasing, done with an eye toward enhancing the report's credibility, ended up causing a lot of trouble. Its inability to dismiss the Iraqi allegations out of hand gave it a simulacrum of balance that left the report open to interpretation. Iqbal Riza, the UN official who accompanied the investigators on their mission, addressed the report's ambiguity at the time by telling journalists that the UN had found evidence of Iraq's chemical weapons use "in each instance" (its missions in 1984, 1986, and 1987), but that "there is no evidence that Iran has used them."[54] In an interview in 2000 he put it even more bluntly: The Iraqi evidence, he charged, "was clearly fabricated." Moreover, he recalled, the investigators had made this clear upon their return, openly talking about it in the UN's hallways, for all the Security Council members to hear. Alastair Hay and Julian Perry Robinson, two independent chemical weapons experts, later declared (interview, 2001) that the allegation that Iran had used gas in the war was unequivocally false, derived solely from the phrasing of the 1987 UN report, which, they said, "some people chose to interpret wrongly."

And so it was that the notion that Iran was equally culpable of chemical warfare took hold and entered the realm of conventional wisdom, often disguised in ambiguous terms. On March 24, 1988, for example, the French daily *Libération*, in reporting on the Halabja attack a week earlier, asserted that, "In June 1987, a UN mission of inquiry confirmed in a report that soldiers of both countries had been the victim of chemical weapons." While technically correct, the phrasing helped perpetuate the theory of shared responsibility.[55]

Iran, Iraq, and Halabja

Iraq's edge in the propaganda war served to shield it from the worst of the Halabja allegations. Initially, the Iraqis did not even bother to deny their crime, except perfunctorily. Only when pressed with their feet to the fire did they go into denial overdrive and attempt to pin the blame on the Iranians. Mostly, Iraq stayed silent. This must be read as an implicit admission of guilt: otherwise, how could a regime so eager to point at Iranian crimes pass up the propaganda coup it would derive from an Iranian atrocity of this magnitude, in the wake of almost five years of Iranian accusations, supported by UN reports, of Iraqi chemical weapons use?

On the evening of March 16, 1988, the independent Radio Monte Carlo in Arabic reported an Iraqi confirmation that a battle was taking place between Iraqi and Iranian forces at Khurmal – which Iran claimed it had taken earlier that morning – but provided no detail. The next day, the Iraqis denied reports of clashes near Khurmal and Halabja as "baseless," but acknowledged their forces' withdrawal from those areas. They made no mention of chemical attacks by either their own or Iranian forces on March 16 or the days that followed.[56]

That first mention of chemical weapons came only a week later, on March 23, when Iraq's permanent representative to the UN, Abd-al-Amir al-Anbari, repeated to Ted Koppel what US State Department spokesperson Charles Redman had suggested earlier that day: that "Iran used chemical shelling against Iraqi territories." But two days later, even Iraqi foreign minister Tariq Aziz, interviewed on Jordanian radio, oddly failed to repeat the State Department's allegation. "There is no doubt," he said, "that the loss of Halabjah is a regrettable thing. . . . This area is neither a strategic area nor a fortified one. . . . The Iranian presence is a formal presence and poses no military threat to the front." On chemical weapons, he said only this: The Iranians "are raising a hue and cry over the war of the cities and over the use of chemical weapons. . . . The people who want to prolong the war at all costs will use these claims as an excuse to prolong it."[57]

All the same, the Iraqis felt pressure to do more to sway public opinion, but they needed an opportunity. This presented itself by the end of the month, when the military situation in northern Iraq had changed dramatically in the regime's favor with the fall of the PUK's headquarters on March 19, itself precipitated by the devastating civilian losses at Halabja three days earlier. Iraq swiftly unleashed the second Anfal, targeting the mountainous area of Qaradagh directly south of Suleimaniyeh and west–northwest of Halabja. It was from here that Dr. Faiq Golpy and his companions had watched Iraqi planes streak overhead from their Kirkuk bases to Halabja, visible against the distant mountains on the Iranian border. On the operation's first day, March 22, an Iraqi artillery barrage rained chemical shells on a series of villages that the PUK and other Kurdish parties had been using as their local headquarters. Close to one hundred civilians and peshmergas were killed, and many more were injured. Another attack followed a week later on Zerda mountain, one of the last rebel strongholds that overlooks the southern Qaradagh region. Now resistance crumbled: On April 1, the peshmergas' local bases in the villages of Takiyeh and Balagjar fell, and they were forced to retreat westward toward the Germian plain, the Iraqis in hot pursuit.

The chemical attack on Zerda mountain on March 30 – while dealing a knockout blow to the rebels in Qaradagh – may have backfired as Iraqi soldiers were caught in the downdraft, but their injuries provided a crucial windfall for the regime. A few days after the attack, Tariq Aziz accused Iran of having carried out gas attacks by air and artillery against Iraqi forces in "the Halabja sector" on March 30–31, injuring eighty-eight Iraqi soldiers.[58] Since there was no significant fighting around Halabja at the time, nor allegations of chemical strikes except from Kurds being flushed out of Qaradagh, the logical assumption is that Iraqi forces had once again managed to injure their own soldiers through the inept use of gas – in Qaradagh, not in Halabja.[59] Now Iraq paraded these soldiers in front of the visiting UN team in Baghdad as Exhibit A of Iranian resort to poison gas, making sure that the victims said as little as possible and only parroted the party line.

When the UN medical expert, Dr. Manuel Domínguez Carmona, met with some of these casualties in a Baghdad hospital, he concluded they had been exposed to mustard gas and possibly also a nerve agent. He did not say that nerve gas would implicate Iraq, as no one at the time was suggesting that Iran had the capability to launch nerve gas attacks. According to the injured, the incident had occurred during air and artillery attacks on their "mountaintop positions north of Halabja" on March 30–31 – information fully consistent with the reported chemical attack on Zerda mountain. This information was insufficient for Dr. Domínguez to draw a conclusion as to how these soldiers had sustained their injuries.[60]

The expert did not visit the affected area, a point that raised the Iranians' ire: "It has been authoritatively and independently established that, owing to certain atmospheric conditions, Iraqi soldiers were in previous cases affected by chemical weapons that the Iraqi régime itself deployed. Therefore, a simple visit to Iraqi soldiers in Baghdad hospitals will not be able to shed any light on the source of responsibility for this inhuman act."[61] A postwar assessment by the US Air Force Intelligence Agency stated unequivocally, despite the carefully worded conclusions in the UN report, that the UN had found "medical evidence to support the Iraqi charge that Iran had used mustard gas against Iraqi soldiers in the Halabjah area." But, it continued, "an independent intelligence source indicates that those casualties resulted from misdirected Iraqi fire."[62]

The March 30 gas attack is the only such attack in "the Halabja sector" about which Iraq claimed that Iran had used chemical weapons. This charge therefore appears to be a belated attempt at rectifying the oversight of having remained silent in the days following March 16 by collapsing the two separate Halabja dates into a single one. This worked.

There are other ways of determining what happened in Halabja and Qaradagh, however. What the Iraqis announced publicly is one thing; what they discussed among themselves – via memoranda circulating throughout the various security agencies – is quite another. Iraq's secret police and intelligence documents are a treasure trove of self-incriminating evidence. For example, a secret police cable of March 16, referring to the situation in Halabja, mentioned the need for "a firm escalation of military might and cruelty."[63] Several days later a military intelligence memo reported that, "as a result of the bombing by our planes and our artillery on the area of Halabja and Khurmal, approximately 2,000 enemy forces of the Persians and Iranian agents [the PUK] were killed."[64] Most damningly, a military intelligence cable several weeks after the attack divulged that videotapes were (secretly) offered for sale in Suleimaniyeh shops, showing, as the cable put it, "the Iraqi chemical attack on Halabja."[65]

Just as certain to indict the Iraqis, another military intelligence cable used a euphemism to refer to the chemical attack on Halabja, speaking of the "recent attack on Halabja with *special* ammunition."[66] As noted earlier, the moniker "special" is used consistently throughout the Iraqi secret police documents to designate the regime's chemical weapons. The two most common usages are "special ammunition" (*'etad khaas*) and "special strikes" (*darabat khaseh*). Iraqi defectors with intimate knowledge of Iraqi chemical attacks, including the former head of military intelligence, Maj.-Gen. Wafiq al-Samarra'i (interview, 1997), have stated that the word "special" in this context could only mean "chemical." Likewise, the 1986 UN experts' report quoted an Iraqi pilot captured in the Faw battles as referring to chemical air strikes as "special missions."[67]

Furthermore, in eighteen metric tons (close to five million pages) of captured Iraqi secret police and intelligence documents, the Iraqis make not a single reference to any supposed Iranian chemical attacks at any point during the war, while repeatedly and unambiguously, if not always explicitly, acknowledging their own chemical weapons use.[68] The documents also contain plenty of references to Iranian and Kurdish claims that Iraq carried out the chemical attack on Halabja without even a hint of denial, an attempt to question the information, or an intimation that Iran was the culprit. A sampling:

- A military intelligence memo, dated March 24, mentions the effects of the chemical attack on Halabja and surrounding areas in which 1,500 inhabitants were either killed or injured. It also refers to journalists from Iran, France, and Italy who, accompanied by an Iranian official and an Islamic Unity Movement of Kurdistan commander, visited Halabja after it was hit with chemical weapons. Moreover, it says fifteen "saboteurs" (peshmergas) were killed and twenty injured in the Halabja attack.[69]
- A military intelligence memo, dated March 25, refers to Iranians providing Kurds with supplies against chemical agents, as well as more than twenty ambulances.[70]
- A military intelligence memo, dated March 27, reports that Iran has been urging Kurds to demonstrate against the Iraqi government for using chemical weapons in Kurdish areas and to claim that thousands of inhabitants of Halabja and surrounding housing complexes were killed.[71]
- A secret police memo, dated April 18, reports that local Kurds are looking for homes for orphaned children, claiming that these children lost their parents when the (Iraqi) government used chemical weapons against the Iranian army in Halabja.[72]

- A military intelligence memo, dated March 15, 1989 (eve of the first anniversary of the Halabja attack), cites an informer's report mentioning a chemical attack in Halabja that killed 5,000 and injured 9,000.[73]
- A memo from the (Kurdish, pro-regime) special brigades (*Mafarez Khaseh*) attached to the secret police, dated March 16, 1989 (the first anniversary), reports that Halabjans are commemorating the chemical attack and threatening to stage antiregime demonstrations. The secret police director notes that if they try to demonstrate, the "traitors'" 'punishment will be "fair."[74]

The accusation that emerges from the pages of these secret police and intelligence documents is corroborated by Iraqis – including staunch Iraqi Arab nationalists who harbored no love for the Kurds. Take, for example, the case of an Iraqi pilot captured after Iranian forces shot down his Sukhoy-22 during the Halabja operation on March 17. His name was Maj. Ahmad Shaker, and a few days after his capture he was paraded at a press conference in Tehran, where he made a declaration – apparently truthful but presumably under duress (he was a prisoner of war) – that Baghdad was responsible for gassing Halabja, that he himself had carried out chemical strikes against Iranian forces massed on the southern front, and that chemical munitions were generally fitted to military jets by plainclothed secret agents at the Balad and Kirkuk air bases in Iraq.[75] Coming from the mouth of a confessed perpetrator, these words were powerful and could not be ignored. However, because they were made in custody, they could be challenged. Yet they were consistent with statements made by POWs (including pilots) captured in previous engagements.

More importantly, Yaser al-Gailani, an Iraqi pilot who left home after the war and could speak freely in exile, largely confirmed Maj. Shaker's story (interview, 2000). He said he had been flying a MiG-21, a one-seater sent out on reconnaissance and intercept missions, for the length of the war. In 1988, he recounted, he learned from fellow pilots that Iraqi Sukhoys flying from Kirkuk airbase had hit Halabja with chemical weapons. He said that Iraqi pilots returning home from Iranian captivity following prisoner exchanges were not harmed by the regime, despite their televised testimonies about Iraqi chemical strikes, which, he said, had been truthful.

Another Iraqi pilot (interview, 2003) explained the regime's motive behind the Halabja attack:

> Halabja is close to the border. Iran invaded, working with local people. They dug in, brought artillery, and occupied Halabja. For us, as Iraqis, this was high treason. Halabja was strategically located on the roads to Suleimaniyeh and Erbil. It was a big shock for Saddam Hussein. He needed to respond. It would have cost greatly if he had used conventional weapons. So he resorted to "special strikes": nerve gas, instant death. But there were still Iraqi troops in the Halabja area, and they were begging: "We're in your range! We're sitting here in the middle!" But Saddam Hussein and Ali Hassan al-Majid didn't care. They just started bombing.

More directly and therefore more damningly, Jawdat Mustafa al-Naqib, an Iraqi Air Force brigadier general and UK-trained pilot with intimate knowledge of Iraq's chemical warfare practices, gave an interview on Radio Free Iraq, a US–funded station broadcasting in Arabic from Prague, following his escape from Iraq in 1998 in which he gave direct evidence of Iraqi culpability for Halabja.[76] He suggested that he was motivated to speak out because of his own relationship to the March 16 events. Apart from any possible moral qualms about the gassing of defenseless civilians, the Halabja attack appeared to fill him with a mix of guilt and anger, given the peculiar circumstance of his lineage: His father was a Turkoman from Kirkuk, while his late mother was a Kurd of the large Jaf tribal confederation who hailed from Halabja. At the time of the attack, he was director of aviation and safety at Air Force headquarters in Baghdad.

In the interview, which aired in December 2000, Gen. al-Naqib recounted that he was on duty as one of the senior officers in the military operations room within the Republican Palace when the order came to strike at Halabja with chemical weapons. Those in the air operations cell received regular updates on the military situation, and now they learned that "Halabjah had been eliminated and the Iranians had taken it with the participation of the Kurdish forces." He said he could not remember the precise date, but it was "on the day that the Iraqi forces left Halabjah." At once, Gen. al-Naqib started making preparations to send warplanes to bomb Halabja, notifying the command centers at Kirkuk, Al-Bakr, and Saddam airbases. But, he said, "chemical bombs do not go out without orders." The main order had to come from Saddam Hussein himself, or sometimes from his then-defense minister, Adnan Khairallah Tulfah. Then the order was telephoned in and the bombing started:

> The first time, the bombing was done using conventional bombs. After that there was a breakthrough from the Iranian sectors and they entered the city. After that chemical bombs were used. We knew the effect of chemical bombs and we were sitting there in the operations room. We knew the effect on human beings and the civilian population, the people and the citizenry, and there was no warning.

Some forty to fifty aircraft participated in the chemical strikes, he said. He did not know what chemicals were used; this was a matter left to "specialists" within the Air Force. But he realized "right away . . . what the effect would be. . . . We had experience from bombing the Iranian sectors and we knew the result." Two months after the radio interview and a full thirteen years after the events in question, Gen. al-Naqib still sounded devastated (telephone interview, 2001): "It was terrible, because I had relatives in the Halabja area at the time. There was nothing I could do."

The most senior Iraqi officer to defect in the 1990s was Gen. Nizar al-Khazraji, who served as army chief of staff in 1987–1990. He has denied any personal role in atrocities committed against the Kurds, blaming Ali Hassan al-Majid instead as the man who had overall responsibility and whose orders could not be disobeyed. He claims that when he heard Halabja had been gassed, he called defense minister Khairallah, who, he said, appeared also to be out of the loop. Khairallah called back a few minutes later, telling Khazraji he had found out that "it was us who bombed the town."[77]

The second most senior Iraqi officer to defect in the 1990s, Staff Maj.-Gen. Wafiq al-Samarra'i, the former head of Iraq's Military Intelligence, also has had little to say about his own role in the atrocities committed by the regime he so loyally served. All the same, he made some important comments that, as statements against interest, have great credibility. Al-Samarra'i was a committed nationalist who fell out with Saddam Hussein after the Kuwait debacle and fled to London. During the Iran–Iraq war he served as the head of the military intelligence section responsible for the prosecution of the war, as well as the counterinsurgency against the Kurds. Following his defection, he signaled his interest in leading the Iraqi opposition, but few of the opposition groups warmed to him, suspecting him of human rights abuses. He became a prolific writer, publishing several books and numerous columns in Arabic–language newspapers, but granted few interviews. It was therefore a rare privilege to be able to interview him at his home in London in June 1997.

A squat man with a heavy moustache and glasses who in some respects bore a superficial resemblance to Saddam Hussein, he carefully steered the discussion away from his own responsibility for specific events while playing up his command responsibility as deputy to military intelligence director Sabr al-Duri during the war. He identified several intelligence documents captured by the Kurds in 1991 as authentic, and pointed out the signatures of his subordinates. On Iraq's chemical warfare, he said that only Saddam Hussein and Ali Hassan al-Majid could order chemical strikes. The attack on Halabja, he said, involved some fifty Iraqi aircraft, each carrying four 500-kg bombs filled with chemical agents the nature of which he could not specify – a total of two hundred chemical bombs.[78] In an astonishing political resurrection, this man – who claimed to have been Saddam Hussein's "only source" on Iran ("he trusted me completely") and who was deputy chief of an agency that oversaw the army's role in detaining thousands of Kurdish civilians during Anfal before handing them over to the secret police (who then killed them) – became security advisor to the new Iraqi president, Jalal Talabani, in 2005.

A high-ranking Iraqi diplomat, who spent four years in Washington in the 1980s, said (interview, 2004) that he first learned about the Halabja gas attack from the media. Then, he said, "the Americans told us that their investigation showed that perhaps Iran was responsible. There was a good deal of factionalism in Washington, with each faction accusing the other country – Iran or Iraq. So in the end, they did not decide who did it." At least not publicly.

The public record shows what the Reagan administration's line was: Iran was also partially to blame for the gas attack. But CIA and military documents from this period do not even hint at this. The CIA's daily brief for March 22, for example (one day before the State Department briefing that fingered Iran), suggested that Iraq did not value the Halabja area sufficiently "to risk a major counterattack that probably would entail heavy casualties," but would instead "use its Air Force and chemical weapons to inflict high casualties on Iranian forces."[79] The CIA thus almost made Iraq's gas use sound routine; it certainly expressed no surprise itself at Iraq's expected response. A Joint Chiefs of Staff document also dated March 22 displayed a similarly laconic view. Referring to Iraq's loss of Halabja, it suggested that the Iraqis, relying on the same doctrine for "the last 4–6 years," will not seek to retrieve the area: "Iraqi use of cluster and chemical munitions is not an unusual way for them to deal with these situations."[80]

On Balance

Did Iran use chemical weapons against Iraqi forces during the war? The answer is: not impossible, but unlikely. If there was any such use, it was, as US intelligence asserts, on a small scale and episodic at most, and possibly only experimental. But so far no persuasive evidence has been presented that Iran did use gas.

In the absence of proof, allegations of Iranian gas use must be considered due either to a misreading of battlefield events (the appearance of Iraqi chemical casualties) or a misinterpretation of UN reports discussing Iraqi chemical victims that did not identify the perpetrator. To the extent that such misinterpretation was deliberate, it may have been part of a calculated effort to relieve pressure on the Iraqi regime by shifting responsibility for gas attacks at least partially onto Iranian shoulders, taking advantage of the fog of war, independent observers' lack of access to the battlefield, and public animus against Iran. In the case of Halabja, they suggest an exceptional attempt at naked deception, necessitated by the exceptional nature of the event – the unprecedented wholesale gassing of an entire Iraqi town and its surroundings with evident intent to inflict maximum civilian casualties.

In any case, Iran's repeated warnings that it might have no choice but to respond in kind to Iraqi gas attacks may have helped create an environment that was more receptive to allegations that Iran was making good on its threats. Soon these accusations took on a life of their own, with few observers demanding concrete evidence. The mere display of Iraqi chemical casualties served to sustain the portrayal of the Iranian regime as on a par with the Iraqis as far as chemical warfare was concerned.

One might argue that everything said here about the Iraqis' attempts at deception – serving up soldiers who were victims of Iraq's own leaking munitions or of poisonous clouds wafting back – could also be applied to the Iranians: Might any of the casualties they presented to the UN have been caused by their misuse of their own chemical agents? Were they above such perfidy in any way? Probably not. But the fact is that no one has come forward with such a claim: no victims, no eyewitnesses, nor Iranian defectors disgusted with the regime and its wartime conduct.

In the final analysis, the only evidence we have for the convenient claim that Iran used chemical weapons during the war is that the US government, with all its intelligence capabilities and diplomatic weight, said so. And the antipathy for Iran was such that no one cared to question that statement.

EIGHT

FIXING THE EVIDENCE

More than a year after [Colin] Powell's [February 2003] speech, after an investigation that extended to three continents, the CIA acknowledged that [an Iraqi defector code-named] Curveball was a con artist who drove a taxi in Iraq and spun his engineering knowledge into a fantastic but plausible tale about secret bioweapons factories on wheels.... Although no American had ever interviewed Curveball, [CIA analysts] believed the informant's technical descriptions were too detailed to be fabrications. "People were cursing. These guys were absolutely, violently committed to it" [dissenting senior CIA officer Tyler], Drumheller said. "They would say to us, 'You're not scientists, you don't understand.'"
           – *Los Angeles Times*, June 25, 2006

The Pentagon and Halabja

Today, few observers question the assertion that it was Iraq that gassed Halabja. Since Iraq's invasion of Kuwait in August 1990, almost no one has suggested that Iran was responsible. In the spring of 2002, as Washington was girding for war, President George W. Bush openly accused Saddam Hussein of being a "man who gassed his own people," a direct reference to the Halabja events.

Speaking to journalists a few months later, a survivor had the following to say about US policy: "In 1988 they closed their eyes to Halabja because Saddam was the enemy of Iran. But now he's the enemy, and they are using my town as an excuse. We feel bitter, used, sickened."[1] This was a fair point, and it had already merited an investigation. In

August 2002, an exposé in the *New York Times* headlined, "Officers Say U.S. Aided Iraq in War Despite Use of Gas," revealed a "covert American program" that "provided Iraq with critical planning assistance at a time when American intelligence agencies knew that Iraqi commanders would employ chemical weapons in waging the decisive battles of the Iran–Iraq war."[2] The writer, the *Times*' Washington bureau chief Patrick Tyler, produced a former senior military intelligence officer, Col. Walter "Pat" Lang of the Defense Intelligence Agency (DIA), who, without disclosing the classified details, justified the program by saying that the US intelligence community was "desperate to make sure" Iraq would not be defeated. Lang declared that the DIA "would have never accepted the use of chemical weapons against civilians." Yet Iraq repeatedly gassed civilians, for well over a year, in a manner known to the DIA, and at least once in full view of the world.

Tyler also quoted Colin Powell and Richard Armitage, both senior Reagan administration officials (and in 2002 secretary of state and his deputy, respectively), as denying the charge that Washington had been complicit in Iraq's use of gas, while quoting former Pentagon chief Frank L. Carlucci as declaring: "I did agree that Iraq should not lose the war, but I certainly had no foreknowledge of their use of chemical weapons" – this, four years after the US first publicly condemned Iraq's use of gas. Armitage, Tyler writes, even went so far as to use "an expletive relayed through a spokesman to indicate his denial that the United States acquiesced in the use of chemical weapons."

Tyler had been covering the story for some time. In March 1988, when he was still working for the *Washington Post*, Tyler was one of the first journalists to visit Halabja. He described finding "more than 100" bodies of civilians, "victims of what Iran alleges is the worst chemical-warfare attack on civilians in more than seven years of the Gulf War." While giving considerable credence to the Iranian claim of Iraqi culpability, Tyler suggested that, "any independent verification . . . would have to examine the question of why Iraqi forces employed such weapons on the civilian population of Halabja after the battle for the city was over."[3]

Two years later, in April 1990, Saddam Hussein made disquieting threats that he would counter any Israeli attack with a chemical response, and stepped up pressure on Kuwait, one of his main wartime creditors. Soon afterward the *Washington Post* ran another story under Tyler's byline in which he described a freshly completed, classified US Defense Department "reconstruction of the final stages of the Iran–Iraq war."[4] The study presented what he quoted unnamed Pentagon analysts as saying was "conclusive intelligence" that the massacre of civilians in Halabja "was caused by repeated chemical bombardments from both belligerent armies." The original allegation, Tyler said, stemmed from Pentagon sources at the time of the attack, but "the details in support of this claim have only emerged with completion of the internal Pentagon study." Tyler was unable to draw the authors out on their sources, but, he noted, they were confident of their findings. The findings were, in Tyler's words:

- "An indeterminate number of Iranian chemical bombs or shells were dropped on Halabja."
- "Iran may have been the first to fire artillery shells filled with deadly cyanide gas into Halabja when Iranian commanders mistakenly believed Iraqi forces were occupying the city."
- Presumed sources for the classified study included "intercepts of battlefield communications as well as accounts from participants and witnesses that reached western intelligence agencies."
- "Kurdish guerrillas infiltrated Halabja on the 16th and prepared for their Iranian allies to enter Halabja the next day. While Iranian commanders reported that the Iraqis were using chemical weapons against the city, Kurdish guerrilla leaders in Halabja determined that they were being fired upon with chemical ordnance from Iranian positions to their east as well as from Iraqi positions to the west."
- "Foreign journalists [supposedly including Tyler himself] and medical teams that visited Halabja the next week saw evidence of many cyanide deaths (blue lips) among the estimated 100 to 200 corpses."
- "Iran's assertion. . . . that many of the Halabja victims died from cyanide poisoning was considered a key piece of evidence" implicating Iran, because US intelligence knew Iran to be using cyanide, and not Iraq.

The 1990 Pentagon after-action report was produced by two analysts at the US Army War College, one of whom, Stephen Pelletière, was a former CIA analyst who had left the agency a few months before the Halabja events. More than anyone else, Pelletière has pressed the claim that Iran was partly responsible for the Halabja gas attack, reaching even the opinion pages of the *New York Times* in the run-up to the 2003 Iraq war.[5] In the study's unclassified version, Pelletière and co-author Doug Johnson even asserted (citing no sources) that "the Iranians perpetrated this attack."[6]

The arguments in Tyler's article and Pelletière's co-authored study closely mirror the contents of a declassified DIA document of October 1988.[7] A background briefing for policy makers, the document presents a thumbnail review of Kurdish history that is laced with errors. More importantly, it advances the argument that "in the fighting for Halabjah and some nearby villages, Iraq and Iran used poison gas. According to special intelligence, at least some of the Kurdish civilian gas casualties observed by the foreign press were caused by Iranian gas attacks. Kurdish military units complained of being gassed by both sides." As head of the DIA's Middle East section in October 1988, Pat Lang signed off on the briefing and therefore likely is the original source of the Iran gassing charge.

The gist of the Tyler piece, the War College study it quotes, and the Lang memo on which the Halabja charge is based, is that in the fog of war Iran fired chemical shells (or bombs), including some containing deadly cyanide gas, in the mistaken belief that Iraqi forces were inside the town, thus contributing to the many civilian deaths that occurred. The analysis is based on three sources: intercepted communications, Kurdish guerrilla leaders or military units on the scene, and an expert finding that the incidence of blue lips suggested the use of cyanide, and that this in turn proved an Iranian hand. These claims all deserve to be scrutinized in full, not just to set the historical record straight, but because if these views prevailed inside the Reagan administration, they fed directly into the US government's policy vis-à-vis the war as the conflict entered its end stages.

Intercepts and Informants

Intercepted battlefield communications, the first source of evidence on Halabja, are a type of signals intelligence, or "sigint." An attempt to pursue records of battlefield intercepts is almost futile; the US agency that harvests, analyzes, and stores communications records is the National Security Agency (NSA), considered one of Washington's most secretive. The very notion that the NSA would pick up information on chemical attacks from the Mesopotamian battlefield is challenged by those familiar with both intercept technology and Iraqi and Iranian countercapabilities. Lt. Col. Rick Francona, who was Pat Lang's deputy at the DIA in 1988 and worked at the NSA before that, explained (interview, 2000) that the Iraqis were more vulnerable to the interception of noncommunicating emissions, that is, electronic intelligence ("elint"), another type of sigint. For example, Francona said, Iranian electronic intercept units would pick up radar emissions from Iraqi artillery batteries (a noncommunicating emission) and pass this information electronically to headquarters. The US, with its superior technology, would intercept these communications and thus pinpoint Iraqi artillery.

These interceptions would yield no information about a chemical attack, however. And the Iraqis were very well protected against a breach of the other type of sigint – communications intelligence, or "comint," Francona said. This would include orders given by radio, for example, concerning chemical attacks. But the Iraqis did not have to use radios to communicate orders for chemical attacks. They could use landlines or fiber optics instead, both non-emanating systems. Or if they did use their radios, they could encrypt messages or use code. Said another former intelligence officer (interview, 2006): "Were there indications of the chemical attacks against the Kurds? I don't recall, but it is certainly possible. We had the capability to [intercept them], but the Iraqis would never have stated it in the clear."

On the other hand, Yaser al-Gailani, the pilot who defected in the 1990s, recalled (interview, 2000) that the Iraqis were so confident of their air superiority that they became lax in their in-air communications: "One of the mistakes we made is that we spoke too much on the RT [the wireless radio–telephone]," so much so that the Iranians "really benefited from our conversations," he said. At the same time, Gailani noted that because the issue of chemical weapons use was top secret, pilots would have been unlikely to discuss it during missions, and he averred he certainly never had. Furthermore, he argued, "Most pilots – no, all of them – were unhappy about using chemical weapons. But they were under orders, and they were *afraid* to discuss it."

Some Kurdish guerrillas disagree. Several local commanders indicated (interviews for HRW, 1992–1993) that they had been able to listen in on Iraqi pilot conversations, using commercially available scanners, and that on numerous occasions they realized that the aircraft overhead were on a chemical mission. One PUK peshmerga, Heresh Baban, recalled the following incident near the town of Koysanjaq in the spring of 1987 (interview, 2002): "There were sixteen jets crossing over us. On our FM radios we overheard the pilots talking about using 'special' weapons and then they gave a code number in English. I didn't know what this meant. Later I learned that the planes had attacked the Khoshnawati area with chemical weapons." If the story is true, what the peshmerga witnessed were planes readying for the chemical attack on Balisan and Sheikh Wasanan (see Chapter 4).

Intercepting Iranian communications apparently was more difficult. Iranian pilots exercised what Gailani referred to as "*al-samt 'ala silki*" – almost absolute silence on the wireless. Because of this, chances of intercepting communications on putative Iranian gas attacks were minimal. More damningly, in relation to the Halabja attack, Francona said (e-mail communication, 2006):

> It is true that at the time, we thought that the Iranians had also used chemical munitions at Halabjah, delivered by artillery. . . . If, that's a big IF, the Iranian communications indicated they were going to fire chemical rounds, it is POSSIBLE that the US SIGINT System would have intercepted it, but . . . my office would have known about it and [I] cannot recall that we ever got that definitive information. It isn't something I'd likely forget.

In short, evidence of chemical warfare derived from intercepted communications during the Iran–Iraq war would, by virtue of the habits of Iraqi versus Iranian pilots, almost certainly implicate the Iraqis, not the Iranians, even if the latter were dropping chemical munitions. But if it was the Iranians, then at least one former DIA officer has disavowed knowledge of it, and Francona in particular questioned the Pelletière–Johnson study's accuracy in his e-mail message.

A second source of evidence is the testimonies of "Kurdish guerrilla leaders in Halabja." Today, there are no Iraqi Kurdish guerrilla leaders who claim that Iran played a chemical role in Halabja. In 1988–1990,

any such testimony could only have come from imprisoned commanders, as no peshmergas strolled freely through Iraqi streets ready to be
interviewed by US intelligence agents. If one assumes, however, that
the witnesses were not guerrilla leaders but other Kurds in Halabja,
one could consider three possibilities. The first is that not peshmergas
but local civilians claimed there was an Iranian role. This would be
easy to prove, because the fact is that some of civilians did claim that,
because Kurds knew the consequences of defying the cardinal rule to
only parrot the government line when asked about chemical attacks.
Jamal Aziz Amin, a government-employed teacher doubling as a PUK
underground leader in Suleimaniyeh in the 1980s, recalled (interview,
1999) that people were expressly prohibited from discussing chemical
attacks on pain of severe punishment. Victims of such attacks not only
had to remain silent about what had caused their injuries – "many were
killed because they told people close to them" – they also were denied
the medical care they so desperately needed.

Dr. Latif Amin, head of the Suleimaniyeh Health Department
responsible for all local hospitals in the 1980s, said (interview, 2002)
that when victims of the Balisan and Sheikh Wasanan attacks found
their way to Suleimaniyeh, he remembered thinking: "We thought it
was Iran. This was the first time and we didn't think the Iraqi regime
would do this." However, after the injured arrived, "we received explicit
instructions from Sheikh Ja'far Barzinji, Suleimaniyeh's governor, not
to treat the people arriving from Balisan. He told me three times that if
we did anyway, I would be killed on orders of Ali Hassan al-Majid. We
then realized that it was Iraq that had carried out the attack."

He said he suggested to doctors that they send patients to their relatives' homes and see them only for daily checkups – in other words,
to turn them into outpatients. There were children among them, he
said:

> These we kept, changing their case sheets to suggest they suffered from
> various other ailments. It was a dangerous decision and a big risk to
> me. But as doctors we could not discharge these patients. At the teach-
> ing hospital we worked side-by-side with military doctors who were
> Arabs. When intelligence investigators came from Baghdad, we told
> them these were victims of environmental poisoning, and our Arab
> colleagues said exactly the same thing. Doctors are doctors!

After Halabja, rather than being forced to remain silent, civilians were instead paraded in front of foreign journalists to declare that it was Iran that had gassed the Kurds. This emerges from Iraq's own secret police files: A police report from January 1989, for example, mentions a French TV team's visit to investigate the Halabja attack. Halabja residents in Suleimaniyeh told them how the Iranians had attacked the town with chemical weapons.[8] After 1991, however, and freed from the yoke of Iraqi control, no Iraqi Kurd has ever again claimed that Iran gassed Halabja. Instead they have stated unequivocally that it was Iraq, and only Iraq.

There is a second possibility: Perhaps the Kurdish guerrilla leaders were not peshmergas but pro-regime militia (jahsh) commanders. The jahsh were split into two parts during the Iranian–peshmerga assault on Halabja. Top commanders – those who had invested in the regime the most and had benefited accordingly – fled with retreating Iraqi forces. They were not in Halabja when the chemical attack occurred, and so could not have offered eyewitness testimony. Other commanders and many of the rank and file switched sides, joining the guerrillas when they defeated the Iraqis. Once the chemical attack started, they fled to Iran with other Halabjans. Many likely returned after the regime announced a general amnesty "for all Iraqi Kurds" in September 1988, rejoining their families in resettlement complexes across Sirwan lake and elsewhere. If they were "interviewed" by Iraqi or US intelligence agents, their testimonies would have the same credibility as those of other Kurds living under government control: none.

A third possibility is the most interesting. What if the guerrilla leaders were not Iraqi but *Iranian* Kurds? There were indeed KDP-Iran and Komala fighters in the mountains above Halabja in March 1988, protected by the Iraqi regime. If they were not the primary reason for the Iranian invasion, they surely were one of its primary targets. Once Iranian troops entered Iraq, a special force made straight for these two groups. But the PUK, which maintained good relations with at least the KDP-I, had alerted both parties to the coming invasion in an effort to nudge them out of the way. On this, all PUK commanders agree. Shawqat Haji Mushir, for example, said (interview, 2002) that he tried to persuade his KDP-I friends, headquartered near PUK fighters in Hawar and Daratu villages, to leave: "I had four meetings with them.

I could not reveal the impending operation. All I could tell them was that Iraq was planning to destroy Halabja, so there would be fighting. They didn't trust us and were, moreover, under Iraqi pressure to stay." The Komala fighters, no friends of the PUK, were in Biyara. Shawqat said he sent them a warning nonetheless that trouble was coming their way.

In any event, neither party heeded the warning. The PUK left the Komala group to its own devices. The Iranians attacked the band of fewer than a hundred fighters, sending them fleeing down the mountains to the edge of Sirwan lake, near the (destroyed) village of Imam Zamen. They remained there for three days, cowering in the tall grass and waiting for Iraqi reinforcements. Before help could arrive, an Iranian patrol decimated the small group. Just one young female peshmerga survived, injured. Shawqat said he found her a doctor, changed her into civilian dress, and later returned her safely to the Komala's main force above Qala Dizeh on the Iraqi side of the border.

The PUK was more generous toward the KDP-I, and Shawqat blamed his role in their rescue for the subsequent dent in his relationship with the Iranians. The Iranian Kurds fought their attackers for two days, losing only three men, and then withdrew toward Khurmal. From there, a small PUK band shepherded the fighters and their families on a perilous journey – traveling at night for three days – along the ridges, around newly established Iranian posts, and across the front line near the town of Sayed Sadeq. This was difficult terrain, saturated with mines. Because the PUK peshmergas had not been in the area for some years, they did not know where the danger lurked. In any event, three KDP-I fighters were injured by mines as they retreated. Before they crossed over to the Iraqi side, they radioed their headquarters in Boleh on Qandil mountain to ask their leaders to tell Iraqi commanders in Sayed Sadeq to hold their fire as they passed.

It is possible that the KDP-I told their Iraqi friends, or the Americans, that Iran had also used chemical weapons in Halabja. The Defense Intelligence Agency maintained a healthy working relationship with Iraq's Military Intelligence Directorate that supported the Iranian opposition. US diplomats in Baghdad also enjoyed excellent access to these groups, often meeting with their political representatives. An embassy political officer, for example, visited an "Iranian Kurdish official" at the

KDP-I Baghdad office in April 1988, according to a declassified cable from which the Kurd's name was redacted. They discussed the Halabja events but the official, according to the US diplomat, "had no evidence to substantiate claims of Iranian use of chemical weapons." This is highly significant, because the official's finding was a virtual statement against interest. After all (as the political officer added in a post-meeting assessment), the KDP-I had "a highly jaundiced view of Iran."[9] If anyone was ready to seize an opportunity to accuse the Iranians, it was these opposition parties. Yet they failed to do so now, just as the Americans were alleging an Iranian role in the Halabja gassing.

Today there is at least one former KDP-I commander who does claim that Iran used gas in the Halabja area. Now living in exile, in March 1988 he was with the small force that was rescued by the PUK. He claimed (e-mail communication, 2002) to have witnessed an Iranian air attack against Iraqi positions near Khurmal and Dojeileh/Sirwan on March 16, both towns that Iraqi Kurds say were hit in the general Iraqi chemical barrage that day. The commander readily agreed that the chemical attack on Halabja itself, which he and his men observed from Shinirweh mountain, was the Iraqis' handiwork. But, he said, later that same day two Iranian planes came and bombed Khurmal and Dojeileh with chemical weapons, hitting "civilians, Iraqi forces, and animals." They came from the direction of Iran and they were not fired at by Iranian troops. Afterward, once the KDP-I fighters had safely reached the Iraqi side, "we reported [to party leaders] that Iranian planes had also bombed Iraqi bases and killed civilians [with chemical weapons], but they refused to hear it and suggested that we not mention it because no one would believe us, because everyone was focusing on the bombing of Halabja by Iraq."

It is conceivable that these KDP-I fighters, having reached their Iraqi safe haven, became the source of the claim that Iran, too, had attacked the area with chemicals. But the exiled commander's testimony is flatly contradicted by several other officers. For example, Hashemi Karimi, a KDP-I commander now living in London (interview, 2003) who readily alleged a separate Iranian chemical attack elsewhere (see Chapter 7), categorically denied that Iranian planes had used gas in the general area of Halabja: "Iran did not use chemical weapons in Halabja.

Whoever said this is wrong. Iran is our enemy, but this is wrong." More-over, the sighting of Iranian planes around Halabja is discounted by a former senior Kurdish advisor to Saddam Hussein, Mukarram Talabani, who stressed (interview, 2003) that in 1988 Iranian aircraft were "not able to reach Iraqi territory" because of Iraqi air superiority. An Iraqi fighter pilot who used to fly reconnaissance missions in the border zone stated likewise (interview, 2003): "Theoretically, an Iranian plane could have been in the Halabja area on March 16, but if I had to bet on it, I'd bet against it." A survivor of the chemical attack on Khurmal did recall (interview, 2005) having seen a couple of Iranian planes peeping over the distant mountain, but he said they were chased away by Iraqi fighter planes, and, he added, they certainly did not use chemical weapons in or around Halabja.

Perhaps most importantly, whomever the Pentagon relied upon among "Kurdish guerrilla leaders in Halabja" for evidence of Iranian culpability in its supposedly definitive reconstruction of the battle, it could not have been the KDP-I commander in Halabja. The study's authors, according to the *Washington Post*, said their sources had been inside Halabja at the time of the Iranian gas attack (not in the hills above it), that the fire was directed at Halabja (rather than at Khurmal and Sirwan/Dojeileh), and that their sources themselves had been fired upon (rather than witnessing the attack from afar) by chemical ordnance from Iranian artillery positions, not with bombs dropped from the air.

Blue Lips versus Red Lips

What about the third basis for the Pentagon's claim that Iran was at least partly to blame for the Halabja deaths by gassing? It relates to the observation by foreign journalists and medical experts touring Halabja in the attack's aftermath that the dead displayed a distinct blue dis-coloration in their extremities, especially their lips and fingertips. The Pentagon interpreted this phenomenon as indicative of cyanide poison-ing. In turn, the Pentagon contended, this finding proved that Iran was the primary culprit, because Iran was known to have used cyanide gas and Iraq was not.

The only truly verifiable element of this claim is that some of the corpses did indeed exhibit a bluish hue. The rest of the claim must be characterized as conjecture based on poor science, or worse.

Early reports from Halabja indeed suggested that the Iraqis had dropped cyanide on the town. Iran's press agency affirmed this, without detail, on March 21.[10] The press agency's probable source was the Iranian frontline military doctor, Abbas Foroutan, who was present in Halabja, where the *Guardian* quoted him as saying that the tableau of instantaneous death indicated cyanide.[11] Foroutan's diagnosis was soon endorsed by Jacques de Milliano and Réginald Moreels, two Western doctors – heads of, respectively, the Dutch and Belgian sections of the nongovernmental organization Médecins sans Frontières (MSF) – who had jumped on an Iran-bound plane immediately after learning of the attack. At a press conference in Tehran on March 26, having returned from a lightning visit to the blighted town, they described some of their clinical findings: "blue faces (cheeks), blue fingers and toe nails, and blisters on the skin of some children." This, and the fact that people appeared to have died instantly, led the doctors to conclude that "a very toxic and fast killing chemical gas" had been used. Moreover, they said, "also taking into consideration the specific features we can conclude with a very high degree of probability that the agent was cyanide." They also found evidence of mustard gas in victims with blisters.[12]

The two doctors carried back samples of body tissue, as well as a dead bird, and transferred these to Aubin Heyndrickx, head of the University of Ghent's toxicology department in Belgium. Heyndrickx, who had been monitoring chemical use in the Iran–Iraq war for several years, is a controversial figure in the scientific community. His findings (which found some support in the US government) of mycotoxin ("yellow rain") poisoning by the Soviets in Cambodia have been dismissed by prominent independent scientists.[13] His conclusions about chemical weapons use in Angola in the 1980s have similarly been rejected as "scientifically unsound."[14] Nor has his assessment that Iraq used the biological agent aflatoxin (a family of mycotoxins) against Iranian troops in the battle over the Majnoun islands in March 1984 been corroborated by his peers.[15]

In April 1988, three weeks after the Halabja attack, Heyndrickx personally visited what had become a ghost town: "We arrived in a completely devastated and dead city," he reported. "Nothing was alive any more." He ascribed the sudden deaths to cyanide, an assessment he said was supported by the blueness of the faces and fingernails in photographs of the dead.[16] He collected more samples in Halabja for analysis – water from an open container, bomb shrapnel, stones found at the site of a bomb's impact, a rag, burned brushwood, a woman's hair. Two weeks later, he produced a report in which he declared that the Halabja victims had died from a cocktail of gases, including mustard gas and cyanide, nerve agents such as tabun, sarin, and soman, and possibly even phosgene and mycotoxins.[17]

The cyanide claim resonated in Washington. As Rick Francona, the DIA's liaison with Iraqi Military Intelligence in 1988, recalled (interview, 2000):

> We gathered as much of the photographic evidence that we could, from private Kurdish as well as official Iranian sources. From the pictures we saw, the US chemical warfare experts (these would be from Ft Detrick and Aberdeen Proving Grounds) drew the conclusion that some of the casualties exhibited symptoms of hydrogen cyanide poisoning – a capability we ascribed to Iran and not to Iraq.... The experts from Ft Detrick cited the appearance of the victims and concluded hydrogen cyanide poisoning – and ruled out nerve gas or mustard in some of the victims.[18] ... We did not credit Iraq with hydrogen cyanide in their arsenal. Bottom line was that most of us at the Pentagon believed that both sides employed some sort of CW at Halabjah.

The Pentagon has never supplied conclusive proof for the cyanide claim, nor for the accusation that Iran had used this type of gas previously. The UN medical expert who carried out the Halabja investigation diagnosed hospitalized patients as victims of mustard gas and an unidentified nerve agent. Concerning cyanide, he said he was "unable to obtain any definitive information about the [reported] use of hydrocyanic gas as an aggressive chemical."[19]

Moreover, the suggestion that blue extremities point to death by cyanide has been challenged by experts. A bluish discoloration of the skin and extremities of cadavers – lips and fingertips, in particular – is called "cyanosis" (from the Greek *kyanosis*, dark blue), a condition caused by lack of oxygen in the blood. Apart from a shared etymological origin, there is no direct relationship between cyanosis and cyanide. Blueness may be an indicator of cyanide, but according to experts it could just as easily suggest the use of a nerve agent. "Cyanosis in the peripheries," Dr. Alastair Hay, a professor of environmental toxicology at the University of Leeds, wrote in an e-mail (2002), "is simply caused by poor oxygen perfusion. So if your heart, or your lungs, are not working properly you can become cyanosed. It is not diagnostic of cyanide poisoning. Nerve agents could affect heart function resulting in cyanosis."

Dr. Frederick Sidell, a former chief of the Chemical Casualty Care Office of the US Army Medical Research Institute of Chemical Defense at Aberdeen Proving Ground in Maryland, concurred. When asked what pictures of dead people with blue lips suggested to him, he responded (interview, 2000), "It would only indicate they are dead. You can't tell anything from blue lips. Somebody with a heart attack might have blue lips. Nerve gas also causes blue lips, because it blocks the lungs and airways, and thereby the oxygen supply, a condition called cyanosis." Could cyanide gas cause blue lips? Cyanide, he said, "normally would cause *reddish* skin and *reddish* lips – cherry red, in fact. But not in all cases."

What is more, Dr. Sidell, like other chemical warfare experts, scoffed at the notion that the type of gas could be gleaned from photographs, insisting: "Photographs are a poor way of determining the cause of death." Aubin Heyndrickx disagreed: "Visual identification from color photographs and the position of the corpses are highly indicative of the type of gas used," he asserted (interview, 2003).

If the cyanosis that occurred in the Halabja victims indicated nerve gas rather than cyanide, the obvious culprit in the gassing would be Iraq, which had repeatedly used nerve agents, and not Iran, which had not been so accused. In the end, though, the victims' discoloration in death is a false issue. Even the proven presence of cyanide gas in Halabja would not necessarily implicate Iran. For one thing, Iraq had been accused of cyanide gas use in earlier battles – allegations that remain unconfirmed. By that logic, Iraq could also be implicated in any Halabja deaths by cyanide.

Abbas Foroutan documented a number of what he initially determined to be Iraqi cyanide gas attacks, first in Iran's 1985 Badr offensive, when he observed the effects of a fast-killing gas unlike anything he had seen. The next year, when Iran captured Faw, he reported that a patient in coma had recovered with administration of amyl nitrite, a serum typically used for the treatment of cyanide poisoning. When he saw more such patients during offensives in the southern marshes in late 1986 and early 1987, Foroutan declared: "Proving cyanide poisoning in a war zone is a very difficult task since due to this agent's very quick evaporation, diagnostic kits cannot detect it. But from a clinical perspective during the war we saw typical cyanide patients several but limited times."[20] This finding was embraced by the Iranians, who began adding amyl nitrite to their forces' standard kit. Fighters belonging to the Iraqi opposition group SCIRI, for example, reported (interview, 2002) that in the battle for Shakh Shemiran overlooking Darbandikhan dam three days after the Halabja events, they protected themselves against a chemical attack by helicopter late one evening by donning their gas masks and self-administering both atropine and amyl nitrite.

The UN experts, however, dismissed the cyanide claim. The unnamed Iranian doctor who made the claim (the experts said in their 1987 report) "based his opinion on the absence of miosis [contraction of the pupils] and successful treatment with the inhalation of amyl nitrite and the injection of thio-sulphate. From our observation we cannot affirm that this gas was used; indeed, its use could have been medically proven only at the time of the attack itself."[21]

Evidence of cyanide would not automatically implicate Iran for a second reason: cyanide is one of tabun's essential ingredients; tabun cannot be produced without cyanide; Iraq therefore must have had cyanide, the Pentagon's reasoning notwithstanding. "It is preposterous to argue that Iraq did not have cyanide," said chemical weapons expert Gordon Burck (interview, 2000). "They built a plant in the early 1970s that could produce it. And besides, it is a very common chemical. Sodium cyanide is a standard chemical in the cleaning of swimming pools."

Because of its connection to tabun, if hydrocyanide is found in a given environment, it could be either the residual effect of poorly manufactured tabun or a breakdown element when tabun decomposes. The UN experts noted this in their 1986 report.[22] In the face of continuing allegations in 1988 they decided to elaborate: "Whenever allegations have been made about the use of hydrocyanic gas, organophosphorous agents [such as tabun] have always been used at the same time, and it is possible that the tabun, which has a molecule containing the CN group, decomposed when the shell exploded, causing characteristic hydrocyanic effects."[23] A CIA report on chemical weapons use in the Iran–Iraq war similarly noted: "Decontamination of tabun can lead to liberation of dangerous cyanide compounds."[24] Whether cyanide thus released could give rise to the types of symptom observed in Halabja is a matter of dispute. The UN experts apparently thought it possible. Experts such as Dr. Sidell disagree: Because there is only a relatively minor amount of cyanide present in tabun, no symptoms associated with cyanide would occur if tabun were used, he said.

The claim, finally, that the DIA showed the photographs of the Halabja dead to chemical warfare specialists at Aberdeen is also challenged by Dr. Sidell, who headed the Chemical Casualty Care Office at that facility in 1988. "I think I would have known if anyone at Aberdeen would have made a different assessment of blue lips [than mine]," he asserted. "So far as I know, Aberdeen did not make that assessment."

Was cyanide used in Halabja? Probably not. Even if it possessed cyanide gas, it is very unlikely that Iran had been able to weaponize the gas and had developed the capability to deliver it effectively on the battlefield. Hydrogen cyanide, said Seth Carus, a chemical weapons expert at the National Defense University in Washington, DC (interview, 2000), is "extremely difficult to use. First of all, it is lighter than air, so it is very difficult to achieve concentrations that are toxic. Secondly, it is an agent that the body detoxifies; it kills only in sufficient concentrations." During World War II, the US military tried to solve the technical difficulties, seeking to find ways of delivering the gas not in artillery shells, but in bombs dropped from planes so as to obtain volume and broad dispersal, but this effort failed – and in any event, no chemical weapons were used during the war. "The notion," said Carus, "that the Iranians would have solved technical problems that the US military was not able to, and in the early stages of a CW program, I find highly implausible." As for possible cyanide gas use by Iraq, Carus contended that UNSCOM, when it dismantled Iraq's vast chemical arsenal in the 1990s, did not find cyanide-based weapons. The implication is, therefore, that Iraq did not use such weapons either. There must therefore be an alternative explanation for the symptoms the Iranian and foreign doctors observed in Halabja.

The most likely explanation is that doctors on the scene mistook the symptoms for those resulting from sarin, a newly deployed nerve agent with which they were not yet familiar. Like cyanide gas, sarin is highly volatile and kills almost instantaneously (depending on the intake dose), then dissipates rapidly. Iraq possessed sarin (UNSCOM identified and destroyed Iraqi stocks) and used it during the war, including against the Kurds. Sarin was found in soil samples taken from a bomb crater in northern Iraq in 1992 that resulted from an incident local villagers said occurred on August 25, 1988, the first day of the Final Anfal.[25] No one, not even the Pentagon, has come near to suggesting that Iran had the capability to produce and use sarin on the battlefield in 1988.

In the years following the Halabja attack, Dr. Foroutan revised his earlier assessment, saying that the symptoms he observed could also have been caused by a fast–acting nerve agent.[26] By 2002, he had ruled out cyanide altogether. The Halabja victims, he asserted in an interview, were probably "fulminant sarin cases" – victims of a gas that caused sudden and severe symptoms. The two MSF doctors also became less certain over time. Jacques de Milliano recalled some of his Halabja observations (telephone interview, 2000): " . . . Then we saw cyanide victims. They had blue lips. There was, for example, a school bus with children. . . . " He stopped suddenly, then retracted what he had just said. "Cyanide causes red lips. Blue lips indicate that these people had suffocated." In any event, he said, these were cases of "instant death, for example a man who was frozen in the position of shaving. Instant death suggests the use of cyanide." Réginald Moreels went further (interview, 2001): "Cyanide paralyses breathing. Death follows in 60–90 seconds. The victim does not even have time to turn blue (cyanotic). These people were *not* blue. This was very striking. They were red under the nails and had red cheeks – totally different from the death color." But now, having matched the color red with cyanide, in direct contradiction to his recorded observations at the time ("blue faces (cheeks), blue fingers and toe nails"), he departed from the cyanide theory: "It could also have been nerve gas," he offered. He attributed the cyanide diagnosis to Aubin Heyndrickx.

Dr. Heyndrickx lives in retirement in Ghent, his living room decorated as a small museum. The large medical trunk that he used to lug around the world in pursuit of chemical and biological weapons takes pride of place. A kindly man, he appeared prone to memory lapses as he described, in impossible chronological order, some of his trips to Iran, scrambling incidents deriving from different events (interview, 2003). But on key claims he was unequivocal. Iraq used a cocktail of gases, one aggravating the effects of the others: cyanosis – blueness – was indicative of cyanide, while redness suggested mycotoxins. Iraq had used mycotoxins first, before switching to cyanide gas to accelerate the immediacy of death. Hemo-perfusion, a controversial procedure involving the "washing" of the blood (much like the work performed by one's kidneys), was an effective treatment of critical cases affected by mycotoxins.

Today Heyndrickx stands alone in all of these views. Independent scientists who tried to replicate his laboratory findings have come up empty handed. Dr. Jan Willems, a military doctor and pharmacologist also living in Ghent, devoted a major empirical study to defeating Heyndrickx's views after he was confronted by what he termed (interview, 2003) "fantastical diagnoses and fantastical treatment" (hemo-perfusion). He concluded after an extensive study of Iranian chemical warfare casualties in Europe in 1985 that these were all mustard gas victims; that there was no evidence of either nerve agents or mycotoxins; and that hemo-perfusion was a medical procedure "without therapeutic effect," but one that "produced several side effects...that should be avoided in these immunocompromised patients"[27] Dr. Heyndrickx, he said, is an example of how bad science can lead to faulty conclusions, which then go on to inform policy decisions.

Inside the Pentagon

Available evidence suggests that Aubin Heyndrickx and the Iranian doctors he influenced were the original source for the cyanide-in-Halabja claim, just as he was of the aflatoxin and cyanide allegations from the mid-1980s onward. As the only Western doctor to make frequent visits to Iran during the war, he was welcomed with open arms by the Iranians who felt shut out by the international community. By default, they valued his expert opinion like none other. "They carried him on their hands," a colleague said.

In March 1988, the DIA seized upon the cyanide allegation (having ignored it until then despite Heyndrickx's efforts to broadcast it) as evidence that Iran was partially to blame for the Halabja atrocity. In a March 23 assessment that State Department spokesperson Charles Redman may have used as a basis for his claim that "Iran may also have used chemical artillery shells in this fighting" (see Introduction), the DIA asserted that "most of the casualties in Halabja were reportedly caused by cyan[o]gen chloride. This agent has never been used by Iraq, but Iran has shown interest in it."[28]

Today, those who used the cyanide claim to accuse Iran hide behind unnamed US military chemical warfare specialists. Without a smoking-gun document or declaration against interest by one of the specialists, disinformation cannot be proven; the experts may have been victims of bad science themselves. But this begs the question: If this is true, why was bad science allowed to contaminate dispassionate analysis of events during the Iran–Iraq war? Why were DIA officials so eager to embrace the "it-was-cyanide-and-therefore-it-must-have-been-the-Iranians" line? And how did they get away with it?

The answer, of course, is that the analysis never was dispassionate: Powerful factions inside the Reagan administration, the DIA in particular, were squarely behind the Iraqi war effort, even if many preferred to keep their distance from the Iraqi regime. Information about any event that could thwart or delay an Iraqi victory, or that held the promise of an Iranian one, had to be suppressed. The Halabja tragedy was a debacle for the anti-Iran lobby because it exposed the dirty underside of a policy that otherwise – infused by the notion of strategic necessity – could have been defensible. It also showed that "engagement" was not in any way moderating the Iraqi dictator's behavior. When the Halabja attack happened, the immediate response was to diffuse responsibility for it, primarily to stifle critics within the administration, the very same who had sought an opening to Iran (their distaste for Saddam Hussein's regime exceeding their distrust of the Islamic revolution), but also human rights defenders and those concerned about proliferation. A bureaucratic battle was on, so the pro-Iraq tilters sharpened their knives and did what had to be done.

This battle, having subsided in the Iran–Iraq war's aftermath, briefly flared during the Kuwait invasion ("Who lost Kuwait? Who empowered the Iraqi dictator by coddling him?") and in the run-up to the 1992 presidential elections ("What was George Bush's role in the Reagan administration's pro-Iraq tilt?"), but it has remained dormant since. The pro-tilters may have adjusted their views during a decade of demonizing Saddam Hussein, but with respect to the Halabja claim they remain stoutly persistent and unrepentant. They are retired now from the US Army War College and Defense Intelligence Agency – the perches from which they made the unsubstantiated allegation that, amplified by media exposure, carried so much force at the time.

The two most visible proponents of the Iran/Halabja thesis are Stephen Pelletière and Col. Walter "Pat" Lang. Pelletière is a journalist by training (with a PhD in political science from the University of California, Berkeley) and a CIA analyst by profession who covered Iraq for the agency until the end of 1987, before moving to the Army War College just before Halabja. At the CIA, Pelletière was the odd man out, a "perpetual malcontent," according to Pat Lang, who expressed great respect for his capabilities (telephone interview, 2000): "The CIA, like the State Department, was pro-Kurdish," Lang said, a statement that must come as a surprise to both the Kurds and the CIA. "Pelletière was not." Pelletière showed himself equally enamored of Lang (interview, 2001): "The DIA had the best analysis of the war, much better than the CIA. Pat Lang was the best analyst in the field."

Pelletière contended that it was "common knowledge" in the profession that it was Iran that had used chemical weapons at Halabja, but that the evidence was contained in a classified annex to his co-authored 1990 book, which in turn was based on the secret War College study. The contents of that study were leaked to Patrick Tyler at the *Washington Post* "by someone in the Pentagon," Pelletière surmised, adding that "Pat Lang was talking to Pat Tyler all the time."

The purpose of the War College study was to assess, based on their battlefield performance, how the Iraqis fought and under what circumstances they used gas. This was critically important, as the US military was girding itself to eject Iraqi forces from Kuwait. Pelletière contended that the Iraqis used gas "only when they needed to, in extreme cases, not prodigally or superficially or just because." Pelletière and his co-author Doug Johnson had together visited the DIA to discuss these matters with their counterparts. The DIA's conclusions about Iranian chemical weapons use were correct, Pelletière determined, and Doug Johnson, the team's main military analyst, "signed off on the study." Pelletière acknowledged, however, that the CIA had dissented from the final draft.

A perusal of CIA National Intelligence daily reports from that time shows knowledge of Iranian accusations of Iraqi chemical weapons use, which the writers did not question.[29] They even mention prospective Iraqi gas use as if it were the most normal thing in the world. For example, a report on March 22 stated, referring to the Halabja events:

> Baghdad may have decided that the area lost in Val-Fajr X is not important enough to risk a major counterattack that probably would entail heavy casualties and might not regain much territory. If so, Iraq will probably commit its ground forces only in an effort to stop further Iranian gains and will use its Air Force and chemical weapons to inflict high casualties on Iranian forces.[30]

The original source for Pelletière's claims was Pat Lang, a Vietnam veteran and the Pentagon's chief of intelligence for the Middle East and South Asia from 1985 to 1992, the favored unnamed official whom many journalists relied upon for comment. Lang has held onto his Halabja claim (interview, 2000), while not denying that Iraq repeatedly used chemical weapons elsewhere, including at Faw in April 1988. "The intent of chemical weapons is to incapacitate, not to kill," he argued. As such it is "a tremendous force multiplier," because enemy troops have to don suits in which they can't move. He condemned the use of gas against civilians as a violation of both international humanitarian law and the ancient military code, but asked: "On the battlefield, why is it [chemical weapons use] worse than other weapons?" In Iraq's case, he said, "We didn't know when the Iraqis would use chemical weapons . . . Plus we didn't really want to know it. We didn't want to be complicit."

In Halabja, Lang claimed, Iran used crop dusters to drop chemical gas, rigging tanks to the plane to spray the gas like an aerosol, but admitted that this "was a deduction on our part; we didn't see them." The hard evidence, he said, was classified. Lang did not mention any chemical shells in the interview. In response to the remark that Iran had also been blamed for Halabja, he said: "That's because I insisted on this."

In an earlier interview by telephone Lang explained he had fought a hard bureaucratic battle over this: "Nobody wanted to hear" about Iran's chemical weapons use. "The Israelis played a considerable role in this." When reports of Iranian chemical weapons use and programs came out, "they pooh-poohed them via their allies inside the

US government." He also blamed the pro-Iran lobby ensconced in the US bureaucracy. Pelletière offered similar sentiments about hostile lobbies, and then ended by posing the bottom–line question: "But who defended the Iraqis? I did. Pat Lang did. But nobody else did."

There is no evidence that Lang's view on Halabja prevailed inside the Reagan administration. Indeed, there is every indication, as he himself has ruefully noted, that his perspective was cast aside after Iraq again gassed Kurdish civilians in August 1988. But the interpretation of events he and his colleagues put forward in interdepartmental meetings, via the State Department spokesperson on March 23, and in their own not–for–attribution interviews with journalists in April–May 1988, caused a momentary confusion about precise responsibility for the attack. The effect was heightened by the legitimization that the DIA's imprimatur represented. And so, after an initial US condemnation of Iraqi culpability, these maneuvers diffused pressure for further action. Instead, Washington began to waffle over who had carried out the attack and worked actively to oppose a strong and unambiguous Security Council condemnation of their Iraqi allies.

And thus the Reagan administration could breathe a sigh of relief as it entered the endgame in the Gulf. A month after Halabja the *New York Times* reported, "Western diplomats and the State Department agree that although Iraq was the first to use chemical weapons, starting in 1984, Iran is now retaliating in kind."[31]

Historical revisionism took over: Journalists were reminded of alleged Iranian chemical attacks that had occurred earlier and somehow had escaped notice.[32] The canard entered the literature on the war, and after that even those who had seen no convincing evidence that Iran had used chemical weapons were compelled to concede that it might have. For example, Gary Sick, a noted Iran scholar and an Iran specialist in President Carter's National Security Council, was quoted as saying in the *New York Times* in the summer of 1988 that the Iranians had used chemical shells "very, very seldom."[33] He later explained (e-mail communication, 2000):

In 1988, in the last stages of the war, there were . . . widespread allegations that Iran was using chemical weapons. I was always skeptical of those reports, but there was no very reliable information available to scholars at the time. . . . Subsequently, and based on other information that has become available, my view has solidified much more that Iran probably did not use such weapons.

More ominously, and around the same time, the *Christian Science Monitor* quoted unidentified US officials as stating that the evidence that Iran had used cyanide-filled artillery shells in Halabja "has undermined the propaganda advantage that Iran has tried to gain by publicizing Iraq's [gas] attacks."[34]

While fully appreciative of the need to prevent an Iraqi collapse on the battlefield, to Peter Galbraith (a Senate staffer who had been monitoring events in Iraqi Kurdistan), this cunning deception by the Reagan administration was far beyond the pale. By muddying the waters, Galbraith said (interview, 2000), Washington preempted robust action that might have kept Iraq from proceeding with its murderous counterinsurgency campaign against the Kurds, one in which hundreds of villages had already been destroyed and in which people now were being shipped off to unknown destinations – a campaign that eventually would be labeled genocide. "Being casual with facts," he remarked, "is one thing; you can't call that deliberate misinformation. But so twisting the facts to fit your purposes as the Reagan administration did, *that* is evil."

NINE

THE ROAD TO KUWAIT

"I came to regard Iraq, once again, as one of the enemy states of the responsible world community."
    – US Secretary of State George Shultz, *Turmoil and Triumph*
        (1993), p. 243

"Preventing" Genocide

By August 1988 the war had ended – but not yet the Kurdish rebellion, even though it, too, was on its last legs. The Iraqis needed one more push to recapture the last remaining patch of Kurdish land, on the border with Turkey, before they could cry victory and start rebuilding. However, war's end transformed Baghdad's relationship with the Reagan administration overnight, and with it the rules of the game. The Iraqi leadership did not realize this when, on August 25, it dispatched its air force and army to finish the rebellion in an operation it confidently dubbed the Final Anfal (*Amaliyat Khatimat al-Anfal*). On that day, Iraqi planes dropped chemical bombs on several strings of Kurdish villages in a KDP–controlled area hugging the Turkish border called Badinan.[1] Within days, as terrified villagers poured into Turkey, the world got wind of Iraq's latest outrage, and this time those in Washington who had been ruing their necessary proximity to the Iraqi regime decided that enough was enough.

At first the administration's understanding of the military operation was stunningly off base. For example, it was characterized as the beginning, rather than the end, of Iraq's counterinsurgency. A typical analysis began like this: "As soon as the war with Iran ended, Iraq announced its determination to crush the Kurdish insurrection" (War College analysts), even if Iraq made no such announcement.[2] Or: "After [the] cease-fire Iraq *began major campaign* to crush Kurdish rebellion by depopulating countryside, including CW use, mass deportations/executions" (State Department memo).[3] Or: "The latest campaign was probably Baghdad's *opening gun* in a concerted postwar effort to subdue the Kurds once and for all, while Iraqi forces are at wartime strength" (State Department memo).[4] This cable went on to say:

> Iraq had planned to follow up this operation with a move against the forces of the Talabani Patriotic Union of Kurdistan farther south in the hills of the Sulaymaniyah district. It is not clear if full-scale suppression operations are still planned for this sector or if the "general amnesty" for Kurds Baghdad proclaimed in response to Turkish concern about the influx of Iraqi Kurds has superseded its military plans.[5]

As millions of Iraqis (who had been absorbing news from Iraq's state-controlled media outlets since March) knew well, the Anfal campaign was in its final, not its opening, days. Anyone with access to Iraqi media could have known the same. The US Library of Congress received copies of Iraq's major newspapers, and the CIA's Foreign Broadcast Information Service routinely provided summaries of Iraqi news in English, including about Anfal.

The reason for this profound misinterpretation of Anfal is probably due to a dual bias: One, the administration's reflex association of the Kurdish parties with the Iranian enemy served to obscure the Kurdish rebellion's indigenous agenda and dynamic, as well as deep differences between the rebels and their Iranian allies. Two, Washington was familiar with Mustafa Barzani's 1970s revolt, which the US supported (Barzani died in US exile in 1979), but with very little since. A typical example of this selective reading of developments in Kurdistan was the observation, in a State Department cable, that KDP leader Masoud Barzani was excluded, along with Jalal Talabani, from Iraq's September 6 amnesty that ended Anfal.[6] In fact, Barzani, unlike Talabani, was not named at all in the amnesty decree; he had not even been in Iraq for thirteen years at that point, and his region merited only one of Anfal's eight stages.

Distorted though their understanding of the Kurdish insurgency may have been, some leaders in Washington did not doubt that Iraq had gassed the Kurds once again. The State Department's Bureau of Intelligence and Research averred in a memo dated September 2 that Iraq, its forces freed up thanks to the ceasefire, "appears poised to deal a decisive blow against the dissident portion of the Kurdish population in northern Iraq":

> Baghdad is likely to feel little restraint in using chemical weapons against the rebels and against villagers that continue to support them. In fact, we now have confirming evidence that the Iraqis used chemical weapons against Kurdish insurgents on August 25.[7]

Emboldened by having been allowed to gas at will, the Iraqis were not about to stop while the insurgency still smoldered, even if the war had ended. This may have been a mistake, because with war's end, US strategic interests changed, and Iraqi moves were now being watched with renewed scrutiny. Meanwhile, a barrage of media reporting about Kurdish refugees streaming into Turkey was putting pressure on the administration.

George Shultz sent tough talking points to April Glaspie, the freshly appointed ambassador in Baghdad, saying Iraq's chemical weapons use and deportations were "causing an international outcry," and instructing her to convey Washington's concerns to the Iraqi government:

> We recognize that the situation is complex, with deep historical roots, and that it involves an armed rebellion in which Kurds allied themselves with Iran. . . . We see little to be gained from lecturing the Iraqis – but we do want to make clear to them that we will not be silent in the face of such human rights abuses, and that this will inevitably have an adverse impact on our ability to promote a closer bilateral relationship.[8]

On September 8, the State Department went public, its spokesperson declaring that the US government was "convinced that Iraq has used chemical weapons in its military campaign against Kurdish guerrillas."[9] At once, journalists began asking Iraqi officials pointed questions and requesting access to northern Iraq. A few reporters went, hosted by the Iraqis and closely escorted by intelligence "minders" on a quick and limited visit to Kurdish towns – not the countryside – aboard Iraqi helicopters. Upon their return, some reporters, like Milton Viorst and Patrick Tyler, openly questioned the evidence of gas attacks.[10]

That same day, September 8, George Shultz called in Iraq's minister of state for foreign affairs, Sa'doun Hammadi, and, in his own words, "blasted him."[11] According to meeting notes, he told Hammadi that, "The international outcry following CW use in World War One kept it 'in a box' for a long time. Now it has re-emerged, and must be suppressed." He then contended that Washington had "incontrovertible proof" that Iraq had gassed the Kurds, and warned that "while we would like to see our bilateral relations develop in a constructive way, there is no way that can happen if Iraq continues to use chemical weapons in Kurdistan or anywhere else." When Hammadi emphatically denied the accusation, Shultz extracted a concession that Iraq would not use chemical weapons again.[12]

As a sanctions debate heated up regardless of the Iraqi concession, Foreign Minister Tariq Aziz was forced to make a further concession: he affirmed publicly and unequivocally that Iraq would abide by its international treaty obligations, including the 1925 Geneva Protocol. In turn, Washington declared Aziz's assurance to be "satisfactory" and a "firm and very important pledge."[13] Nonetheless, detecting a loophole, Washington asked Baghdad for a clarification that its pledge also covered the Kurds, as the protocol does not apply to internal armed conflict. Tariq Aziz conceded on October 3, as the sanctions debate raged. He did not, however, admit to Iraq's use of gas[14] and he rejected a US-supported request for a UN investigation as an unacceptable infringement on Iraq's sovereignty.

Here, for the first time, was tough language. The irony is this: Although the Reagan administration displayed increased sensitivity to chemical weapons use now that the war had ended, Iraq's gas attacks in Badinan produced fewer fatalities than in previous Anfal stages, especially the first (Jafati valley), second (Qaradagh), and fourth (the mass deaths at Goktapa/Askar), or the massive gas attack on Balisan valley in April 1987, or of course Halabja. In fact, the apparent absence of actual fatalities from these later attacks, despite an abundance of refugees' reports, led some to claim that they had not occurred at all.

Measured in effectiveness, however, Iraq's chemical weapons use was once again spectacular. As in previous Anfal stages, airplanes dropped chemicals on the operation's first day, targeting KDP command centers and villages alike. Although there were relatively few direct casualties from these attacks – Human Rights Watch estimates at most two dozen[15] – the terror effect was huge. The KDP's resistance collapsed within hours, and in mass panic villagers throughout the region picked up whatever they could carry and ran north toward the Turkish border. As many as 80,000 refugees entered Turkey, though many of them returned the next month after the Iraqi regime announced a thirty-day general amnesty for all Kurds.

The refugee crisis caused problems for Turkey. As a memo from Assistant Secretary of State Richard Murphy put it: "The campaign against civilians – forced relocation of thousands and reported use of chemical weapons – appears to involve serious violations of international human rights standards, and puts our ally Turkey in a difficult position."[16] Turkey was indeed an important ally, and it was apprehensive that Iraq's brutal campaign to settle its Kurdish problem would foment trouble in Turkey's own Kurdish region. Turkey's denial of cultural and linguistic rights to its large Kurdish minority and strong–arm suppression of any manifestations of dissent had triggered a Kurdish rebellion led since 1984 by the Kurdish Workers Party (PKK), a group the State Department had designated as terrorists out of deference to its Turkish ally.

Facing waves of refugees, the Turkish government tried to conceal the truth by denying that Iraq had used chemical weapons. However, in telling the US government it had found "no evidence of Iraqi use of 'lethal' CW in northern Iraqi Kurdistan," Turkey was playing with words. Doctors reported cases of nausea and eye irritation – evidence of gas, if perhaps not lethal gas.[17] Victims of lethal gas could be expected to have died along the way, before reaching the border. Eyewitness testimony and soil samples taken by human rights organizations in following years showed unambiguously that Iraq had used chemical weapons, including the highly lethal nerve agent sarin, and that most of those affected never reached safety.[18]

Turkey also tried to block independent observers' access to the refugees. But it could not prevent visits by US diplomats. One of these was Peter Galbraith, an aide to Senate Foreign Relations Committee Chairman Claiborne Pell. Galbraith had visited Iraq in 1984 and 1987 (see Chapter 4), and had written a damning report about the village destruction campaign. Together with colleague Christopher van Hollen, Galbraith traveled to the border on September 10 to interview Kurdish refugees and collect other evidence of chemical warfare. The report the two wrote, while riddled with the errors and exaggerations that reflected the usual accounts of refugees who had left their homes in chaos and panic, was effective in telling the world that Iraq had once again resorted to gas, but now without an Iranian threat as its excuse.[19] Galbraith promptly received a call from Richard Schifter, the official in charge of the State Department's human rights desk. Iraq, Galbraith recalled Schifter as saying (interview, 2000), fit the designation of "committing a consistent pattern of gross violations of human rights," the standard required for Congress to cut US aid.

Apart from riling those who had human rights concerns, Iraq's chemical attacks (and the phenomenal advances in capability the attacks exhibited) at last set off alarm bells about potential proliferation. "Particularly heavy Iraqi [gas] attacks in recent weeks, and the concomitant flow of refugees/victims into Turkey, has [sic] given what has been standard Iraqi practice increased visibility," said a State Department memo.[20] Now bureaucratic weight was turning against Iraq. The Reagan administration knew it had leverage over the Iraqis, who no longer had their backs against the wall and were desperate for US economic assistance to help rebuild their war-weakened country. But the administration had no interest in taking recriminations too far, as US business interests were at stake.

For two months, Washington was atwitter with talk of sanctions. Would punishing Iraq yield the desired result – a cessation of chemical weapons use? Or would it anger the Iraqis to the point of breaking off relations? Would "raising the cost to Iraq of using CW" (as one State Department official offered) "... make an example of Iraq that could deter other potential users, like Libya, while endowing the U.S. stand with greater credibility"?[21] Should punitive action be linked only to Iraq's gassing of Kurds (reprehensible conduct that responded not to an existential threat, but to a "lesser" one – what one State Department memorandum referred to as "convenience use" where other military means could have done the job)?[22] Or, for the sake of global interests, should the language of US sanctions make reference to international standards and explicitly mention Iraq's use of gas not only against the Kurds (a violation of the Geneva Conventions' Common Article 3, which governs internal armed conflict) but also against Iran?[23] Referring to the sanctions legislation pending before Congress, a State Department memo argued:

> With regard to the Bill's focus, we believe reference should also be made to Iraq's use of chemical weapons in its war with Iran, in violation of the 1925 Protocol. Several UN teams have confirmed this CW use, and the U.S. has repeatedly condemned Iraq by name for illegal use of chemical weapons. By omitting reference to Iraqi CW use in the Iran–Iraq war, the Bill may give the impression that we consider use against Iran of less concern than use against Kurds. Such a distinction does not serve U.S. global interests in raising barriers against CW use, and in reaffirming applicability of the 1925 Geneva Protocol in the Iran–Iraq War. In addition, the Bill should make clear that use of CW against Kurdish civilians is a violation of Common Article 3 of the 1949 Geneva Conventions on Protection of Victims of War.

What kind of action might yield the desired result? Should Washington sever diplomatic relations, recall the US ambassador for consultations, declare the Iraqi ambassador *persona non grata*, lower the level of diplomatic representation? Should the administration agree to meet with Kurdish representatives (thus ending an informal ban on such meetings)? Should Washington again designate Iraq as a country supporting terrorism? Should the US withhold trade, credits, and other economic benefits? Should it embargo imports of Iraqi crude? Should it impose a full arms embargo, including on dual-use goods? And should the US link punitive action only to the use of chemical weapons, or also to the production of chemical and biological weapons? The menu of options included, moreover, multilateral actions: a UN ban on exports of chemical products and equipment to Iraq (and Iran), and expanding the efforts of the Australia Group, a coalition of Western countries seeking to limit trade in precursor chemicals.[24]

On September 9, in a direct slap at Iraq, the Senate adopted the "Prevention of Genocide Act." An identical bill was presented in the House, and if the joint bill had passed both houses it would have banned US exports, credits, credit guarantees, and other forms of assistance, it would have prohibited Iraqi oil imports, and it would have required the US to oppose loans to Iraq from international financial institutions. But the word "genocide" acted as a red flag. That apparent stretching of the available information undermined support for the bill and provided ammunition to its detractors.[25] Galbraith has defended the report's title and thrust as follows (interview, 2000): "We knew of the systematic destruction of Kurdish villages, the targeting of cultural institutions and orchards, chemical weapons attacks against the Kurds, killings (both from chemical weapons and by execution), and refugee flows to Turkey in what appeared to be an act of genocide." Galbraith's assessment, however – sound as it may have been – was made on the basis of indicators that, themselves, did not prove genocide. Real evidence of genocide – the mass killing of Kurds – became available only after 1991, when independent investigators could visit Kurdistan freely. And only in 1995 did the State Department's legal advisor determine that what had happened during Anfal constituted genocide.[26]

On October 21, the bill perished after the administration argued strongly against it and several senators, who had originally supported the bill, changed their minds.[27] The State Department declared that it opposed sanctions "as a general principle"[28] and said it found the bill "too sweeping in content." Instead, officials suggested a nonbinding resolution condemning Iraq.[29] In the end, nothing happened. Galbraith, who rubbed many officials in Washington the wrong way with his somewhat (at least in style) quixotic campaign, later (interview, 2000) declared bitterly: "Something outrageous happened; it's completely unequivocal: The response in Washington was not just to do nothing but to block the efforts by others to do something, arguing that unilateral sanctions do not work."

Here is a second irony: In the fall of 1988, Washington finally condemned Iraq's chemical weapons use, but it did so only after the war had ended. Noticeably livid at this public reprimand, the Iraqis were forced to make a concession. But what kind of concession? By the first week of September, not only the war but the counterinsurgency, too, was over, and no significant military threats loomed on Iraq's horizon. This made chemical weapons use redundant. Still the Reagan administration claimed credit for the cessation. On September 10, after she received assurances that Iraq had not used chemical weapons in the north, and that military operations would be over "in a few days" anyway,[30] Ambassador Glaspie cabled Washington to say that, "Iraq has not used and is not using lethal chemical weapons against Kurds." Further, she said, "the remarkably moderate and mollifying mode of its presentation, leads us to conclude that Saddam Hussein has got the message and put a halt to the use of chemical weapons in Kurdistan."[31] This, however, was a full four days after the amnesty that closed the door on Anfal and more than two weeks after Iraq last used gas. Iraq's promise to Washington, therefore, was cost free.

Moreover, even if the Reagan administration and Congress had opted for more robust action, they could only have prevented future atrocities – not a trifling thing, of course – because if the aim, as Galbraith wanted, was to prevent genocide, their actions came (as did Galbraith's trip to Turkey in early September) only after Anfal had ended and the guns had fallen silent on the regime's killing fields.

A Transcendent Interest

In hindsight, what is most astonishing is that Iraq got away with nothing more than a humbling pledge that it would desist from further chemical weapons use. To understand this, we must view the sanctions debate in the context of the pro-Iraq tilt.

First of all, how did George Shultz himself see things? Writing in the early 1990s, well after Iraq's invasion of Kuwait that shook Washington and pitched the pro-Iraq tilt out of the window, Shultz said he recalled that, "There had been a period of twelve to eighteen months in the mid-1980s when I, and American foreign policy, gave the benefit of the doubt to the Iraqi regime of Saddam Hussein." Soon it became clear, however, that the regime was not reforming as Shultz had hoped:

> When Abu Abbas was allowed to leave Italy in October 1985 following the hijacking of the *Achille Lauro*, he . . . made his way to Baghdad. *This was followed* by Iraq's use of chemical weapons and our increasing

awareness that Saddam Hussein had not only given up his pursuit of a 'military option' against Israel but was seeking to construct a regionally dominant military machine that could not be explained by his fear of Iran alone. I came to regard Iraq, once again, as one of the enemy states of the responsible world community. . . . This is the context in which we sought, in one of the transition books we prepared at the State Department for the incoming Bush administration, to point out that a new and tougher policy toward Saddam Hussein's Iraq was now appropriate.[32]

Shultz's account smacks of revisionism. A different reading would go as follows: Shultz and his colleagues gave the Iraqi regime the benefit of the doubt during the war with Iran, not because it looked like it might reform – it did not at all look like it would – but because it played a useful role in maintaining the balance of power in the Gulf. Shultz knew of Iraq's use of chemical weapons at least as early as the fall of 1983 – not two years later, as he claims in his book – highlighting CW's value in countering Iranian human-wave attacks. While concerned about proliferation, the Reagan administration considered it a lesser threat than the one posed by Iranian expansionism and so closed its eyes to Iraq's continued gas use, especially because it offered hope of persuading Iran to accept a ceasefire. Once the war was over, in September 1988, Shultz could say what he may have thought all along: that gassing Kurds was "abhorrent and unjustifiable. . . . It is a grim reminder of the dangers which the proliferation of chemical weapons presents."[33]

These were strong words, even if expressed only in an internal memo. Not even two months earlier, Washington had deemed Iraq's chemical weapons use *justifiable* (however abhorrent) and had allowed it to proceed. Then things changed. By now, however, Iraq had been allowed to demonstrate to would–be users and proliferators how powerful a terror weapon poison gas could be. As a CIA analysis put it: "The Iraqis demonstrated the effectiveness of chemical weapons on the battlefield, particularly the negative effect on enemy morale. . . . The implications of the Iraqis' success in introducing CW to the Middle East battlefield extend beyond that region to the rest of the world."[34] How does one put a demonstration effect back in the bottle?

The answer was unclear. Nonetheless, Shultz now declared it to be a "transcendent interest" to do so,[35] in part to prevent further damage to US relations with Iraq and the rest of the Arab world, and in part because he realized that US tolerance had wrought real harm to its own interests. In a meeting with (likely bemused) Arab League ambassadors in the third week of September, senior State Department officials explained Washington's sudden new posture:

> The U.S. has worked long and hard to contain nuclear weapons but ... in some respects chemical weapons are even more danger-ous. They destroy huge numbers of people, they can be produced cheaply, they can be hidden, and they can be acquired by ter-rorists. Thus the U.S. has taken the strong position to use moral suasion to prevent their proliferation. The world must see CW as reprehensible.[36]

And so the Reagan administration, in its dying days, decided to redou-ble its efforts to bring about a global chemical weapons ban. One result was the Paris Conference on the Prohibition of Chemical Weapons, a broad forum convened to discuss chemical weapons proliferation, in January 1989. Another was the Chemical Weapons Convention, a com-prehensive ban on the production, stockpiling, trade, and use of chem-ical weapons negotiated by successive US administrations and com-pleted in 1993. Neither exercise would have stopped Iraq, though. What put an end to that country's development of chemical and other deadly weapons was its foolish decision to invade Kuwait, followed by its sub-sequent expulsion and the resulting destruction of its chemical, biolog-ical, and nuclear arsenal, as well as its ballistic missiles. Even in March 1990, the CIA had made the sobering assessment that, "Treaties, such as the Geneva Protocol, which prohibit the use of chemical weapons do not ensure against an enemy's use of CW," and the superpowers "are unwilling, or unable, to stop the flow of needed technical assistance, chemical precursors, and process equipment, or to prevent or stop the use of chemical weapons in a war."[37]

In late 1988, despite having taken its new anti-chemical-weapons crusade to a global level, Washington was still stuck with an Iraqi regime that had gained significant military capabilities (integrated chemical fire, medium-range ballistic missiles, a biological weapons program in progress, and a nuclear program suspected to be in its early stages) with nothing to balance it. At the same time, Iraq faced a huge wartime debt and had longstanding designs on Gulf territory, not only Warba and Bubiyan islands, but also Kuwait – a limb of the Iraqi nation unfairly severed, in Iraq's view, by the British colonial power after the collapse of the Ottoman Empire.

Iraq, in other words, posed a potential danger. Yet the US would be better off keeping the Iraqis on its side. The answer was "constructive engagement," a new title for the same old tilt, set in motion by the Reagan administration once the brouhaha over the sanctions bill had died down, and enshrined by the Bush administration in National Security Decision Directive 26 in October 1989. It was, President George H. W. Bush and National Security Advisor Brent Scowcroft wrote later, not only "an attempt to encourage acceptably moderate behavior on the part of Saddam Hussein." It was also "a hope of securing a significant role for American business in what we assumed would be a substantial Iraqi reconstruction effort."[38] "Human rights and chemical weapons aside," reminded a State Department memo in September 1988, "in many respects our political and economic interests run parallel with those of Iraq." What were these interests? US business access to Iraq's market and "constructive" use of Iraqi influence in the Arab world, along with Egypt, Jordan, and Saudi Arabia, against Syria and Libya over the Palestinian question and other issues. Sanctions, by contrast – the memo presented several possible levers – "would have a sharp negative impact on our ability to influence the Iraqi regime, and set in motion a downward spiral of action and reaction which would be unpredictable and uncontrollable." Anyway, the memo queried, what good would sanctions do now that the Kurdish insurgency had been suppressed and Iraq therefore needed no further recourse to chemical weapons?[39]

"Constructive engagement" was set in motion as soon as the sanctions bill foundered in Congress in mid-October. Within days Ambassador Glaspie reported on Iraqis' delight over the end to public humiliation, and suggested ways of promptly mending the "erosion of our relationship caused by the sanctions bill," most importantly the extension of EXIM financing."[40] In other words, rather than reducing the tilt and assuming a more evenhanded approach now that the war was over, constructive engagement sent the tilt into a sharp pitch, as expressed in skyrocketing US aid in the form of $1 billion in loan guarantees, the sale of dual-use goods (which helped Iraq in developing its chemical, biological, and nuclear weapons programs), and the import of Iraqi crude to the tune of 1.1 million barrels a day in 1990, more than a quarter of Iraq's exports, at a value of $3 billion. Flush with money, Saddam was able to build up the impressive arsenal – including chemical, biological, and nuclear weapons programs – that the US was forced to destroy in 1991 and the UN Special Commission on Iraq (UNSCOM) was subsequently mandated to dismantle.

Shultz's assertion (cited above) that he advised the incoming Bush administration to toughen its stance against the regime therefore cannot be taken seriously. Zalmay Khalilzad, a member of the State Department's policy planning staff who had supported the Iraq tilt during the war, wrote an internal memorandum in the fall of 1988 in which he warned that Iraq was emerging as the preeminent military power in the Gulf and cautioned against the tilt's continuation, given the weakness of neighboring Iran. In 1993 Shultz claimed credit for this memo in his book, but according to Khalilzad (interview, 2001), in 1988, when the memo was leaked to the media as a pro-Iran initiative, Shultz summoned Khalilzad to his office, read out the memo in front of him, then wrote the word "NO" in large print across it.

Rather than acknowledging the dangerous mix of Iraq's military prowess, economic desperation, and declared regional ambitions, Shultz advocated continuing the tilt. As Khalilzad recalled, key State Department officials such as Richard Haass, Richard Armitage, and Richard Murphy declared that Saddam Hussein had changed – that after eight years of war he was not going to attack his neighbors again, and that he certainly would not go after his friends who had sustained him throughout the war. Instead, Saddam was going to rebuild his country, and the US would have an important piece of the pie. If Iraq indeed emerged as the preeminent power in the Gulf, Washington should work with it and seek to influence it. "My memo was rejected and the United States continued on the Saddam Hussein bandwagon," said Khalilzad, who left government with the outgoing Reagan administration, only to be brought back hastily, in a personal vindication, after Iraq invaded Kuwait twenty months later.

Chemical Legacy

Forced to swallow public humiliation and threatened with US sanctions for actions Washington had theretofore condoned if not encouraged, Iraqis could perhaps be excused for feeling betrayed. In an interview in October 1988, Tariq Aziz reconfirmed a statement he had made earlier that Iraq had used chemical weapons against Iran, but he steadfastly denied any gas use against the Kurds. No one presented even "one shred of evidence substantiating the allegation," he said. "So far, they have failed to provide even a sparrow killed by gas." Then, in a poke at European suppliers of Iraq's chemical arsenal (and perhaps not to anger the Americans even further), he added: "They sold us these weapons, and now they are shedding crocodile tears. The Europeans are hypocrites. They will sell you any weapon that you want."[41]

Iraq's defense minister, Adnan Khairallah, went even further, first drawing a logical analogy between the threat Iraq had faced from Iranian human-wave assaults and the menace of further mass casualties during World War II when the US decided to use the atomic bomb: "Why did the U.S. Senator [Claiborne Pell] not ask his government: Why were nuclear bombs dropped on two innocent cities with their children, women, and elderly?" he asked. Then on to Vietnam: "Before the U.S. senator denounces and creates against Iraq a media clamor without any evidence, do you not agree with me that the United States was the first to use gases on a very large scale in Vietnam?"[42]

Whatever trust had governed Washington's relationship with Baghdad – pieced back together by US diplomats and military and intelligence officers after the first betrayal, Iran–Contra – it now appeared irrevocably broken. The Iraqi leadership saw itself as the junior partner in a hot-and-cold relationship, getting pushed and pulled at the superpower's whim. There was a good deal of injured pride as well, as Saddam Hussein himself pointed out to Ambassador Glaspie two years later: Iraq had protected US interests in the Gulf by keeping the Shi'ite–Persian hordes from overrunning Saudi Arabia and the Gulf states, making huge sacrifices ("we gave rivers of blood"). "You are not the ones who protected your friends during the war with Iran," he reminded Glaspie. "I assure you, had the Iranians overrun the region, the American troops would not have stopped them, except by the use of nuclear weapons."[43] As reward, Iraq received a slap on the wrist (and the threat of worse) over a policy that was integral to its success in protecting US interests. It didn't make sense to the Iraqis, who saw it as grossly unfair.

Here was the germ for future conflict. One can, in fact, detect a linear thread between the distrust built into the US–Iraqi relationship in 1986 (Iran–Contra), reinforced in 1988 (public rebuke and the sanctions bill), and Saddam Hussein's decision to invade Kuwait. In July 1990, the regime's perception was that the US was fighting a war by other means against Iraq, using its Gulf proxies, in particular Kuwait and the United Arab Emirates. These states were driving down the price of oil at a time when Iraq was trying to recover from the war with Iran and facing large debts to these very same states, and the US was not stopping them. "We understand America saying that it seeks friendship with the States in the region, and to encourage their joint interests," the Iraqi leader told Glaspie. "But we cannot understand the attempt to encourage some parties to harm Iraq's interests." When Glaspie expressed concern that Iraq was poised to invade Kuwait, Saddam responded by more explicitly accusing the US of inciting the Kuwaitis: "What we ask is not to express your concern [about the escalating situation in the Gulf] in a way that would make an aggressor [i.e., Kuwait] believe that he is getting support for his aggression."

The rest is history. Glaspie told the Iraqi leader that tensions between Iraq and Kuwait were an issue for them and other Arab states to sort out: ("We have no opinion on the Arab–Arab conflicts, like your border disagreement with Kuwait"). When Iraq, its back against the wall, failed to gain the economic concessions it was seeking, its forces rushed into the Gulf sheikhdom, setting off the first major international crisis of the post-Cold War world. Looking back at Washington's record, Saddam Hussein may have felt he could not trust the US when it professed its innocence (Glaspie: "President Bush is an intelligent man. He is not going to declare an economic war against Iraq.") and even a desire to forge a stronger bond with the Iraqis (Glaspie: "I have a direct instruction from the President to seek better relations."). If Washington was not deliberately squeezing the Iraqis, it failed to get this across for reasons directly related to its past policy.

Having been forgotten for two years, the chemical issue boomeranged on Washington only after the Kuwait invasion, when war planners realized suddenly they might face a problem: Iraq might use poison gas (and perhaps even engage in germ warfare) against US troops set to liberate Kuwait. Analysts working overtime produced a flurry of intelligence assessments of Iraqi capabilities. Concerning WMD, this is what they concluded:

- "By the end of the war [with Iran] Iraq had developed a large, robust, and sophisticated CW capability that was fully integrated into its military system. Iraq's chemical weapons played an important if not decisive role in the climactic battles in the spring of 1988 that finally forced Iran to agree to a cease-fire.... Iraq also has an aggressive biological weapon development program.... Iraq has developed and combat tested a wide variety of tactical chemical weapon delivery means, chiefly artillery shells, rockets, and bombs.... Iraq has also produced some ballistic missile warheads with chemical and possibly biological agent fills, but these strategic delivery systems have not been tested in combat."[44]
- Chemicals in the Iraqi arsenal included mustard gas, sarin, tabun, cyclosarin (GF), and possibly hydrogen cyanide and phosgene. Iraq "probably" also produced and weaponized small quantities of VX.[45] By the end of the war, Iraq was "able to produce about 1,000 tons each per year of blister and nerve agents."[46] It also produced "binary" chemical weapons, which fuse precursor chemicals – that do little or no harm individually – inside their munitions only after a weapon's launch, thereby solving the perennial problem of toxic leakage during storage. Moreover, Iraq developed a precursor production infrastructure, reducing its dependence on foreign suppliers.[47]
- Iraq possessed a number of delivery means for its chemical weapons, including at the least:
  - ❖ fixed-wing aircraft (250-kg and 500-kg bombs, 55-gallon drums)
  - ❖ helicopters (1,000-liter spray tanks, 90-mm air-to-surface rockets)
  - ❖ 82-mm and 120-mm mortars (each with 1-kg to 3-kg rounds)
  - ❖ 122-mm, 130-mm, 152-mm, and 155-mm howitzers (ditto)
  - ❖ 122-mm rockets (with an 8-kg warhead).[48]

- On biological weapons: "We believe [Iraq] has now developed and stockpiled biological weapons," producing two biological agents: botulinum (a toxin that attacks the nervous system) and anthrax (which causes pulmonary failure).[49]
- Iraq was also believed to have a nuclear research and development program.[50]

Independent investigations conducted after August 1990 showed that Western companies and governments, including the US, had been instrumental in funding and supplying materials to Iraq's WMD programs throughout the 1980s up until the Kuwait invasion. What emerges from these studies, which have been presented to a wider audience in an extensive literature,[51] is a frightening picture of a country arming itself to the teeth simply because it was able and willing to pay for it.

The upshot of US policy in the 1980s is that it helped create a regional behemoth out of a nation run by a one–time, tin–pot dictator, a state with awesome capabilities, reckless ambitions, and pressing needs, and a leader whose understanding of the US and how it worked was known to be limited. That understanding was so limited, in fact, that Saddam failed to anticipate Washington's response to his decision to seize Kuwait.

As Iraq and the US faced off in the months following the Kuwait invasion, the US military took all necessary preparations for a chemical defense. "The principal concern," recalled Gen. Bernard Trainor, a retired Marine Corps commander who covered the Gulf war for ABC television (e-mail communication, 2000), "was Iraqi artillery (of which there was plenty) firing chemical weapons. . . . It was on the top of the coalition's target list." In the end, Washington's privately communicated threat that it might use nuclear weapons should Iraq resort to chemical or biological warfare was effective; there is no evidence Iraq used either weapon. This was fortunate. The subsequent dismantling of Iraq's WMD programs was even more salutary, given not only what the Iraqis were found to possess but the utter lack of compunction they had exhibited in using their terrifying chemical arsenal, including against civilians.[52]

Iraq's suspected chemical capability played a role even as late as 2003. In the run-up to the US invasion of Iraq, the key argument that US officials presented in favor of removing the regime, according to an official present in these meetings (interview, 2006), was that Saddam Hussein not only had weapons of mass destruction (which officials publicly intimated were nuclear weapons but knew very well to be only chemical and perhaps also biological weapons), but that he had the skill to use them, as proven during the Iran–Iraq war. The point they made was that Iraq was not a nonstate actor such as the Japanese group Aun Shirikyo that had released sarin into the Tokyo subway, but a nation–state that had the capability to strike abroad and had the knowledge, skill, and experience to do it right. In support of the new Bush administration's war drive, this argument proved particularly effective in bringing around those who had remained skeptical.

CONCLUSION

FALLOUT

"We found the weapons of mass destruction. We found biological laboratories. They're illegal. They're against the United Nations resolutions, and we've so far discovered two."
— US President George W. Bush, Polish TV/CBS News,
May 31, 2003

"They are weapons of mass destruction. They are harmful to human beings. And they have been found." (Referring to 500 newly discovered degraded and unusable chemical munitions in Iraq.)
— US Secretary of Defense Donald Rumsfeld, Associated Press,
June 23, 2006

"We know he's got those weapons of mass destruction. We've got the receipts."
— Comedian Mark Russell, *International Herald Tribune*, December
31, 2002

The Kurds: Resurgent Nationalism

For many years after Halabja, the lives of ordinary Kurds were governed by fear – fear of a repressive state that punished harshly anyone who rejected its writ (as many Kurds did), and a much deeper, gut–wrenching fear that could empty out whole towns at the mere mention of two words: gas attack! The massive chemical bombardment of Halabja induced such mass panic that a few chemical strikes on a single subsequent day were sufficient to precipitate an instantaneous and nearly total evacuation of a large territory, even if few inhabitants died from the gas. Thus did the regime, understanding the terrorizing potency of its weapon, inaugurate every stage of its Anfal campaign. Tens of thousands of people were lost to this tactic and today lie scattered in mass graves under western Iraq's desert sands, waiting to be uncovered and returned to their homeland for identification and proper burial – for a measure of closure.

The Halabja attack set in motion a continuum of fear from which Kurds have not known how to truly free themselves. In April 1991, after Iraqis rose in wholesale protest against a regime weakened by defeat in Kuwait, rumors that Iraqi forces would gas Kurdish towns triggered mass flight into Iran and Turkey. Three months earlier, people in Suleimaniyeh reported hearing Izzat Ibrahim al-Duri, the regime's number two, declare: "If you have forgotten Halabja, I would like to remind you that we are ready to repeat the operation."[1] Whether al-Duri actually uttered these dire words did not matter. "During the uprising, every day I expected the Iraqis to attack us with chemical weapons," said Jamal Aziz Amin, a leader of the PUK underground in Suleimaniyeh (interview, 1999). Once the tide turned, when tanks began rumbling northward and helicopters opened up their guns on all that moved, Halabja came right back as a potential, imminent reality. The Kurds' revolt collapsed overnight, prompting a mass exodus without parallel. Never before, concluded the UN High Commissioner for Refugees, had the world experienced such large numbers of people – almost 1.5 million – leaving their country in a matter of days.

Again in March 2003, as war loomed, Kurds preemptively evacuated their towns, fearing that the regime would turn what remained of its chemical arsenal – after a decade of disarmament and sanctions – against them in revenge for their treasonous support of the invaders. As a US intelligence assessment put it, "reports of possible WP [white phosphorus] chemical weapon attacks spread quickly among the Kurdish populace in Erbil and Dohuk. As a result, hundreds of thousands of Kurds fled from these two areas and crossed the Iraqi border into Turkey."[2]

Only liberation could break the continuum. But even now, deep in the recesses of the Kurdish unconscious still lies this fear, equivalent to an unmovable conviction, that no central government can ever be trusted not to repeat such abominations. This is one reason why Kurdish leaders have placed all their postwar energies into creating long-term protections for their people. In so doing, they have sought to parlay the Halabja and Anfal tragedies into the foundations of their hoped-for state. Architecturally, the monument to Halabja's victims rises from dark interior walls bearing the names of the dead to form a triumphal spire hoisting the Kurdish flag. (At least it did, until it was torched on March 16, 2006, the annual commemoration, by Halabjans themselves. They were infuriated by official neglect and the parties' exploitation of this national disaster for partisan gain, whisking foreign dignitaries from burial grounds to memorial but carefully shielding them from the town itself, its hospitals, or its people – disturbing numbers of whom appear afflicted with diseases that doctors attribute to delayed mustard gas effects.)

Through the Kurds' weight in drafting Iraq's permanent constitution in 2005, Halabja and Anfal took pride of place in the lexicon of the ousted regime's outrages enumerated in its preamble, which refers to "the massacres of Halabja, Barzan, Anfal and the Fayli Kurds." These massacres, Kurds contend, were committed to thwart their tenacious quest for nationhood.[3] The Kurds thus cannot be blamed for their desire to put a stop behind the legacy of the twentieth century – an era that was filled by national disasters and recurrent betrayals – and to pursue a decisive settlement to the troubled question of their status as a people. Denied statehood after the Ottoman Empire's dismemberment, the Kurds became an instrument in the hands of more powerful players and were led along a trail of broken promises and agreements. The latest guarantor of Kurdish rights and security, the United States, has come in for the same criticism – of hardly having Kurdish interests at heart but pursuing its own goals at the Kurds' expense, on the back of pledges honored mainly in the breach.

Perceived betrayals are the insult added to the injuries of repeated defeats and tragedies, which are recited as a litany of woes by the Kurds but are little known outside Kurdistan. Thus, Halabja and Anfal have largely been known only to regional experts, and even then their histories have often been distorted in the slowly growing literature. Nor has the extent of their suffering been fully acknowledged. The international community's inability to comprehend the transformative significance of Anfal and Halabja to the Kurds is roughly equivalent to failing to grasp how the events of 9/11 affected the American psyche, or how crushing were any of the 20th century genocides to those who survived them. It is easy to forget, ignore, or deny that Anfal indeed constituted genocide.

It is out of such deep emotions and national traumas that identities are forged or reinforced and, sometimes, that nations are born. These are certainly the factors that have given rise to the Kurds' strong sense of entitlement today. But with their new political and military power in a post-Saddam Iraq, they have started pressing to obtain (or, in their view, retrieve) territories they claim are historically Kurdish; in so doing, they have started to overreach, alienating their political partners, angering the other communities living in these territories, and stretching their resources in a situation of continuing economic dependency on Iraq as well as on neighboring states. It is Kirkuk, in particular, on which they have set their sights, realizing the importance of its oil wealth (some 12 percent of Iraq's proven reserves) to their quest for independence. Their stubborn refusal to compromise and pursue a negotiated solution is dictated by the memory of these past traumas and the need to secure a safer future for their children. As a consequence, civil strife and foreign intervention loom in Kirkuk, developments that would likely unmake all the gains of the past decade and contribute to growing instability and civil war in Iraq.

Today Iraqi Kurdistan, isolated for so long, is linking up with the world, its many young people gaining knowledge and skills and adopting ideals and ambitions that are unfamiliar to the old *maquis*-based generation, and just a little threatening. We can only hope they will succeed, by democratic means, to spawn new leadership that can make the compromises Kurdish society will need to survive in a difficult regional environment, without trading away the protections and guarantees that Anfal and Halabja taught the Kurds they cannot do without.

Iran: Nuclear Quest

If to the Kurds events in the 1980s culminated in a tragedy that ultimately gave way to a resurgent Kurdish nationalism, Iran's experience was different and so had a dissimilar outcome. The "imposed" war left

Iranians deeply scarred – no more, perhaps, than were the Iraqis. It bears emphasizing that in terms of atrocities the two countries were easily each other's equals. Nor can Iran claim a moral high ground, certainly not after 1982 when, having booted out the invaders, it rejected a cease-fire and prolonged the war for six senseless years.

Yet, unlike the Iraqis, the Iranians felt deeply wronged, at least on the chemical weapons issue, as well as unfairly ostracized and abandoned, if not betrayed, by an international community that was proud of its universal norms but remained silent when the victim of these norms' systematic breach was its enemy. Iran suffered thousands of dead from poison gas alone. Many others survived but succumbed to increasingly debilitating illnesses. In January 1989, Iran's foreign minister, Ali Akbar Velayati, devoted a major speech to Iraq's chemical weapons use. "Over 50,000 Iranians suffered severe and moderate injuries," he said bitterly. "About ten percent of the Iranian wounded died, 10–20 percent from mustard, 10 percent from cyanide and the rest from nerve agents. Over half of the dead were civilians."[4] An Iranian medical census later identified 34,000 survivors of mustard gas attacks.[5]

Iran drew two important lessons from this episode: never again to allow itself to be so strategically vulnerable, and to distrust all multilateral agreements, even those to which it was party. This legacy survives today, with a vengeance, and has helped upturn the system of multilateral arms control.

Israel's nuclear quest may have been the original spark for the spread of WMD in the Middle East, but Iraq's wartime gas use gave proliferation both a fresh impulse and a new dynamic. Chemical weapons have come to be seen as useful, effective especially when an opponent lacks a superior deterrent such as nuclear weapons and can be staved off or even vanquished with the use or threat of terror. By 1990, six Middle Eastern countries were suspected or proven to have a chemical warfare capability: Israel, Egypt, Iraq, Iran, Syria, and Libya.[6] Moreover, Iran started a nuclear program that today, from all appearances, looks like it is military in nature. "You'd have to blame the Iraqis for this," commented Gideon Gera, the head of research at Israel's Mossad intelligence agency in 1987–1988 (interview, 2000). "Iran started developing nuclear weapons after UNSCOM revealed Iraq's nuclear program. It cannot afford to be the weaker party in the Gulf."

Just as the experience of World War I gave rise to the 1925 Geneva Protocol, so gas warfare against battlefield soldiers and innocent civilians alike provoked a reenergized effort to address this escalating problem. The US recognized the need as well – belatedly. In September 1988, as Iraq faced the possibility of sanctions legislated by Congress, a key State Department analysis concluded:

> Iraq's use of CW during the war and the failure of the international community to mobilize an effective response has lowered the inhibitions on CW use and may have conferred a measure of legitimacy on use of these weapons in the region and elsewhere. It has also encouraged other states to acquire a CW capability. . . . The worldwide spread of CW capabilities poses a serious threat to international security and in particular to U.S. friends in the Middle East including Israel, Saudi Arabia, and the smaller Arab Gulf states. In short, as a result of CW use during the Iran–Iraq war, the credibility and effectiveness of our global CW policy has been weakened. It is imperative, therefore, that we act now to shore up our CW non-proliferation policy.[7]

If only these words had been written five years earlier, when they could have led to action that would have made a real difference in the lives of Iraqis and Iranians.

The first multilateral initiative to control the spread of chemical weapons was launched in 1985 by the government of Australia, which established a voluntary body known as the Australia Group to coordinate industrial states' exports of precursor chemicals, banning sales to Iran and Iraq. While it was an important initiative, the group's effectiveness was challenged by enforcement problems: Some chemical shipments slipped through the net owing to corruption and negligence. Moreover, states outside the group were not similarly bound to embargo the two belligerents.

More than a year after the war, in January 1989, the Reagan administration and the French government of François Mitterand organized the Paris Conference on the Prohibition of Chemical Weapons, expressly to bolster a ban on chemical weapons use severely eroded by Iraq's five-year record. One hundred and forty-nine governments solemnly reaffirmed their commitment to the Geneva Protocol, agreed to strengthen the UN's role in investigating violations, and endorsed stepped-up efforts to conclude a comprehensive chemical weapons ban. But tellingly, Iraq was not named even once during the proceedings, a powerful testimony to Western nations' continuing Iraq tilt.

Negotiations for a comprehensive chemical weapons ban, initiated in the 1960s, continued throughout the 1980s under the auspices of the UN Conference on Disarmament. The United States promoted these talks as a way of convincing the Soviet Union and China to get rid of their chemical weapons. Like its older cousin the 1972 Biological Weapons Convention (BWC), the Chemical Weapons Convention (CWC) arose from the consideration that in a nuclear world ruled by two superpowers, lesser nonconventional weapons offered no added value while they spurred proliferation among actors unconstrained by the "mutually assured destruction" paradigm.

Even if the Iranians found no audience for their pleadings, said chemical weapons expert Julian Perry Robinson (interview, 2001), the Iran–Iraq war nonetheless fueled a critical debate, almost despite the Iranians. This was not only because escalating chemical weapons use posed a new threat (with Halabja as symbolic turning point), but because states realized that Iraq had outgrown its dependency on the Soviet Union, acquiring precursor chemicals, tools, and equipment from private Western companies to create its own indigenous production program. And so the treaty, which bans chemical weapons production, trade, stockpiling, and use, was signed in 1993, entering into force four years later. Iran was one of its early signatories and has similarly adhered to the BWC, as well as the nuclear Non-Proliferation Treaty (NPT).

Whence Iran's vigorous and somewhat surprising commitment to multilateral restraints? Originally, the Shah had launched research programs aimed at developing weapons of mass destruction, but the 1979 Islamic revolution interrupted his efforts. So when Iraq, with its back against the wall in 1983, introduced chemical weapons on the battlefield, Iran had to scramble to start its own program. It is now generally accepted that Iran gained the capability to field chemical weapons toward war's end. Parliamentary speaker Ali Akbar Hashemi Rafsanjani declared two months after the ceasefire that "chemical bombs and biological weapons are poor man's atomic bombs and can easily be produced. We should at least consider them for our defense. . . . Although the use of such weapons is inhuman, the war taught us that international laws are only drops of ink on paper."[8] It is likely that, had the war con-tinued, Iran too would have resorted to this weapon.

In signing the CWC, Iran assumed the obligation to fully account for and then liquidate its chemical stockpiles and production facilities. In due time Iran did report possessing (unspecified) chemical agents, and the agency charged with implementing the CWC – the Organi-zation for the Prohibition of Chemical Weapons – subsequently over-saw their destruction. Nevertheless, some governments and chemical weapons experts continue to suspect Iran of concealing an active chem-ical weapons program. This, if true, would indisputably be a legacy of the Iran–Iraq war and the international community's unwillingness to stop Iraq's gas use. Moreover, the world's ability to challenge Iran is reduced dramatically by the Iranian perception, based on its sense of having been abandoned during the war, that it has no one to protect it from weapons of mass destruction except its own WMD deterrent. "They were traumatized both by chemical weapons use and the lack of an international response," said Seth Carus, a chemical weapons expert (interview, 2000). "They did not realize the extent to which they had been demonized, and so now they make every effort to actively engage with the international community. They reckon they can talk their way out of trouble in case of a challenge inspection under the CWC."

Although Iran has not faced such inspections, its maneuvering on the nuclear question may be emblematic of its posture on WMD more broadly. Following revelations about clandestine nuclear research in 2002, Iran initially pledged cooperation with the International Atomic Energy Agency (IAEA) as part of its NPT obligations, then denied the agency access to undeclared sites. Having suspended uranium enrich-ment for over a year following high-level negotiations with Britain, France, and Germany, Iran resumed enrichment in 2006, insisting its intentions were peaceful and aimed at creating nuclear energy, not a nuclear bomb. In making this claim, Iranian officials have suggested Iran is inspired by its experiences in the war with Iraq: "As the only victims of the use of weapons of mass destruction in recent history," declared Javad Zarif, Iran's ambassador to the UN, "[Iranians] reject the devel-opment and use of all these inhuman weapons on ideological as well as strategic grounds."[9] All the same, Iran itself admitted in the 1990s that it had developed chemical weapons.

Iranian officials have said that the country wants to follow the Japanese model. Japan has mastered the complete fuel cycle as part of its peaceful nuclear program, but it has done so in a fully transparent manner, cooperating with the IAEA. By contrast, with its dodges, half–truths, and quasi-concessions, Iran looks like it is in dogged pursuit of nuclear weapons under the guise of playing the compliance game. This is the lesson it learned in the 1980s and subsequently, in a different way, during the sanctions decade, when Iraq's WMD programs were dismantled by the most extensive and intrusive disarmament regime in history: hide, evade, and dissemble to protect strategic interests. But now Iran is led by a theocratic regime that is as entrenched at home as it is despised and distrusted abroad. It thrives on high oil prices and the power to cause trouble for US interests in Iraq and elsewhere. And it counts on its new deterrents, whether actual or suspected, to prevent a repeat of its traumatic war with Iraq and, perhaps, regain its standing as the preeminent power in the Gulf.

The United States: Failure to Intervene Early

After all is said and done the question must be asked: Could things have been done differently? Could US policy have been adjusted to respond to unexpected and undesirable events – Iraq's resort to weaponry abhorrent to humanity and potentially harmful to long-term US interests – while preserving US priorities: keeping Iran dammed in, oil flowing at a reasonable price, and Israel, America's strategic asset, safe?

The Iraq tilt was occasioned by the overthrow of the Shah, who had served as the West's guardian of the Gulf's riches. He had combined two vital traits: one, a shared perception of "the nature of the Soviet threat . . . the need to preserve the political status quo in the Gulf and . . . the importance of Israel's security"; and two, the military capability to protect the Gulf from both Soviet domination and Arab radicalism.[10] Iraq, too, had considerable military capability, but it did not share Washington's vision of the balance of power in the Middle East, having become the most vocal opponent of the Camp David peace accord. Saudi Arabia and Kuwait, by contrast, had plenty of shared interest with the West, whose energy needs they fulfilled at an affordable price. Given their internal weakness as rentier states, though, they themselves needed protection.

With the Shah gone, Washington not only lost its sheriff in the Gulf, but it also witnessed the rise of a militant regime with a lot of oil and a desire to oust the Gulf's calcified monarchies. The West's primary objective then became to contain the Islamic revolution. This required mobilizing all those who could help protect the region, even if they did not fully share Washington's vision. Iraq was first courted, patiently, then inducted as a partner in 1984. The country was perhaps not the most trustworthy ally, but Washington tried to make the best of it, using a menu of incentives to bring Iraq more tightly into the fold. With each outrage in Lebanon (the bombings of the US Marine barracks and the US and French embassies, the taking of Western hostages), and with each Iraqi setback in the war, the embrace became more intimate.

Iraqi concessions on the Israeli–Arab conflict helped, as did a commitment to manage US economic and financial aid responsibly. The Iraqis were "on their best behavior," said David Newton, America's first ambassador in Baghdad (interview, 2001). "It's a command system: You send a signal, you get a quick response." The Iraqis got rid of terrorist leader Abu Nidal, and the Department of Agriculture gave them "a clean bill of health in terms of how the money was used. Had there been massive corruption, we would have had to shut the credit program down," according to Newton. Moreover, even if Baghdad's Arab nationalist pretensions prevented a closer rapprochement with Washington, the same nationalism also kept the Soviet Union at arm's length. Finally, many in Washington hoped that the Iraqi regime would reform over time, cut off all its support for terrorism, and engage in limited democratization – that it would become a "moderate" Arab state, in other words. "It made sense," explained Newton, "to try to make as many common threads with Iraq as possible to maximize the incentives for behaving responsibly and maximize the disincentives for behaving irresponsibly." Iraq's chemical weapons use was ignored as a justified act of war against fanatical foot soldiers of an irredeemable regime that was just as brutal as Iraq's, if not more. "We did everything possible to make sure Iraq would not collapse," said Newton, "thus to protect Saudi Arabia and Kuwait."

It is reasonable to ask what might have happened if Iraq had been constrained in its wartime conduct and, as a result, if Iran had succeeded in overwhelming Iraqi defenses, seized Basra, and precipitated the regime's ouster. Iran might then have occupied Iraq, installed a pro-Iranian Shi'ite government modeled on its own regime, taken control of Iraqi oil fields (and thus driven up oil prices), put the neighboring oil sheikhdoms on the military and economic defensive, raised anti-Israel rhetoric to new heights. . . . Would this have been better?

The question, as posed, is a false one. The US and its allies had two strategic objectives: To block Iranian expansionism and, at the same time, to prevent the emergence of a victorious but undependable Iraq as the new regional superpower – a policy, in other words, of dual containment, foreshadowing US policy in the 1990s. Washington's anti-Iranian animus was such, however, that the scales were tipped in Iraq's favor. Events in the Gulf, said a retired CIA official (interview, 2000), "made the government utterly breathless. They didn't understand Islamic fundamentalism. They didn't want to listen to advice, as in: 'Khomeini means what he says.' It was a paradigm shift. Everyone had assumed that modernism and a Western elite would lead this part of the world. Their policy decisions reflected this thinking. It is as if we lost our balance when the Shah fell."

And so the Reagan administration overreacted. In failing to distinguish between pragmatists and radicals in Iran, the administration missed an opportunity, which almost certainly existed, to strengthen the former at the latter's expense. Instead, its policies drove the two factions into each other's arms; in Washington's own bureaucratic struggles those who maintained that the Iranian regime could be reformed were driven underground; and the Iran–Contra fiasco ensued. Support of Iraq, furthermore, elicited no significant opposition, certainly not after Iran–Contra. And so an important question was not asked: Could the US have helped Iraq enough to protect itself from being overrun, short of allowing it to use a weapon as horrifying in its effects and as dangerous in its implications as poison gas – or put differently, could Iraq have survived without using gas?

The answer is a matter of speculation. Military experts seem to disagree about the potency and effectiveness of battlefield chemical weapons. But a case can be made that a more robust international response to the war (laying down the rules – the 1949 Geneva Conventions and related humanitarian agreements – monitoring each side's compliance, and sanctioning violations) could have enabled negotiations aimed at ending the conflict under conditions that both Iran and Iraq might have accepted, without either's recourse to chemical weapons.

Pressure on Iraq to modify its behavior need not have entailed a change in the pro-Iraq tilt, but Washington's lack of confidence in the strength of the relationship may have militated against an unequivocal condemnation of Iraq's conduct. Throughout this period, the Reagan administration had three distinct opportunities to intervene and successfully extract an Iraqi commitment to refrain from further chemical weapons use: in 1983–1984, when the Iraqis began experimenting with gas; immediately after Halabja, in March 1988; and following the Badinan attacks in August 1988. In each case, public revelation of Iraq's gas use prompted scrutiny of the relationship; repeated revelations had a cumulative effect that, over time, increased pressures on Washington to change its approach to Iraq. But that first opportunity, in 1983, was the most important one, when the US had both knowledge of what was happening and leverage to affect Iraq's behavior, and when Iraq's chemical conduct was still in its early stages and thus vulnerable to international pressure. Understanding what went wrong on that occasion is critical for understanding what happened later.

In late 1983 US policy makers were well informed of battlefield developments. The CIA was aware both of chemical weapons use and Iraq's testing of chemical agents on animals. It also knew that the Iraqis, using cutout companies and a cover story, were buying precursor chemicals and equipment in Germany and other European countries, but also in the US. Hamstrung by its inability to divulge intelligence information, the administration was able to act only after Saddam Hussein's public threat to use "insecticide" against the Iranians in February 1984. The argument the State Department presented to the National Security Council was couched in terms of interest, not morality: Iraq's chemical weapons use ran counter to US objectives because it might trigger a dangerous escalation, deter the Iranians from negotiating, and hand them a "potent propaganda weapon."[11]

Nor did Washington share Iraq's perception that only chemical weapons, with their force-multiplier effect, could compensate for its disadvantage in numbers. "Chemical weapons were not needed to prevent an Iranian victory," asserted the State Department's Jim Placke (interview, 2000), "though I'm not sure we ever made that sort of calculation." A 1986 CIA document concluded that the effectiveness of Iraq's chemical attacks had been decreasing as a result of poor tactical deployment, the lessened element of surprise, increased Iranian preparedness, and a series of technical problems.[12] And the DIA's Pat Lang, who accused Iran of partial responsibility for the Halabja chemical attack, noted (interview, 2000), concerning Iraq's 1988 Tawakkulna 'ala Allah campaign, that even "if you had deducted chemical weapons from the fire package, Iraq would still have won these battles anyway." In his view this was not a military calculation, however: "The commander goes for maximum overkill."

Diverging perceptions between the US and Iraq may be the reason why Washington failed to get its message across. In the fall of 1986, Tariq Aziz warned Javier Pérez de Cuéllar of a possible breakup of Iraq, with the Shi'ite south falling under Iran's sway: "If it means that we have to use all – and I mean all – kinds of weapons, we shall use them, no matter what the convention or what anybody says. We are fighting a war for you as well."[13] Only in September 1988 did the State Department seem to acknowledge Iraq's perspective. "Iraq's insistence that chemical weapons were essential to its national survival," it observed, "suggests why U.S. and [UN Security Council] efforts to halt Iraqi CW use, in the context of the ongoing war, were ineffective."[14]

The punishment Washington chose for Iraq in 1984 was an embargo on precursor chemicals to both Iran and Iraq, demarches to European capitals to institute the same, and a diplomatic message to the Iraqis to halt gas use. This was considered effective, because Iraq's chemical industry remained heavily dependent on precursor imports. Interviews and documents show, however, that the embargo's limited scope and voluntary nature rendered it largely unsuccessful. The demarches were derisively referred to as "demarchemallows" – pieces of candy bereft of nutritional value. Iraqi imports continued from Europe and the East Bloc, and the diplomatic message was ignored by the Iraqis, who claimed their survival was at stake. The same 1986 CIA assessment concluded:

> Because the political costs of continued CW use have been so small, we doubt that Iraq will abandon its use of chemical weapons in the foreseeable future. Furthermore, Iraq probably has now made sufficient progress in its chemical weapons program to render it relatively immune to the foreign trade restrictions. US and Western nations' efforts to embargo Western precursor chemicals have not, and probably will not, curtail Iraq's CW progress.[15]

Washington's solution in 1984, in other words, was to dampen public outrage by preemptively condemning Iraq's behavior – before the media could grab hold of the issue and expose the administration's complicity. This meant, however, that the administration diffused pressure before it could build. As a result, its subsequent actions may have been weaker than they could have been. Washington could, for example, have threatened to link Iraq's chemical weapons use to the resumption of diplomatic relations, the strongest lever it had. Instead, US diplomats expressed satisfaction afterward that *despite* the uproar over Iraq's gas use, they had been able to execute what they considered an overriding US interest.

The Reagan administration could also have bolstered the norm against gas use. Seth Carus, who testified before Congress in 1991 on Iraq's chemical weapons capabilities and the US role in strengthening them, contended that a political message reinforcing the norm could have had substantial results. The Iraqis were approaching lots of chemical companies in the US and many had cold feet; some backed out. A stronger norm, he said, would have reduced the field even further, and the Iraqis, subject to pressure, "would have backed off."

Limited sanctions and mild diplomatic signals persuaded the Iraqis instead that all remained well and that all the Americans had done was set the volume control. Donald Rumsfeld's two visits to Baghdad only reinforced this message. When Washington subsequently agreed to restore diplomatic relations, how else to interpret this but as a reward for Iraqi sacrifices in holding back the Islamic hordes? And so, in 1984, a critical opportunity was passed over. This set the stage for escalating chemical weapons use that culminated, four years later, in the Halabja tragedy.

The uproar the chemical attack on Halabja caused might have forced a change in US policy. The event was so dramatic as to warrant this, but the timing was terrible: After Iran–Contra, Washington had promised it would help the Iraqis get the ceasefire they so desperately needed, and in March 1988 it looked like the Iraqis might succeed if their scheduled offensives aimed at recapturing lost territories were executed according to plan.

There is no doubt that the Reagan administration had the necessary real–time information to make a judgment about Iraq's chemical weapons use. Documents show that the CIA, for example, had forewarning of impending air attacks involving chemical weapons. A report from July 1988 provided the following intelligence, remarkable for its detail:

> Iraqi forces continue to withdraw from the central battle sector while an Iranian counter-offensive is producing heavy fighting in the southern battle sector. In addition, preparations were continuing at Tallil airfield in Iraq for the possible use of air deployable chemical weapons (CW) munitions. . . . One longbed trailer associated with Iraqi chemical weaponry remained in the CW-associated storage bunker and at least five additional trailers were outside of the storage bunker. At least two of the thirteen [Sukhoy-22] Fitter fighter-bombers in the dispersal area had munitions-handling dollies in the area.[16]

That being the case, would intelligence not also have seen preparations for the Halabja attack a month earlier, one that involved fifty aircraft flying from a known airbase? A Kuwaiti-born US military officer, moreover, recalled (interview, 2000) having been told by US intelligence officers, including a lieutenant colonel, that they had been present inside the Iraqi military operations room at Faw in April 1988, a particularly advantageous view of the battlefield, where they shared US satellite intelligence with their Iraqi allies. Thus they would have been aware of gas use not only after the battle – from the absence of animal life and the abundance of dispensed atropine injectors that the DIA's Lt. Col. Rick Francona reported – but *as it was taking place*. "US intelligence were tracking what was going in [imports] and what was happening at production facilities, and they were monitoring the battlefield very closely," said Seth Carus, who had high-level security clearance.

Immediately after the Halabja atrocity reached television screens, Ted Koppel, the host of Nightline, asked Alastair Hay, a noted chemical weapons expert, whether he saw any way "to put this genie back in the bottle again, any way to prevent their [CW] use . . . ?" Hay replied: "I think we really need tougher sanctions from other countries. I think we need the world community to be condemnatory of the use of chemical–warfare agents, and I think they need to . . . have that position put over loud and clear. I don't think it has been said effectively so far."[17]

Nor would it be. A signal that gas use was taboo precisely when it promised to be the qualitative factor ensuring an Iranian retreat would have negatively affected the Iraqis' morale. Although Halabja brought home the shocking consequences of earlier indulgence of gas use, the stakes were now so high that Washington's unquestioned support had to continue – with eyes closed and a tighter pinch of the nose.

Reagan administration officials were undoubtedly worried about the Halabja attack's possible fallout. As a retired US intelligence officer recalled (interview, 2000):

When the attacks on Halabja became public thanks to a well-executed public relations campaign by the Iranians, both Wolfowitz and Armitage wanted to stop our support, concerned over the potential public backlash if it was learned that the U.S. was providing intelligence to Iraq while they were using CW on their own people. In the end, it was determined in an interagency forum – I think it was a "deputies" meeting, a meeting of the cabinet deputies and DDCI [Deputy Director of Central Intelligence] – that it was more important that Iran not win the war.

Evidence shows that the US, fully aware it was Iraq that had gassed Halabja, accused Iran of being at least partly responsible, and then instructed its diplomats to propagate Iran's partial culpability. The response to Halabja, in other words, was not preemptive condemnation, as in 1984, but disinformation designed to diffuse responsibility for the crime and thus prevent collective punitive action.

This ploy, while successful in getting the Iraqis off the hook, had an important consequence: the Iraqis saw another green light and took immediate advantage. Using gas tactically on the first day of every Anfal stage, they were able to gather up and methodically kill tens of thousands of Kurds. This surely was not a US policy objective; nevertheless, it resulted directly from failing to call the Iraqis to a halt.

By September 1988, the Reagan administration, with some delay, finally intervened. But at this point it was too late. The war was over, the Kurdish insurgency was crushed, and the Iraqi leadership was fully convinced that its new military power could help it settle some outstanding bills. Kuwait was next.

Targeting Civilians: A Growing Culture of Impunity

In an op-ed article in October 2003, six months after the Iraqi regime's ouster, US Secretary of Defense Donald Rumsfeld put out a rallying cry for Washington's war on terrorism. US troops faced a growing insurgency in Iraq, and he now wanted to remind Americans of a significant anniversary. Twenty years earlier, he wrote, he had visited Beirut as Ronald Reagan's personal envoy shortly after Hezbollah operatives had driven a truck bomb into the US Marine barracks, killing 241 servicemen. The Lebanon experience had taught him two lessons. First, the US troop withdrawal six months later had emboldened terrorists worldwide to contemplate more devastating attacks against the United States, and that therefore America should bring the war to the terrorists, smoke them out, deny them safe haven, and "make clear to states that sponsor and harbor them that such actions will have consequences." And furthermore, he wrote, the world had seen the development of ever more dangerous weapons, and these could be turned against America by terrorists. This required a forceful response: "If the world does not deal with the emerging nexus between terrorist networks, terrorist states and weapons of mass murder," he argued, "terrorists could one day kill not more than 240 people, as in Beirut, or more than 3,000 people, as on Sept. 11, but tens of thousands – or more."[18]

Rumsfeld's recounting of the Lebanon story elided both an uncomfortable reality and his own role in developments that have given rise to a more dangerous world. It is, first of all, important to recall why

US soldiers were in Lebanon and why fighters of the nascent Hezbollah movement saw fit to target them with unconventional means. A month earlier, in September 1983, US forces, part of a multinational peace-keeping force that also included French, British, and Italian troops, had abandoned their neutrality in the civil war by throwing their support behind the Christian Phalange militia and the government of Amin Gemayel against a coalition of Palestinian, Druze, and other pro-Syrian groups. This involved subjecting Druze front lines in the Shouf mountain range to a naval bombardment in which, almost inevitably, villages were hit as well. Hezbollah's twin suicide attacks against the US Marine barracks and the French battalion headquarters came as a direct response to US and French intervention on behalf of an unpopular, unrepresentative regime in Beirut. The organization chose its targets (both of them military, not civilian) as well as its means (suicide car bombers) to maximize the impact, given limited resources. If these means were unconventional, they were no more deadly than the US battleship *New Jersey*'s lobbing of Volkswagen–sized munitions (one–ton bombs) at civilian areas in the Shouf.[19] Countering overwhelming conventional firepower with unconventional tactics is a time–honored guerrilla tradition, their "asymmetric threat" constituting a force multiplier – a sort of equalizer that by creating a balance of fear restores a sense of fairness in the eyes of the militarily weaker party.[20]

Rumsfeld also failed to mention the other leg of his 1983 Middle East trip. Not only did he visit Beirut and Jerusalem, he also made the first visit to Saddam Hussein by a US official of Rumsfeld's stature. In paving the way for the resumption of diplomatic relations (Iraq's reward for fighting Iran) and closing an eye to Iraq's chemical warfare, Rumsfeld gave the Iraqis a green light to intensify their gas use. US support of the unleashed dictator, in turn, gave rise to the very terrorist regime and proliferation specter that Rumsfeld was to decry twenty years later. George Shultz recognized this, albeit belatedly, in the fall of 1988, when he remarked that the combination of ballistic missiles and chemical weapons in the hands of a country with a terrorist history was his worst nightmare.[21] After all, six months earlier Iraq had threatened to attack Tehran and other Iranian cities with chemically tipped missiles. This must have given Shultz a premonition. Only three years later, in January 1991, Iraq would fire Scud missiles at Israel amid widespread fears it had filled the warheads with chemical agents. This did not happen, but Iraq did have the capability. Only the threat of a nuclear response is thought to have deterred Saddam Hussein.

We have now arrived in the age of terror, a time of suicide bombers dispatched by merciless handlers in shadowy organizations. Not to see its antecedents in the actions of states, however, would be a serious error, crippling any effort to formulate an effective response. It is easy to blame guerrilla groups for failing to adhere to international conventions to which they are not party. It is true that basic norms of humanity apply to all, regardless of signature, but it is the world's governments, with all their resources and representing organized societies based on moral standards and the rule of law, that must set the example. Yet it is major states that have been the prime violators of the very treaties they themselves were in the forefront to negotiate and sign. In doing so, they have sent a very dangerous message.

Take, for example, the Chemical Weapons Convention, a treaty accomplished largely by strong diplomatic leadership during successive US administrations and ratified by President Clinton in 1997. In passing the necessary implementing legislation in 1998, the US Congress – over the Clinton administration's opposition – entered reservations that directly violated the treaty, which prohibits signatories from attaching conditions. These reservations – the president's right to refuse challenge inspections, a prohibition on taking abroad samples collected during an inspection, limits on the number of industrial facilities required to declare their activities involving banned chemicals – effectively rendered US adherence to the treaty meaningless.

The trampling of multilateral treaties, such as the Geneva Protocol, the Geneva Conventions, and the CWC, and the undermining of international institutions such as the United Nations has real consequences. It erodes the very norms on which these treaties and institutions are based, the most fundamental of which is the prohibition on targeting civilians in warfare. Although it is often nonstate actors (like Iraqi insurgents, Palestinians fighting Israel's military occupation, al-Qaeda terrorists) that bear the brunt of moral condemnation, it is states (like Israel in Palestine and Lebanon, the United States in Iraq) that have set the example by using superior firepower in populated areas and then hiding behind the convenient pretext of "targeted assassinations," "proportionate response," and "collateral damage." Well-disciplined, professional militaries equipped with precision weapons may not target civilians outright, but if the result of their actions, repeatedly, is many civilian deaths, they have lost both the moral high ground and the battle for hearts and minds.

If the US did not lose its credibility in the Middle East by bombing Lebanese villages in 1983, by accusing Saddam Hussein of being "a man who gassed his own people" after giving him the green light, by ejecting Iraqi forces from Kuwait while financing and otherwise supporting Israel's brutal and predatory military occupation of Palestine, or by propping up authoritarian regimes while declaiming the virtues of democracy and human rights, then surely a statement by Madeleine Albright, Clinton's UN ambassador (later his secretary of state), clinched it. In 1996 Leslie Stahl asked Albright on CBS's "60 Minutes" whether the human cost of international sanctions against Iraq was justified: "We have heard that half a million children have died. I mean, that is more than died in Hiroshima. . . . Is the price worth it?" Stahl asked. "I think this is a very hard choice," Albright replied, "but the price, we think the price is worth it."

An earlier prime example of how universal norms were dangerously weakened is presented in this book, also involving Iraq. The failure to act against Iraqi chemical weapons use when action was possible and could have made a difference, in 1983–1984, nurtured an environment of impunity, one that was clearly recognized as such by the regime. Predictably, impunity led to worse abuses, amounting to international crimes: war crimes (the targeting of civilians in warfare), crimes against humanity (the gassing of Halabja), and genocide (the systematic killing of Kurdish civilians in areas marked for Arabization). Under these circumstances, Washington's wink-and-nod policy amounted to culpable complicity. In the late 1990s, the State Department showed a belated concern for the implications of this policy, when its lawyers ordered a documents review as part of a debate about whether its Iraq policy in the 1980s, especially regarding chemical weapons use, would disqualify the US from participating in efforts to put the Iraqi leadership in the dock. In the end, there was no international tribunal, or one combining Iraqi and international expertise, but a strictly Iraqi one that was funded and directed by Washington, in part to prevent unpleasant surprises. It is also because of this history that one of the incoming Bush administration's first actions in 2001 was to cancel President Clinton's signature to the Rome treaty establishing the International Criminal Court. Today unilateralism and impunity are the order of the day.

Senior Iraqi leaders have been tried in front of an Iraqi tribunal in 2005 and 2006. Saddam Hussein was sentenced to death for his role in a massacre in the Shi'ite town of Dujeil in 1982, and was hanged at the end of 2006. In 2007, the trial of those implicated in the crimes committed during the Anfal campaign continued, with Ali Hassan al-Majid and Sabr al-Duri, among others, facing justice, but no longer Saddam Hussein (nor, for different reasons, Wafiq al-Samarra'i). The trial for the gassing of Halabja was in preparation. These trials will be far too late, however, to send the kind of message that, had it been delivered during the early stages of chemical weapons use, could have prevented worse. Moreover, those who were complicit in these crimes by supplying the means, giving the green light, and covering up their actions through deceit, will never stand trial. To the contrary, today they are the very architects of both the war in Iraq and the Bush administration's gutting of multilateral engagement.

It bears remembering that the horrors of World War II gave the impetus for updating and amplifying an elaborate treaty regime that, by establishing rules based on fundamental norms, has served to prevent the recurrence of such mayhem. Without a renewed commitment to these conventions and the values they embody, we can be certain that the world we, and our children, inhabit can grow only more dangerous.

EPILOGUE

United States, August 2006

I am sitting on a couch in a suburban living room, surrounded by men, women, and children, including my own family. The conversation flits between English (the language of the children and increasingly of the adults), Arabic (so that I can communicate with my friends), and Kurdish (which I don't speak, but which binds all in this room together). We talk about Iraq, Kurdish food, minor illnesses, and life in Kurdistan, and I am transported back to the day, ten years ago, when I was sitting in a US army vehicle on the bridge over the Khabur river, which marks the border between Turkey and Iraq. The sun was beating down and the wait was long; I was not certain that the party I had arranged to meet would find its way to the border from Suleimaniyeh, their starting point.

It was November 1996. Three months earlier, Iraqi forces had slammed into Erbil, the capital of the Kurdish region, with the help of the KDP, which had temporarily switched sides to defeat the common enemy, the PUK, in a bitter four-year internecine conflict. The operation cost the lives of a number of Iraqi opposition fighters, who had been preparing to overthrow the regime (an initiative that failed to gain US support and was therefore doomed from the moment it was conceived). It also put an end to four years of hard work by the US government and US-funded nongovernmental organizations to resurrect rural Kurdistan following its destruction before, during, and after Anfal. Within a month, the Clinton administration had begun to airlift its intelligence operatives, as well as its citizens, out of the area. Soon, the administration decided to also evacuate all those associated with US-funded projects. This included thousands of Kurds, an emergent well-trained elite, the cream of their society, who were thus siphoned off in a virtual brain drain. By November, this operation was going full tilt.[1]

In addition to this well-publicized effort, a parallel secret initiative was under way. Acting on a request by Human Rights Watch and at the behest of the Clinton White House, the US military, working in close coordination with the government of Turkey, agreed to evacuate a small group of Iraqi Kurds and their families from Iraqi Kurdistan for the purpose of bringing to safety key witnesses in any future trial of Saddam Hussein and his regime – witnesses to the Anfal killing grounds. They were five men and one boy. At the height of the Anfal campaign in 1988, the Iraqi security police packed them, separately, into minibuses with their friends and relatives and delivered them to execution sites in the country's western desert. Here they were made to disembark, pushed toward freshly dug trenches, and summarily shot. Miraculously, each in his own way, these five men and the boy survived and, under cover of darkness, blessed with a good deal of luck and using their wits, they managed to return to Kurdistan, where they hid until Iraqi forces withdrew in October 1991.

The reunion on the middle of the bridge was joyful but brief. Having been identified, three of the men as well as the teenage boy were allowed to cross with their families, and at once they were whisked away and flown to Guam, where they joined the many other Kurdish evacuees for several months of acclimatization and language training, before being resettled in America. The two other Anfal survivors were brought to the US two years later.

The transition from rural Kurdistan to suburban America proved challenging to these Kurds, who had only an elementary education and, aside from serving in the Iraqi military at the war front, had seen little of the world beyond Germian, where they grew up. Yet, today, a decade hence, they are thriving. While the men have taken low-paying jobs in fast–food franchises and car washes, their children have become proficient in the essential requirements of modern life, such as the internet, and are completing high school and entering college. They are safe, at last, and hopeful for the future.

NOTES

PREFACE

1. "Poison Gas: Iraq's Crime," Editorial, *New York Times*, March 26, 1988.
2. Julian Perry Robinson and Jozef Goldblat, "Chemical Warfare in the Iraq-Iran War" (SIPRI Fact Sheet, Stockholm International Peace Research Institute, May 1984), p. 3.
3. Human Rights Watch, *Iraq's Crime of Genocide: The Anfal Campaign against the Kurds* (New Haven and London: Yale University Press, 1995), Chapter 9, "The Firing Squads."

INTRODUCTION: THE HALABJA CONTROVERSY

1. In two separate shipments in May 1992 and August 1993, the US military brought eighteen metric tons of Iraqi secret police documents seized by Kurdish rebel parties during the short-lived 1991 uprising to the United States for safekeeping and analysis. They were housed in a facility of the US National Archives under supervision of the US Senate Foreign Relations Committee. The nongovernmental organization Human Rights Watch received exclusive access to these documents in 1992–1994 to sift for evidence of human rights crimes. This author supervised this project for Human Rights Watch during this period (and escorted the second shipment in August 1993). The principal results are contained in two publications by Middle East Watch: *Genocide in Iraq: The Anfal Campaign against the Kurds* (1993), and *Bureaucracy of Repression: The Iraqi Government in Its Own Words* (1994), available at: http://www.hrw.org/reports/1993/iraqanfal/ and http://www.hrw.org/reports/1994/iraq/, later combined into one book and published by Human Rights Watch as *Iraq's Crime of Genocide: The Anfal Campaign against the Kurds* (New Haven and London: Yale University Press, 1995).
2. Physicians for Human Rights and Human Rights Watch, "Scientific First: Soil Samples Taken from Bomb Craters in Northern Iraq Reveal Nerve Gas – Even Four Years Later." Press statement (April 29, 1993), available from http://www.phrusa.org.

3. US government and intelligence documents cited in this book were obtained either through this author's own requests under the Freedom of Information Act, the Washington–based nongovernmental National Security Archive (http://www.nsa.org), or Gulflink (http://www.gulflink.osd.mil), an initiative by US veterans of the 1991 Gulf war to obtain information about prior Iraqi WMD capabilities in pursuit of the unexplained Gulf war syndrome. Accordingly, the source of official US documents will here be indicated as follows: FOIA–Author, FOIA–NSA, or FOIA–Gulflink.

4. Cited in "Téhéran accuse Bagdad d'avoir utilisé des armes chimiques contre une ville Kurde irakienne," Agence France Presse, March 16, 1988.

5. Bernard E. Trainor, "Iranians' Strike Isn't the Feared Winter Offensive," *New York Times*, March 27, 1988.

6. Alan Cowell, "Iran–Iraq Tactics: Waging War Far from Front," *International Herald Tribune*, March 24, 1988.

7. "Plus de 2.000 kurdes tués par des bombardements chimiques, selon un dirigeant kurde," Agence France Presse, March 18, 1988.

8. Iraqi News Agency, March 17, 1988, in *FBIS-NES-88–052*, p. 31.

9. Letters from Mohammad Mahallati, S/19637 (March 17, 1988), S/19639 (March 17, 1988), and S/19647 (March 18, 1988).

10. Cited in "Iran Says Iraq Used Nerve Gas – 5,000 Kurds Die, Tehran Tells UN," Associated Press, March 21, 1988, and Letter from Mahallati, S/19664, March 21, 1988.

11. Paul Koring, "Poison-Gas Victims Recall Bombing Horror," *Globe and Mail*, March 22, 1988.

12. Letter from Mahallati, S/19669, March 22, 1988.

13. David Hirst, "Iran Puts Dead on Show after Gas Raid," *Guardian*, March 22, 1988.

14. *Jerusalem Post*, March 23, 1988, based on wire stories.

15. US Department of State, "Daily Press Briefing," March 23, 1988.

16. Quoted in Jim Muir, "Iraqi Gas Attacks Revive Horrors of the Great War," *Sunday Times*, March 27, 1988.

17. "Use of Chemical Weapons in Iran–Iraq War," transcript of "Nightline" show of March 23, 1988.

18. *Christian Science Monitor*, April 13, 1988.

19. "Secretary-General and Red Cross Consult on Question of Chemical Weapons," UN Press Release, SG/SM/4103, March 25, 1988.

20. Iraqi News Agency, March 29, 1988.

21. Letter from Mahmoud Madarshahi, S/19741, April 5, 1988.

22. Cited in *Al-Ra'i* (Jordan), March 29, 1988, in *FBIS-NES-88–060*, p. 34.

23. Letter from Ismat Kittani, S/19730, April 5, 1988.

24. "Spokesman Denies Chemical Weapons Accusations," Iraqi News Agency, April 5, 1988, in *FBIS-NES-88–067*, p. 17; and "UN Team Departs after Mission on CW Victims," Iraqi News Agency, April 11, 1988, in *FBIS-NES-88–072*, p. 32. Emphasis added.

25. Patrick E. Tyler, "Both Iraq and Iran Gassed Kurds in War, U.S. Analysis Finds," *Washington Post*, May 3, 1990. Tyler later moved to the *New York Times*.

26. Letter from Madarshahi, S/19741, April 5, 1988.

27. UN Security Council, *Report of the Mission Dispatched by the Secretary-General to Investigate Allegations of the Use of Chemical Weapons in the Conflict between the Islamic Republic of Iran and Iraq*, S/19823, April 25, 1988.

28. Director of Central Intelligence, "Impact and Implications of Chemical Weapons Use in the Iran–Iraq War," undated, late 1987 – early 1988 (FOIA–Gulflink).

29. David Ignatius, "Reaching Out to Iran," *Washington Post*, June 2, 2006.

30. *Time*, March 19, 1984.

31. "Aziz Confirms Use of 'Poison Gas' in Gulf War," Hamburg DPA, in *FBIS-NES-88–127* (July 1, 1988), p. 17. Iraq's UN representative promptly issued a denial, claiming that "the allegations mendaciously imputed to a high–ranking Iraqi official . . . are completely unfounded." Letter from Ismat Kittani, S/20076, August 1, 1988.

32. Patrick E. Tyler, "Well–Armed Iraq Takes Aggressive Stance," *Washington Post*, May 11, 1988.

33. Gordon M. Burck and Charles C. Flowerree, *International Handbook on Chemical Weapons Proliferation* (New York: Greenwood Press, 1991), p. 117. This is otherwise an invaluable source, offering a great amount of very useful detail.

34. US Central Intelligence Agency, "Iraq's Potential for Chemical and Biological Warfare," September 1990 (FOIA–Gulflink).

35. UN Security Council, *Report of the Mission Dispatched by the Secretary-General to Investigate Allegations of the Use of Chemical Weapons in the Conflict between the Islamic Republic of Iran and Iraq*, S/18852 (May 26, 1987), pp. 2 and 5–6.

36. State of the Union address, January 28, 2003.

37. Letter from J. Edward Fox, Assistant Secretary for Legislative Affairs, US Department of State, to Dante B. Fascell, Chairman, House Foreign Affairs Committee, September 13, 1988 (FOIA–NSA).

38. Quoted in James Bamford, *Body of Secrets: Anatomy of the Ultra–Secret National Security Agency from the Cold War through the Dawn of the New Century* (New York: Doubleday, 2001), p. 544.

39. "Overview of the Kurdish Insurgency," unsigned document contained in an Action Memorandum, "U.S. Policy toward Iraqi CW Use," from H. Allen Holmes and Paul Hare to Secretary of State George P. Shultz, September 13, 1988 (FOIA–NSA).

1. CROSSING THE CHEMICAL THRESHOLD

1. UN Security Council, "Decisions," September 23, 1980.

2. Cameron R. Hume, *The United Nations, Iran, and Iraq: How Peacemaking Changed* (Bloomington: Indiana University Press, 1994), p. 38.

3. UN Security Council, Resolution 479, September 28, 1980.

4. H. Allen Holmes and Paul Hare to Secretary of State, "U.S. Policy Toward Iraqi CW Use," September 13, 1988 (FOIA–NSA).

5. Victor L. Wolfe, Thomas C. D'Isepo, and William E. Myers, "Chemical and Biological Warfare Capabilities – Middle East Countries," DIA Task Unit PT-I600-04-77 (August 10, 1981), pp. 133 and 136 (FOIA–NSA).

6. W. Andrew Terrill, Jr., "Chemical Weapons in the Gulf War," *Strategic Review* (Spring 1986), p. 53.

7. Rather than responding spontaneously to questions, Dr. Foroutan read relevant segments from a manuscript he was preparing about Iraq's chemical weapons use. It has since been published as Abbas Foroutan, *Jange Shimiaeeye Aragh va Tajarobe Bezeshkie Aan* (*Medical Experiences of Iraq's Chemical Warfare*) (Tehran: 2003, in Persian).

8. J. P. Perry Robinson, "Chemical and biological warfare: developments in 1984." *World Armaments and Disarmament: SIPRI Yearbook 1985* (London and Philadelphia: Taylor & Francis, 1985), Appendix 6A, pp. 207–8.

9. Terrill, "Chemical Weapons," p. 53.

10. Anthony H. Cordesman and Abraham R. Wagner, *The Lessons of Modern War: Volume II* (Boulder: Westview Press, 1990), p. 166.

11. Abbas Foroutan, "Medical Notes on Chemical Warfare," *Kowsar Medical Journal*, Fall 1375 (1996), vol. 1, p. 94.

12. *Al-Iraq* (Baghdad), September 13, 1983.

13. The episode is described in Human Rights Watch, *Iraq's Crime of Genocide: The Anfal Campaign against the Kurds* (New Haven and London: Yale University Press, 1995), pp. 25–27.

14. Cordesman and Wagner, *Lessons of Modern War*, p. 176.

15. Perry Robinson, "Chemical and biological warfare," pp. 208–09.

16. Julian Perry Robinson and Jozef Goldblat, "Chemical Warfare in the Iraq–Iran War" (SIPRI Fact Sheet, Stockholm International Peace Research Institute, May 1984), p. 4.

2. US RESPONSE: SETTING THE VOLUME CONTROL

1. "General Quizzed on Swamp Battles, CW Use," *Foreign Broadcast Information Service (FBIS), Middle East and Africa*, March 7, 1984.

2. Don Oberdorfer, "Iran Moves 500,000 up to Front; Biggest Offensive of War with Iraq Viewed Under Way," *Washington Post*, March 3, 1984.

3. At the time of the interview, in November 2000, Ricciardone was Secretary of State Madeleine Albright's Special Coordinator for the Transition of Iraq. In 2006, he was US ambassador to Egypt.

4. *New York Times*, March 6, 1984.

5. *Time*, March 19, 1984.

6. Cable from US Interests Section, Baghdad, to Secretary of State, BAGHDA 00879, April 4, 1981 (FOIA–NSA).

7. Cable from US Secretary of State to US Interests Section, Baghdad, SECTO 02076, April 8, 1981 (FOIA–NSA).

8. Cable from US Interests Section, Baghdad to Secretary of State, BAGHDA 00972, April 12, 1981 (FOIA–NSA).

9. Wafiq al-Samarra'i, *Hotam al-Bawaba al-Sharqiya* (*The Destroyer of the Eastern Gate*) (London: publisher and year unlisted), pp. 82–83.

10. George P. Shultz, *Turmoil and Triumph: My Years as Secretary of State* (New York: Charles Scribner's Sons, 1993), p. 236.

11. Cable from US Secretary of State to various US Embassies, STATE 042566, February 15, 1983 (FOIA–NSA).

12. Shultz, *Turmoil and Triumph*, p. 237.

13. Cable from US Interests Section, Baghdad, to Secretary of State, BAGHDA [correspondence code illegible], June 13, 1983 (FOIA–NSA).

14. Cable from US Interests Section, Baghdad, to Secretary of State, BAGHDA 01836, August 1, 1983 (FOIA–NSA).

15. Nicholas A. Veliotes, "Iran–Iraq War: Analysis of Possible U.S. Shift from Position of Strict Neutrality," Information Memorandum, US Department of State (October 7, 1983), p. 7 (FOIA–NSA).

16. Shultz, *Turmoil and Triumph*, p. 238.

17. Jonathan T. Howe, "Iraq [sic] Use of Chemical Weapons," Information Memorandum, US Department of State, November 1, 1983 (FOIA–NSA). Emphasis added.

18. Jonathan T. Howe and Richard W. Murphy, "Iraqi Use of Chemical Weapons," Action Memorandum, US Department of State, November 21, 1983 (FOIA–NSA).

19. Francis J. Ricciardone, "Deterring Iraqi Use of Chemical Weapons," US Department of State, November 10, 1983 (FOIA–NSA).

20. Francis J. Ricciardone, "Background on Iraqi Use of Chemical Weapons," US Department of State, November 10, 1983 (FOIA–NSA).

21. The White House, "U.S. Policy toward the Iran–Iraq War," National Security Decision Directive 114, November 26, 1983 (FOIA–NSA).

22. US Department of State, "Iraqi Illegal Use of Chemical Weapons (CW)," Briefing paper, November 16, 1984 (FOIA–NSA).

23. Cable from US Interests Section, Baghdad, to US Embassy, Amman, BAGHDA 03101, December 14, 1983 (FOIA–NSA).

24. *Harper's Magazine*, October 2003, p. 13, citing the *Times* (London).

25. Cable from US Embassy, London, to Secretary of State, LONDON 27572, December 21, 1983 (FOIA–NSA).

26. Cable from US Embassy, London, to Secretary of State, LONDON 27592, December 21, 1983 (FOIA–NSA).

27. Quoted in Michael Dobbs, "U.S. Had Key Role in Iraq Buildup," *Washington Post*, December 30, 2002.

28. Cable from US Interests Section, Baghdad, to US Embassy, Amman, BAGHDA 03163, December 26, 1983 (FOIA–NSA).

29. Cable from US Secretary of State to US Consulate, Jerusalem (Rumsfeld's team), STATE 012251, January 14, 1984 (FOIA–NSA).

30. Cable from US Interests Section, Baghdad, to US Embassy, Amman, BAGHDA 00392, February 22, 1984 (FOIA–NSA).

31. Press statement reproduced in cable from US Secretary of State to US Mission, Geneva, STATE 074411, March 14, 1984 (FOIA–NSA),

32. Cable from US Interests Section, Baghdad, to US Embassy, Amman, BAGHDA 00461, March 7, 1984 (FOIA–NSA).

33. Cable from US Interests Section, Baghdad, to US Embassy, Amman, BAGHDA 00525, March 7, 1984 (FOIA–NSA).

34. Francis J. Ricciardone, "Briefing Notes for Rumsfeld Visit to Baghdad," US Department of State, March 24, 1984 (FOIA–NSA).

35. Transcript from US Senate Armed Services Committee hearing, September 19, 2002.

36. Cable from US Secretary of State to US Mission, Geneva, STATE 074411, March 14, 1984 (FOIA–NSA).

37. The White House, "Measures to Improve U.S. Posture and Readiness to Respond to Developments in the Iran–Iraq War," National Security Decision Directive 139, April 5, 1984 (FOIA–NSA).

38. Cable from US Secretary of State to various US Embassies, STATE 093714, March 31, 1984 (FOIA–NSA).

39. Anthony Cordesman, *The Iraq–Iran War and US–Iraq Relations: An Iraqi Perspective – An Interview with Iraqi Foreign Minister Tariq Aziz* (Washington, DC: National Council on US–Arab Relations, August 1984), p. 39.

40. Seymour Hersh, "U.S. Aides Say Iraqis Made Use of a Nerve Gas," *New York Times*, March 30, 1984.

41. Shultz, *Turmoil and Triumph*, p. 240.

42. Ibid.

43. Cable from US Secretary of State to US Embassy, Baghdad, STATE 352124, November 29, 1984 (FOIA–NSA).

44. Cable from US Embassy, Damascus, to Secretary of State, DAMASC 02601, April 23, 1985 (FOIA–NSA).

45. Reported in *International Review of the Red Cross*, May–June 1984, p. 168.

46. While the Geneva Protocol lacks a mechanism to investigate alleged use, General Assembly resolution 37/98 of December 13, 1982 seeks to fill the gap by requesting the secretary-general to investigate, with the aid of experts, any such allegations.

47. UN Security Council, *Report of the Specialists Appointed by the Secretary-General to Investigate Allegations by the Islamic Republic of Iran Concerning the Use of Chemical Weapons*, S/16433, March 26, 1984.

48. Cable from US Mission, New York, USUN N 00626, March 28, 1984 (FOIA–NSA).

49. Ibid.

50. Cable from US Secretary of State to US Embassy, Amman, STATE 094420, April 6, 1984 (FOIA–NSA).

51. UN Security Council, S/16454, March 30, 1984.
52. Giandomenico Picco, *Man without a Gun* (New York: Times Books, 1999), p. 61.
53. W. Andrew Terrill, Jr., "Chemical Weapons in the Gulf War," *Strategic Review* (Spring 1986), p. 56.
54. Shultz, *Turmoil and Triumph*, pp. 238–41, and interviews with US State Department officials.
55. The court's ruling is available in English at: http://www.rechtspraak.nl/ljn.asp?ljn=AX6406.
56. US Department of State, "Iraqi Illegal Use of Chemical Weapons (CW)," Briefing paper, November 16, 1984 (FOIA–NSA).
57. Terrill, "Chemical Weapons," p. 56.
58. Cable from US Mission, New York, to Secretary of State, USUN N 01615, July 6, 1984 (FOIA–NSA).
59. Defense Intelligence Agency, "Prospects for Iraq," Defense Estimative Brief, September 25, 1984 (FOIA–NSA).
60. Julian Perry Robinson and Jozef Goldblat, "Chemical Warfare in the Iraq–Iran War" (SIPRI Fact Sheet, Stockholm International Peace Research Institute, May 1984), pp. 4–5.

3. CHEMICAL INTERLUDE

1. *Kowsar Medical Journal*, Spring 1376 (1997), vols. 1 and 2.
2. Gordon M. Burck and Charles C. Flowerree, *International Handbook on Chemical Weapons Proliferation* (New York: Greenwood Press, 1991), p. 105; and letter from the UN Secretary-General, S/17127 (April 24, 1985), p. 4.
3. Letter from Said Rajaie Khorassani, S/17046, March 21, 1985.
4. Letter from Khorassani, S/17088 and S/17089, April 9, 1985.
5. "There Can Be No Military Resolution of This Coflict [sic]," from prepared statement by Assistant Secretary of State for Near Eastern and South Asian Affairs [Richard W.] Murphy, April 4, 1985, Document No. 255, *American Foreign Policy: Current Documents 1985* (Washington, DC: US Department of State, 1986), pp. 551–52.
6. "Report of the Secretary-General on his Visit to Iran and Iraq," S/17097, April 12, 1985.
7. Letter from the UN Secretary-General, S/17127, April 24, 1985.
8. "Note by the President of the Security Council," S/17130, April 25, 1985.
9. Letter from Khorassani, S/17864, February 25, 1986.
10. UN Security Council, *Report of the Mission Dispatched by the Secretary-General to Investigate Allegations of the Use of Chemical Weapons in the Conflict between the Islamic Republic of Iran and Iraq*, S/17911, March 12, 1986.
11. "Note by the President of the Security Council," S/17932, March 21, 1986. Emphasis added.
12. Letter from Fereidoun Kamali, S/17925, March 18, 1986.

13. Letter from Ismat Kittani, S/17934, March 23, 1986.
14. US Defense Intelligence Agency, "Prospects for Iraq (U)," Defense Estimative Brief, DEB-85–84, September 25, 1984 (FOIA–NSA).
15. William Myers and Richard Wilson, "Expanding Chemical Warfare Capabilities: A Cause for Concern," US Army Intelligence Agency, *U.S. Army Scientific and Technical Intelligence Bulletin*, AST-2660R-074–86 (December 1986), p. 25 (FOIA–NSA).
16. "Curbing Proliferation of Chemical Weapons," June 19, 1985 (FOIA–NSA).
17. Central Intelligence Agency, "Iran–Iraq: Chemical Warfare Continues," An Intelligence Assessment, November 1986 (FOIA–NSA).
18. Richard W. Murphy, "IRAQ: CPPG Meeting of Wednesday, July 23," Briefing Memorandum, US Department of State, July 23, 1986 (FOIA–NSA).
19. "Present Status in Saga Regarding the Movement of TOW Missiles," inter-agency memorandum, January 25, 1986 (FOIA–NSA).
20. Richard W. Murphy, "U.S.–Iraqi Relations: Picking Up the Pieces," Action Memorandum, US Department of State, December 5, 1986 (FOIA–NSA).
21. Michael H. Armacost, "Letter to Dr. [Alton] Keel [acting assistant to the President for National Security Affairs]: Commerce Licenses for Iraq," US State Department, Action Memorandum, December 12, 1986 (FOIA–NSA).
22. Quoted in A. P. Burleigh, "U.S. Intelligence for Iraq," US State Department, December 15, 1986 (FOIA–NSA).
23. Anthony Cordesman and Abraham R. Wagner, *The Lessons of Modern War: Volume II* (Boulder: Westview Press, 1990), p. 250.

4. WAR IN KURDISTAN

1. UN Security Council, *Mission to Inspect Civilian Areas in Iran and Iraq Which Have Been Subject to Military Attack*, S/15834, June 20, 1983.
2. Quoted in letter from Khorassani, S/18800, April 13, 1987.
3. Letter from Khorassani, S/18819, April 21, 1987.
4. UN Security Council, *Report of the Mission Dispatched by the Secretary-General to Investigate Allegations of the Use of Chemical Weapons in the Conflict between the Islamic Republic of Iran and Iraq*, S/18852 (May 26, 1987), p. 5.
5. Note by the Security Council President, S/18863, May 14, 1987. The UN team's finding that Iraqi troops also suffered chemical injuries, which contributed to the note's balanced tone, is examined in Chapter VII.
6. Interviewed by Delphine Minoui, a freelance journalist, in Serdasht in June 2006. She kindly shared transcripts of her interviews.
7. Mustafa Ghanei, S. Khateri, A. Jalali, and J. Aslani, "Outcome [sic] of civilian population of Sardasht city after chemical warfare bombardment," paper presented at a medical conference in Switzerland, May 2002 (in Persian, summary in English). See also Farnoosh Hashemian et al., "Anxiety, Depression, and

Posttraumatic Stress in Iranian Survivors of Chemical Warfare, *Journal of the American Medical Association*, no. 296 (2006), pp. 560–66.

8. Quoted in letter from Khorassani, S/19029, August 10, 1987.

9. The people of Serdasht ardently seek to keep the memory of the attack alive. Aside from the annual commemoration, some survivors have written books. See, for example, Hossein Mohammadian, *Bou Ná Ashená (An Unknown Smell)* (Tehran: Ahed, 2001, in Persian). Mohammadian, a survivor who received treatment in Spain, is the president of the Organization for Defending the Victims of Chemical Weapons in Serdasht.

10. Joint Staff of the Army and Islamic Revolution, Operations Department, *Atlas Jank Iran wa 'Iraq (Atlas of the Iran–Iraq War)* (Tehran: The Center for War Studies and Research, 2001), p. 92.

11. *Le Monde*, March 19, 1988.

12. Human Rights Watch, *Iraq's Crime of Genocide: The Anfal Campaign against the Kurds* (New Haven and London: Yale University Press, 1995), p. 39.

13. Ibid., p. 254.

14. Ibid.

15. Ibid., p. 40.

16. Ibid., pp. 52–56.

17. Giandomenico Picco, *Man without a Gun* (New York: Times Books, 1999), p. 73.

18. Memorandum R 040918Z to intelligence branches, August 4, 1987 (FOIA–NSA). Emphasis in the original.

19. Director of Central Intelligence, "Impact and Implications of Chemical Weapons Use in the Iran–Iraq War," undated, late 1987 – early 1988 (FOIA–Gulflink).

20. Ibid.

21. Haywood Rankin, "Travels with Galbraith – Death in Basra, Destruction in Kurdistan," US Government Memorandum (September 27, 1987), pp. 11, 15, 19, and 22.

22. US Department of State, *Country Reports on Human Rights Practices for 1987* (Washington, DC, 1988).

23. Reuters, October 19, 1987. See Chapter VII for an analysis of claims that Iran used chemical weapons during the war.

5. HALABJA

1. Shawqat Haji Mushir, *Karasati Kimiabarani Halabja bi Hari 1988 (The Sad Events of the Chemical Bombing in Halabja in the Spring of 1988)*. (Suleimaniych: 1998.) Shawqat was killed by militants of the radical Islamist group Ansar al-Islam in February 2003.

2. Director of Central Intelligence, "National Intelligence Daily, Saturday, 12 March 1988," p. 15 (FOIA–Author).

3. Director of Central Intelligence, "National Intelligence Daily, Saturday, 1 March 1988," p. 11 (FOIA–Author).

4. Director of Central Intelligence, "National Intelligence Daily, Monday, 28 March 1988," p. 3 (FOIA–Author).

5. See also, cable from US Embassy in Baghdad to Secretary of State, 1988BAGHDA01888, April 6, 1988 (FOIA–Author).

6. *FBIS-NES-88–058* (March 25, 1988), p. 64.

7. *FBIS-NES-88–057* (March 24, 1988), pp. 69–71.

8. *FBIS-NES-88–049* (March 14, 1988), pp. 63–68.

9. *FBIS-NES-88–051* (March 16, 1988), pp. 64–65.

10. *FBIS-NES-88–052* (March 17, 1988), pp. 56–59.

11. *FBIS-NES-88–053* (March 18, 1988), p. 52.

12. *FBIS-NES-88–058* (March 25, 1988), p. 64.

13. *FBIS-NES-88–052* (March 17, 1988), p. 59.

14. Human Rights Watch, *Iraq's Crime of Genocide: The Anfal Campaign against the Kurds* (New Haven and London: Yale University Press, 1995), p. 70.

15. *FBIS-NES-88–061* (March 30, 1988), p. 49.

6. THE HALABJA DEMONSTRATION EFFECT

1. *New York Times*, March 25, 1988.

2. Cable from US Mission, New York, to Secretary of State, 1988USUNN00926, March 31, 1988 (FOIA–Author).

3. Cable from US Embassy, London, to Secretary of State, 1988LONDON07498, April 5, 1988 (FOIA–Author). The characterization "apparent" is that of the cable's author and does not necessarily reflect the language the UK government used with the Iraqi ambassador.

4. Cable from Secretary of State to US Mission, New York, 1988STATE109519, April 7, 1988 (FOIA–Author). Emphasis added.

5. Cable from Secretary of State to US Embassies, 1988STATE118615, April 15, 1988 (FOIA–Author). Emphasis added.

6. Cable from US Embassy, Lisbon, to Secretary of State, 1988LISBON03202, April 11, 1988 (FOIA–Author).

7. Cable from Secretary of State to US Mission, New York, 1988STATE139494, May 3, 1988 (FOIA–Author).

8. Cable from Secretary of State to US Mission, New York, 1988STATE146514, May 7, 1988 (FOIA–Author).

9. Cameron R. Hume, *The United Nations, Iran, and Iraq: How Peacemaking Changed* (Bloomington: Indiana University Press, 1994), p. 154.

10. *FBIS-NES-88–054* (March 21, 1988), pp. 22–23.

11. *Al-Thawra*, March 20, 1988.

12. Mudiriyat al-Amn al-'Ameh, Suleimaniyeh, April 25, 1988, Human Rights Watch ref. 413/4-A.

13. Mudiriyat al-Istikhbarat al-Askariya al-'Ameh, Baghdad, April 6, 1988, HRW ref. 880/8-A.

14. *FBIS-NES-88–064* (April 4, 1988), p. 22.

15. Middle East Watch, *Bureaucracy of Repression: The Iraqi Government in Its Own Words* (New York: Human Rights Watch, 1994), document 9, pp. 49–52.

16. For a description of events in Qaradagh, see Human Rights Watch, *Iraq's Crime of Genocide: The Anfal Campaign against the Kurds* (New Haven and London: Yale University Press, 1995), Chapter 4.

17. Ibid., p. 91.

18. Ibid., pp. 117–120.

19. Ibid., Chapter 7.

20. Ibid., Chapter 9.

21. Ibid., p. xvii.

22. Ziad Abd-al-Rahman (pseudonym for Najmaddin Rashid Abdullah Fakeh), *Death Crematorium: The Anfal Operations from the Iraqi Regime's Documents* (*Tuni Merg* in Kurdish, *Mahraqet al-Mawt* in Arabic) (Erbil: Committee for the Defense of Anfal Victims' Rights, 1995).

23. Jonathan C. Randal, *After Such Knowledge, What Forgiveness? My Encounters with Kurdistan* (New York: Farrar, Straus and Giroux, 1997), p. 214.

24. See Joost Hiltermann, "Elusive Justice: Trying to Try Saddam," *Middle East Report*, no. 215 (Summer 2000), pp. 32–35.

25. Cable from US Embassy, Baghdad, to Secretary of State, 1988BAGHDA01888, April 6, 1988 (FOIA–Author). The Iranian Kurdish official's name was redacted from the document.

26. "Iraq: The Campaign against the Kurds," attached to: Morton I. Abramowitz, "Iraq's Use of Chemical Weapons on the Kurds," Information Memorandum, September 17, 1988 (FOIA–NSA).

27. US Department of the Army, CFICI intelligence summary, April 11, 1988 (FOIA–NSA).

28. US Department of Defense, "Baghdad's Repressive Measures against the Kurds," a Joint Chiefs of Staff memorandum, April 19, 1988 (FOIA–NSA).

29. Richard Schifter, "The Human Rights Aspect of Iraq's Measures against the Kurds," Information Memorandum, US Department of State, September 13, 1988 (FOIA–NSA).

30. Morton I. Abramowitz, "Swan Song for Iraq's Kurds?" Information Memorandum, US Department of State, September 2, 1988 (FOIA–NSA).

31. Stephen C. Pelletiere, Douglas V. Johnson II, and Leif R. Rosenberger, *Iraqi Power and U.S. Security in the Middle East* (Carlisle Barracks, PA: US Army War College, Strategic Studies Institute, 1990), p. 53.

32. US Defense Intelligence Agency, "Kurdistan: Resistance Forces at Peril," October 6, 1988 (FOIA–NSA).

33. Elaine Sciolino, "How the U.S. Cast Off Neutrality in Gulf War," *New York Times*, April 24, 1988.

34. Director of Central Intelligence, "National Intelligence Daily, Monday, 23 April 1988," p. 2 (FOIA–Author).

35. Pelletiere et al., *Iraqi Power*, p. 36. They state (p. 31): "Because of the secrecy that surrounds everything in Iraq it is impossible to make definitive judgments about the Iraqi tactics" during the campaign.

36. *FBIS-NES-88–075* (April 19, 1988), p. 65.

37. Patrick E. Tyler, "Officers Say U.S. Aided Iraq in War Despite Use of Gas," *New York Times*, August 17, 2002.

38. Rick Francona, *Ally to Adversary: An Eyewitness Account of Iraq's Fall from Grace* (Annapolis: Naval Institute Press, 1999), p. 23.

39. US Air Force Intelligence Agency, "Iran/Iraq Chemical Warfare Casualties," para. 6G (undated), obtained from US Central Command (FOIA–Author).

40. "Scud Chemical Agent Coverage Patterns," August 1990 (FOIA–Gulflink).

41. "Iraqi Air Force Capability to Deliver Chemical Weapons," December 1, 1990 (FOIA–Gulflink).

42. Quoted in the *Independent* (London), July 3, 1998.

43. See, for example, US Defense Intelligence Agency, "Iraqi Chemical Weapons Trends," August 8, 1990 (FOIA–Gulflink).

44. Foroutan reports these cases in "Medical Notes on Chemical Warfare," *Kowsar Medical Journal*, Winter 1377 (1999), vol. 3, no. 4; and Spring 1378 (1999), vol. 4, no. 1

45. Letter from Mohammad Mahallati, S/19967, June 27, 1988.

46. UN Security Council, *Report of the Mission Dispatched by the Secretary-General to Investigate Allegations of the Use of Chemical Weapons in the Conflict Between the Islamic Republic of Iran and Iraq*, S/20060 (July 20, 1988), paras. 9–11.

47. UN Security Council, *Report of the Mission Dispatched by the Secretary-General to Investigate Allegations of the Use of Chemical Weapons in the Conflict Between the Islamic Republic of Iran and Iraq*, S/20134 (August 19, 1988).

48. *FBIS-NES-88–069* (April 11, 1988), p. 30.

49. Foroutan, "Medical Notes," Summer 1377, p. 218.

50. *Jordan Times*, March 30, 1988, citing wire agencies. See also Patrick E. Tyler, "Iraq Targets Bigger Missile on Tehran; More Powerful Warheads Raise the 'Terror' Factor," *Washington Post*, March 28, 1988.

51. Director of Central Intelligence, "National Intelligence Daily, Tuesday, 5 April 1988," p. 9 (FOIA–Author).

52. *New York Times*, April 2, 1988.

53. US Central Intelligence Agency, "Issues (U)", DST-1620S-464–90, March 1, 1990 (FOIA–Gulflink).

54. US Central Intelligence Agency, "Iraq's National Security Goals," an Intelligence Assessment, December 1988 (FOIA–NSA).

7. IRAN AND THE USE OF GAS

1. Letter, S/15934, August 18, 1983.

2. Letter, S/19193, October 9, 1987.

3. Letter, S/19029, August 10, 1987. Emphasis added.

4. Letter, S/19892, May 19, 1988.

5. Letter, S/17088, April 9, 1985.

6. Examples of the use of these terms abound in Iran's communications to the UN. For war crimes, see Letter, S/18555, January 5, 1987. For crimes against humanity, Letter, S/18577, January 11, 1987. For genocide (Halabja), Letter, S/19696, March 28, 1988. This was mere sloganeering, as Iran made no serious attempt to argue that Iraqi conduct amounted to such crimes.

7. Letter, S/16340, February 14, 1984.

8. Letter, S/17949, March 27, 1986.

9. Letter, S/17028, March 13, 1985.

10. UN Security Council, *Report of the Mission Dispatched by the Secretary-General to Investigate Allegations of the Use of Chemical Weapons in the Conflict between the Islamic Republic of Iran and Iraq*, S/20060 (July 20, 1988), p. 6.

11. Letter, S/18800, April 13, 1987.

12. Letter, S/19696, March 28, 1988.

13. Letter, S/18757, March 19, 1987.

14. Letter, S/18800, April 13, 1987.

15. Letter, S/19942, June 16, 1988.

16. Letter, S/17217, May 24, 1985.

17. Letter, S/19193, October 9, 1987.

18. Letter, S/17829, February 14, 1986.

19. Letter, S/19029, August 10, 1987.

20. For example, Letter, S/15743, May 4, 1983.

21. Letter, S/16342, February 15, 1984, at the height of the first tabun attacks during the Khaybar operation. Emphasis added.

22. Letter, S/15743, May 4, 1983. Chapter 1 of the UN Charter (1945) reads in part: "The Purposes of the United Nations are: 1. To maintain international peace and security, and to that end: to take effective collective measures for the prevention and removal of threats to the peace, and for the suppression of acts of aggression or other breaches of the peace, and to bring about by peaceful means, and in conformity with the principles of justice and international law, adjustment or settlement of international disputes or situations which might lead to a breach of the peace." (Art. 1.1.) And: "All Members shall settle their international disputes by peaceful means in such a manner that international peace and security, and justice, are not endangered." (Art. 2.3.) And: "All Members shall refrain in their international relations from the threat or use of force against the territorial integrity or political independence of any state, or in any other manner inconsistent with the Purposes of the United Nations." (Art. 2.4.)

23. Letter, S/16213, December 12, 1983.

24. "Report of the Secretary-General on His Visit to Iran and Iraq," S/17097, April 12, 1985.

25. UN report, S/23273, December 1991.

26. Letter, S/17922, March 17, 1986, and Letter, S/17934, March 23, 1986.

27. For example, Letter, S/16120, November 3, 1983.

28. Letter, S/19730, April 5, 1988. Emphasis added.

29. Letter, S/19029, August 10, 1987.

30. Chris Kutschera, "Le général perdu du rais," *Le Point*, March 21, 2003, based on an interview conducted in Denmark on December 2, 2002.

31. US Central Intelligence Agency, "Iraq's Potential for Chemical and Biological Warfare," September 1990 (FOIA–Gulflink).

32. US Defense Intelligence Agency, "Chemical and Biological Warfare in the Kuwait Theater of Operations; Iraq's Capability and Posturing (U)," undated (FOIA–Gulflink).

33. US Central Intelligence Agency, "Report on the Use of Chemical Weapons during the Iran–Iraq War," February 1989 (FOIA–Gulflink).

34. Anthony Cordesman, "Creating Weapons of Mass Destruction," *Armed Forces Journal International* (February 1989), pp. 54–57.

35. William Myers and Richard Wilson, "Expanding Chemical Warfare Capabilities: A Cause for Concern," US Army Intelligence Agency, *U.S. Army Scientific and Technical Intelligence Bulletin*, AST-2660R-074–86 (December 1986), p. 23 (FOIA–NSA). Emphasis added.

36. Baghdad Domestic Service, September 26, 1988, in *FBIS-NES-88–188*, p. 28.

37. Cited in Gordon M. Burck and Charles C. Flowerree, *International Handbook on Chemical Weapons Proliferation* (New York: Greenwood Press, 1991), pp. 242–43.

38. IRNA in English, "Shifting Smog Makes Iraq's Chemically Tainted Record More Darker [sic]," September 2, 1988, in *FBIS-NES-88–173*, p. 54, and Iranian letters to the UN secretary-general: S/16139 of November 10, 1983, and S/16154 of November 16, 1983.

39. Letter, S/17824, February 13, 1986.

40. Reuters, October 19, 1987.

41. Letters, S/18806, April 15, 1987, and S/18810, April 16, 1987.

42. UN Security Council, *Report of the Mission Dispatched by the Secretary-General to Investigate Allegations of the Use of Chemical Weapons in the Conflict between the Islamic Republic of Iran and Iraq*, S/18852 (May 26, 1987), paras. 40–54 and 64B(a).

43. Ibid., para. 66.

44. Letter, S/18870, May 18, 1987.

45. Burck and Flowerree, *International Handbook*, p. 112.

46. US Central Intelligence Agency, "CW Use in Iran–Iraq War," undated (FOIA–Gulflink). Emphasis added.

47. US Central Intelligence Agency, "Iraqi Chemical Weapons and Defense Capabilities," undated (FOIA–Gulflink).

48. UN Security Council, *Report of the Mission* (1987), paras. 59–62.

49. Ibid., p. 2. Emphasis added.

50. Two examples: Letters, S/20013, July 13, 1988, and S/20077, August 1, 1988.

51. The secretary-general noted "with regret that the evidence obtained by the specialists points to an ever increasing presence of different types of weapons associated with aggressive chemical agents in the conflict between Iran and Iraq." UN Security Council, *Report of the Mission Dispatched by the Secretary-General to Investigate Allegations of the Use of Chemical Weapons in the Conflict between the Islamic Republic of Iran and Iraq*, S/20063 (July 25, 1988), p. 2.

52. Ibid., paras. 17–32.

53. Letter, S/19029, August 10, 1987.

54. Quoted in the *Atlanta Constitution*, July 9, 1987.

55. In an interesting footnote, the UN team reported that, according to senior Iraqi officials, the alleged chemical attacks against their forces that had yielded mustard and phosgene casualties were "the first that Iraq had experienced during the course of the conflict." If this is so, it certainly pulls the rug out from underneath earlier Iraqi allegations of Iranian gas use, as well as to the claim made by Tariq Aziz in July 1988 that Iran had been the first to resort to this weapon, namely at the war's start. UN Security Council, *Report of the Mission* (1987), para 62.

56. *FBIS-NES-88–052* (March 17, 1988), pp. 30–31.

57. Sawt al-Sha'ab, *FBIS-NES-88–058* (March 25, 1988), pp. 38–39.

58. Letter, S/19730, April 5, 1988.

59. The Iranians, too, reported the chemical attacks in the Qaradagh area, giving as dates March 21, 22, 23, 26, and 31. Letter, S/19733, April 4, 1988.

60. UN Security Council, *Report of the Mission Dispatched by the Secretary-General to Investigate Allegations of the Use of Chemical Weapons in the Conflict between the Islamic Republic of Iran and Iraq*, S/19823 (April 25, 1988), paras. 33–53.

61. Letter, S/19741, April 5, 1988.

62. US Air Force Intelligence Agency, "Iran/Iraq Chemical Warfare Casualties" (undated), paras. 4 and 6F (FOIA–author).

63. Mudiriyat al-Amn al-'Ameh, secret cable to Amn headquarters in Erbil, March 16, 1988. Document on file with Human Rights Watch (HRW).

64. Mudiriyat al-Istikhbarat al-Askariyeh al-'Ameh, Suleimaniyeh, March 27, 1988, HRW ref. 2106/4-I.

65. Mudiriyat al-Istikhbarat al-Askariyeh al-'Ameh, Suleimaniyeh, April 11, 1988, HRW ref. 2107/2-A.

66. Mudiriyat al-Istikhbarat al-Askariyeh al-'Ameh Eastern Sector, Kirkuk, April 2, 1988, HRW ref. 2123/5-H. Emphasis added.

67. UN Security Council, *Report of the Mission Dispatched by the Secretary-General to Investigate Allegations of the Use of Chemical Weapons in the Conflict between the Islamic Republic of Iran and Iraq*, S/17911 (March 12, 1986), para. 43.

68. For a discussion, see Middle East Watch, *Bureaucracy of Repression: The Iraqi Government in Its Own Words* (New York: 1994), pp. 10–12.

69. HRW ref. 2099/1-P.

70. HRW ref. 2099/1-O.

71. HRW ref. 2099/1-N.

72. HRW ref. 1040/8-B.
73. HRW ref. 478/13-A.
74. HRW ref. 1060/6-A.
75. IRNA reported on March 18 that Iranian forces had shot down an Iraqi Sukhoy-22 around noon the previous day and had captured the pilot, a man by the name of Ahmad Shaker Ahmad Helaleh. *FBIS-NES-88–054*, p. 56. The press conference was held in Tehran on April 1 in front of Iranian and foreign reporters. IRNA, *FBIS-NES-88–064*, p. 55. Earlier, Iran had dragged before the camera Iraqi army officers who had been captured by Iranian forces in Halabja and inadvertently became targets of the Iraqi chemical attack themselves. "I saw with my own eyes the Iraqi warplanes come and use chemical bombs against the city," one POW said, who added that he survived because his captors gave him a gas mask. "Iraqi POWs admit use of gas," *The Times* (London), March 25, 1988.
76. "Former Iraqi Air Force Officer Discusses Halabjah, Current State of Iraqi Air Force," Radio Free Iraq, December 4, 2000.
77. Kutschera, "Le général perdu."
78. See also, Wafiq al-Samarra'i, *Hotam al-Bawaba al-Sharqiya* (*The Destroyer of the Eastern Gate*) (London: publisher and date unlisted), p. 104.
79. Director of Central Intelligence, "National Intelligence Daily, Tuesday, 22 March 1988," p. 5 (FOIA–Author).
80. Cable from Joint Chiefs of Staff, Washington, DC, to various US agencies (including the Department of State and the Defense Intelligence Agency), March 22, 1988 (FOIA–NSA).

8. FIXING THE EVIDENCE

1. Agence France Presse, October 22, 2002.
2. *New York Times*, August 17, 2002.
3. Patrick E. Tyler, "Poison Gas Attack Kills Hundreds; Iran Accuses Iraq of Atrocity in Kurdish Region Near Border City," *Washington Post*, March 24, 1988.
4. Patrick E. Tyler, "Both Iraq and Iran Gassed Kurds in War, U.S. Analysis Finds," *Washington Post*, May 3, 1990.
5. Stephen C. Pelletiere, "A War Crime or an Act of War?" *New York Times*, January 31, 2003.
6. Stephen C. Pelletiere and Douglas V. Johnson II, *Lessons Learned: The Iran–Iraq War*, Volume I (Quantico, VA: US Marine Corps, 1990), p. 100.
7. US Defense Intelligence Agency, "Kurdistan: Resistance Forces at Peril," October 6, 1988 (FOIA–NSA).
8. Human Rights Watch ref. 244/7-A.
9. Cable from US Embassy, Baghdad, to Secretary of State, 1988BAGHDA01888, April 6, 1988 (FOIA–Author).
10. Cited in "Iran Says Iraq Used Nerve Gas – 5,000 Kurds Die, Tehran Tells UN," Associated Press, March 21, 1988.

11. David Hirst, "Iran Puts Dead on Show after Gas Raid," *Guardian*, March 22, 1988. IRNA referred to "personnel" of the Pasdaran's "anti-chemical units" speaking to foreign reporters in Halabja on March 20. *FBIS-NES-88-055*, p. 66.

12. Artsen Zonder Grenzen – MSF Holland, "Assessment of the [sic] by Chemical War Affected Population: Report mission Kurdistan 24 – 27 March 1988" (Amsterdam: MSF, undated), pp. 4–5; and MSF, *Ten Years Emergency Aid Worldwide* (Amsterdam: MSF, undated).

13. T. D. Seeley, J. W. Nowicke, M. Meselson, J. Guillemin, and P. Akratanakul, "Yellow Rain," *Scientific American*, no. 253 (1985), pp. 122–31; and Julian Robinson, Jeanne Guillemin, and Matthew Meselson, "Yellow Rain in Southeast Asia: The Story Collapses," in Susan Wright, ed., *Preventing a Biological Arms Race* (Cambridge, MA: MIT Press, 1990), pp. 220–38.

14. Jan L. Willems, "Difficulties in Verifying the Use of Chemical Weapons and the Implications: Some Brief Case Studies," *The PSR Quarterly*, vol. 1, no. 4 (December 1991), p. 204.

15. For his own analysis, see A. Heyndrickx, N. Sookvanichsilp, and M. van den Heede, "Detection of Triochothecene Mycotoxins (Yellow Rain) in Blood, Urine, and Faeces of Iranian Soldiers Treated as Victims of a Gas Attack," *Rivista di Tossicologia Sperimentale e Clinica*, vol. 19, nos. 1–3 (1989), pp. 7–11. For a systematic study countering Heyndrickx's allegations, see Jan L. Willems, "Clinical Management of Mustard Gas Casualties," *Annales Medicinae Militaris Belgicae*, vol. 3/supplement, 1989.

16. Quoted by Olivia Ward, "Expert Urges Tough Action against Chemical Weapons, Stop 'Murder of Minorities,'" *Toronto Star*, November 13, 1988.

17. A. Heyndrickx, "Clinical Toxicological Reports and Conclusion of the Biological Samples of Men and of the Environmental Samples, Brought to the Department of Toxicology at the State University of Ghent, for Toxicological Investigation," Report no. 88/KU2/PJ881, Department of Toxicology, University of Ghent, April 27, 1988.

18. Francona may have misidentified Ft. Detrick, which specializes in biological warfare. Aberdeen Proving Ground, by contrast, covers chemical warfare.

19. UN Security Council, *Report of the Mission Dispatched by the Secretary-General to Investigate Allegations of the Use of Chemical Weapons in the Conflict between the Islamic Republic of Iran and Iraq*, S/19823 (April 25, 1988), paras. 21–23.

20. Abbas Foroutan, "Medical Notes on Chemical Warfare," *Kowsar Medical Journal* (Tehran), vol. 2, no. 1 (Spring 1376–1997); vol. 2, no. 2 (Summer 1376–1997); and vol. 2, no. 4 (Winter 1376–1998), pp. 293–94 and 299–300.

21. UN Security Council, *Report of the Mission Dispatched by the Secretary-General to Investigate Allegations of the Use of Chemical Weapons in the Conflict between the Islamic Republic of Iran and Iraq*, S/18852 (May 26, 1987), para. 17.

22. UN Security Council, *Report of the Mission Dispatched by the Secretary-General to Investigate Allegations of the Use of Chemical Weapons in the Conflict between the Islamic Republic of Iran and Iraq*, S/17911 (March 12, 1986), para. 26.

23. UN Security Council, *Report of the Mission Dispatched by the Secretary-General to Investigate Allegations of the Use of Chemical Weapons in the Conflict between the Islamic Republic of Iran and Iraq*, S/20060 (July 20, 1988), para. 31.
24. Director of Central Intelligence, "Impact and Implications of Chemical Weapons Use in the Iran–Iraq War," undated, late 1987 – early 1988, para. 17 (FOIA–Gulflink).
25. Physicians for Human Rights and Human Rights Watch, "Scientific First: Soil Samples Taken from Bomb Craters in Northern Iraq Reveal Nerve Gas – Even Four Years Later," Press statement, April 29, 1993, available from http://www.phrusa.org.
26. Abbas Foroutan, "Medical Notes on Chemical Warfare," *Kowsar Medical Journal* (Tehran), vol. 3, no. 2 (Summer 1377–1998), p. 218.
27. Willems, "Clinical management."
28. Cited in Roger Trilling, "Fighting Words," *Village Voice*, May 1–7, 2002. According to Jean Pascal Zanders (e-mail, January 2007), who has long studied the Halabja question, the assessment was conveyed from the DIA's Special Security Office, carrying the document code PTTSZYUW RUEKJCS2867 0850428-SSS-RUEALGX.
29. For example, Director of Central Intelligence, "National Intelligence Daily, Friday, 18 March 1988," p. 5 (FOIA–Author).
30. Director of Central Intelligence, "National Intelligence Daily, Tuesday, 22 March 1988," p. 5 (FOIA–Author).
31. "'Poor Man's Bomb' Is Once Again Used in Battle," *New York Times*, April 17, 1988.
32. For example, David Ottoway, "In Mideast, Warfare with a New Nature," *Washington Post*, April 5, 1988, looking back to Iraq's claim that Iran used phosgene and mustard gas at Fish lake during Karbala V. Also, Jim Muir, "Iraqi Gas Attacks Revive Horrors of the Great War," *Sunday Times*, March 27, 1988, quoting an unnamed US State Department official as saying Iran had used chemical shells on "very limited occasions" in 1987 and 1988.
33. *New York Times*, July 22, 1988.
34. *Christian Science Monitor*, April 13, 1988.

9. THE ROAD TO KUWAIT

1. For a description of the Final Anfal, see Human Rights Watch, *Iraq's Crime of Genocide: The Anfal Campaign Against the Kurds* (New Haven and London: Yale University Press, 1995), Chapter 10.
2. Stephen C. Pelletiere, Douglas V. Johnson II, and Leif R. Rosenberger, *Iraqi Power and U.S. Security in the Middle East* (Carlisle Barracks, PA: US Army War College, Strategic Studies Institute, 1990), p. 51.
3. Memorandum from Assistant Secretary of State Richard W. Murphy to Secretary of State George P. Shultz, September 7, 1988 (FOIA–NSA). Emphasis added.

4. Cable from Secretary of State George Shultz to various recipients, September 21, 1988 (FOIA–NSA). Emphasis added.

5. On September 6 the regime announced a thirty–day "general and comprehensive amnesty for Iraqi Kurds inside and outside Iraq," excluding Jalal Talabani. *Al-Thawra*, September 7, 1988. The English translation of the Revolutionary Command Council's full statement can be found in *FBIS-NES-88–174*, pp. 38–39.

6. Memorandum from Morton I. Abramowitz, director of the State Department's Bureau of Intelligence and Research, to George Shultz, September 13, 1988 (FOIA–NSA).

7. Morton I. Abramowitz, "Swan Song for Iraq's Kurds?" US Department of State, September 2, 1988 (FOIA–NSA).

8. Cable from secretary of state to US embassy, Baghdad, September 3, 1988 (FOIA–NSA).

9. US Department of State briefing, Federal News Service, September 8, 1988.

10. Milton Viorst, "Poison Gas and Genocide: The Shaky Case Against Iraq," *Washington Post*, October 5, 1988; and Patrick E. Tyler, "The Kurds: It's Not Genocide," *Washington Post*, September 25, 1988.

11. George P. Shultz, *Turmoil and Triumph: My Years as Secretary of State* (New York: Charles Scribner's Sons, 1993), p. 241.

12. Cable from secretary of state to US embassy, Baghdad, September 10, 1988 (FOIA–NSA).

13. Cable from secretary of state to various recipients, September 22, 1988 (FOIA–NSA).

14. Baghdad Domestic Service, in *FBIS-NES-88–185* (September 23, 1988), p. 15.

15. Human Rights Watch, *Iraq's Crime*, p. 264.

16. Briefing memorandum from Richard Murphy to George Shultz, September 7, 1988 (FOIA–NSA).

17. Cable from US embassy, Baghdad, to secretary of state, September 9, 1988 (FOIA–NSA).

18. See Physicians for Human Rights and Human Rights Watch, "Scientific First: Soil Samples Taken from Bomb Craters in Northern Iraq Reveal Nerve Gas – Even Four Years Later," Press statement, April 29, 1993, available at: http://www.phrusa.org. See also, Physicians for Human Rights, *Winds of Death: Iraq's Use of Poison Gas Against Its Kurdish Population* (Boston: PHR, 1989).

19. Peter W. Galbraith and Christopher Van Hollen, Jr., *Chemical Weapons Use in Kurdistan: Iraq's Final Offensive.* Staff Report to the Committee on Foreign Relations, US Senate (Washington, DC: US Government Printing Office, 1988).

20. US Department of State, Bureau of Intelligence and Research, "Chemical Weapons Use," September 13, 1988 (FOIA–NSA).

21. H. Allen Holmes and Paul Hare, "U.S. Policy Toward Iraqi CW Use," action memorandum to George Shultz, September 13, 1988, pp. 6–7 (FOIA–NSA).

22. Curtis W. Kamman, "US–Iraqi Relations: Implications of Passage of Economic Sanctions Bill," memorandum to George Shultz, October 18, 1988 (FOIA–NSA).

23. US Department of State, Letter from J. Edward Fox, assistant secretary for legislative affairs, to Dante B. Fascell, chairman of the House Foreign Affairs Committee, September 13, 1988 (FOIA–NSA).

24. Some of these options are laid out in US State Department memorandum, "Export Controls on Chemical Weapons (CW) and Related Items," September 8, 1988 (FOIA–NSA); and in US State Department memorandum, "Overview of U.S.–Iraqi Relations and Potential Pressure Points," September 9, 1988 (FOIA–NSA).

25. Holmes and Hare, "U.S. Policy."

26. See Joost Hiltermann, "Elusive Justice: Trying to Try Saddam," *Middle East Report*, no. 215 (Summer 2000).

27. For the best description of this episode, see Samantha Power, "*A Problem From Hell*": *America and the Age of Genocide* (New York: Basic Books, 2002), Chapter 8.

28. Memorandum from Murphy to Shultz, October 3, 1988 (FOIA–NSA).

29. Holmes and Hare, "U.S. Policy," p. 3.

30. Cable from April Glaspie, Baghdad, to George Shultz, September 4, 1988 (FOIA–NSA).

31. Cable from Glaspie to Shultz, September 10, 1988 (FOIA–NSA).

32. Shultz, p. 243. Emphasis added.

33. US Department of State, "Public Diplomacy," September 13, 1988 (FOIA–NSA).

34. US Central Intelligence Agency, "Section II: Issues (U)," DST-1620S-464–90, March 15, 1990 (FOIA–Gulflink).

35. Quoted in Richard Murphy, "U.S. Policy towards Iraq and CW Use," action memorandum to Michael Armacost, September 19, 1988 (FOIA–NSA).

36. US Department of State, "Deputy Secretary's Meeting with Arab League Ambassadors on Iraqi CW Use," September 22, 1988 (FOIA–NSA).

37. CIA, "Section II: Issues (U)."

38. George Bush and Brent Scowcroft, *A World Transformed* (New York: Vintage Books, 1998), p. 305.

39. US Department of State, "Overview."

40. Cable from Glaspie to Shultz, November 5, 1988 (FOIA–NSA).

41. Quoted by Adil Ilyas in *Al-Qabas* (Kuwait), October 31, 1988, reproduced in BBC, Middle East, ME/0299/A/1, November 3, 1988.

42. Baghdad news conference reported in *Al-Jumhuriya*, September 18, 1988, in *FBIS-NES-88-189*, pp. 27–36.

43. "The Glaspie Transcript: Saddam Meets the U.S. Ambassador (July 25, 1990)," in Micah L. Sifry and Christopher Cerf, eds., *The Gulf War Reader: History, Documents, Opinions* (New York: Random House, 1991), pp. 122–33.

44. US Central Intelligence Agency, "Iraq's Potential for Chemical and Biological Warfare," September 1990 (FOIA–Gulflink).
45. Ibid.
46. US Central Intelligence Agency, "Iraq's Chemical Warfare Program: More Self-Reliant, More Deadly," research paper, August 1990 (FOIA–Gulflink).
47. US Department of the Air Force, "Iraq's Efforts to Improve Its Chemical Weapons (CW) for a Desert Environment," information memorandum, October 23, 1990 (FOIA–Gulflink).
48. US Central Intelligence Agency, "Iraq's Potential for Chemical and Biological Warfare," September 1990 (FOIA–Gulflink); and unnamed agency, "Iraqi Air Force Capability to Deliver Chemical Weapons," December 1, 1990 (FOIA–Gulflink).
49. CIA, "Iraq's Potential."
50. "Defense Intelligence Assessment: Iraqi Military Developments Through 1992," undated–1989 (FOIA–Gulflink).
51. One of the best books on the subject is Alan Friedman's *Spider's Web: The Secret History of How the White House Illegally Armed Iraq* (New York: Bantam Books, 1993).
52. The full extent of Iraq's WMD programs can be gleaned from the record of their dismantlement by the UN Special Commission on Iraq (UNSCOM), established in the aftermath of the Gulf war under UN Security Council Resolution 687 of April 3, 1991, available from http://www.un.org/Depts/unscom/.

CONCLUSION: FALLOUT

1. Cited by Jonathan C. Randal, "Rebel Kurds Say They Are Ready to Strike at Iraq," *Washington Post*, January 24, 1991.
2. US Department of Defense, "Possible Use of Phosphorus Chemical," April 17, 1991 (FOIA–Gulflink). See also C.J. Chivers with David Rohde, "Thousands of Kurds Flee Front–Line Cities," *New York Times*, March 18, 2003.
3. Some of what follows was published in International Crisis Group, *War in Iraq: What's Next for the Kurds?* (Brussels: ICG, March 2003), available from http://www.crisisgroup.org.
4. IRNA, January 7, 1989, in *FBIS-WEU-89-005*, p. 7.
5. David Ignatius, "Reaching Out to Iran," *Washington Post*, June 2, 2006.
6. US Air Force Intelligence Agency, "Iran/Iraq Chemical Warfare Casualties," undated (FOIA–Author).
7. H. Allen Holmes and Paul Hare, "U.S. Policy toward Iraqi CW Use," action memorandum to Secretary of State George Shultz, September 13, 1988, pp. 1–2 (FOIA NSA).
8. IRNA in English, October 19, 1988, *FBIS-NES-88-202*, p. 55.
9. Quoted by Reuters, "UN Council Demands Iran Suspend Nuclear Work," July 31, 2006.

10. US Joint Chiefs of Staff, "Thinking about a Policy for Iraq," January 3, 1990 (FOIA–NSA).
11. Jonathan T. Howe and Richard W. Murphy, "Iraqi Use of Chemical Weapons," US Department of State, November 21, 1983 (FOIA–NSA).
12. US Central Intelligence Agency, "Iran–Iraq: Chemical Warfare Continues," November 1986 (FOIA–Gulflink).
13. Quoted in Giandomenico Picco, *Man without a Gun* (New York: Times Books, 1999), p. 74.
14. Holmes and Hare, "U.S. Policy," p. 6.
15. CIA, "Iran–Iraq: Chemical Warfare Continues."
16. US Central Intelligence Agency, "Iran–Iraq Frontline," July 27, 1988 (FOIA–Gulflink).
17. "Use of Chemical Weapons in Iran–Iraq War," transcript of "Nightline" show of March 23, 1988.
18. Donald H. Rumsfeld, "Take the Fight to the Terrorists," *Washington Post*, October 26, 2003.
19. For an account, read Robert Fisk, *Pity the Nation: Lebanon at War* (Oxford: Oxford University Press, 2001), Chapter 14.
20. See, for example, Greg Myre, "Rockets Create a 'Balance of Fear' with Israel, Gaza Residents Say," *New York Times*, July 9, 2006.
21. *Washington Post*, October 30, 1988.

EPILOGUE

1. See Joost R. Hiltermann, "The Demise of Operation Provide Comfort," *Middle East Report*, no. 203 (Spring 1997). While those working on US-funded projects left, other Kurds, working with the UN or the European Union, or on projects funded by them, stayed and continued to rebuild Kurdistan.

BIBLIOGRAPHY

Abd-al-Rahman, Ziad (pseudonym for Najmaddin Rashid Abdullah Fakeh), *Death Crematorium: The Anfal Operations from the Iraqi Regime's Documents* (*Tuni Merg* in Kurdish, *Mahraqet al-Mawt* in Arabic). Erbil: Committee for the Defense of Anfal Victims' Rights, 1995.

Aburish, Saïd K., *Saddam Hussein: The Politics of Revenge*. New York: Bloomsbury Publishing, 2000.

Ali, Javed, "Chemical Weapons and the Iran–Iraq War: A Case Study in Non-Compliance." *The Nonproliferation Review* (Monterey, CA), vol. 7, no. 1 (Spring 2001), 1–16.

Angeli, Claude, and Stéphanie Messier, *Notre Allié Saddam*. Paris: Olivier Orban, 1992.

Ardestani, Hussein, "Imposed War: The Impact of the Conflict on Great Powers Strategies." *Discourse: An Iranian Quarterly*, vol. 1, no. 4 (Spring 2000), 123–52.

Ashworth, George, Gerald E. Connolly, and Peter W. Galbraith, *War in the Persian Gulf: The U.S. Takes Sides*. Staff Report to the Committee on Foreign Relations, United States Senate. Washington, DC: US Government Printing Office, 1987.

Axelgard, Frederick W., *A New Iraq? The Gulf War and Implications for US Policy*. New York: Praeger Publishers, 1988.

Ayalon, Ami, "The Iraqi–Iranian War." *Middle East Contemporary Survey*, vol. 4 (1979–80), 14–29.

Bakhash, Shaul, *The Reign of the Ayatollahs: Iran and the Islamic Revolution*. New York: Basic Books, 1984.

Balta, Paul, *Iran–Irak: Une Guerre de 5000 Ans*. Paris: Editions Anthropos, 1988.

Bamford, James, *Body of Secrets: Anatomy of the Ultra-Secret National Security Agency from the Cold War through the Dawn of the New Century*. New York: Doubleday, 2001.

Baram, Amatzia, *Culture, History and Ideology in the Formation of Ba'thist Iraq, 1968–89*. Basingstoke, U.K.: Macmillan Ltd., 1991.

Baram, Amatzia, and Barry Rubin, editors, *Iraq's Road to War*. New York: St. Martin's Press, 1993.

Baran, David, *Vivre la Tyrannie et Lui Survivre: L'Irak en Transition*. Paris: Mille et Une Nuits, 2004.

Al-Barazi, Tammam, *Al-Iraq wa Amrika 1983–90 (Iraq and the United States 1983–90)*. Cairo: Maktabet Madbouli (year unlisted).

Batatu, Hanna, *The Old Social Classes and the Revolutionary Movements of Iraq*. Princeton, NJ: Princeton University Press, 1978.

Bellaigue, Christopher de, *In the Rose Garden of the Martyrs: A Memoir of Iran*. New York: HarperCollins, 2006.

Bengio, Ofra, "Iraq." *Middle East Contemporary Survey*, vol. 4 (1979–80), 501–36; vol. 5 (1980–81), 578–604; vol. 6 (1981–82), 582–630; vol. 7 (1982–83), 560–94; vol. VIII (1983–84), 465–96; vol. IX (1984–85), 460–86; vol. X (1986), 361–96; vol. XI (1987), 423–59; vol. XII (1988), 500–42; and vol. XIII (1989), 372–418.

Bengio, Ofra, "The Iraqi Kurds: The Struggle for Autonomy in the Shadow of the Iran–Iraqi Conflict." *Immigrants and Minorities*, vol. 9, no. 3 (November 1990), 249–68.

Bennis, Phyllis, and Michel Moushabeck, *Beyond the Storm: A Gulf Crisis Reader*. New York: Olive Branch Press, 1991.

Beres, Louis Rene, "Iraqi Deeds and International Law: The Question of Punishment." *The Jerusalem Journal of International Relations*, vol. 14, (Summer 1992), 22–43.

Bergquist, Ronald E., *The Role of Airpower in the Iran–Iraq War*. Honolulu, HI: University Press of the Pacific, 1988.

Binnendijk, Hans, et al., *War in the Gulf*. Staff Report prepared for the Committee on Foreign Relations, United States Senate. Washington, DC: US Government Printing Office, 1984.

Bloom, Mia, "The Case of Iraq: The Glorious Anfal Campaign to eradicate and eliminate the Kurds." In Jongman, Albert J., ed., *Contemporary Genocides: Causes, Cases, Consequences* (Leiden, NL: Projecten Interdisciplinair Onderzoek naar de Oorzaken van Mensenrechtenschendingen (PIOOM), 1996), 79–94.

Bruinessen, Martin van, *Agha, Shaikh and State: The Social and Political Structures of Kurdistan*. London: Zed Books Ltd., 1992.

Bruinessen, Martin van, *Kurdish Ethno-Nationalism Versus Nation-Building States*. Istanbul: The Isis Press, 2000.

Bulloch, John, and Harvey Morris, *No Friends But the Mountains: The Tragic History of the Kurds*. New York: Oxford University Press, 1992.

Burck, Gordon M., and Charles C. Flowerree, *International Handbook on Chemical Weapons Proliferation*. New York: Greenwood Press, 1991.

Bush, George, and Brent Scowcroft, *A World Transformed*. New York: Vintage Books, 1998.

Carus, Seth, *The Genie Unleashed: Iraq's Chemical and Biological Weapons Program*. Washington, DC: Washington Institute for Near East Policy, 1989.

Chaliand, Gerard, ed., *A People Without a Country: The Kurds and Kurdistan*. Brooklyn, NY: Olive Branch Press, 1993.

Chandler, Robert W., *Tomorrow's War, Today's Decisions: Iraqi Weapons of Mass Destruction and the Implications of WMD-Armed Adversaries for Future U.S. Military Strategy*. McLean, VA: AMCODA Press, 1996.

Charny, Israel W., "Intervention and Prevention of Genocide." In Israel W. Charny, ed., *Genocide: A Critical Bibliographic Review*. London: Mansell Publishing Ltd., 1988.

Christison, Kathleen, "The Arab–Israeli Policy of George Shultz." *Journal of Palestine Studies*, vol. 18, no. 2 (Winter 1989), 29–47.

Chubin, Shahram, *Iran's National Security Policy: Capabilities, Intentions & Impact*. Washington, DC: The Carnegie Endowment for International Peace, 1994.

Chubin, Shahram, and Charles Tripp, *Iran and Iraq at War*. Boulder, CO: Westview Press, 1988.

Cockburn, Andrew, and Patrick Cockburn, *Out of the Ashes: The Resurrection of Saddam Hussein*. New York: HarperCollins, 1999.

Colhoun, Jack, "How Bush Backed Iraq." *Middle East Report*, no. 176 (May–June 1992), 35–37.

Conason, Joe, "The Iraq Lobby: Kissinger, the Business Forum & Co.," in Micah L. Sifry and Christopher Cerf, eds., *The Gulf War Reader: History, Documents, Opinions* (New York: Times Books, 1991), 79–84.

Cordesman, Anthony, "Creating Weapons of Mass Destruction." *Armed Forces Journal International*, February 1989.

Cordesman, Anthony H., *The Iran–Iraq War and Western Security 1984–87: Strategic Implications and Policy Options*. London: Jane's Publishing Company Limited, 1987.

Cordesman, Anthony, *The Iraq–Iran War and US–Iraq Relations: An Iraqi Perspective – An Interview with Iraqi Foreign Minister Tariq Aziz*. Washington, DC: National Council on US–Arab Relations, August 1984.

Cordesman, Anthony H., and Abraham R. Wagner, *The Lessons of Modern War: Volume II*. Boulder, CO: Westview Press, 1990.

Creighton, John, *Oil on Troubled Waters: Gulf Wars 1980–91*. London: Echoes, 1992.

Dann, Uriel, "Iraqi–Iranian War." *Middle East Contemporary Survey*, vol. 6 (1981–82), 309–14; vol. 7, (1982–83), 256–60; vol. VIII (1983–84), 183–87; vol. IX (1984–85), 168–77; and vol. X (1986), 157–62.

Darwish, Adel, and Gregory Alexander, *Unholy Babylon: The Secret History of Saddam's War*. New York: St. Martin's Press, 1991.

Dodge, Toby, *Inventing Iraq: The Failure of Nation Building and a History Denied*. New York: Columbia University Press, 2003.

Eddington, Patrick, *Gassed in the Gulf: The Inside Story of the Pentagon – CIA Cover-up of Gulf War Syndrome*. Washington, DC: Insignia Publishing Company, 1997.

Eisenstadt, Mike, *"The Sword of the Arabs": Iraq's Strategic Weapons*. Washington, DC: The Washington Institute for Near East Policy, 1990.

Emin, Noshrwan Mustafa, *Khulanawwa la Now Baznada (Going Around in Circles: The Inside Story of Events in Iraqi Kurdistan, 1984–88)*. Berlin: Awadani b.v., 1999.

Ezell, Walter K., "Newspaper Responses to Reports of Atrocities: Burundi, Mozambique, Iraq." In Helen Fein, ed., *Genocide Watch* (New Haven and London: Yale University Press, 1992), 87–112.

Farouk–Sluglett, Marion, and Peter Sluglett, *Iraq Since 1958: From Revolution to Dictatorship*. London: I.B. Tauris & Co., Ltd., 2001.

Fisk, Robert, *Pity the Nation: Lebanon at War*. Oxford: Oxford University Press, 2001.

Foroutan, Abbas, *Jange Shimiaeeye Aragh va Tajarobe Bezeshkie Aan (Medical Experiences of Iraq's Chemical Warfare)*.Tehran: 2003, originally published in *Kowsar Medical Journal* (Tehran), in twelve installments from the Fall 1375 (1996), vol. 1, issue to the Summer 1378 (1999), vol. 4 (2), issue.

Francona, Rick, *Ally to Adversary: An Eyewitness Account of Iraq's Fall from Grace*. Annapolis: Naval Institute Press, 1999.

Friedman, Alan, *Spider's Web: The Secret History of How the White House Illegally Armed Iraq*. New York: Bantam Books, 1993.

Galbraith, Peter W., *Kurdistan in the Time of Saddam Hussein*. Staff Report prepared for the Committee on Foreign Relations, United States Senate. Washington, DC: US Government Printing Office, 1991.

Galbraith, Peter W., and Christopher Van Hollen, Jr., *Chemical Weapons Use in Kurdistan: Iraq's Final Offensive*. Staff Report to the Committee on Foreign Relations, United States Senate. Washington, DC: US Government Printing Office, 1988.

Gander, Terry J., "Iraq – the Chemical Arsenal." *Jane's Intelligence Review*, September 1992.

Gates, Robert M., *From the Shadows: The Ultimate Insider's Story of Five Presidents and How They Won the Cold War*. New York: Touchstone, 1996.

Gera, Gideon, "The Iraqi–Iranian War." *Middle East Contemporary Survey*, vol. XI (1987), 180–98.

Ghanei, Mustafa, S. Khateri, A. Jalali, and J. Aslani, "Outcome [sic] of Civilian Population of Sardasht City after Chemical Warfare Bombardment." Paper presented at a medical conference in Switzerland, May 2002 (in Persian, summary in English).

Gillard, Emanuela–Chiara, "What's Legal? What's Illegal?" In Lora Lumpe, ed., *Running Guns: The Global Black Market in Small Arms*. London and New York: Zed Books, 2000.

Goldberg, Jeffrey, "A Reporter at Large: The Great Terror." *New Yorker*, March 25, 2002.

Gordon, Michael R., and Bernard E. Trainor, *The Generals' War: The Inside Story of the Conflict in the Gulf*. Boston: Little, Brown and Company, 1995.

Gutman, Roy, and David Rieff, eds., *Crimes of War: What the Public Should Know*. New York: Norton, 1999.

Hamdoon, Nizar, "Iraq–U.S. Relations." *American–Arab Affairs*, no. 95 (Fall 1985), 95–97.

Hamza, Khidir, with Jeff Stein, *Saddam's Bombmaker: The Terrifying Inside Story of the Iraqi Nuclear and Biological Weapons Agenda*. New York: Scribner, 2000.

Harris, Robert, and Jeremy Paxman, *A Higher Form of Killing: The Secret History of Chemical and Biological Warfare*. New York: Random House, 2002.

Haselkorn, Avigdor, *The Continuing Storm: Iraq, Poisonous Weapons, and Deterrence*. New Haven: Yale University Press, 1999.

Hashemian, Farnoosh, Kaveh Khoshnood, Mayur M. Desai, Farahnaz Falahati, Stanislav Kasl, and Steven Southwick, "Anxiety, Depression, and Post-traumatic Stress in Iranian Survivors of Chemical Warfare, *Journal of the American Medical Association*, no. 296 (2006), 560–66.

Hassanpour, Amir, "The Kurdish Experience." *Middle East Report*, no. 189 (July–August 1994), 2–7, 23.

Henderson, Simon, *Instant Empire: Saddam Hussein's Ambition for Iraq*. San Francisco: Mercury House, 1991.

Helms, Christine Moss, *Iraq: Eastern Flank of the Arab World*. Washington, DC: The Brookings Institution, 1984.

Herby, Peter. *The Chemical Weapons Convention and Arms Control in the Middle East*. Oslo: International Peace Research Institute, 1992.

Heyndrickx, A., "Clinical Toxicological Reports and Conclusion of the Biological Samples of Men and of the Environmental Samples, Brought to the Department of Toxicology at the State University of Ghent, for Toxicological Investigation." Report no. 88/KU2/PJ881, Department of Toxicology, University of Ghent, April 27, 1988.

Heyndrickx, A., N. Sookvanichsilp, and M. van den Heede, "Detection of Trichothecene Mycotoxins (Yellow Rain) in Blood, Urine, and Faeces of Iranian Soldiers Treated as Victims of a Gas Attack." *Rivista di Tossicologia Sperimentale e Clinica*, vol. 19, nos. 1–3(1989), 7–11.

Hiltermann, Joost, "Elusive Justice: Trying to Try Saddam." *Middle East Report*, no. 215 (Summer 2000), 32–35.

Hiltermann, Joost R., "Genocide, Complicity, Silence: The Case of Iraq and the Kurds." Paper presented at the conference on "Ten Years after Anfal: Causes and Consequences of the Politics of Genocide in Iraq," in Amsterdam, June 5, 1998, and published in Dutch in *Soera*, vol. 6, no. 2 (May 1998).

Hiltermann, Joost R., "Outsiders as Enablers: Consequences and Lessons from International Silence on Iraq's Use of Chemical Weapons during the Iran–Iraq War." In Lawrence G. Potter and Gary G. Sick, eds., *Iran, Iraq and the Legacies of War* (New York: Palgrave Macmillan, 2004), 151–66.

Hiltermann, Joost R., "The Demise of Operation Provide Comfort," *Middle East Report*, no. 203 (Spring 1997).

Hiltermann, Joost R., "The Men Who Helped the Man Who Gassed His Own People." In Micah L. Sifry and Christopher Cerf, eds., *The Iraq War Reader: History, Documents, Opinions* (New York: Touchstone, 2003), 41–44.

Hiro, Dilip, *The Longest War: The Iran–Iraq Military Conflict*. New York: Routledge, Chapman, and Hall, Inc., 1991.

Hopwood, Derek, Habib Ishow, and Thomas Koszinowski, editors, *Iraq: Power and Society*. Reading, UK: Ithaca Press, 1993.

Human Rights Watch, *Iraq's Crime of Genocide: The Anfal Campaign Against the Kurds*. New Haven and London: Yale University Press, 1995. Originally published by Middle East Watch as *Genocide in Iraq: The Anfal Campaign Against the Kurds*. New York: HRW, 1993, available from http://www.hrw.org.

Hume, Cameron R., *The United Nations, Iran, and Iraq: How Peacemaking Changed*. Bloomington: Indiana University Press, 1994.

Institut Kurde de Paris, *Halabja: Ville Martyre*. Paris: Institut Kurde, 1988.

Institut Kurde de Paris, *Les Vents de la Mort*. Paris: Institut Kurde, 1988.

International Crisis Group, 2003, *War in Iraq: What's Next for the Kurds?* Brussels: ICG, 2003, available from http://www.crisisgroup.org.

Jabbar, Faleh A., "Why the Uprisings Failed." In Fran Hazelton, ed., *Iraq Since the Gulf War: Prospects for Democracy*. London: Zed Books, 1994, 97–117.

Jentleson, Bruce, *With Friends Like These: Reagan, Bush and Saddam, 1982–1990*. New York: W. W. Norton, 1994.

Joint Staff of the Army and Islamic Revolution, Operations Department, *Atlas Jank Iran wa 'Iraq (Atlas of the Iran–Iraq War)*. Tehran: The Center for War Studies and Research, 2001.

Jupa, Richard, and Jim Dingeman. *Gulf Wars*. Cambria, CA: 3W Publications, 1991.

Kadivar, Hooshang, and Stephen C. Adams, "Treatment of Chemical and Biological Warfare Injuries: Insights Derived from the 1984 Iraqi Attack on Majnoon Island." *Military Medicine*, vol. 156 (April 1991), 171–77.

Karsh, Efraim. *The Iran–Iraq War 1980–1988*. Oxford: Osprey Publishing, Ltd., 2002.

Karsh, Efraim. *The Iran/Iraq War: Impact and Implications*. Tel Aviv: The Jaffee Center for Strategic Studies, 1987.

Keddie, Nikkie, and Mark Gasiorowski, eds. *Neither East nor West: Iran, the Soviet Union, and the United States*. New Haven and London: Yale University Press, 1990.

Khadduri, Majid. *The Gulf War: The Origins and Implications of the Iraq–Iran Conflict*. New York: Oxford University Press, 1988.

Al-Khafaji, Isam, "State Terror and the Degradation of Politics in Iraq." *Middle East Report*, no. 176 (May–June 1992), 15–21.

Khateri, Shahriar, "La Guerre Chimique Pendant le Conflit Iran–Irak." In Chris Kutschera, ed., *Le livre noir de Saddam Hussein*. Paris: Oh editions, 2005, 455–70.

King, Ralph. *The Iran–Iraq War: The Political Implications*. Adelphi Papers #219. London: The International Institute for Strategic Studies, 1987.

Kinzer, Stephen. *All the Shah's Men: An American Coup and the Roots of Middle East Terror*. New York: John Wiley & Sons, 2003.

Klare, Michael T., "Prelude to Desert Storm: Arms Transfers to Iran and Iraq during the Iran–Iraq War of 1980–1988 and the Origins of the Gulf War." Paper prepared for the conference "Reassessing the Gulf War," Boston University, February 21, 2001.

Krasno, Jean E., and James S. Sutterlin, *The United Nations and Iraq, Defanging the Viper*. Westport, CT: Praeger Publishers, 2003.

Kreyenbroek, Philip G., and Stefan Sperl, editors, *The Kurds: A Contemporary Overview*. London: Routledge, 1992.

Krosney, Herbert, *Deadly Business: Legal Deals and Outlaw Weapons: The Arming of Iran and Iraq, 1975 to the Present*. New York: Four Walls Eight Windows, 1993.

Kutschera, Chris, *Le défi kurde ou le rêve fou de l'indépendance*. Paris: Bayard Editions, 1997.

Kutschera, Chris, "Le général perdu du rais." *Le Point*, March 21, 2003.

Kutschera, Chris, *Le mouvement national Kurde*. Paris: Flammarion, 1979.

Lavoy, Peter R., Scott D. Sagan, and James J. Wirtz, *Planning the Unthinkable: How New Powers Will Use Nuclear, Biological, and Chemical Weapons*. Ithaca: Cornell University Press, 2000.

Lawyers Committee for Human Rights, *Asylum under Attack: A Report on the Protection of Iraqi Refugees and Displaced Persons One Year after the Humanitarian Emergency in Iraq*. New York: LCHR, 1992.

MacDonald, Charles. "The Impact of the Gulf War on the Iraqi and Iranian Kurds." *Middle East Contemporary Survey*, vol. 7 (1982–83), 261–72.

Makiya, Kanan, "The Anfal: Uncovering an Iraqi Campaign to Exterminate the Kurds." *Harper's Magazine*, May 1992.

Makiya, Kanan, *Cruelty and Silence: War, Tyranny, Uprising and the Arab World*. New York: W. W. Norton, 1993.

Makiya, Kanan, *Republic of Fear: The Politics of Modern Iraq*. Berkeley and Los Angeles: University of California Press, 1998.

Marr, Phebe, *The Modern History of Iraq*. Boulder: Westview Press, 2004.

McDowall, David, *A Modern History of the Kurds*. London: I. B. Tauris, 2000.

McNaugher, Thomas L., "Ballistic Missiles and Chemical Weapons: The Legacy of the Iran–Iraq War." *International Security*, vol. 15, no. 2 (Fall 1990), 5–34.

Médecins sans Frontières, *Ten Years Emergency Aid Worldwide* (Amsterdam: MSF, undated).

Meiselas, Susan, *Kurdistan: In the Shadow of History*. New York: Random House, Inc., 1997.

Menashri, David. "Iran." *Middle East Contemporary Survey*, vol. X (1986), 323–60; vol. XI (1987), 391–422; and vol. XII (1988), 469–99.

Middle East Research and Information Project, *Crisis in the Gulf*. Washington, DC: MERIP, 1990.

Middle East Watch, *Bureaucracy of Repression: The Iraqi Government in Its Own Words*. New York: Human Rights Watch, 1994, available from http://www.hrw.org.

Middle East Watch, *Human Rights in Iraq*. New Haven and London: Yale University Press, 1990, available from http://www.hrw.org.

Middle East Watch and Physicians for Human Rights, *The Anfal Campaign in Iraqi Kurdistan: The Destruction of Koreme*. New York: Human Rights Watch, 1993, available from http://www.hrw.org.

Miller, Judith, "Iraq Accused: A Case of Genocide." *New York Times Magazine* (January 3, 1993), 12–17, 28, 31–36.

Miller, Judith, and Laurie Mylroie, *Saddam Hussein and the Crisis in the Gulf*. New York: Times Books, 1990.

Mohammadian, Hossein, *Bou Ná Ashená. (An Unknown Smell)*. Tehran: Abed, 2001.

Moushabeck, Michel, "Iraq: Years of Turbulence," in Phyllis Bennis and Michel Moushabeck, eds., *Beyond the Storm: A Gulf Crisis Reader*. (New York: Olive Branch Press, 1991), 25–36.

Mushir, Shawqat Haji, *Karasati Kimiabarani Halabja bi Hari 1988 (The Sad Events of the Chemical Bombing in Halabja in the Spring of 1988)*. Suleimaniyeh: 1998 (publisher unlisted).

Mylroie, Laurie, "After the Guns Fall Silent: Iraq in the Middle East." *Middle East Journal*, vol. 43, no.1 (Winter 1989), 51–67.

Mylroie, Laurie, "The Baghdad Alternative." *Orbis*, no. 32 (Summer 1988), 339–54.

Mylroie, Laurie, "The Superpowers and the Iran–Iraq War." *American–Arab Affairs* (Summer 1987), 15–26.

Neff, Donald, "The U.S., Iraq, Israel, and Iran: Backdrop to War." *Journal of Palestine Studies*, vol. 20, no. 4 (Summer 1991), 23–41.

O'Ballance, Edgar, *The Gulf War*. London: Brassey's Defence Publishers Ltd., 1988.

Pelletière, Stephen, *Iraq and the International Oil System: Why America Went to War in the Gulf*. Westport: Praeger, 2001.

Pelletière, Stephen C., *The Iran–Iraq War: Chaos in a Vacuum*. New York: Praeger, 1992.

Pelletière, Stephen C., and Douglas V. Johnson II, *Lessons Learned: The Iran–Iraq War*. Volume I. Quantico, VA: US Marine Corps, 1990.

Pelletière, Stephen C., Douglas V. Johnson II, and Leif R. Rosenberger, *Iraqi Power and U.S. Security in the Middle East*. Carlisle Barracks, PA: US Army War College, Strategic Studies Institute, 1990.

Pérez de Cuéllar, Javier, *Pilgrimage for Peace*. New York: St. Martin's Press, 1997.

Perry Robinson, J. P., "Chemical and biological warfare: developments in 1984." *World Armaments and Disarmament: SIPRI Yearbook 1985*. London and Philadelphia: Taylor & Francis, 1985.

Perry Robinson, Julian, and Jozef Goldblat, "Chemical Warfare in the Iraq–Iran War." SIPRI Fact Sheet, Stockholm International Peace Research Institute, May 1984.

Physicians for Human Rights, *Winds of Death: Iraq's Use of Poison Gas Against Its Kurdish Population*. Boston: PHR, 1989, available from http://www.phrusa.org.

Physicians for Human Rights and Human Rights Watch, "Scientific First: Soil Samples Taken from Bomb Craters in Northern Iraq Reveal Nerve Gas – Even Four Years Later." Press statement, April 29, 1993, available from http://www.phrusa.org.

Phythian, Mark, *Arming Iraq: How the U.S. and Britain Secretly Built Saddam's War Machine*. Boston: Northeastern University Press, 1997.

Picco, Giandomenico, *Man without a Gun*. New York: Times Books, 1999.

Pipes, Daniel, and Laurie Mylroie, "Back Iraq: Why Iran's Enemy Should Be America's Friend." *New Republic*, April 27, 1987.

Potter, Lawrence G., and Gary G. Sick, editors. *Iran, Iraq and the Legacy of War*. New York: Palgrave Macmillan, 2004

Power, Samantha, *"A Problem from Hell": America and the Age of Genocide*. New York: Basic Books, 2002.

Rajaee, Farhang, ed., *The Iran–Iraq War: The Politics of Aggression*. Gainesville: University Press of Florida, 1993.

Ramazani, R.K., *Revolutionary Iran: Challenge and Response in the Middle East*. Baltimore and London: The Johns Hopkins University Press, 1988.

Randal, Jonathan C., *After Such Knowledge, What Forgiveness: My Encounters with Kurdistan*. New York: Farrar, Straus and Giroux, 1997.

Rankin, Haywood, "Travels with Galbraith – Death in Basra, Destruction in Kurdistan." US Government Memorandum, September 27, 1987.

Ratner, Steven R., and Jason S. Abrams, *Accountability for Human Rights Atrocities in International Law: Beyond the Nuremberg Legacy* (Second Edition). Oxford: Oxford University Press, 2001.

Resool, Shorsh M., *Anfal: Kurdu Dawlati Iraq (Anfal: The Kurds and the Iraqi State)*. London: Al-Rafid, 2003.

Resool, Shorsh, *The Destruction of a Nation*. London: Patriotic Union of Kurdistan, April 1990 (unpublished report).

Ritter, Scott, *Endgame: Solving the Iraq Problem—Once and For All*. New York: Simon and Schuster, 1999.

Roberts, Adam, and Richard Guelff, eds., *Documents on the Laws of War*. Oxford: Oxford University Press, 2000.

Roberts, Brad, ed., *Terrorism with Chemical and Biological Weapons: Calibrating Risks and Responses*. Alexandria, VA: Chemical and Biological Arms Control Institute, 1997.

Robinson, Julian, Jeanne Guillemin, and Matthew Meselson, "Yellow Rain in Southeast Asia: The Story Collapses." In Susan Wright, ed., *Preventing a Biological Arms Race* (Cambridge, MA: MIT Press, 1990), 220–38.

Russell, Richard L., "Iraq's Chemical Weapons Legacy: What Others Might Learn from Saddam," *The Middle East Journal*, vol. 59, no. 2 (Spring 2005), 187–208.

Sahebjam, Freidoune, *Je N'ai Plus de Larmes Pour Pleurer*. Paris: Editions Grasset & Esquelle, 1985.

Al-Samarra'i, Wafiq, *Hotam al-Bawaba al-Sharqiya (The Destroyer of the Eastern Gate)*. London (publisher and date unlisted).

Al-Samarra'i, Wafiq, *Tariq al-Jahim: Haqa'eq 'an al-Zaman al-Seye' fi al-'Iraq (The Road to Hell: Facts about the Bad Era in Iraq)*. London: 1998 (publisher unlisted).

Schabas, William A., "Enforcing international humanitarian law: Catching the accomplices." *International Review of the Red Cross*, vol. 83, no. 842 (June 2001), 439–59.

Scott, Richard, *Report of the Inquiry into the Export of Defence Equipment and Dual-Use Goods to Iraq and Related Prosecutions.* London: HMSO, 1996.

Seeley, T. D., J. W. Nowicke, M. Meselson, J. Guillemin, and P. Akratanakul, "Yellow Rain." *Scientific American*, no. 253 (1985), 122–31.

Segal, David, "The Iran–Iraq War: A Military Analysis." *Foreign Affairs*, no. 66 (Summer 1988), 946–63.

Shultz, George P., *Turmoil and Triumph: My Years as Secretary of State.* New York: Charles Scribner's Sons, 1993.

Sick, Gary, *All Fall Down: America's Tragic Encounter with Iran.* New York: Random House, 1985.

Sick, Gary, "Iran's Quest for Superpower Status." *Foreign Affairs* (Spring 1987), 697–715.

Sick, Gary, "Moral Choice and the Iran–Iraq Conflict." *Ethics & International Affairs*, vol. 3 (1989), 117–33.

Sick, Gary, "Slouching toward Settlement: The Internationalization of the Iran–Iraq War, 1987 1988." In Nikkie Keddie and Mark Gasiorowski, eds., *Neither East nor West: Iran, the Soviet Union, and the United States* (New Haven and London: Yale University Press, 1990), 219–46.

Sifry, Micah L., and Christopher Cerf, eds., *The Gulf War Reader: History, Documents, Opinions.* New York: Times Books, 1991.

Sifry, Micah L., and Christopher Cerf, eds., *The Iraq War Reader: History, Documents, Opinions.* New York: Touchstone, 2003.

Simons, Lew, "Genocide and the Science of Proof." *National Geographic*, January 2006.

Sweeney, John, *Trading with the Enemy: Britain's Arming of Iraq.* London: Pan Books Ltd., 1993.

Talabany, Nouri, *Arabization of the Kirkuk Region.* London: Khak Press and Media Center, 1999.

Tarock, Adam, *The Superpowers' Involvement in the Iran–Iraq War.* Commack, NY: Nova Science Publishers, Inc., 1998.

Teicher, Howard, and Gayle Radley Teicher, *Twin Pillars to Desert Storm: America's Flawed Vision in the Middle East from Nixon to Bush.* New York: William Morrow, 1993.

Terrill, W. Andrew, "Chemical Warfare and 'Desert Storm': The Disaster that Never Came." *Small Wars & Insurgencies*, vol. 4, no. 2 (Autumn 1991), 263–79.

Terrill, W. Andrew, Jr., "Chemical Weapons in the Gulf War." *Strategic Review* (Spring 1986), 51–58.

Timmerman, Kenneth R., *The Death Lobby: How the West Armed Iraq*. Boston: Houghton Mifflin Company, 1991.

Trevan, Tim, *Saddam's Secrets: The Hunt for Iraq's Hidden Weapons*. London: HarperCollins, 1999.

Trilling, Roger, "Fighting Words," *Village Voice*, May 1–7, 2002.

Tripp, Charles, *A History of Iraq*. Cambridge: Cambridge University Press, 2000.

United Nations, Security Council, *Mission to Inspect Civilian Areas in Iran and Iraq Which Have Been Subject to Military Attack*, S/15834 (June 20, 1983).

United Nations, Security Council, *Report of the Specialists Appointed by the Secretary-General to Investigate Allegations by the Islamic Republic of Iran Concerning the Use of Chemical Weapons*, S/16433 (March 26, 1984).

United Nations, Security Council, *Letter Dated 17 April 1985 from the Secretary-General Addressed to the President of the Security Council*, S/17127 (April 24, 1985).

United Nations, Security Council, *Report of the Mission Dispatched by the Secretary-General to Investigate Allegations of the Use of Chemical Weapons in the Conflict between the Islamic Republic of Iran and Iraq*, S/17911 (March 12, 1986); S/18852 (May 26, 1987); S/19823 (April 25, 1988); S/20060 (July 20, 1988); S/20063 (July 25, 1988); S/20134 (August 19, 1988).

US Committee for Refugees, *Mass Exodus: Iraqi Refugees in Iran*. Washington, DC: American Council for Nationalities Services, 1991.

US Department of State, *American Foreign Policy: Current Documents 1985*. Washington, DC: US Department of State, 1986.

US Department of State, *Country Reports on Human Rights Practices for 1987*. Washington, DC: US Department of State, 1988.

Velayati, Ali Akbar, *Tarikh Siyasi Jank Tahmili Iraq 'alei Jumhuri Islami Iran* (*The Political History of the Iraqi Imposed War against the Islamic Republic of Iran*). Tehran: Daftar Nashr Farhank Islami, Isl. 1374 (1995–1996).

Viorst, Milton, "Iraq at War." *Foreign Affairs* (Winter 1986–87), 349–65.

Willems, Jan L., "Clinical management of mustard gas casualties," *Annales Medicinae Militaris Belgicae*, vol. 3/supplement, 1989.

Willems, Jan L., "Difficulties in Verifying the Use of Chemical Weapons and the Implications: Some Brief Case Studies," *The PSR Quarterly*, vol. 1, no. 4 (December 1991), p. 204.

Yahia, Latif, and Karl Wendl, *I Was Saddam's Son*. New York: Arcade Publishing, 1994 and 1997.

Yildiz, Kerim, *The Kurds in Iraq: The Past, Present and Future*. London: Pluto Press, 2004.

Zanders, Jean Pascal, *The 2nd Gulf War and the CBW Threat: Proceedings of the 3rd Annual Conference on Chemical Warfare.* Brussels: Centrum voor Polemologie, Vrije Universiteit, 1995.

Zanders, Jean Pascal, and Eric Remacle, editors, *Chemical Weapons Proliferation: Policy Issues Pending an International Treaty.* Brussels: Centrum voor Polemologie and Groupe de Recherche et d'Information sur la Paix, 1991.

Zarif, Mohammad Javad, and Mohammad Reza Alborzi, "Weapons of Mass Destruction in Iran's Security Paradigm: The Case of Chemical Weapons." *The Iranian Journal of International Affairs*, vol. XI, no. 4 (Winter 1999), 511–23.

INTERVIEWS CONDUCTED FOR THIS BOOK

Mahmoud **Abassi**, head nurse, internal medicine, at Baghyatollah Military Hospital, Tehran, May 20, 2002

Mullah Ali **Abd-al-Aziz**, head of Islamic Unity Movement of Kurdistan, Halabja, May 25, 2002

Najmeddin Faqi **Abdallah**, Iraqi Kurdish political and human rights activist in 1980s and 1990s, Rotterdam, November 19, 2000 and January 30, 2006

Faridoun **Abd-al-Qader**, Political Bureau member of Patriotic Union of Kurdistan, senior PUK commander in 1980s, Suleimaniyeh, May 23 and 27, 2002

Mu'ath **Abd-al-Rahim**, member Iraqi National Accord, Iraqi Ministry of Information official during 1980s, Amman, August 26, 2000

Taymour **Abdullah**, Anfal survivor, Washington, DC, March 31, 2001

Taghi **Aghaei**, travel agent who served as Basiji frontline reporter, Tehran, May 18, 2002

Hero Ibrahim **Ahmad**, head of PUK TV, Suleimaniyeh, May 24, 2002

Abbas Abd-al-Razzaq **Akbar** ("Abbas Video"), PUK guerrilla and videographer, Suleimaniyeh, May 23, 2002

Aras Abed **Akram**, official with Kurdish Save the Children, Halabja, May 27, 2002

Kosrat Rasoul **Ali**, senior PUK commander in 1980s, Washington, DC, July 6, 2000

Jamal Aziz **Amin**, PUK official, London, December 16, 1999 and April 16, 2000, and Suleimaniyeh, May 22, 2002

Khaled Reza **Amin**, PUK guerrilla responsible for communications in 1980s, Rotterdam, November 19, 2000

Dr. Latif **Amin**, head of Suleimaniyeh Health Department in 1980s, Suleimaniyeh, May 23, 2002

Mahmoud Reza **Amin**, PUK guerrilla in 1980s, Rotterdam, November 19, 2000

Neywshirwan Mustafa **Amin**, deputy leader of PUK, Washington, DC, May 2, 1993

Abu Mehdi **al-Asadi**, Badr Corps fighter in 1980s, Tehran, June 11, 2002

Dr. Ja'fer **Aslani**, pulmonologist, Baghyatollah Military Hospital, Tehran, May 20, 2002

Dr. Fuad **Baban**, Iraqi Kurdish medical doctor who saw civilian CW victims in 1980s, Suleimaniyeh, May 23, 2002

Heresh **Baban**, PUK peshmerga in 1980s, Suleimaniyeh, May 24, 2002

Salahuddin **Bahauddin**, leader of Kurdistan Islamic Union, Erbil, April 6, 2006

Ahmed **Bamarni**, PUK representative in France, Paris, April 14, 2000

Amatzia **Baram**, professor at Haifa University, reserve office in Israel's Military Intelligence in 1980s, Haifa, August 31, 2000

Abu Zahra **al-Basri**, Badr Corps fighter in 1980s, Tehran, June 11, 2002

Miqdad **Bayes**, Kurd living in Kirkuk during 1986 PUK–Pasdaran raid on oil installations, Kirkuk, September 21, 2005

Ofra **Bengio**, researcher at Dayan Center, Tel Aviv, September 4, 2000

Brig. Gen. Shlomo **Brom**, senior research associate at Jaffee Center for Strategic Studies, Israeli Air Force intelligence officer in 1980s, Tel Aviv, August 31, 2000

Wa'el Yusef **Bourachi**, Iraqi tank mechanic in 1980s, Kirkuk, June 8, 2003

Hamit **Bozarsan**, French academic, Paris, April 13, 2000

Gordon **Burck**, editor of *Chemical Weapons Convention Bulletin* in 1980s, Washington, DC, June 17, 2000, and e-mail communications, May 20, 2002 and March 10, 2003

Seth **Carus**, professor for counterproliferation research at US National Defense University, Washington, DC, July 20, 2000

Patrick **Clawson**, deputy director for research at Washington Institute for Near East Policy, Washington, DC, June 20, 2000

Ann **Clwyd**, member of Parliament, London, April 17, 2000, and Paris, April 13, 2000

Raf'at Ali Aziz **Diwana**, Iraqi Kurdish head of pro-government militia in 1980s, Halabja, May 25, 2002

Dr. Manuel **Domínguez Carmona**, a colonel in Spain's Army Medical Corps, WMD expert and professor of preventive medicine in 1980s, Madrid, by telephone, February 17, 2003

Hamid **Effendi**, senior official of Kurdistan Democratic Party, Erbil, June 7, 2003

Hadi **Farajvand**, Basiji platoon commander in Iran–Iraq war, later official at Iranian Foreign Ministry's CWC National Authority, Tehran, May 21, 2002, and e-mail communications, November 19 and 23, 2002

Col. Munqedh **Fathi**, Iraqi army officer in 1980s, Baghdad, September 5, 2003

Omar **Fattah**, PUK head of internal intelligence and member PUK Political Bureau, Suleimaniyeh, May 24, 2002

Shai **Feldman**, director of Jaffee Center for Strategic Studies, Tel Aviv, September 6, 2000

Dr. Abbas **Foroutan**, physiologist, Beheshti Center for Medical Science, Tehran, June 8, 2002. Rather than directly answering questions, Dr. Foroutan read from his draft manuscript on Iran's chemical warfare experience

Charles **Forrest**, director of NGO Indict, London, by telephone, November 13, 2001

Lt. Col. Rick **Francona**, officer in US Defense Intelligence Agency in 1987–1990 and liaison to Iraqi military intelligence in 1988, Oregon, by telephone, June 20, 2000, and e-mail communications, July 3 and 31, 2000, March 11, 2003, and July 2006

Staff Col. Yaser **al-Gailani**, Iraqi Air Force pilot, defected in 1990s, Amman, August 28, 2000

Peter **Galbraith**, staff member of Senate Foreign Relations Committee in 1980s, Washington, DC, January 13, 2000

Hamid Haji **Gali**, PUK commander in 1980s, Schiedam, Netherlands, November 17, 2000

Gideo **Gera**, Mossad's head of research in 1980s, Tel Aviv, September 5, 2000

Dr. Mustafa **Ghanei**, pulmonologist and associate professor of internal and pulmonary medicine, Baghyatollah University, Tehran, May 19, 2002

Yaghoub **Ghotsian**, head of nursing at Baghyatollah Military Hospital, Tehran, May 20, 2002

Dr. Faiq Muhammad **Golpy**, PUK guerrilla in 1980s, Suleimaniyeh, May 23, 2002

Sarah **Graham-Brown**, researcher/writer, London, by telephone, September 13, 1999

Alain **Gresh**, editor of Le Monde Diplomatique, Paris, April 11, 2000

Ayatollah Muhammad Baqr **al-Hakim**, leader of Supreme Council for the Islamic Revolution in Iraq, Tehran, June 3, 2002

Mohammed **Hanon**, private first class in Iraqi army in 1980s, Baghdad, September 3, 2003

Efrat **Harel**, Israeli graduate researcher on Iran, Tel Aviv University, Tel Aviv, September 5, 2000

Ahmed **Hashim**, US military analyst, Washington, DC, August 3, 2000

Alastair **Hay**, professor of molecular epidemiology, University of Leeds, New York, October 21, 2001, and e-mail communications, June 1 and 22, 2002

Aubin **Heyndrickx**, Belgian toxicologist, Gent, January 8, 2003, and by telephone, February 17, 2003

Ghoncheh **Hosseini**, Iranian Kurdish woman injured in 1987 Serdasht attack, Tehran, May 18, 2002

Sherdel Abdullah **Howeizi**, PUK minister of Peshmerga Affairs, Iraqi air defense field artillery specialist in 1970s, and PUK guerrilla in 1980s, Suleimaniyeh, May 24, 2002

Muhammed Ali **Husein**, Badr Corps fighter in 1980s, Tehran, June 11, 2002

Mam Hadi Yusef **Hussein**, retired guerrilla from Halabja area, Suleimaniyeh, and Halabja, May 28, 2002

Nour-al-Din **Isma'il**, Iraqi Kurdish surgeon who treated injured from 1986 Faw battle, Erbil, March 30, 2006

Abu Elyas **al-Jabari**, Badr Corps fighter in 1980s, Tehran, June 11, 2002

Ahmad Abd-al-Aziz **al-Jassim**, Kuwaiti ambassador to Iran in 1979–1983, Kuwait City, August 22, 2000

Col. Ephraim **Kam**, deputy director of Israel's Military Intelligence in 1983–1987, Tel Aviv, September 5, 2000

Dr. Adel **Karim**, general practitioner and manager of Halabja Hospital, Halabja, May 25, 2002

Jamal Hama **Karim**, PUK guerrilla in 1980s, Schiedam, Netherlands, November 19, 2000

Hashemi **Karimi**, member of Kurdistan Democratic Party of Iran, London, by telephone, February 16, 2003

Dr. Saeed **Keshavarz**, dermatologist and director of Baghyatollah Military Hospital, Tehran, May 20, 2002

Isam **al-Khafaji**, Iraqi sociologist, University of Amsterdam, Amsterdam, November 18, 2000

Zalmay **Khalilzad**, special assistant to the President for Gulf, Southwest Asia, and other Regional Issues at National Security Council, Washington, DC, July 18, 2001

'Awn **al-Khasawneh**, Jordanian judge at International Court of Justice, legal advisor to King Hussein in 1980s, Amman, August 27, 2000

Amb. Sa'id Rajaie **Khorassani**, Iran's permanent representative to the UN in 1981–1987, Tehran, June 2 and 3, 2002

Ismat **Kittani**, Iraq's Permanent Representative to UN in 1980s, Geneva, November 13, 2000

Chris **Kutschera**, French researcher/writer, Paris, April 13, 2000

Col. Walter P. **Lang**, head of Middle East section at US Defense Intelligence Agency in 1980s, Washington, DC, July 25, 2000, and by telephone, July 21 and August 1, 2000

Hama Haji **Mahmoud**, leader of Kurdistan Socialist Party, Suleimaniyeh, written communication, December 5, 2001

Robert **Mikulak**, official at Bureau of Arms Control at US Department of State, Washington, DC, by telephone, June 30, 2000

Jacques de **Milliano**, head of Médecins sans Frontières Netherlands in 1980s, Amsterdam, by telephone, November 16, 2001

Réginald **Moreels**, head of Médecins sans Frontières Belgium in 1980s, Nairobi, November 19, 2001

Sheikh **Mowla**, senior SCIRI official and Badr Corps officer in 1980s, Tehran, June 10, 2002

Hania **Mufti**, Iraq researcher for Amnesty International (later for Human Rights Watch), London, December 16, 1999

Barzan Qader **Muhammad**, PUK guerrilla in 1980s, Suleimaniyeh, January 14, 2004

Jim **Muir**, BBC and London *Times* correspondent, e-mail communication, October 17, 2000

Shawqat Haji **Mushir**, PUK commander leading Halabja operation in March 1988, Suleimaniyeh, May 26, 2002

Ghanim **Najjar**, Kuwaiti journalist in 1980s, Kuwait City, August 20, 2000

Salama **Na'mat**, journalist, Amman, August 24, 2000

Brig. Gen. Jawdat Mustafa **al-Naqib**, Iraqi Air Force pilot in 1980s who served in Air Operations Room at Presidential Palace during Halabja attack, Amman, by telephone, January 27, 2001

Ahmad **Nateghi**, chief of photography, Islamic Republic News Agency in 1984–1988, Tehran, June 1, 2002

David **Newton**, US ambassador to Iraq, November 1984–July 1988, Washington, DC, April 5, 2001

Kendal **Nezan**, president of Institut Kurde de Paris, Paris, April 13, 2000

Dr. Jiya Abbas **Nouri**, doctor who observed civilian CW victims in Kurdistan in 1987, Rotterdam, November 19, 2000

Dr. Mahmoud **Osman**, long–time Kurdish guerrilla, negotiator, and politician, London, April 17, 2000

Stephen **Pelletière**, CIA and US Army War College analyst working on Iraq in 1980s, Washington, DC, January 21, 2001

Julian P. **Perry Robinson**, CW proliferation expert at University of Sussex and co-editor of the *CBW Bulletin*, New York, October 21, 2001

Giandoménico **Picco**, UN assistant secretary-general for Political Affairs in 1980s, New York, June 26, 2000

James **Placke**, senior associate at Cambridge Energy Research Associates, US Deputy Assistant Secretary of State for Near Eastern and South Asian Affairs in 1980s, Washington, DC, August 7, 2000

Ja'far Mustafa **Qaradaghi**, senior PUK commander, Suleimaniyeh, May 27, 2002

Jon **Randal**, writer, *Washington Post* correspondent in 1980s, Paris, by telephone, April 12, 2000

Shorsh **Resool**, guerrilla in PUK information department in 1980s, London, September 13, 1999, April 15, 2000, April 15, 2004, and by telephone August 14, 2000

Francis J. **Ricciardone**, US ambassador to Egypt, country officer for Iraq at State Department in 1980s, and special coordinator for transition of Iraq in 2000, Washington, DC, November 1, 2000, and e-mail communication, November 23, 2002

Kevin **Riddell**, aid worker with Swedish NGO Individual Relief, Erbil, October 31, 2004, and Amman, Jordan, November 2, 2004

Iqbal **Riza**, chief of staff to UN Secretary-General Kofi Annan until 2004, official in UN General Secretariat in 1980s, New York, July 12, 2000

Gwynne **Roberts**, filmmaker, London, December 15, 1999

Staff Col. Abd-al-Wahab Abd-al-Zahra **al-Saeidy**, former instructor at Iraq's Staff College, Baghdad, September 5, 2003

Hama Hama **Sa'id**, PUK guerrilla in 1980s, Halabja, May 25 and 27, 2002, and written communication, May 5, 2002

Waleed **Saleh**, Iraqi professor at Universidad Autónoma de Madrid, Madrid, October 24, 2005

Dr. Atya Hama Sa'id **Salhi**, Iraqi Kurdish doctor who witnessed Erbil arrival of 1987 Balisan gas attack victims, Erbil, March 18, 2005

Barham **Salih**, PUK prime minister of Kurdistan Regional Government, Suleimaniyeh, May 28, 2002, and Washington, DC, July 6 and 31, 2000

Wafiq **al-Samarra'i**, former head of Iraqi Military Intelligence, deputy head in 1980s, defected in 1994, London, June 22, 1997

Mustafa Naqib **Serdashti**, former mayor of Serdasht, Tehran, May 19, 2002

Jean-François **Seznec**, adjunct professor at Georgetown University, Washington, DC, June 12, 2001

Yigal **Sheffy**, head of Iraq branch at Israel's Military Intelligence in 1986–1988, Tel Aviv, September 6, 2000

Gen. Muhammad **Shiyab**, Jordanian military strategist and proliferation expert, deputy Air Force commander and director of Air Force Intelligence in 1980s, Amman, by telephone, August 27, 2000

Dany **Shoham**, Israeli research associate at Besa Center for Strategic Studies, officer in Military Intelligence on chemical and biological weapons in 1980s, Tel Aviv, September 1, 2000

Gary **Sick**, executive director of Gulf/2000 and director of Middle East Institute at Columbia University, who was National Security Council official on Iran during Carter administration, New York, June 26, 2000, and e-mail communication, August 27, 2000

Dr. Frederick **Sidell**, former chief of Chemical Casualty Care Office at US Army Medical Research Institute of Chemical Defense (Edgewood/Aberdeen), by telephone, July 27, 2000

Dr. Serwer Aref **Sitar**, general practitioner, Halabja Hospital, Halabja, May 27, 2002

Dr. Hamid **Sohrabpour**, pulmonologist, Labafi Nezhad Hospital, Tehran, May 18, 2002

Dr. Muhammad Reza **Soroush**, Basiji doctor in Iran–Iraq war, director of Medical Engineering Research Institute, Tehran, June 2, 2002

Max van der **Stoel**, former Dutch foreign minister, UN Special Rapporteur for Iraq, The Hague, November 18, 1998

Bahman and Khosrow **Sultani**, brothers who witnessed chemical attacks on Iranian Kurdish villages, Tehran, June 5, 2002

Mowloud **Swara**, member of KDP-Iran, London, by telephone, February 16, 2003

Amb. S. R. **Tabatabaei**, secretary of CWC National Authority at Iranian Ministry of Foreign Affairs, Tehran, May 21, 2002

Mukarram **Talabani**, Iraqi Kurd, former advisor to Saddam Hussein and regime liaison with Kurdish rebel parties, Baghdad, May 24, 2003

Gen. Avraham **Tamir**, strategic advisor to Israeli governments, Tel Aviv, September 7, 2000

Muhammad **Tawfiq**, Iraqi Kurdish teacher collecting folk tales in Qaradagh and Halabja in 1980s, Suleimaniyeh, April 3, 2006

Gen. Bernard **Trainor**, former US Marine Corps commander with extensive combat experience in Vietnam who covered Iran–Iraq war for *New York Times*, e-mail communications, July 5, 20 and 22, 2000

Patrick **Tyler**, Washington bureau chief of *New York Times*, who as *Washington Post* correspondent visited Halabja in 1988, e-mail communication, September 22, 2000

Pervin Karimi **Vahed**, Iranian Kurdish woman injured in 1987 Serdasht attack, Tehran, May 18, 2002

Dr. Jan **Willems**, Belgian chemical weapons expert, Department of Public Health, Ghent University, Gent, January 8, 2003

Judith **Yaphe**, historian at US National Defense University who was at CIA in 1980s, Washington, DC, June 29, 2000

Mohamed **Zahidi**, nurse, Baghyatollah Military Hospital, Tehran, May 20, 2002

Jean Pascal **Zanders**, a WMD proliferation expert at Stockholm International Peace Research Institute (SIPRI), e-mail communication, January 2007

Sadeq **Zarza**, member of KDP-Iran, Groningen, NL, by telephone, June 23 and September 3, 2002

NOT-FOR-ATTRIBUTION INTERVIEWS

Colonel in Iranian Air Force, a tactical control officer who trained on Hawk missile use in Texas in 1970s, Tehran, June 2002

European Businessman living in Baghdad in 1990s, March 29, 2006

Former KDP-Iran commander in Halabja area, e-mail communication, September 9, 2002

Iranian CW expert, May 13, 2002

Iranian Pasdaran soldier, Tehran, May 20, 2002

Iraqi battalion commander, Kirkuk, November 2, 2004.

Iraqi brigadier general, Baghdad, January 11, 2004.

Iraqi cardiologist, military doctor in 1980s, Baghdad, May 24, 2003

Iraqi Kurdish witness to Halabja/Khurmal CW attack, Halabja, March 16, 2005

Iraqi opposition activist, Amman, August 24, 2000

Iraqi pilot who defected in 1990s, by telephone, March 2003

Iraq scholar, Washington, DC, July 3, 2000

Iraqi soldier, Erbil, January 17, 2004.

Senior CIA proliferation analyst in 1980s, Washington, DC, August 8, 2000

Senior ICRC official, Geneva, November 13, 2000

Senior Kurdish officer in Bradosti tribal militia who participated in 1983 Haj Omran battles, August 2000

Senior Iraqi diplomat, Baghdad, January 2004.

Two officers in Kuwaiti Army in 1980s, Kuwait City, August 22, 2000

US Congressional staffer, Washington, DC, August 5, 2006

US diplomat, Washington, DC, 2000

US government contractor, Washington, DC, February 2001

US intelligence analyst, Washington, DC, July 2000

US intelligence analyst, by telephone, August 1, 2001

US intelligence analyst, 2001

US State Department official, Washington, DC, 2000

INDEX